NOW

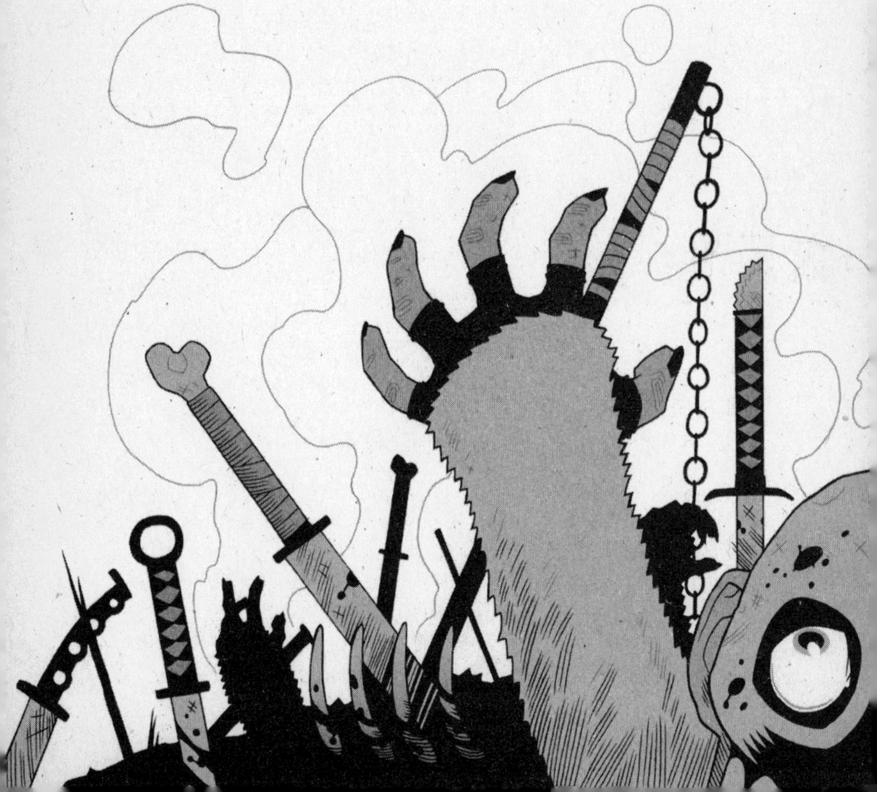

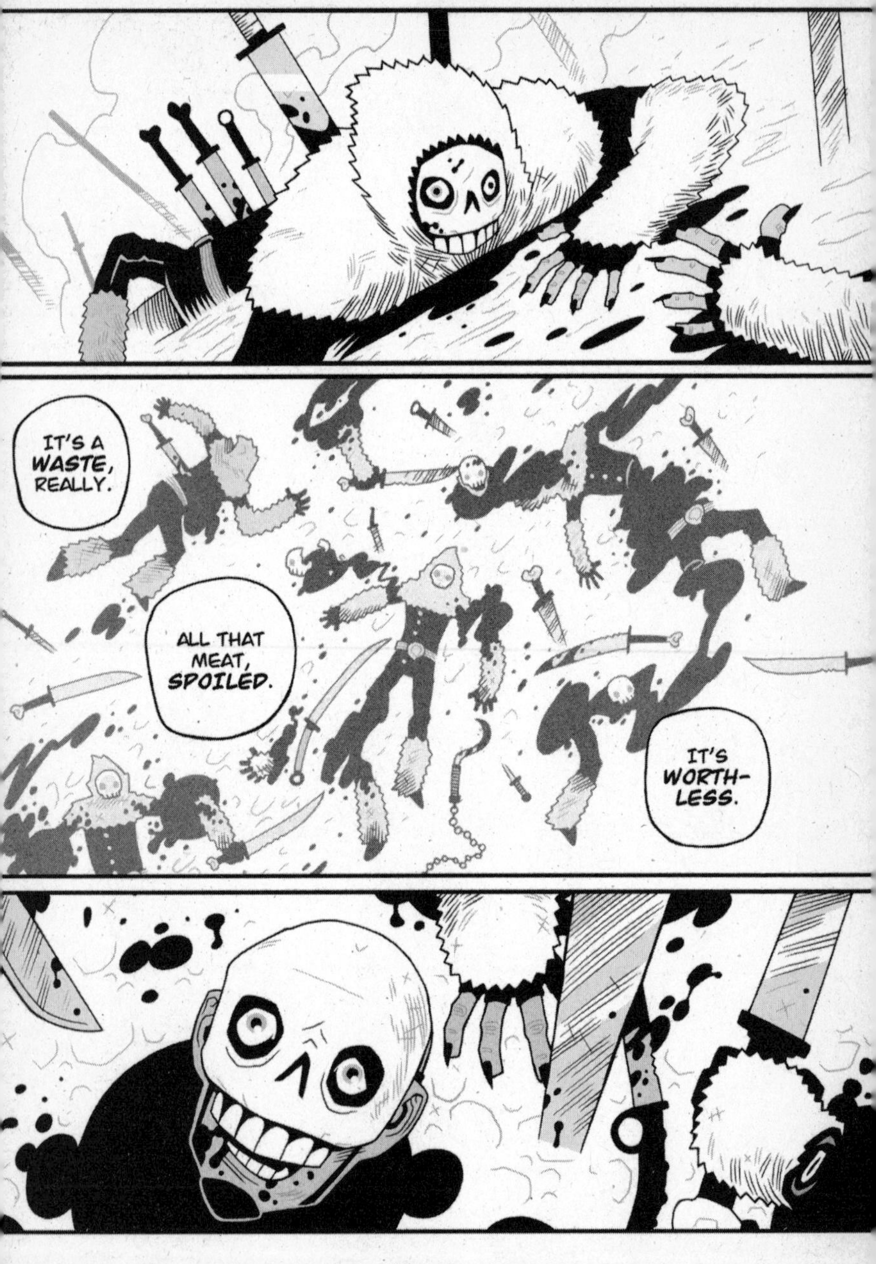
IT'S A WASTE, REALLY.
ALL THAT MEAT, SPOILED.
IT'S WORTH-LESS.

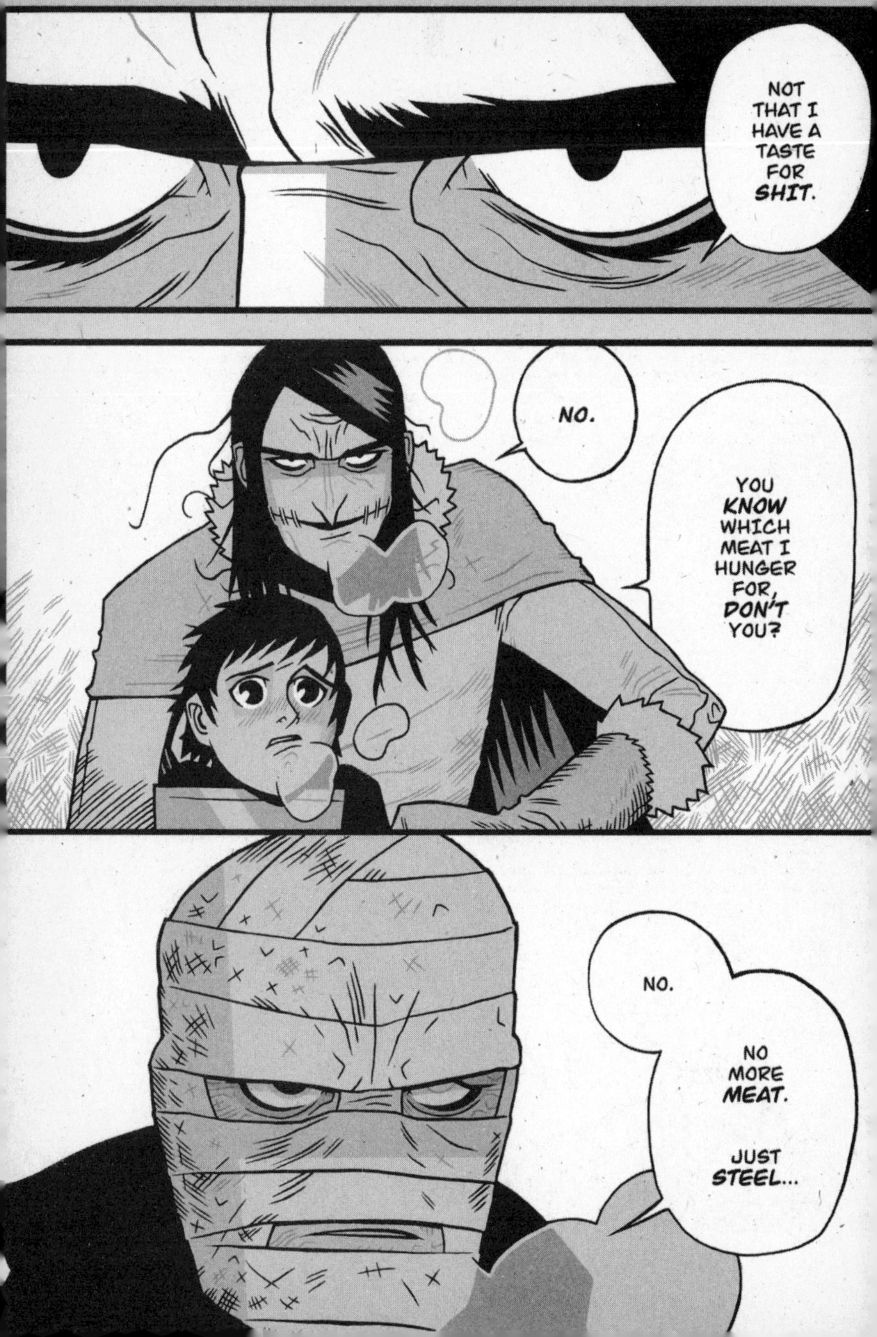
NOT THAT I HAVE A TASTE FOR SHIT.
NO.
YOU KNOW WHICH MEAT I HUNGER FOR, DON'T YOU?
NO.
NO MORE MEAT.
JUST STEEL...

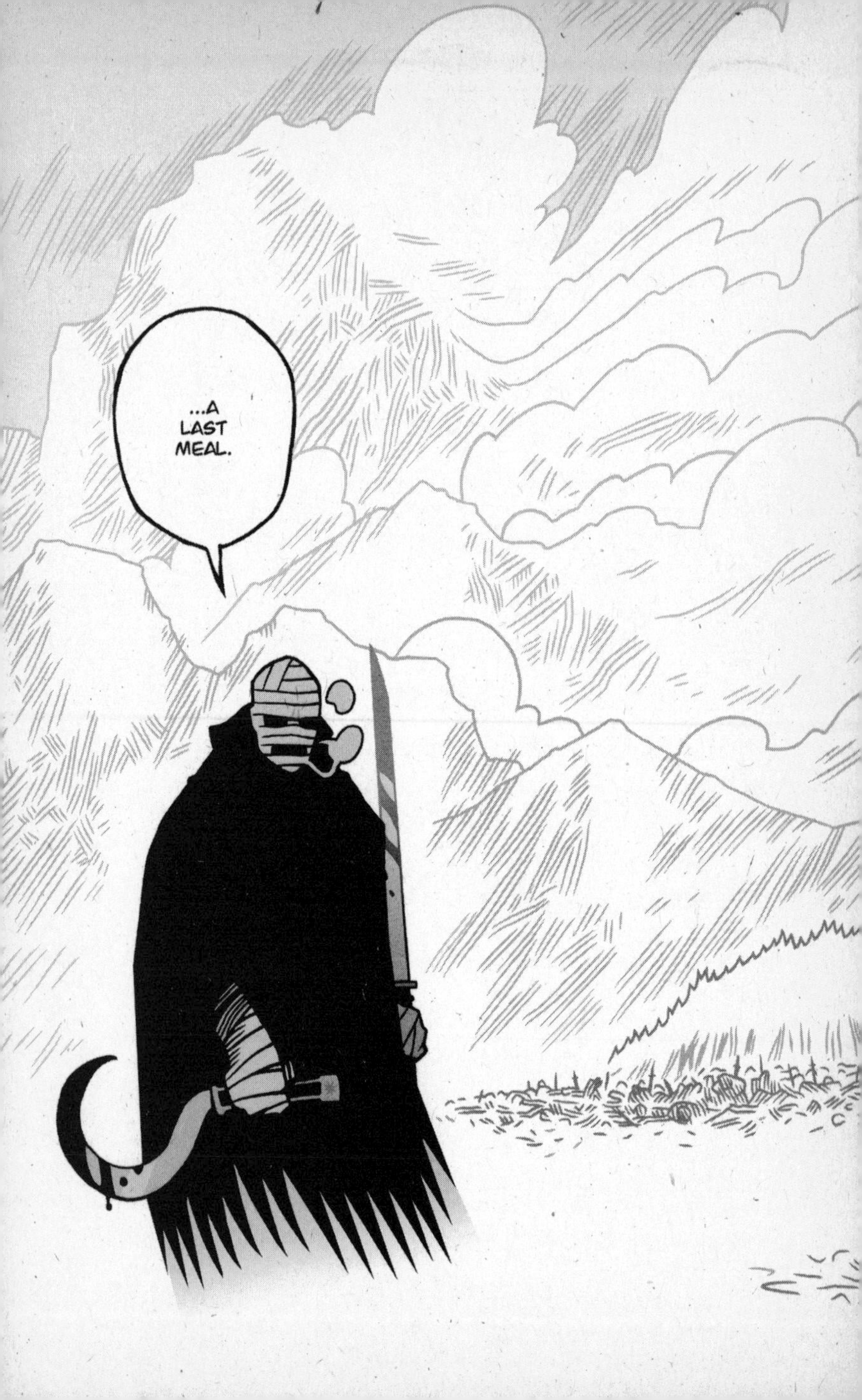
...A LAST MEAL.

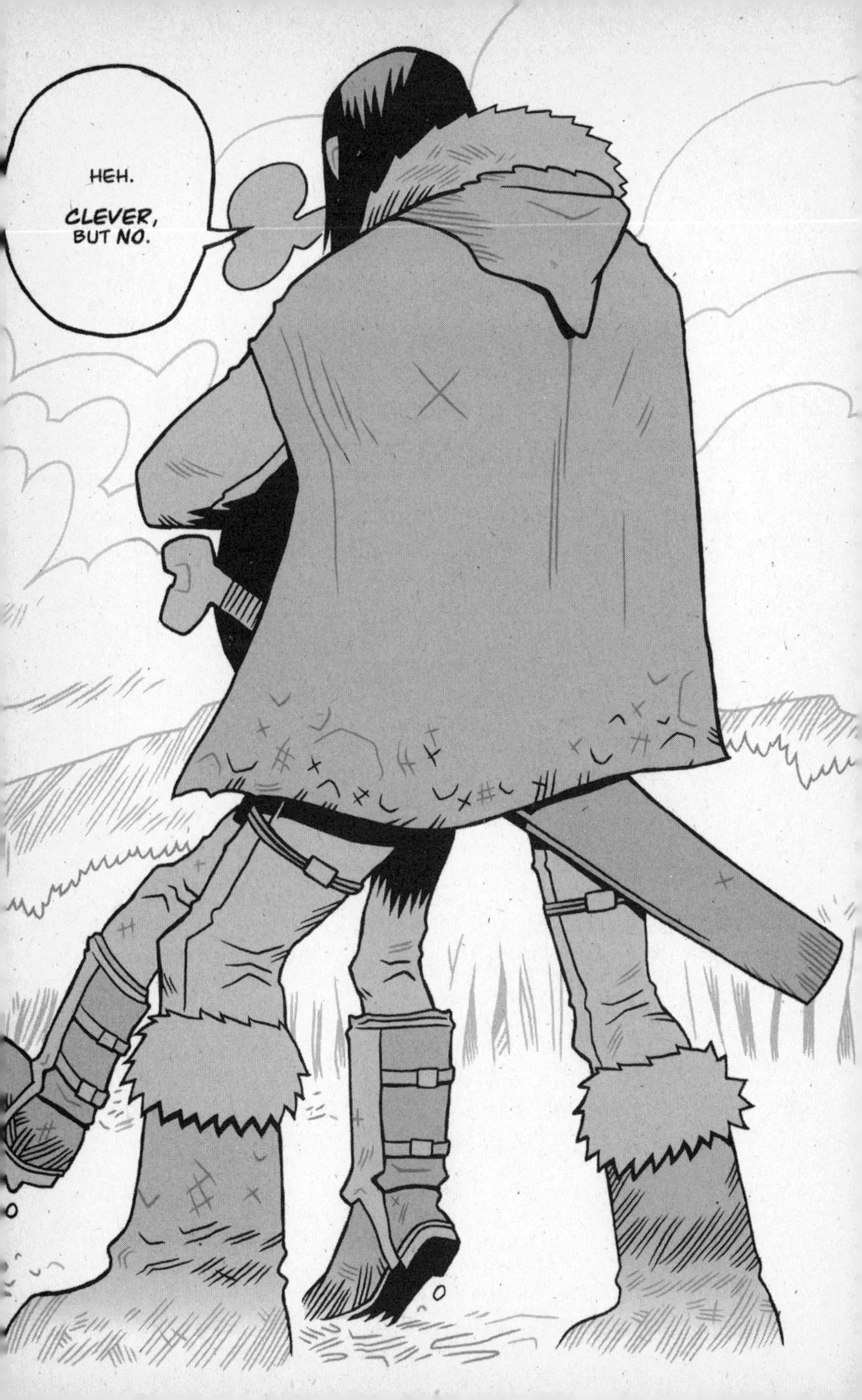
HEH.
CLEVER, BUT NO.

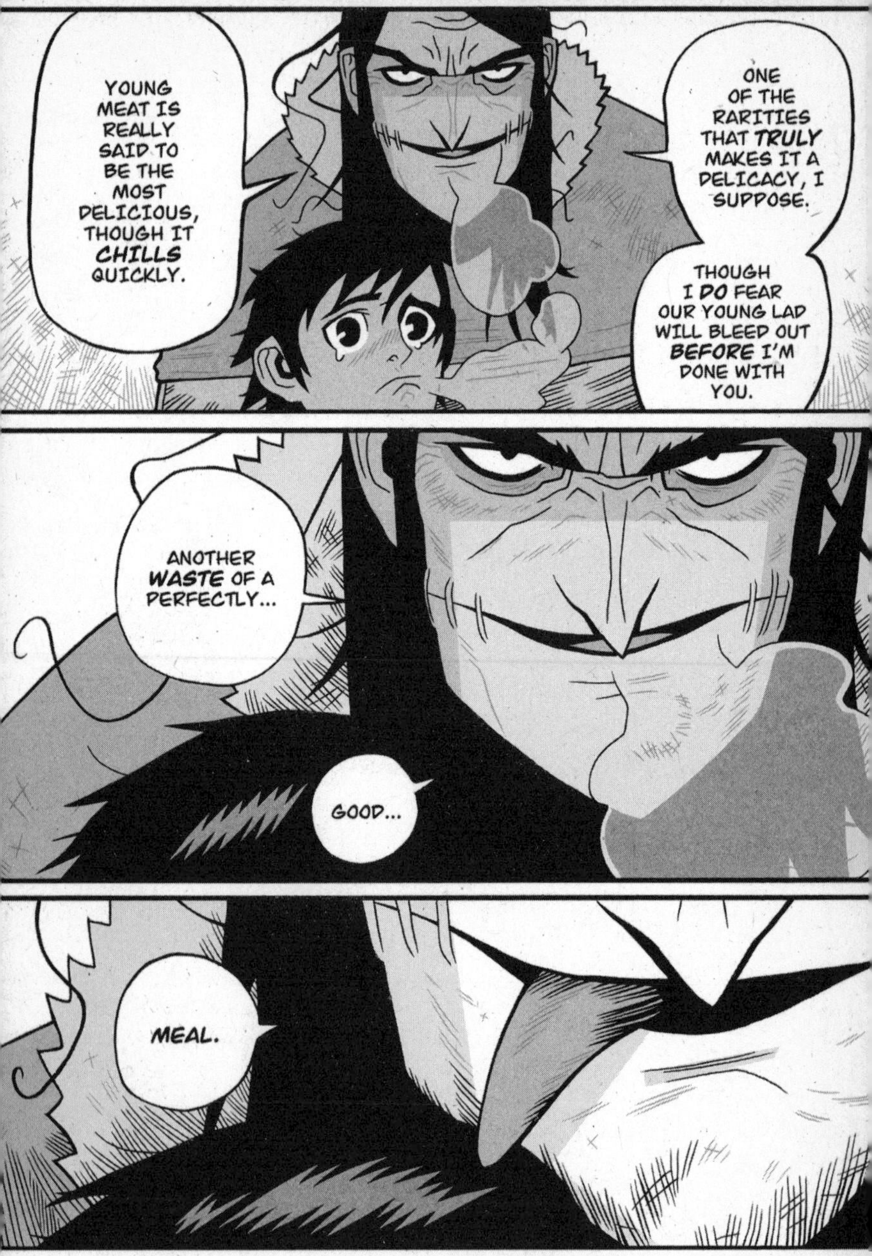
YOUNG MEAT IS REALLY SAID TO BE THE MOST DELICIOUS, THOUGH IT CHILLS QUICKLY.
ONE OF THE RARITIES THAT TRULY MAKES IT A DELICACY, I SUPPOSE.
THOUGH I DO FEAR OUR YOUNG LAD WILL BLEED OUT BEFORE I'M DONE WITH YOU.
ANOTHER WASTE OF A PERFECTLY...
GOOD...
MEAL.

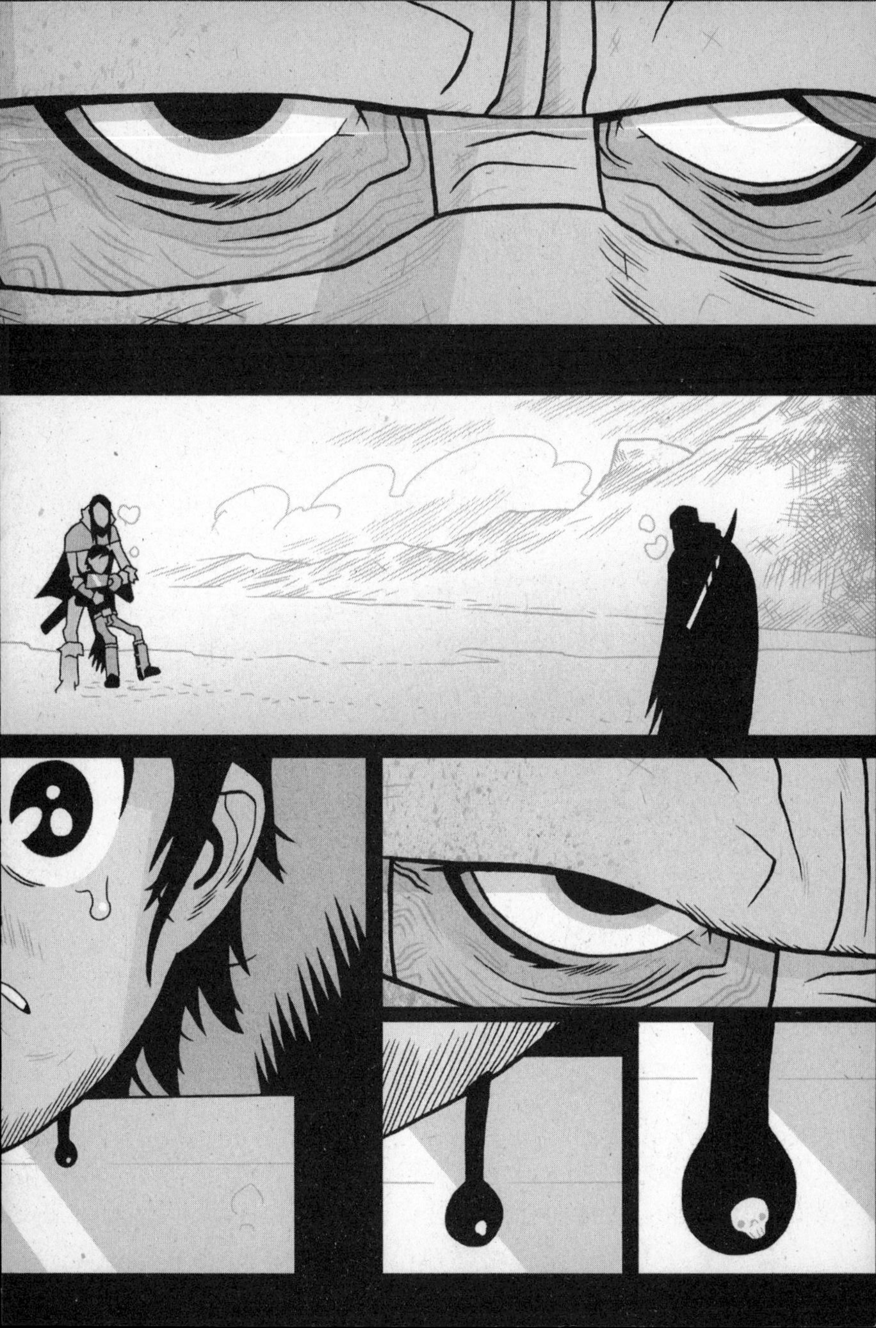

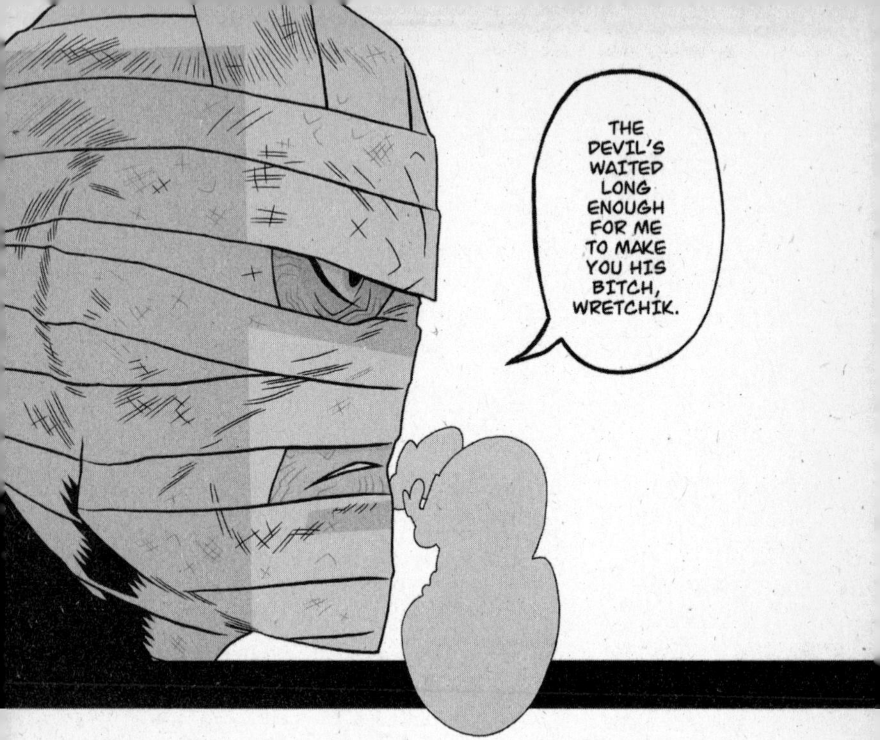
THE DEVIL'S WAITED LONG ENOUGH FOR ME TO MAKE YOU HIS BITCH, WRETCHIK.

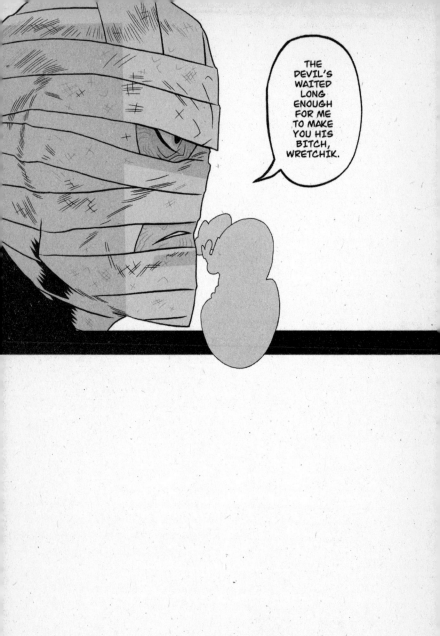

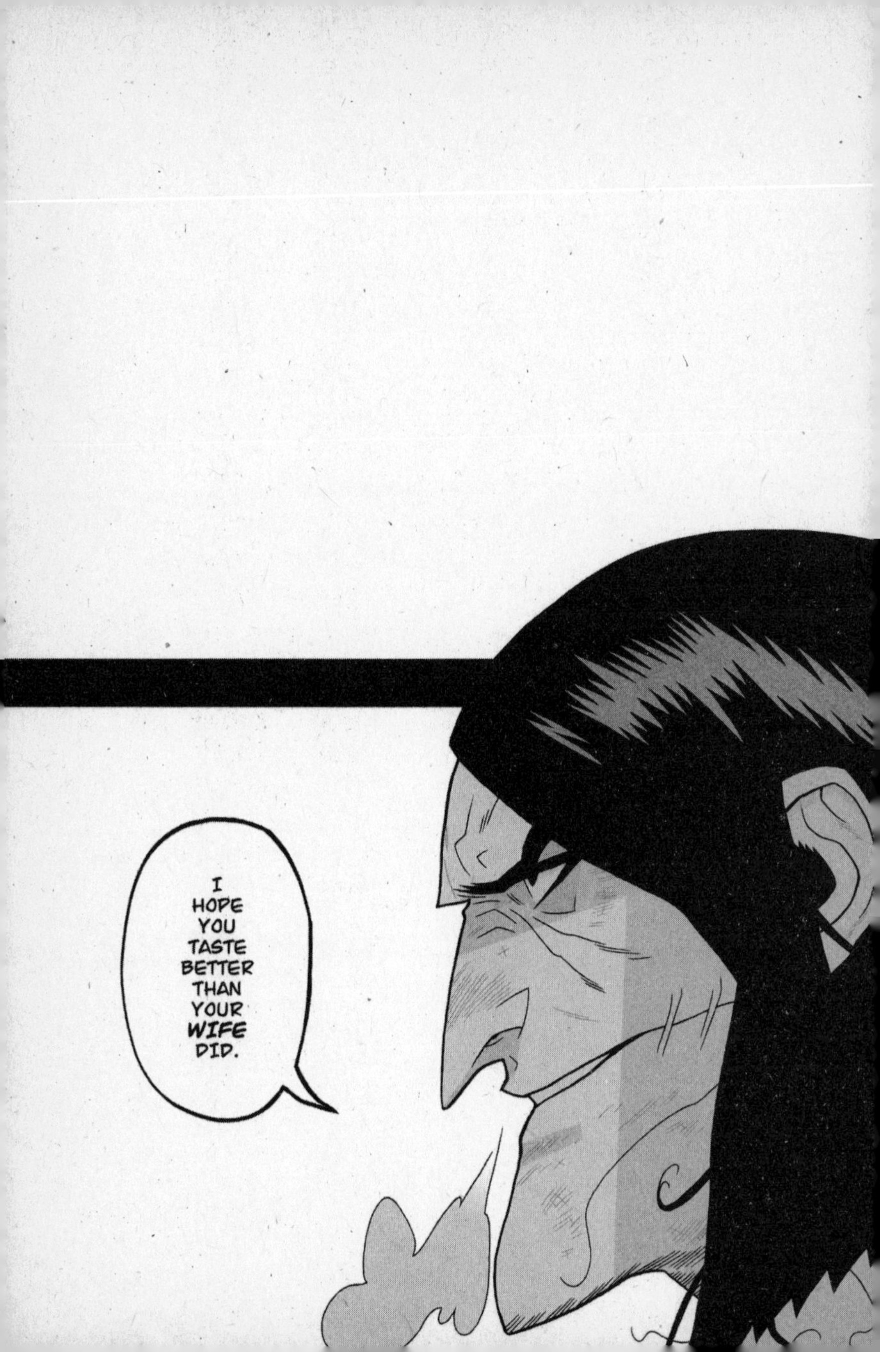
I HOPE YOU TASTE BETTER THAN YOUR WIFE DID.

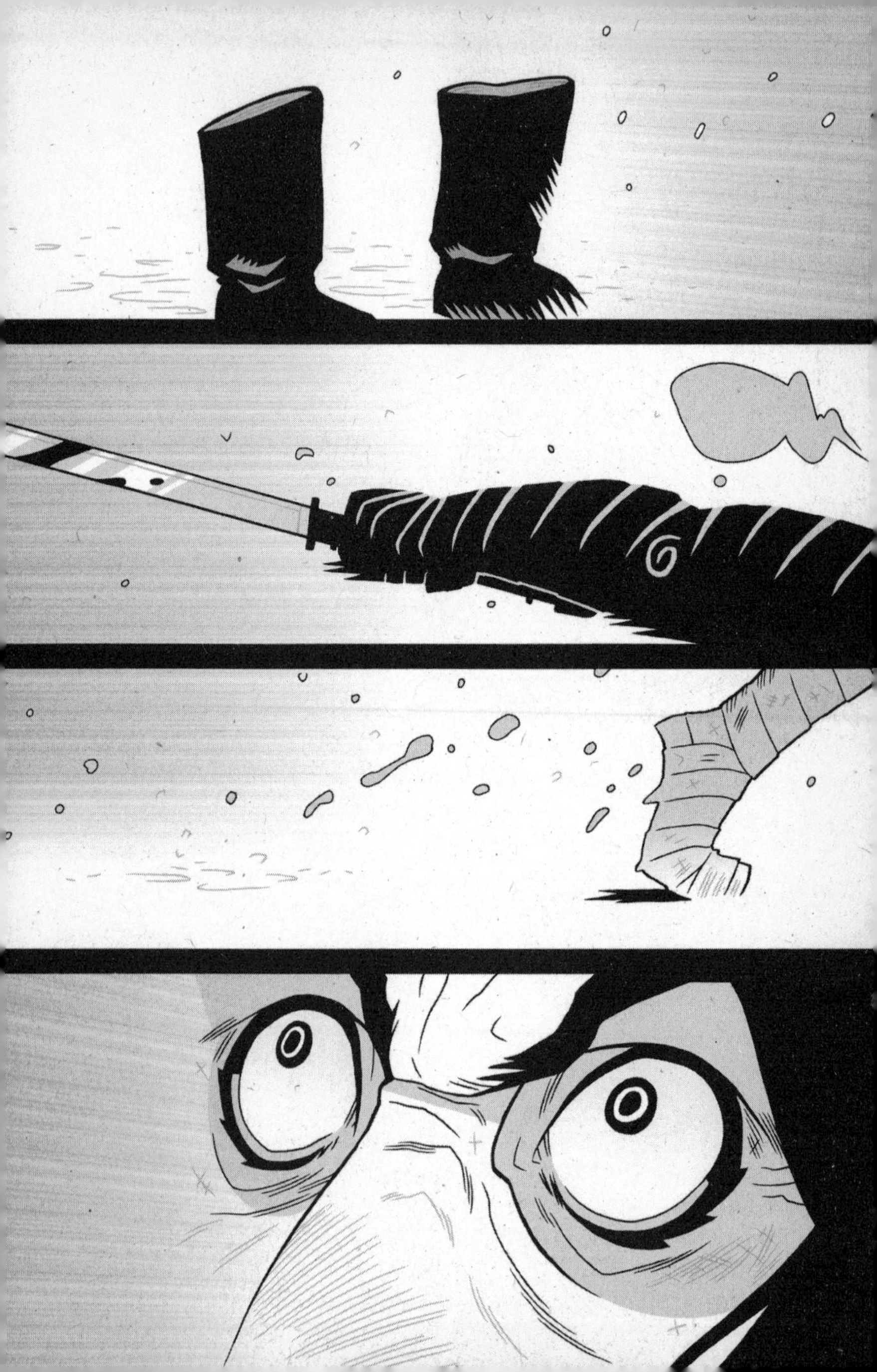

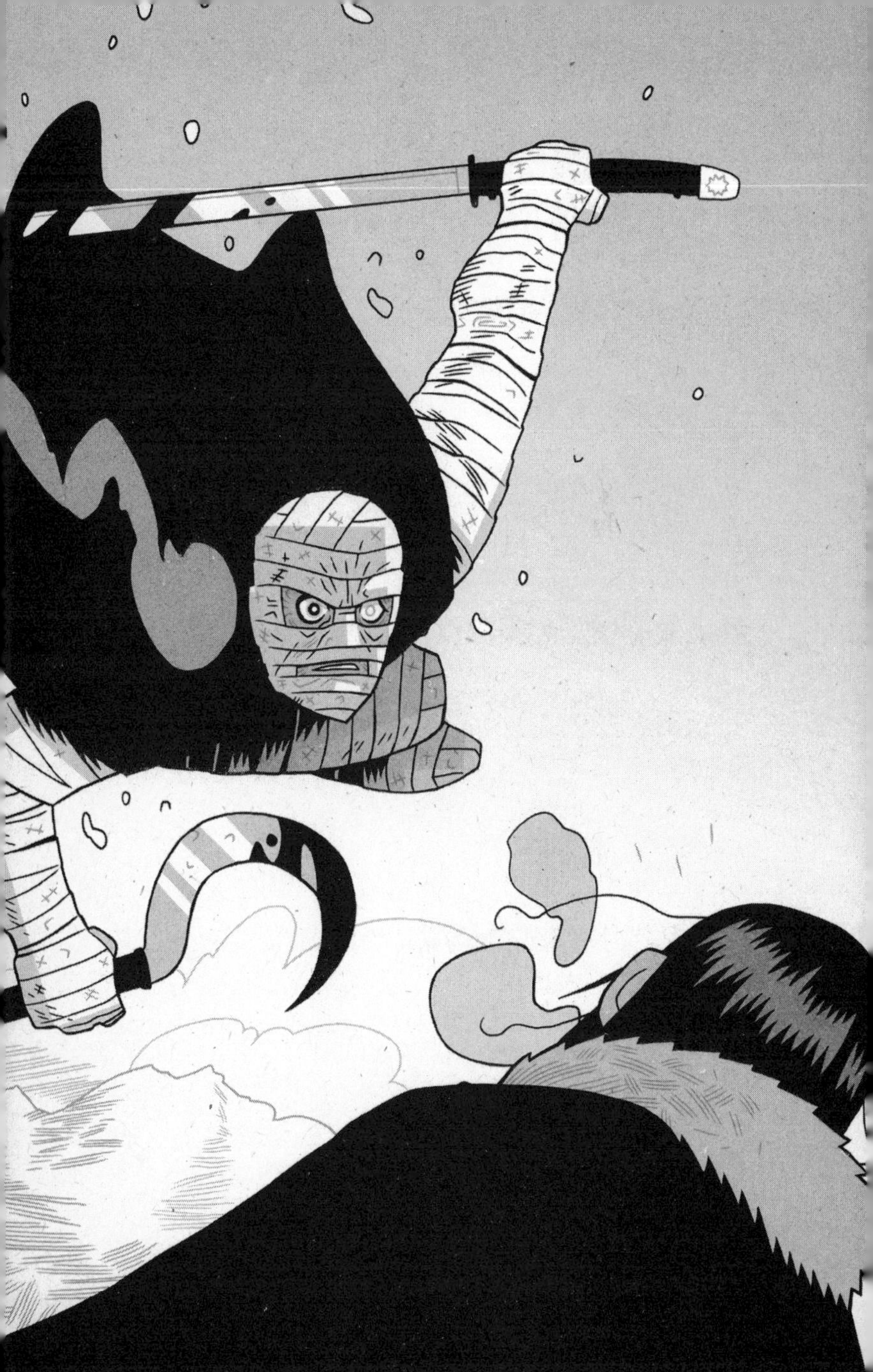

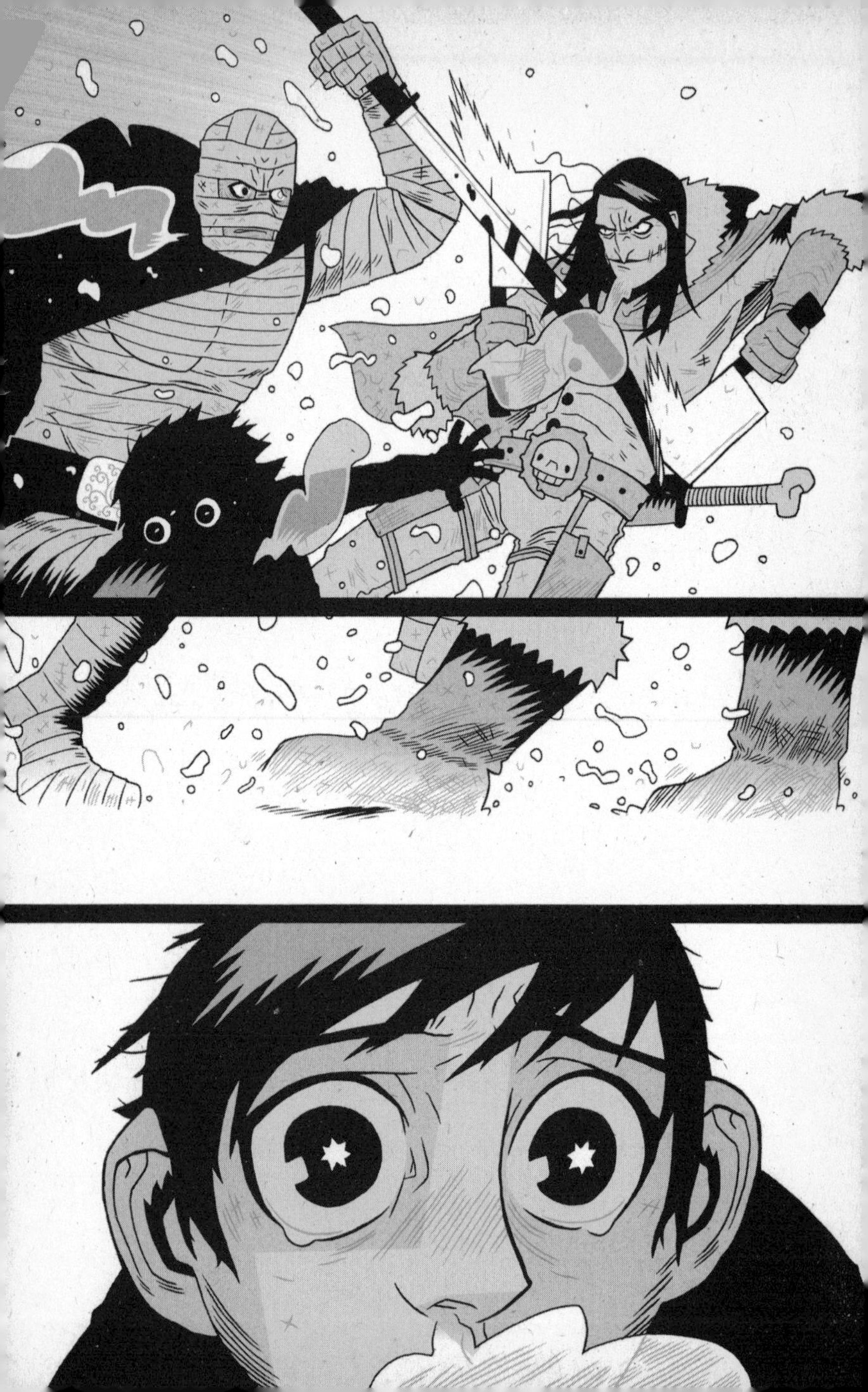

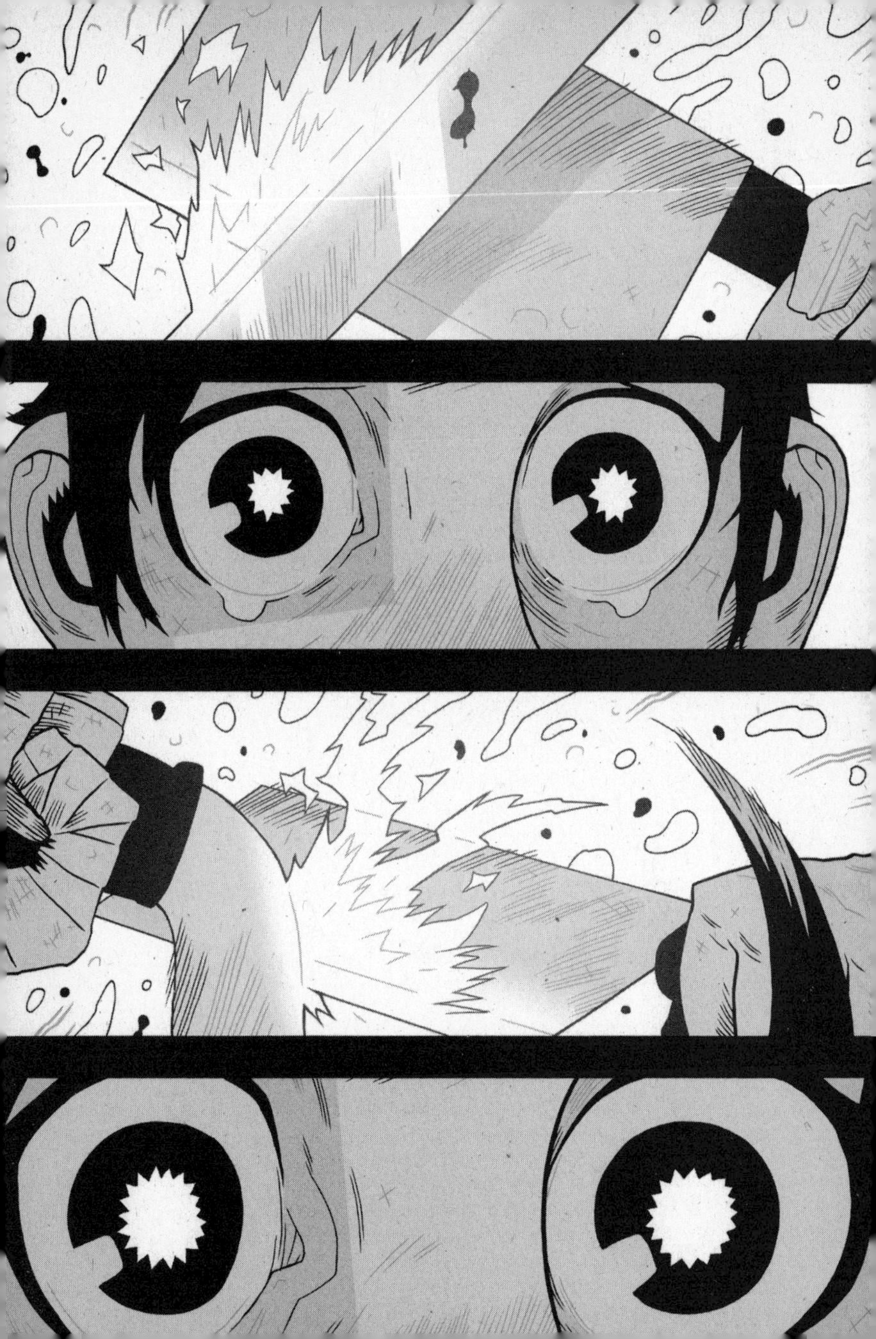

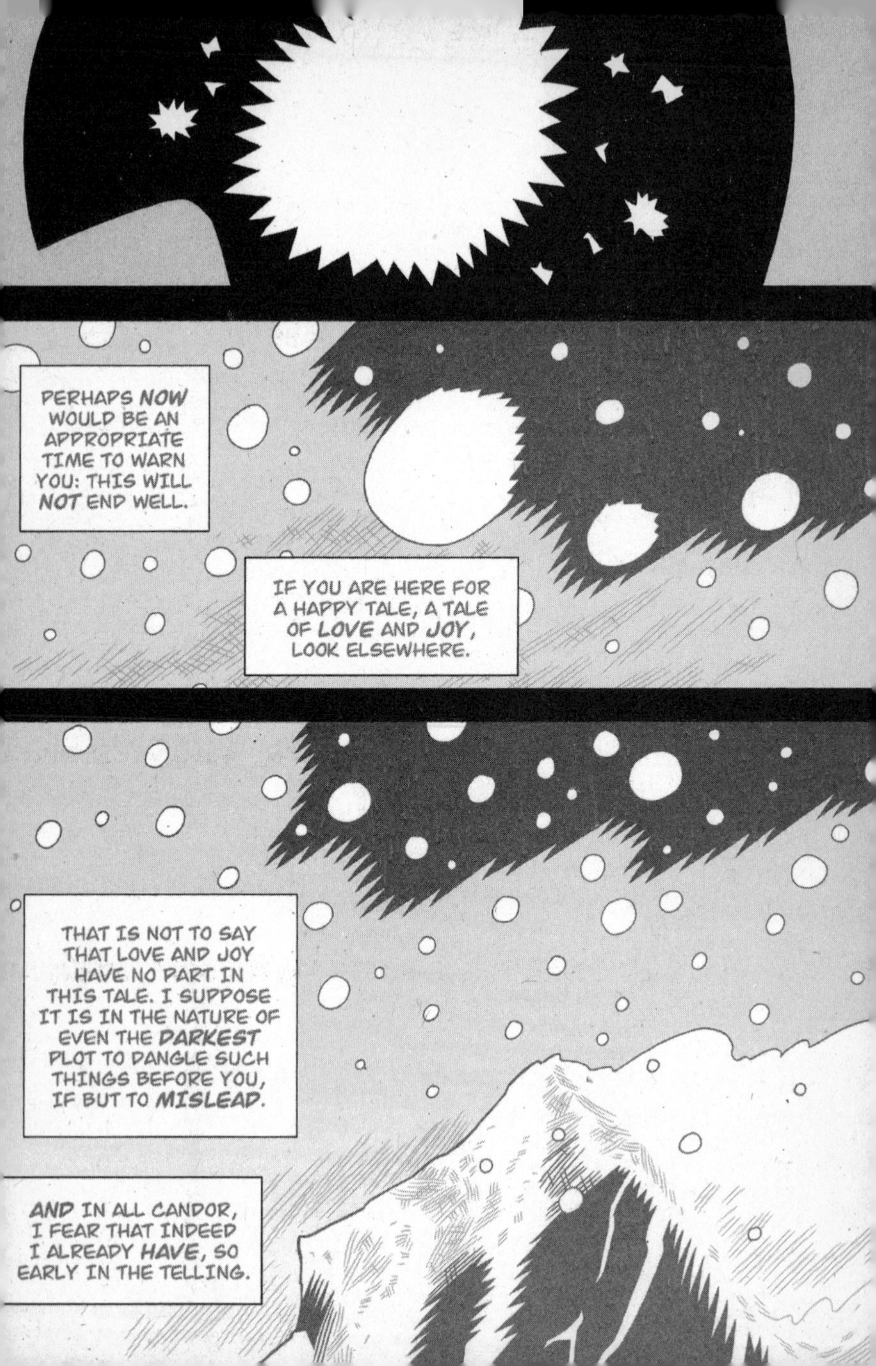
PERHAPS NOW WOULD BE AN APPROPRIATE TIME TO WARN YOU: THIS WILL NOT END WELL.
IF YOU ARE HERE FOR A HAPPY TALE, A TALE OF LOVE AND JOY, LOOK ELSEWHERE.
THAT IS NOT TO SAY THAT LOVE AND JOY HAVE NO PART IN THIS TALE. I SUPPOSE IT IS IN THE NATURE OF EVEN THE DARKEST PLOT TO DANGLE SUCH THINGS BEFORE YOU, IF BUT TO MISLEAD.
AND IN ALL CANDOR, I FEAR THAT INDEED I ALREADY HAVE, SO EARLY IN THE TELLING.

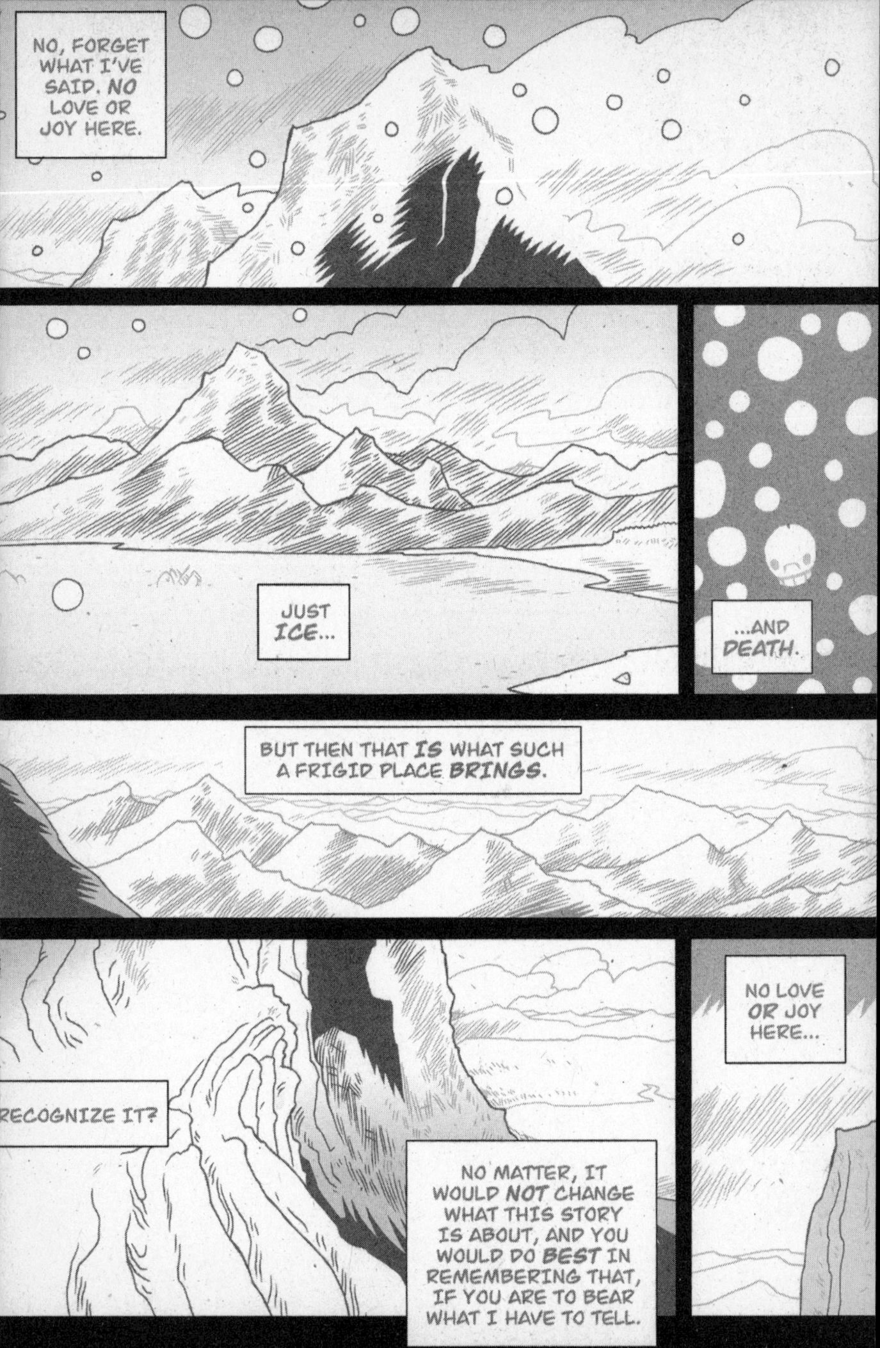
NO, FORGET WHAT I'VE SAID. NO LOVE OR JOY HERE.
JUST ICE...
...AND DEATH.
BUT THEN THAT IS WHAT SUCH A FRIGID PLACE BRINGS.
RECOGNIZE IT?
NO MATTER, IT WOULD NOT CHANGE WHAT THIS STORY IS ABOUT, AND YOU WOULD DO BEST IN REMEMBERING THAT, IF YOU ARE TO BEAR WHAT I HAVE TO TELL.
NO LOVE OR JOY HERE...

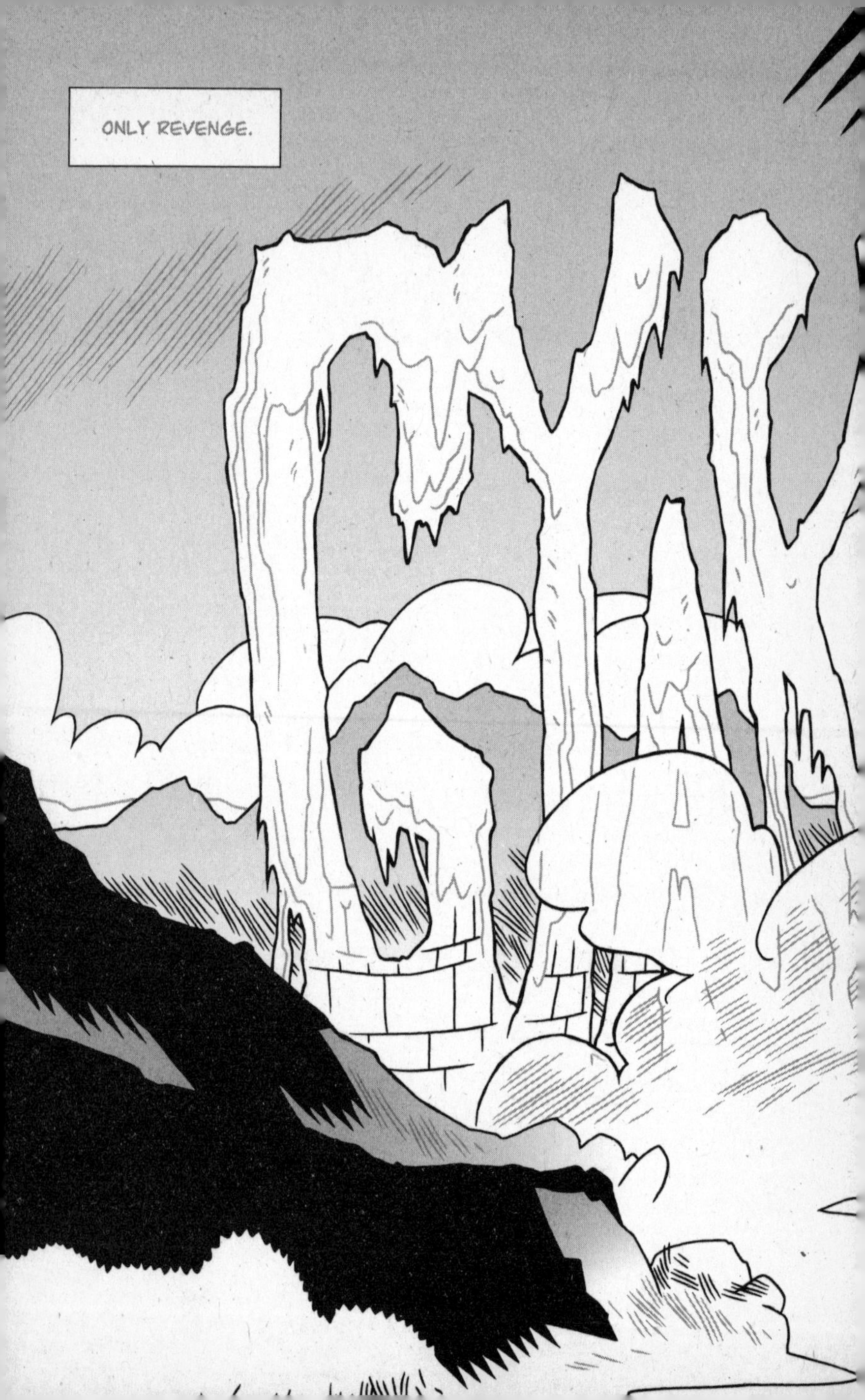
ONLY REVENGE.

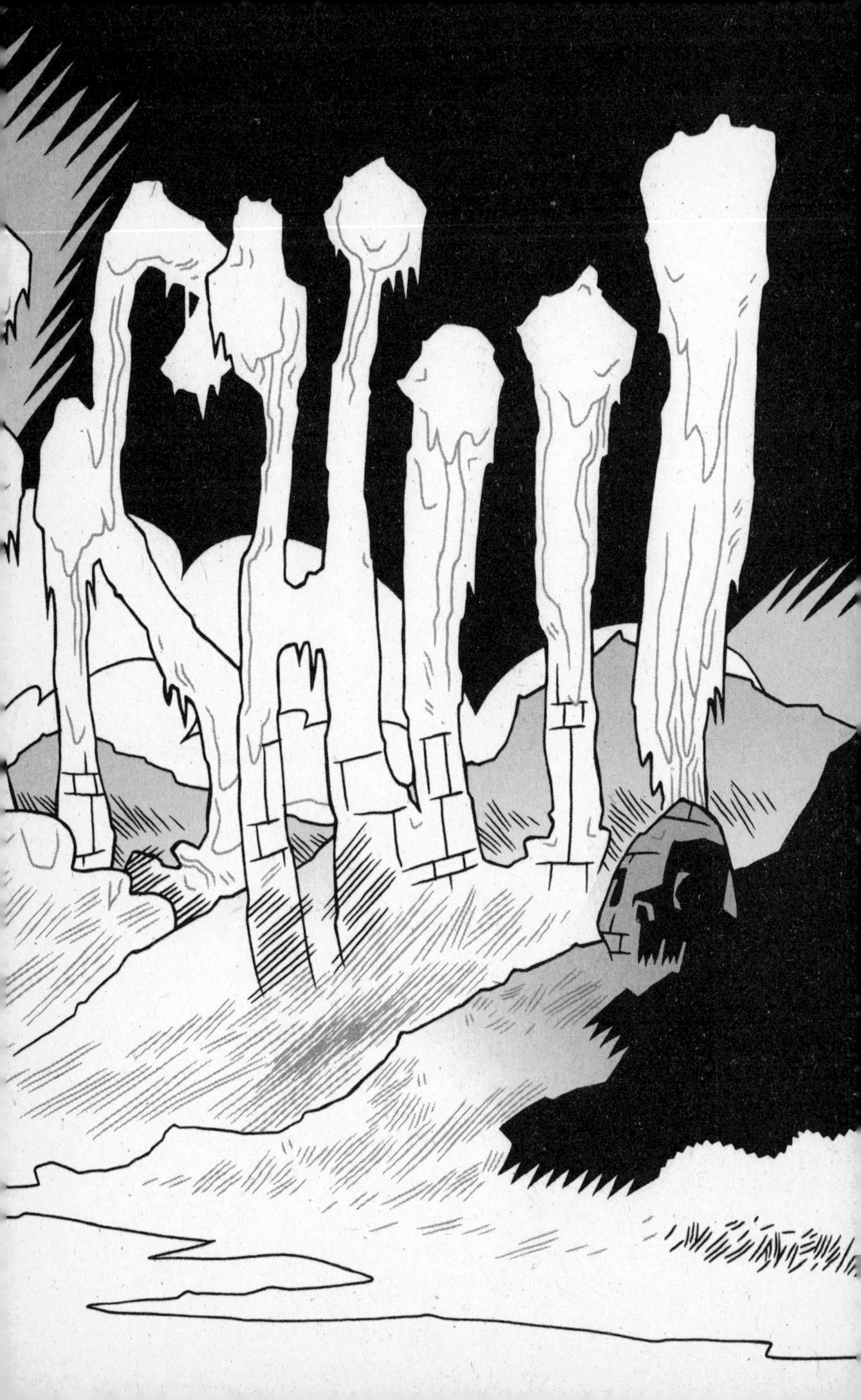

STOP!

This is the back of the book.
You wouldn't want to spoil a great ending!

This book is printed "manga-style," in the authentic Japanese right-to-left format. Since none of the artwork has been flipped or altered, readers get to experience the story just as the creator intended. You've been asking for it, so TOKYOPOP® delivered: authentic, hot-off-the-press, and far more fun!

DIRECTIONS

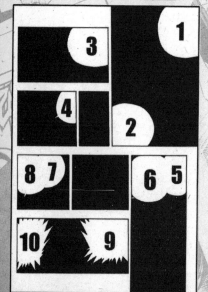

If this is your first time reading manga-style, here's a quick guide to help you understand how it works.

It's easy… just start in the top right panel and follow the numbers. Have fun, and look for more 100% authentic manga from TOKYOPOP®!

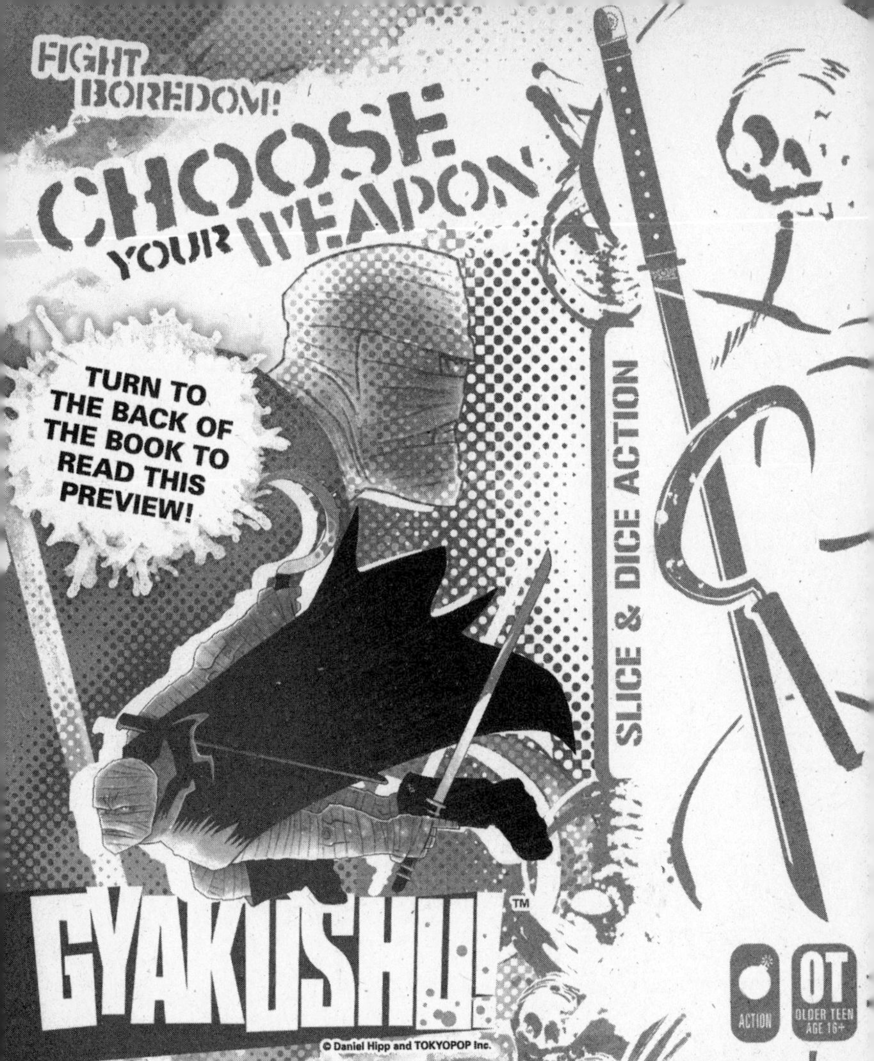
FIGHT BOREDOM!
CHOOSE YOUR WEAPON
TURN TO THE BACK OF THE BOOK TO READ THIS PREVIEW!
SLICE & DICE ACTION
GYAKUSHU!™
ACTION
OT
OLDER TEEN AGE 16+
© Daniel Hipp and TOKYOPOP Inc.

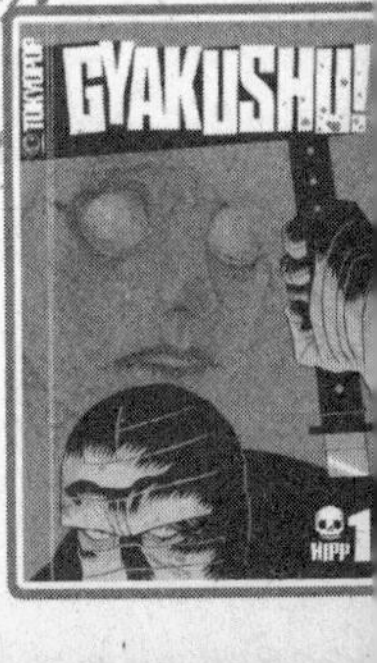
TOKYOPOP
GYAKUSHU!
HIPP
1

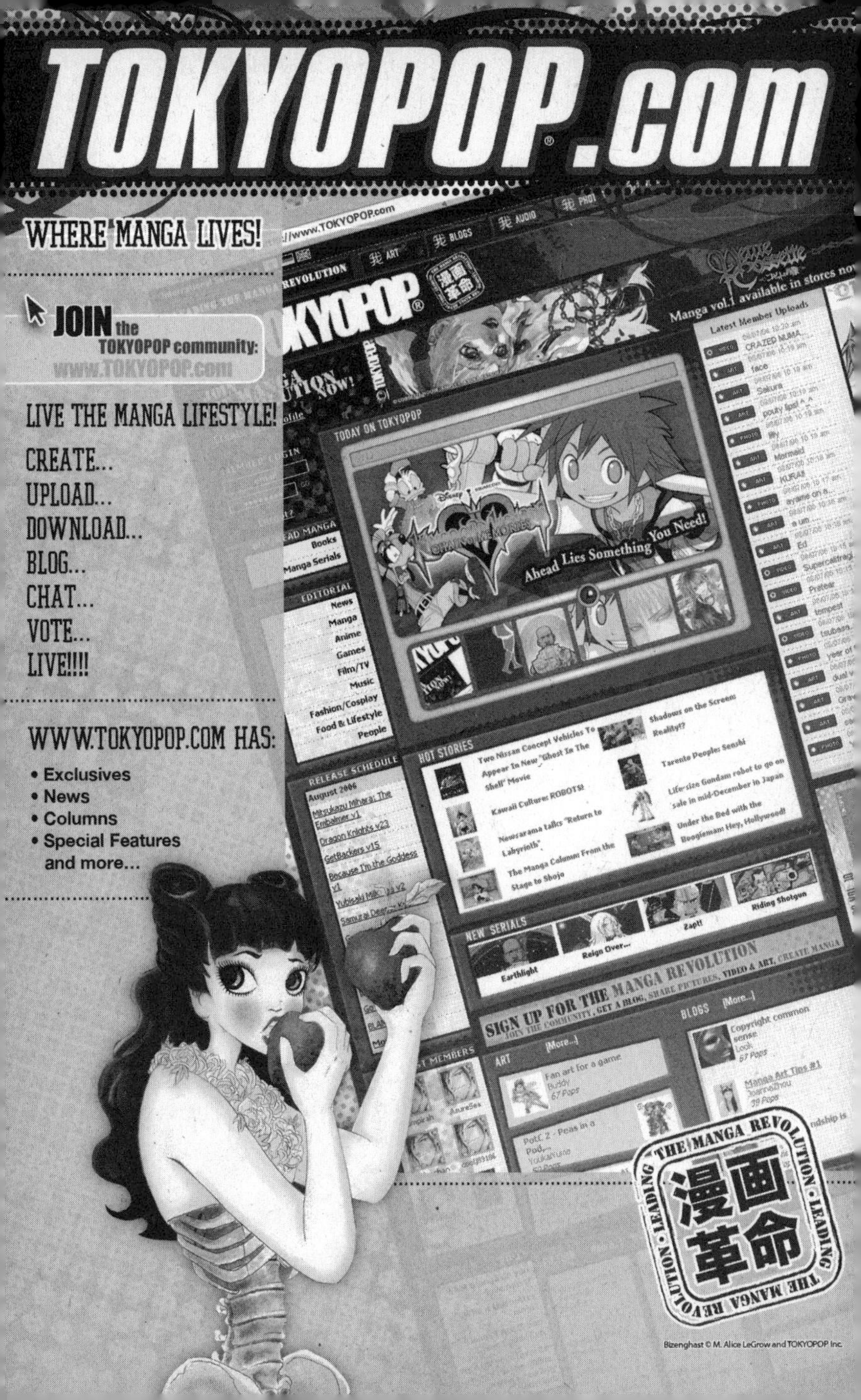
TOKYOPOP®.com
WHERE MANGA LIVES!
JOIN the TOKYOPOP community:
www.TOKYOPOP.com
LIVE THE MANGA LIFESTYLE!
CREATE...
UPLOAD...
DOWNLOAD...
BLOG...
CHAT...
VOTE...
LIVE!!!!
WWW.TOKYOPOP.COM HAS:
• Exclusives
• News
• Columns
• Special Features
and more...
THE MANGA REVOLUTION • LEADING • 漫画革命
Bizenghast © M. Alice LeGrow and TOKYOPOP Inc.

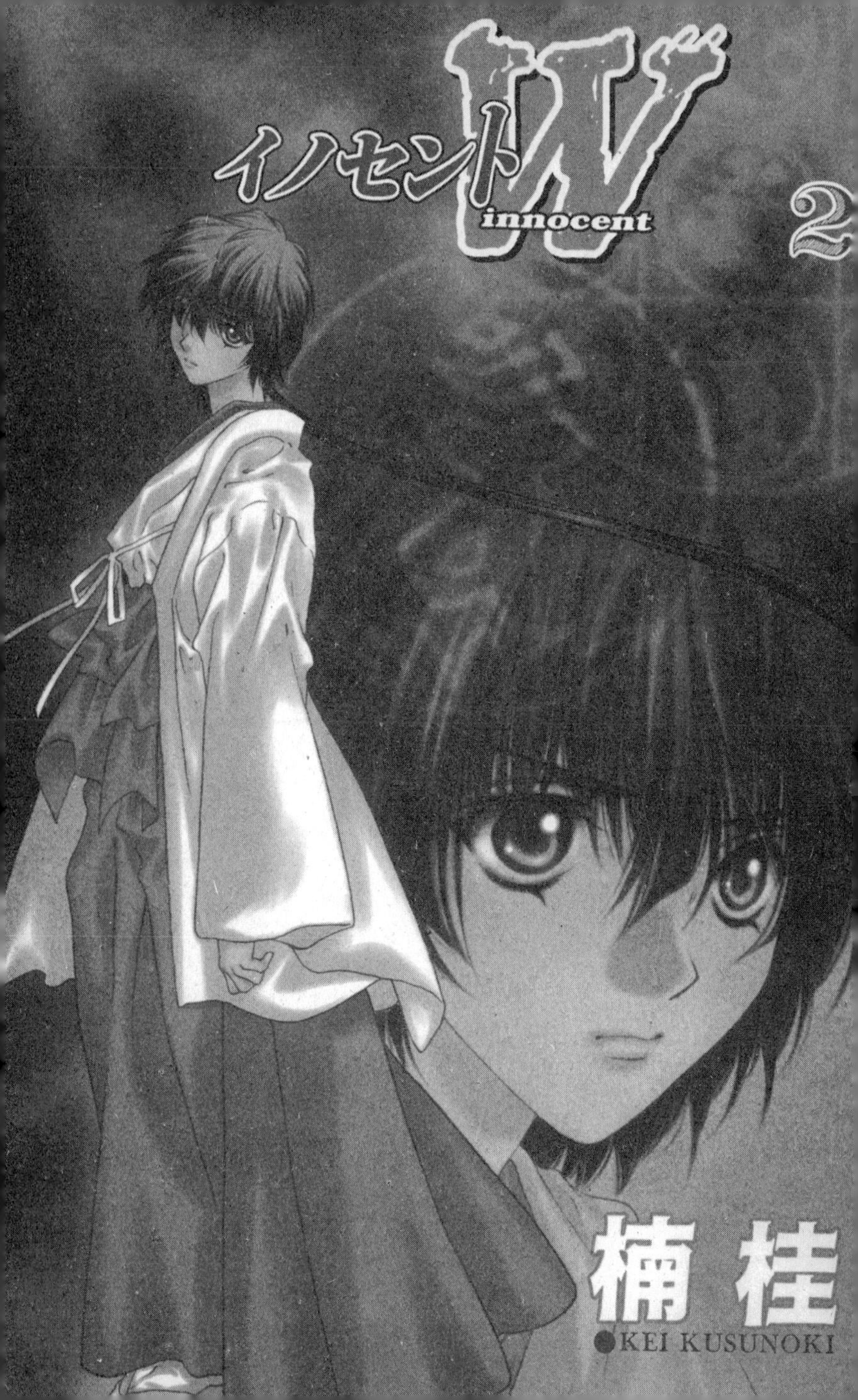
イノセントW
innocent
2
楠桂
●KEI KUSUNOKI

THE STORY SO FAR...

Private detective Makoto Hirasaka was hired to find a "real live Wiccan witch" by riding a certain city bus to its final stop. Although Makoto was sure his special powers would give him an edge, the bus soon crashed; and he learned that every single passenger was some kind of witch. Lost in the mountains, Makoto and the mysterious young ladies discovered that the place was teeming with "witch hunters" all responding to an Internet invitation to come kill off the stranded witches. Now a simple assignment has become a deadly fight for survival.

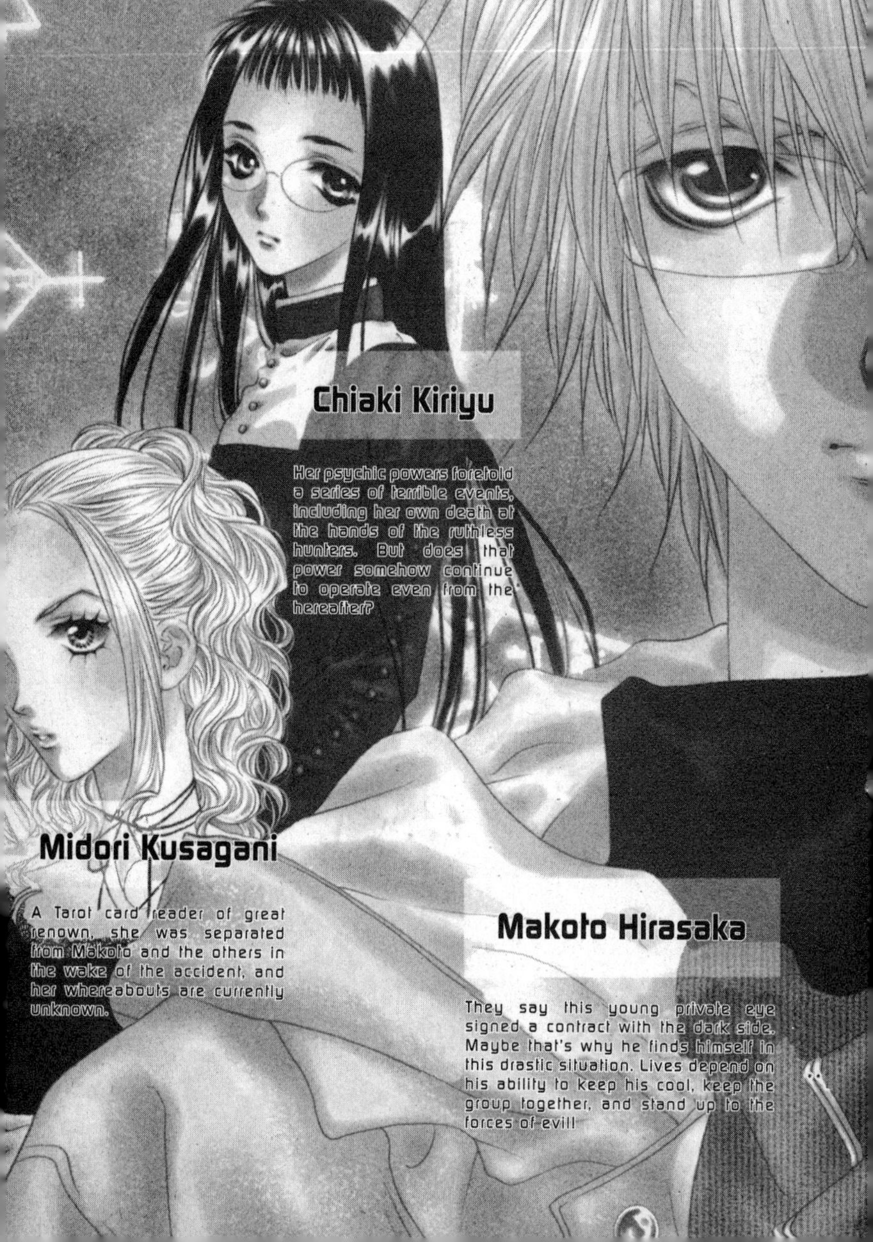

Chiaki Kiriyu

Her psychic powers foretold a series of terrible events, including her own death at the hands of the ruthless hunters. But does that power somehow continue to operate even from the hereafter?

Midori Kusagani

A Tarot card reader of great renown, she was separated from Makoto and the others in the wake of the accident, and her whereabouts are currently unknown.

Makoto Hirasaka

They say this young private eye signed a contract with the dark side. Maybe that's why he finds himself in this drastic situation. Lives depend on his ability to keep his cool, keep the group together, and stand up to the forces of evil!

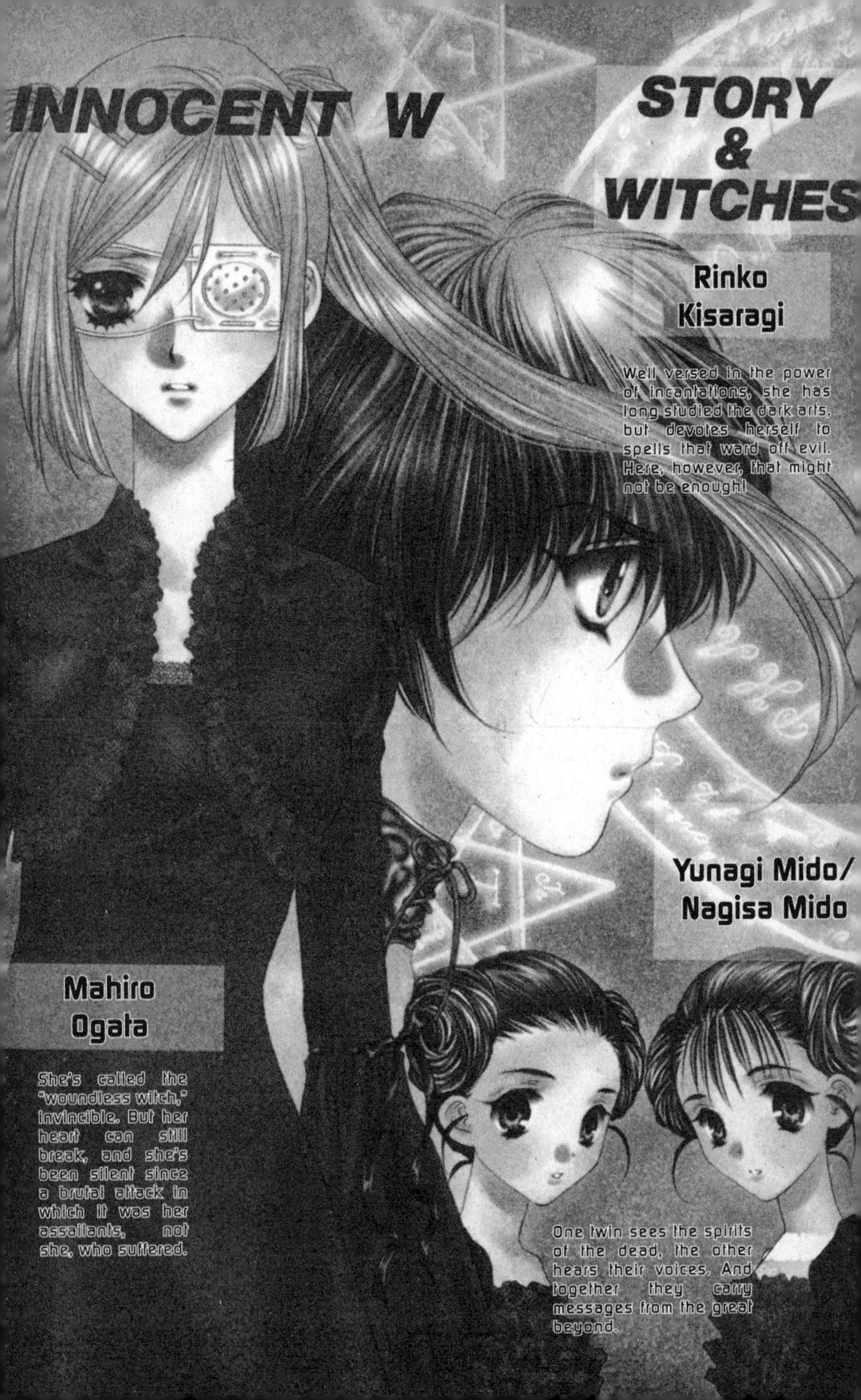
INNOCENT W
STORY & WITCHES
Rinko Kisaragi
Well versed in the power of incantations, she has long studied the dark arts, but devotes herself to spells that ward off evil. Here, however, that might not be enough!
Yunagi Mido/ Nagisa Mido
One twin sees the spirits of the dead, the other hears their voices. And together they carry messages from the great beyond.
Mahiro Ogata
She's called the "woundless witch," invincible. But her heart can still break, and she's been silent since a brutal attack in which it was her assailants, not she, who suffered.

CONTENTS

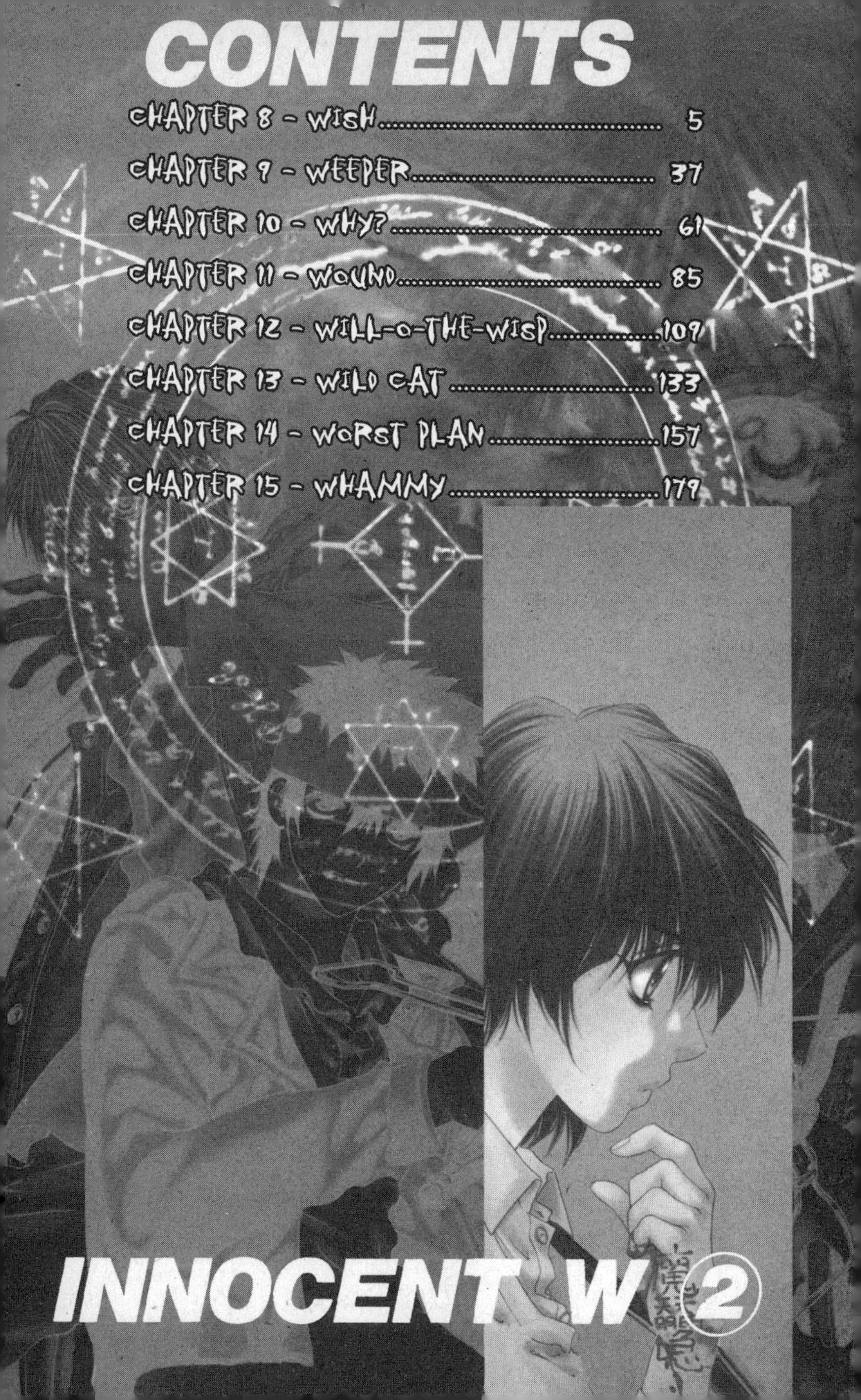

INNOCENT W 2

第8話
Soothsayer
Chiaki Kiriyu
LOOKING FOR A WITCH AMONG WITCHES ...
Tarot Reader
Midori Kusanagi

WHISH-WHAASH-WHISPER-WAIL
WHAT IS THIS PLACE? WHERE ARE WE?
"Woundless Witch" Mihiro Ogata
WONDERFUL. PERFECT. AND THIS WAS SUPPOSED TO BE EASY MONEY.
Private Detective Makoto Hirasaka

Spirit Mediums Yunagi and Nagisa Mido
STOP THE SPELL, RINKO, PLEASE...!
IT'S THE ONLY WAY... I HAVE TO DO IT...!
AND SO, FORWARD THEY FELL, INTO...
DEFEAT THE POWERS OF DARKNESS BY CASTING A SPELL OF MY OWN...!!
Incantation Expert Rinko Kisaragi

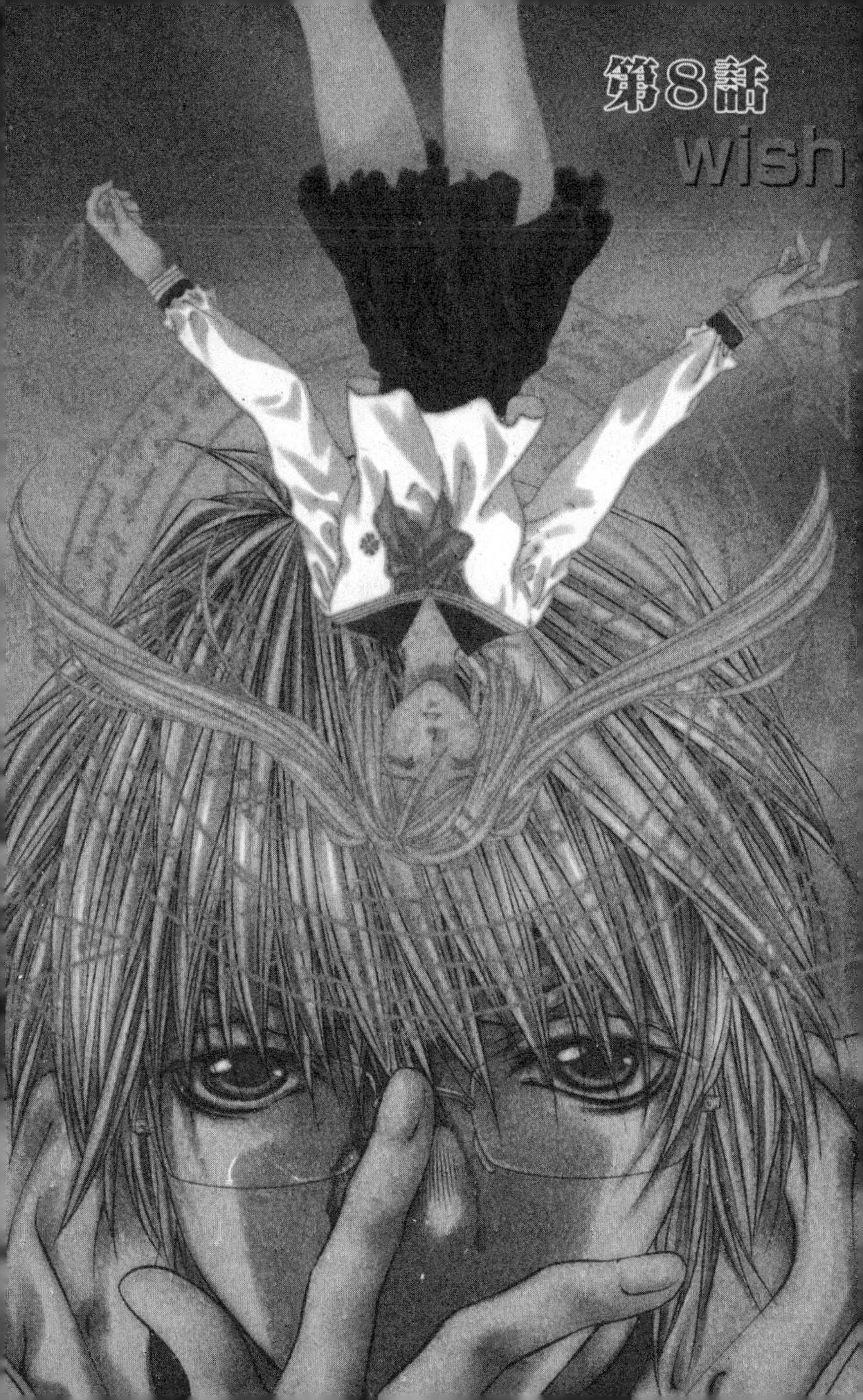
第8話
wish

VOLUME 2
BY
KEI KUSUNOKI

HAMBURG // LONDON // LOS ANGELES // TOKYO

Innocent W Vol.2
Created by Kei Kusunoki

Translation - Christopher North
English Adaption - Daniel Mishkin
Layout and Lettering - Star Print Brokers
Cover Layout - Louis Csontos

Editor - Paul Morrissey
Digital Imaging Manager - Chris Buford
Pre-Production Supervisor - Erika Terriquez
Art Director - Anne Marie Horne
Production Manager - Elisabeth Brizzi
Managing Editor - Vy Nguyen
VP of Production - Ron Klamert
Editor-in-Chief - Rob Tokar
Publisher - Mike Kiley
President and C.O.O. - John Parker
C.E.O. and Chief Creative Officer - Stuart Levy

A  Manga

TOKYOPOP Inc.
5900 Wilshire Blvd. Suite 2000
Los Angeles, CA 90036

E-mail: info@TOKYOPOP.com
Come visit us online at www.TOKYOPOP.com

ISBN: 978-1-59816-842-6

First TOKYOPOP printing: January 2007
10 9 8 7 6 5 4 3 2 1
Printed in the USA

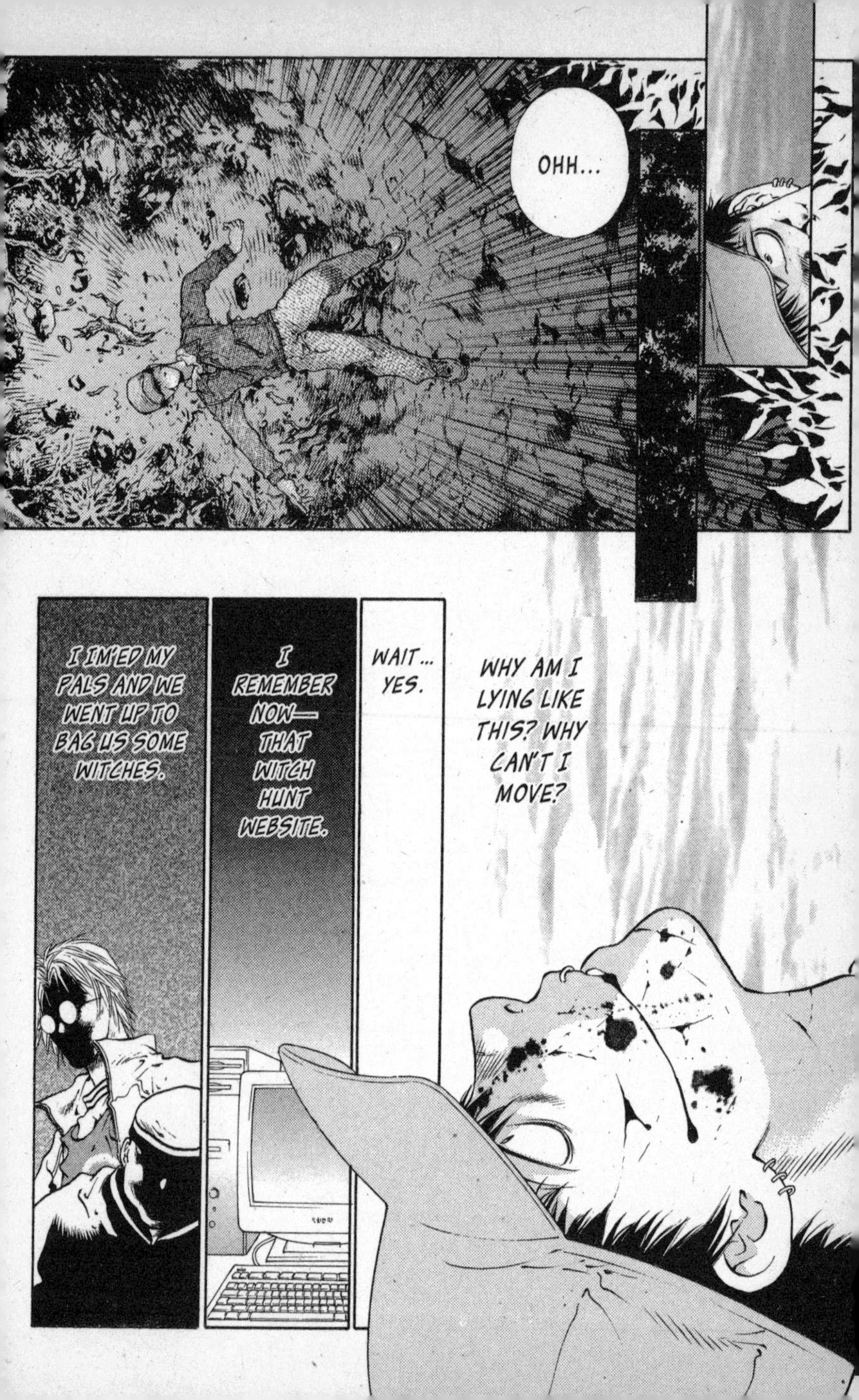
OHH...
WHY AM I LYING LIKE THIS? WHY CAN'T I MOVE?
WAIT... YES.
I REMEMBER NOW—THAT WITCH HUNT WEBSITE.
I IM'ED MY PALS AND WE WENT UP TO BAG US SOME WITCHES.

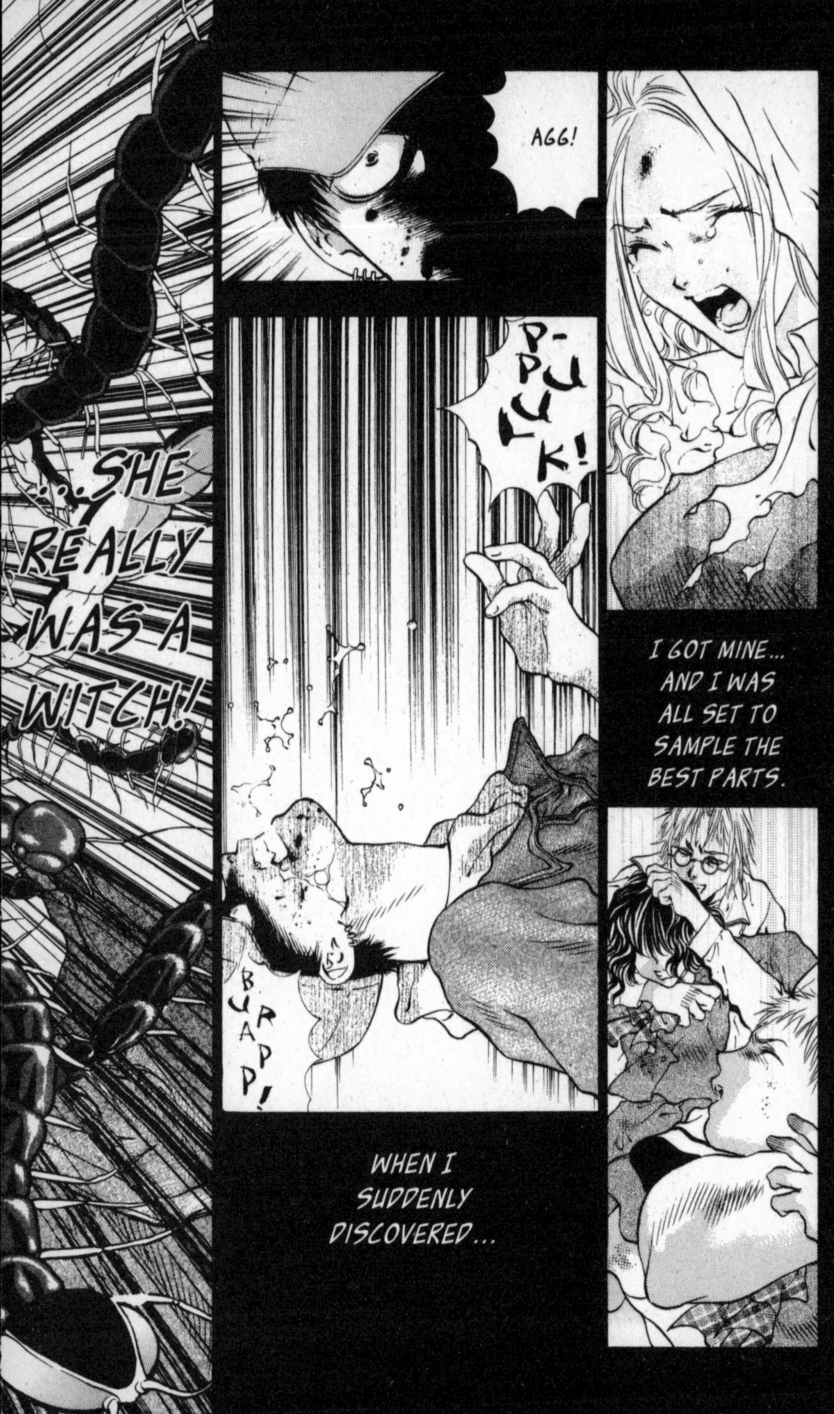

I GOT MINE... AND I WAS ALL SET TO SAMPLE THE BEST PARTS.
AGG!
P-PUJUK!
BURAPP!
WHEN I SUDDENLY DISCOVERED...
...SHE REALLY WAS A WITCH!

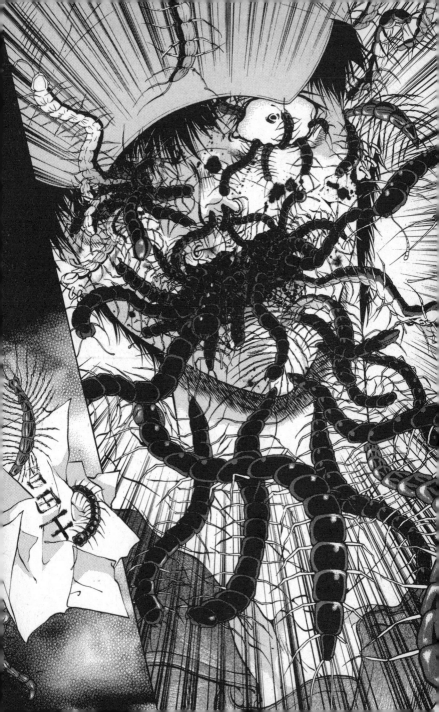

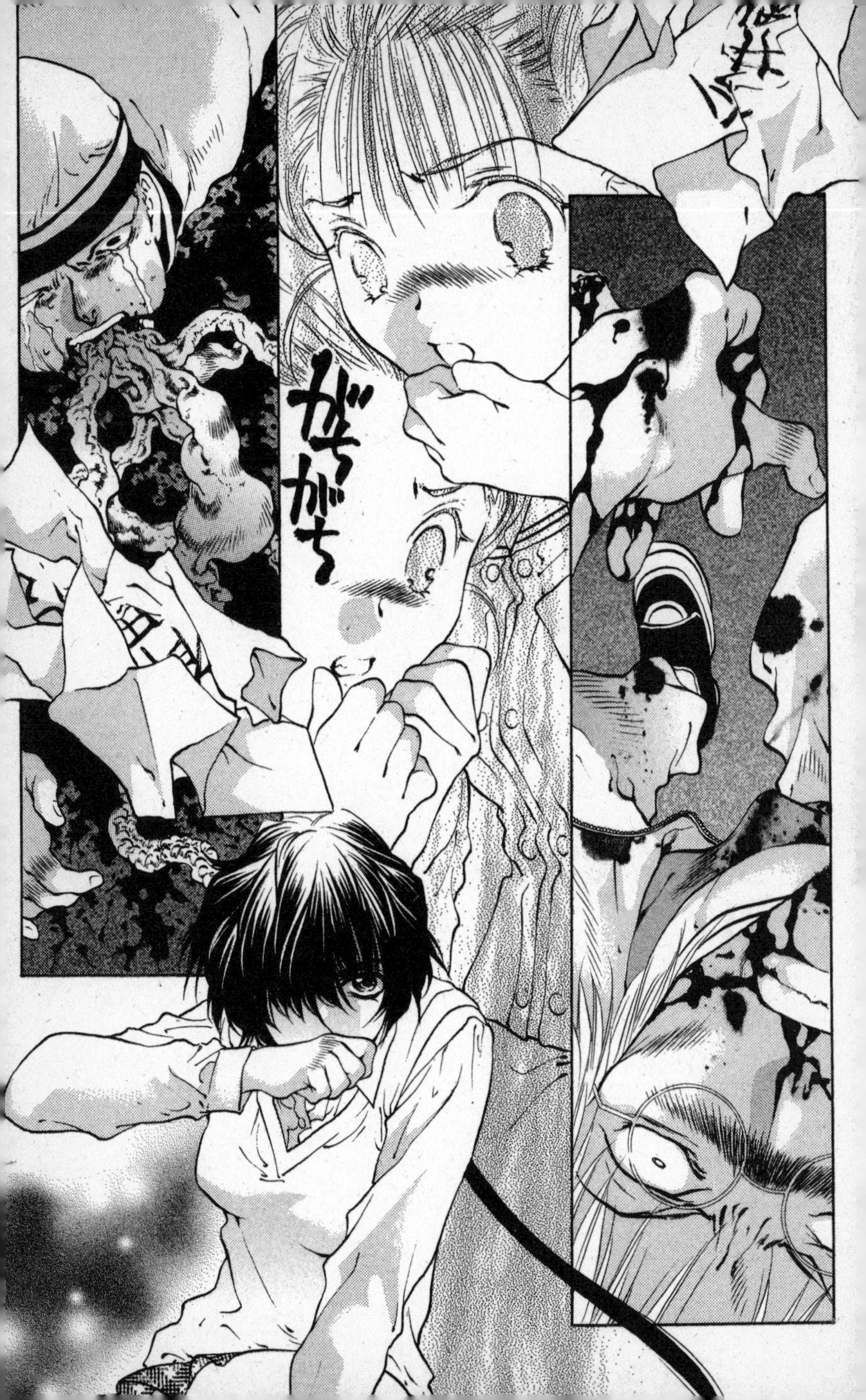
がちがち

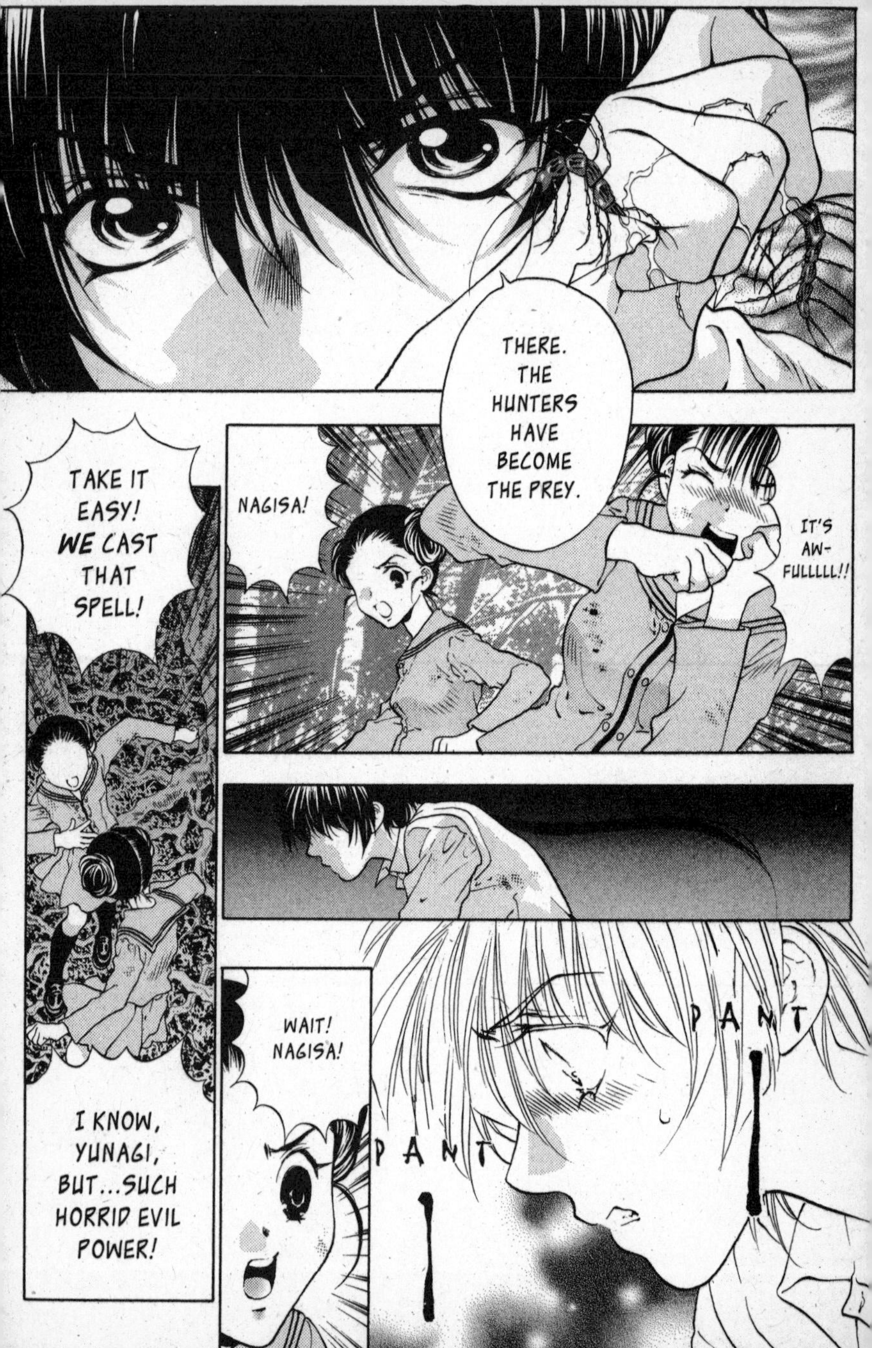

THERE. THE HUNTERS HAVE BECOME THE PREY.
IT'S AW-FULLLLLL!!
NAGISA!
PANT
WAIT! NAGISA!
PANT
TAKE IT EASY! **WE** CAST THAT SPELL!
I KNOW, YUNAGI, BUT...SUCH HORRID EVIL POWER!

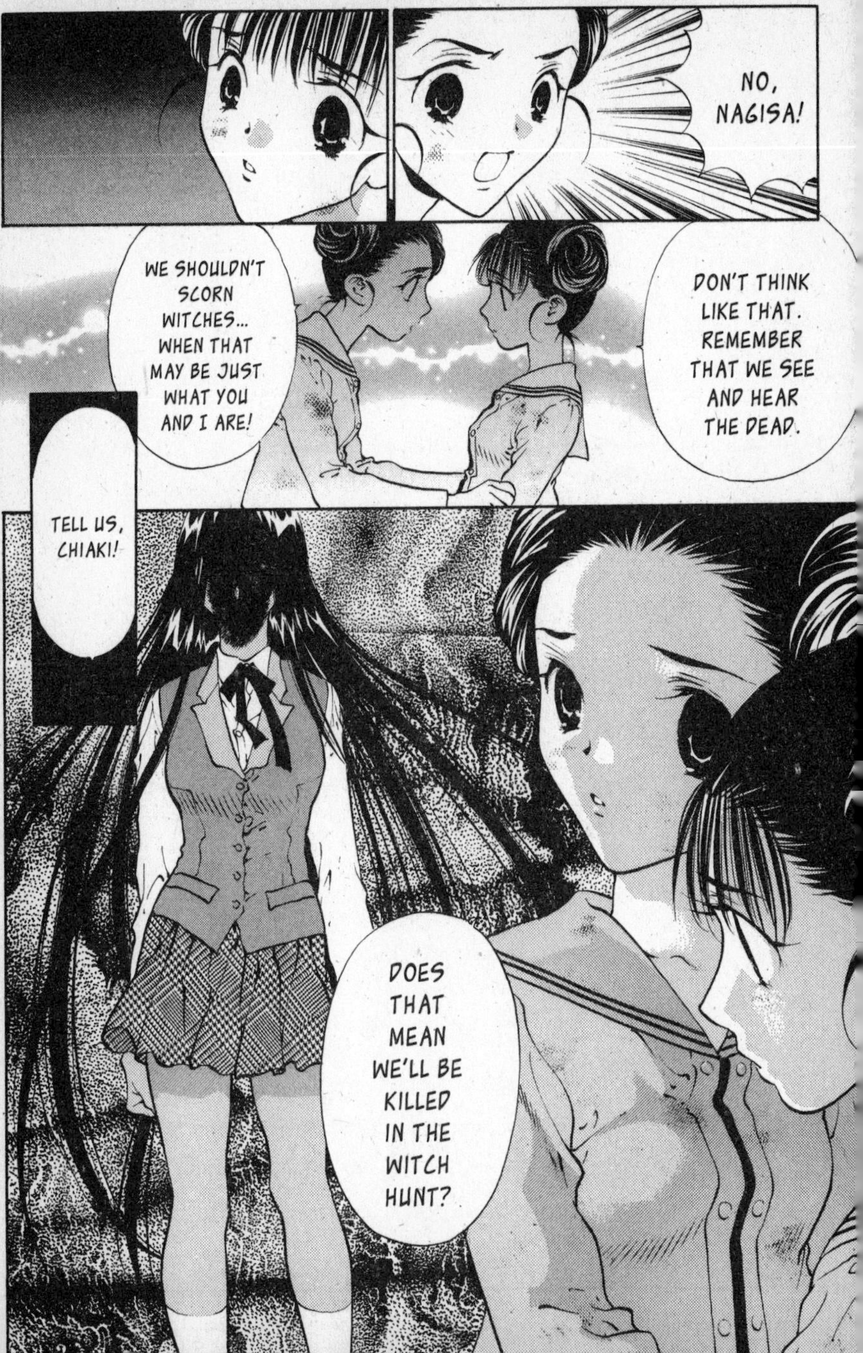
NO, NAGISA!
DON'T THINK LIKE THAT. REMEMBER THAT WE SEE AND HEAR THE DEAD.
WE SHOULDN'T SCORN WITCHES... WHEN THAT MAY BE JUST WHAT YOU AND I ARE!
DOES THAT MEAN WE'LL BE KILLED IN THE WITCH HUNT?
TELL US, CHIAKI!

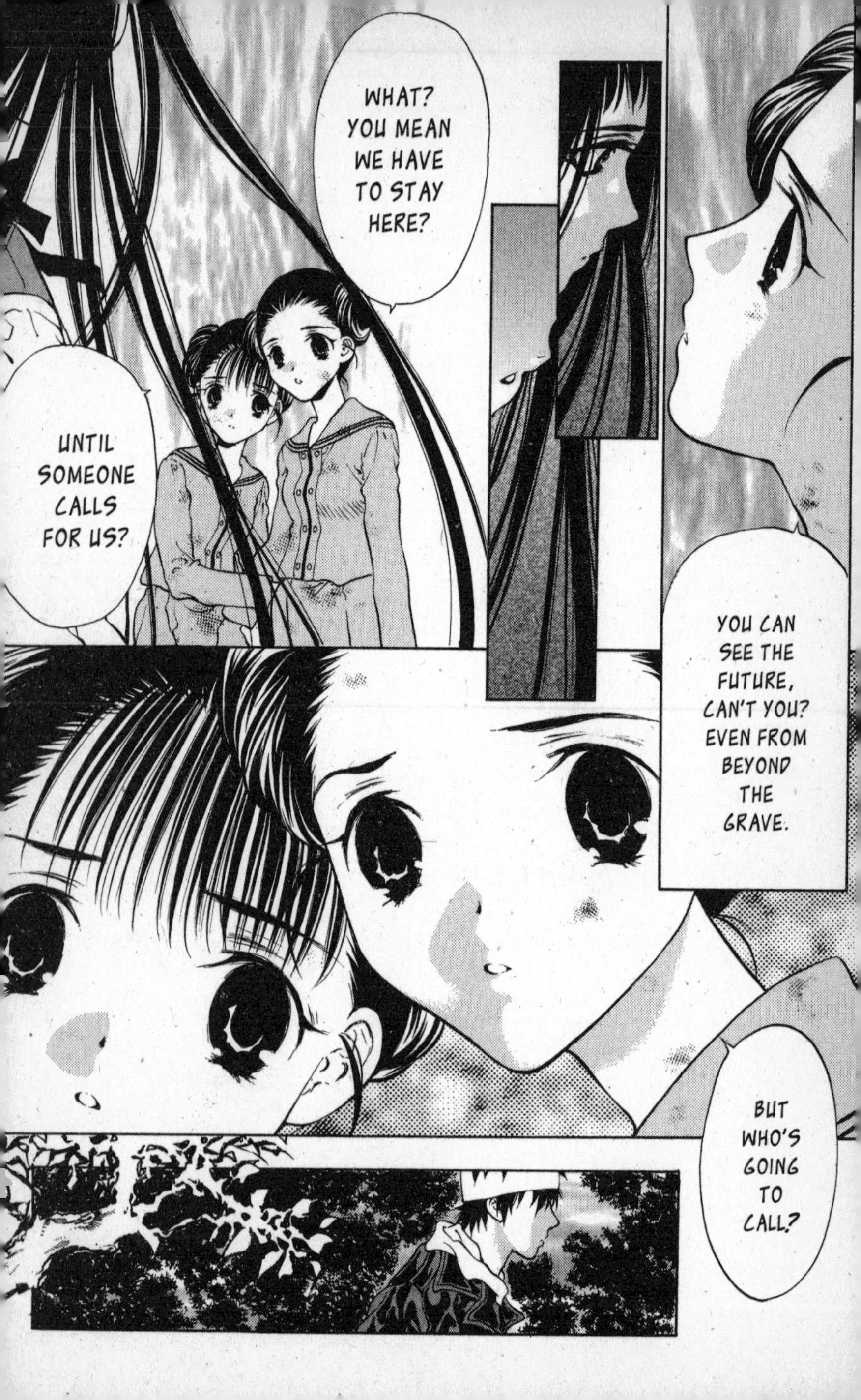
WHAT? YOU MEAN WE HAVE TO STAY HERE?
UNTIL SOMEONE CALLS FOR US?
YOU CAN SEE THE FUTURE, CAN'T YOU? EVEN FROM BEYOND THE GRAVE.
BUT WHO'S GOING TO CALL?

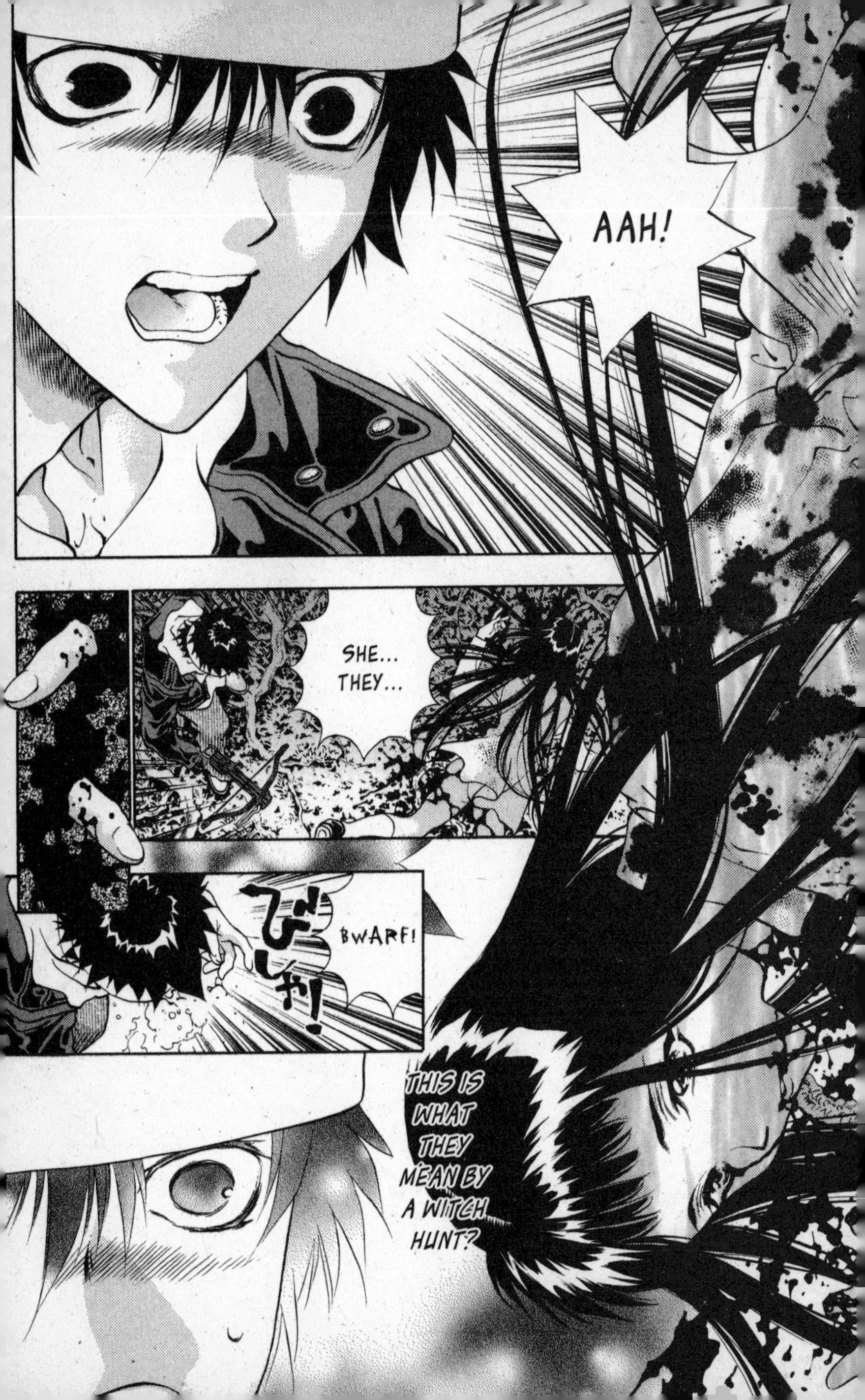
AAH!
SHE... THEY...
BWARF!
THIS IS WHAT THEY MEAN BY A WITCH HUNT?

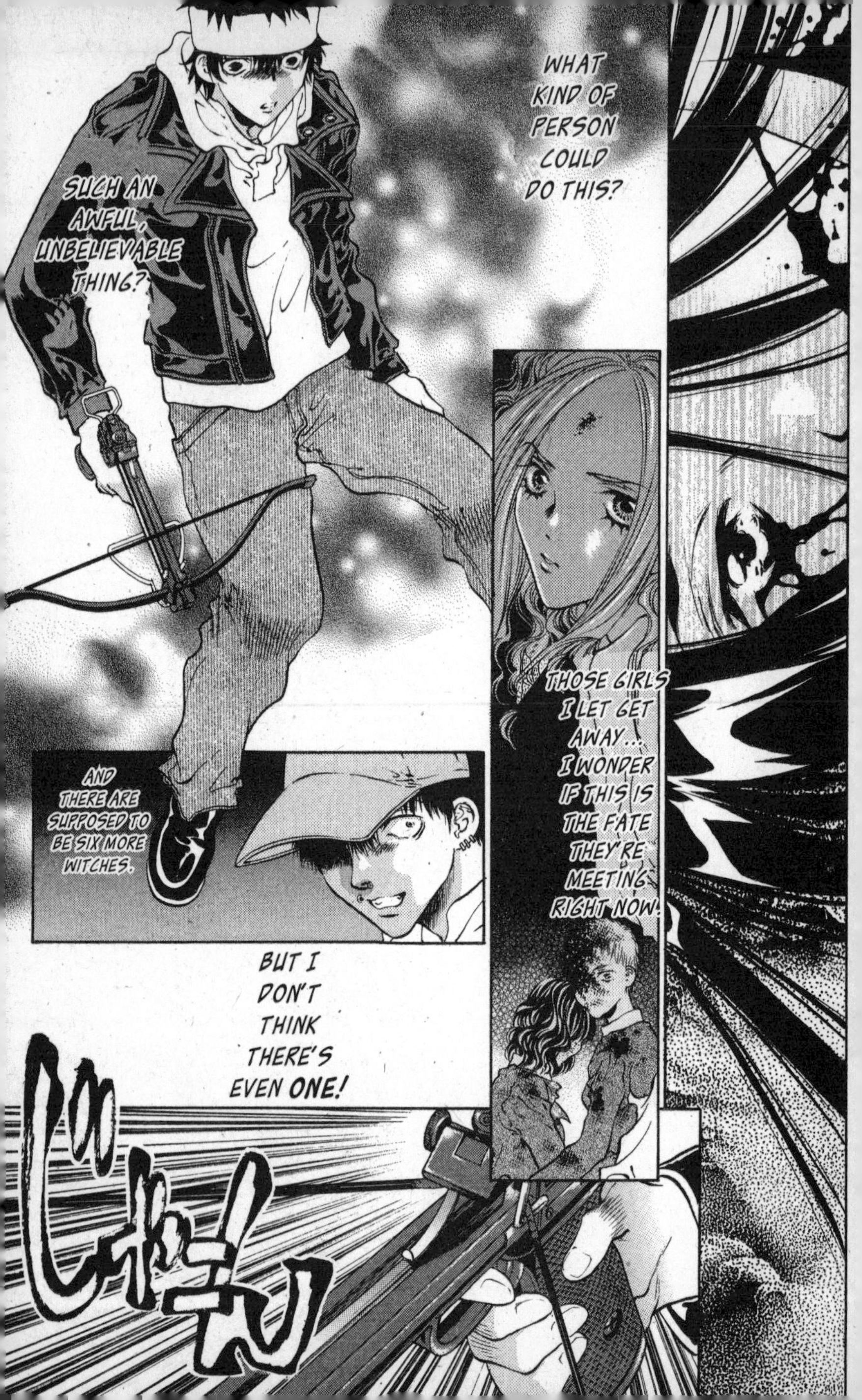
WHAT KIND OF PERSON COULD DO THIS?
SUCH AN AWFUL, UNBELIEVABLE THING?
THOSE GIRLS I LET GET AWAY... I WONDER IF THIS IS THE FATE THEY'RE MEETING RIGHT NOW!
AND THERE ARE SUPPOSED TO BE SIX MORE WITCHES.
BUT I DON'T THINK THERE'S EVEN ONE!

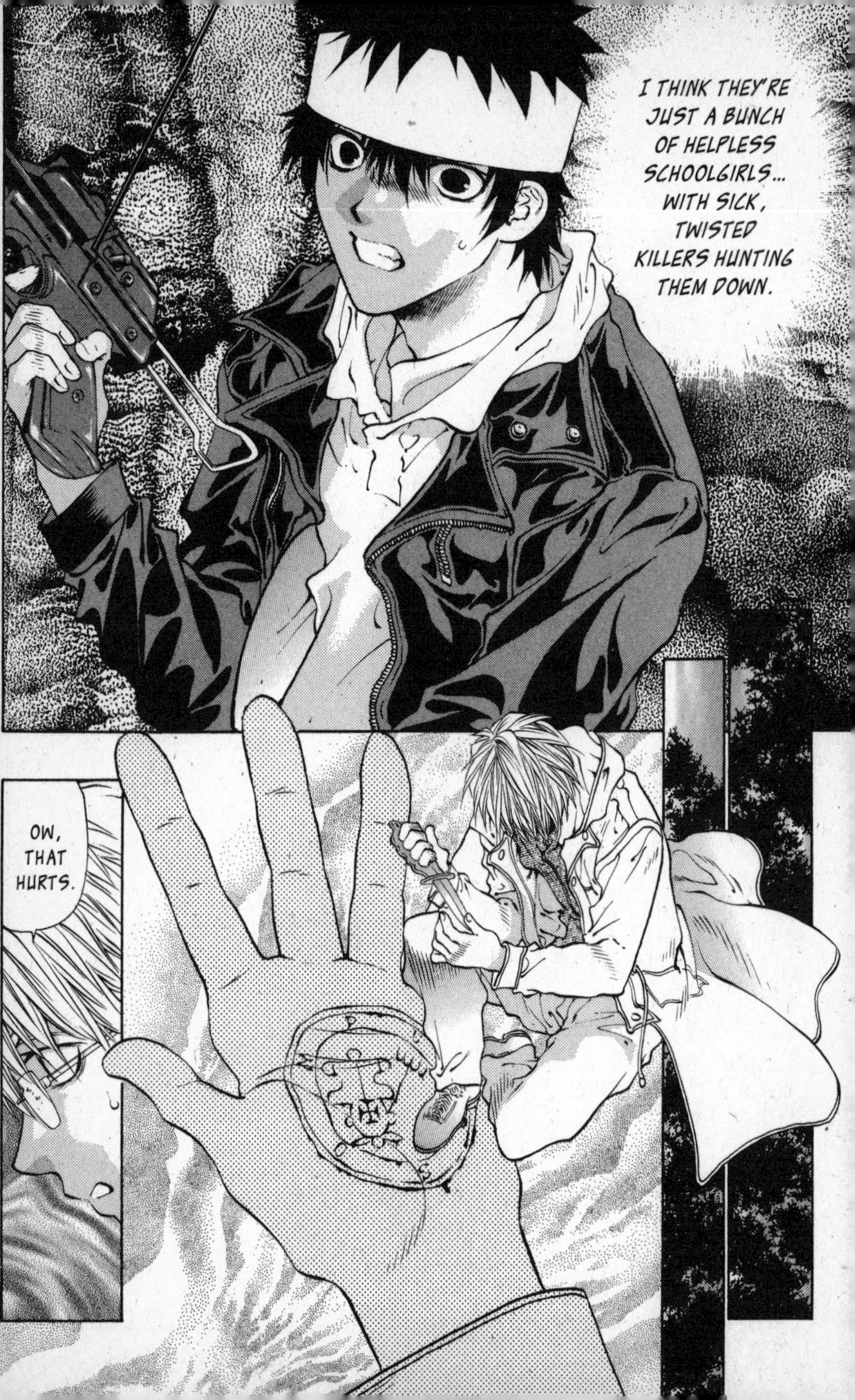
I THINK THEY'RE JUST A BUNCH OF HELPLESS SCHOOLGIRLS... WITH SICK, TWISTED KILLERS HUNTING THEM DOWN.
OW, THAT HURTS.

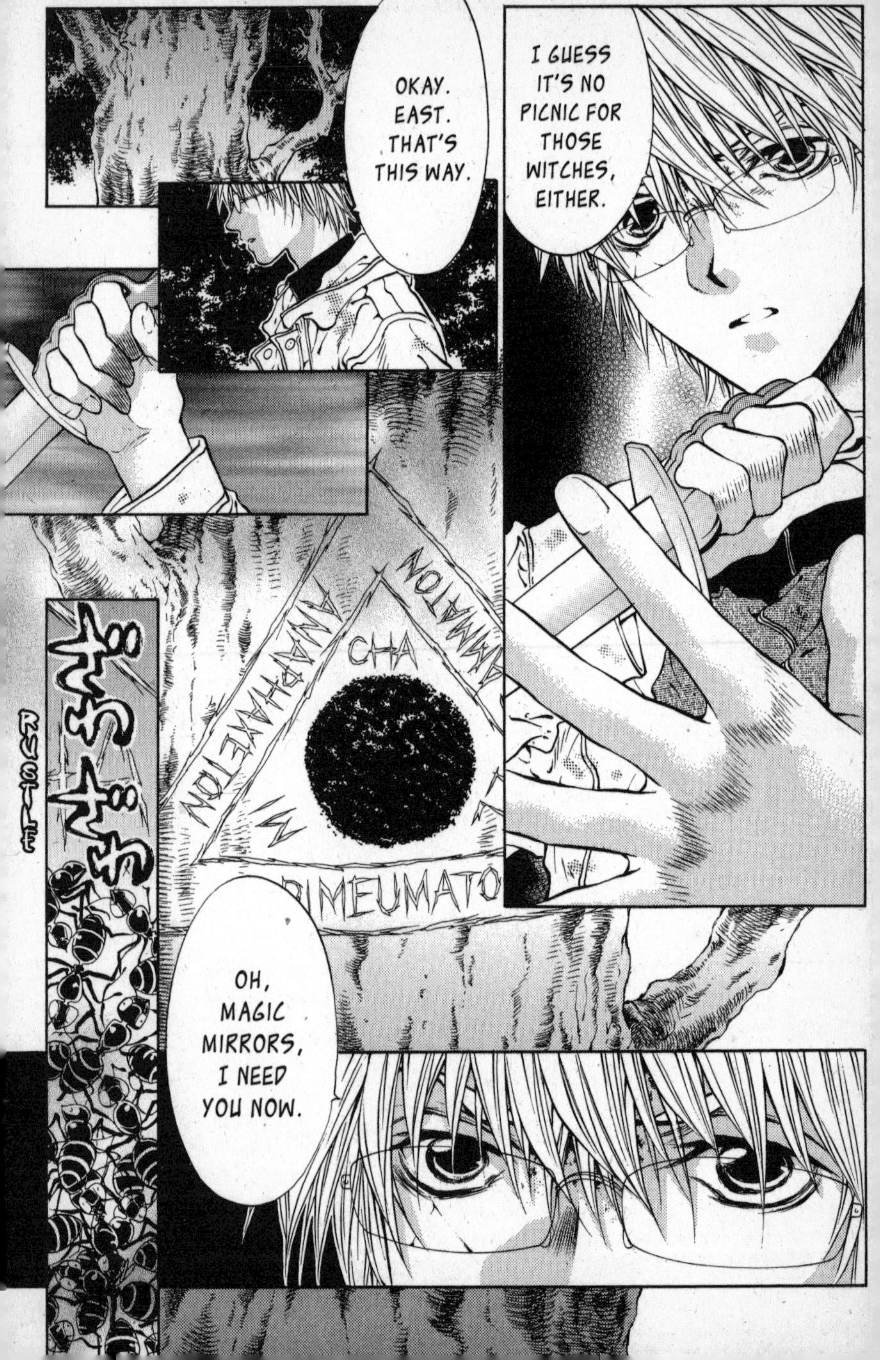
I GUESS IT'S NO PICNIC FOR THOSE WITCHES, EITHER.
OKAY. EAST. THAT'S THIS WAY.
OH, MAGIC MIRRORS, I NEED YOU NOW.

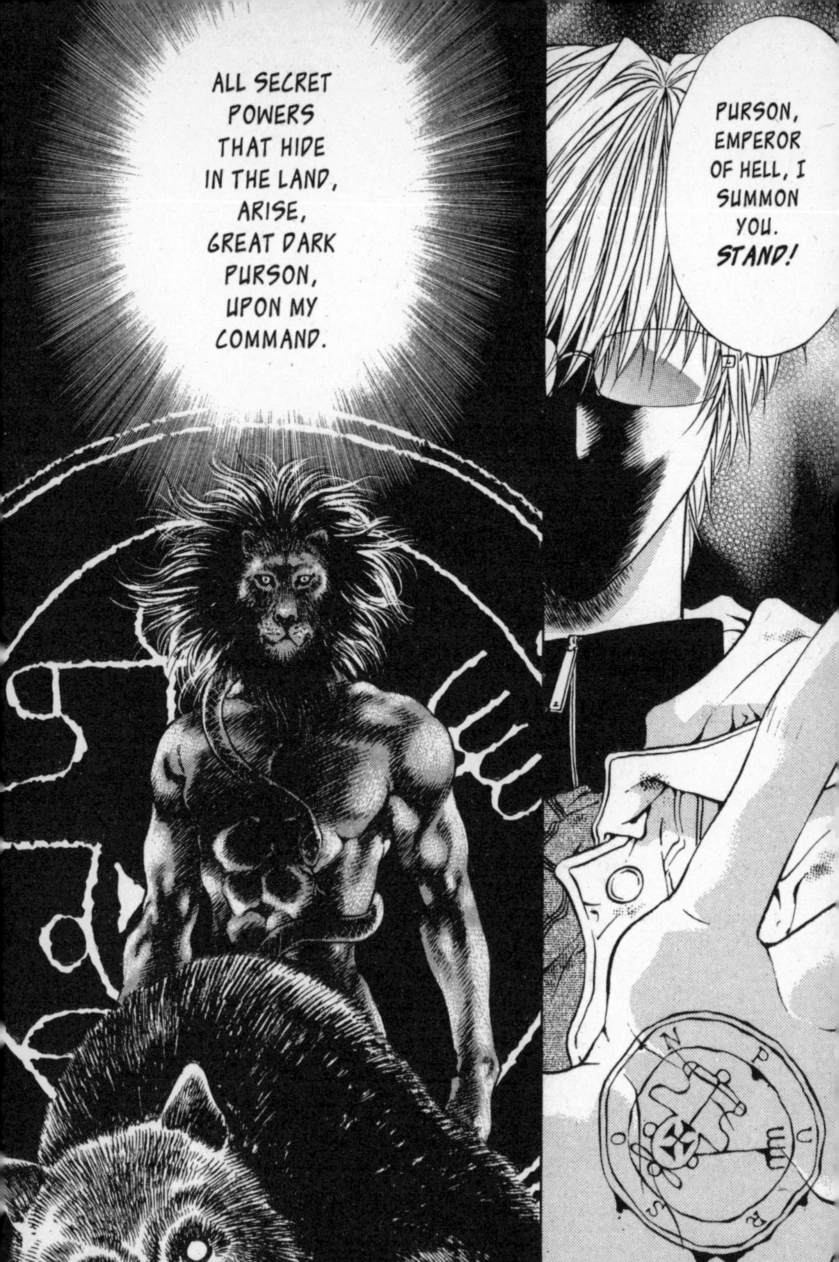
PURSON, EMPEROR OF HELL, I SUMMON YOU. **STAND!**
ALL SECRET POWERS THAT HIDE IN THE LAND, ARISE, GREAT DARK PURSON, UPON MY COMMAND.

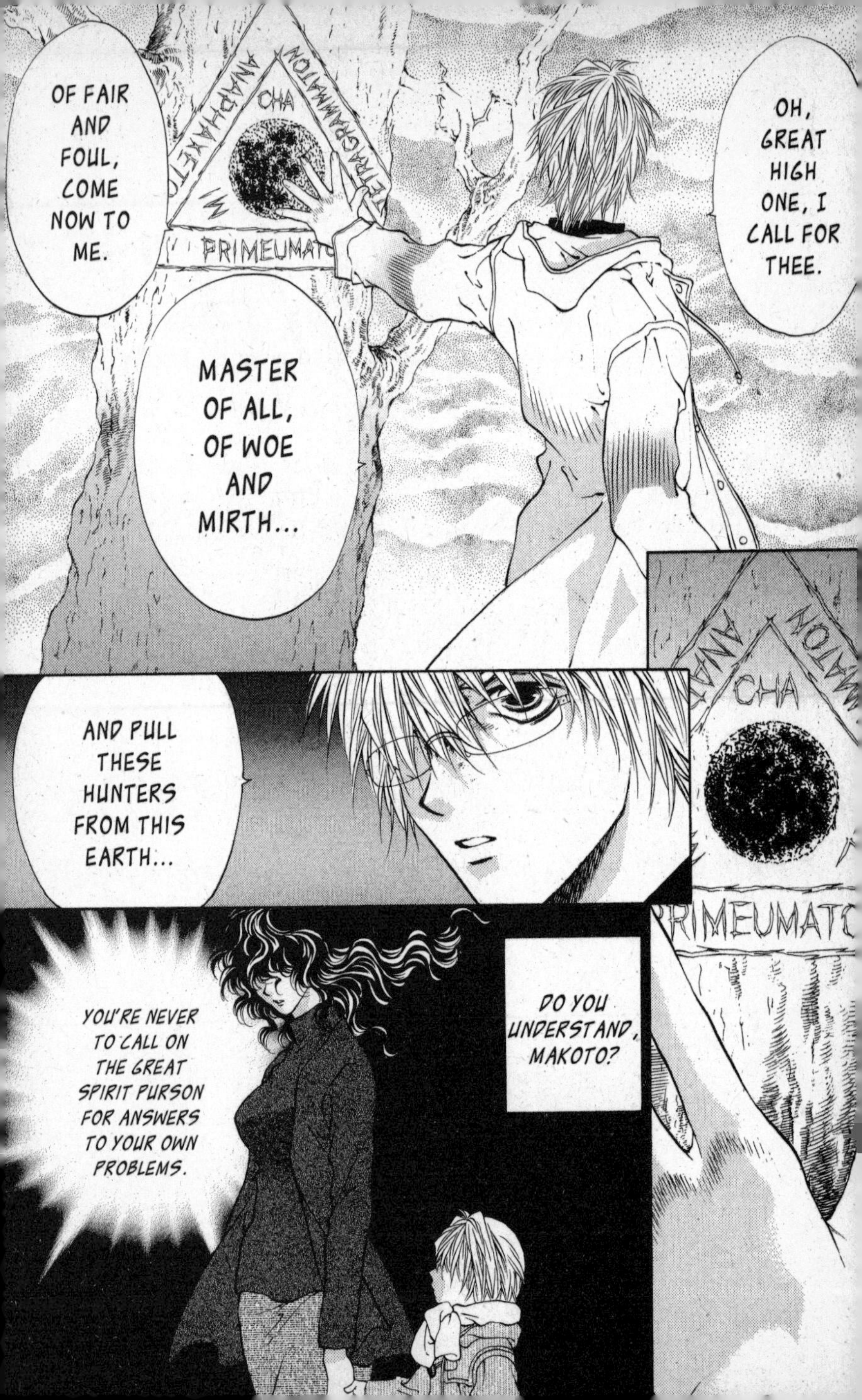
OH, GREAT HIGH ONE, I CALL FOR THEE.
OF FAIR AND FOUL, COME NOW TO ME.
CHA
PRIMEUMATO
MASTER OF ALL, OF WOE AND MIRTH...
CHA
PRIMEUMATO
AND PULL THESE HUNTERS FROM THIS EARTH...
DO YOU UNDERSTAND, MAKOTO?
YOU'RE NEVER TO CALL ON THE GREAT SPIRIT PURSON FOR ANSWERS TO YOUR OWN PROBLEMS.

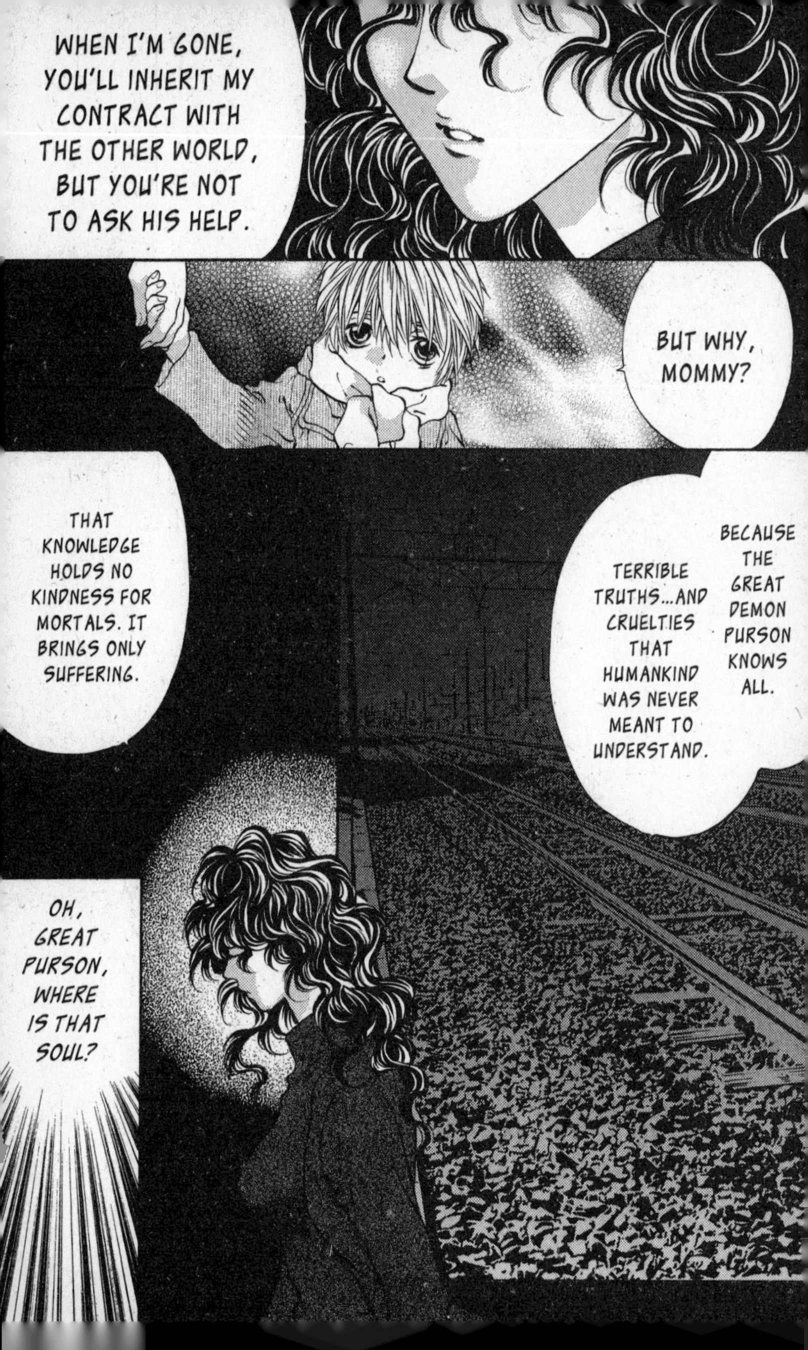
WHEN I'M GONE, YOU'LL INHERIT MY CONTRACT WITH THE OTHER WORLD, BUT YOU'RE NOT TO ASK HIS HELP.
BUT WHY, MOMMY?
BECAUSE THE GREAT DEMON PURSON KNOWS ALL.
TERRIBLE TRUTHS...AND CRUELTIES THAT HUMANKIND WAS NEVER MEANT TO UNDERSTAND.
THAT KNOWLEDGE HOLDS NO KINDNESS FOR MORTALS. IT BRINGS ONLY SUFFERING.
OH, GREAT PURSON, WHERE IS THAT SOUL?

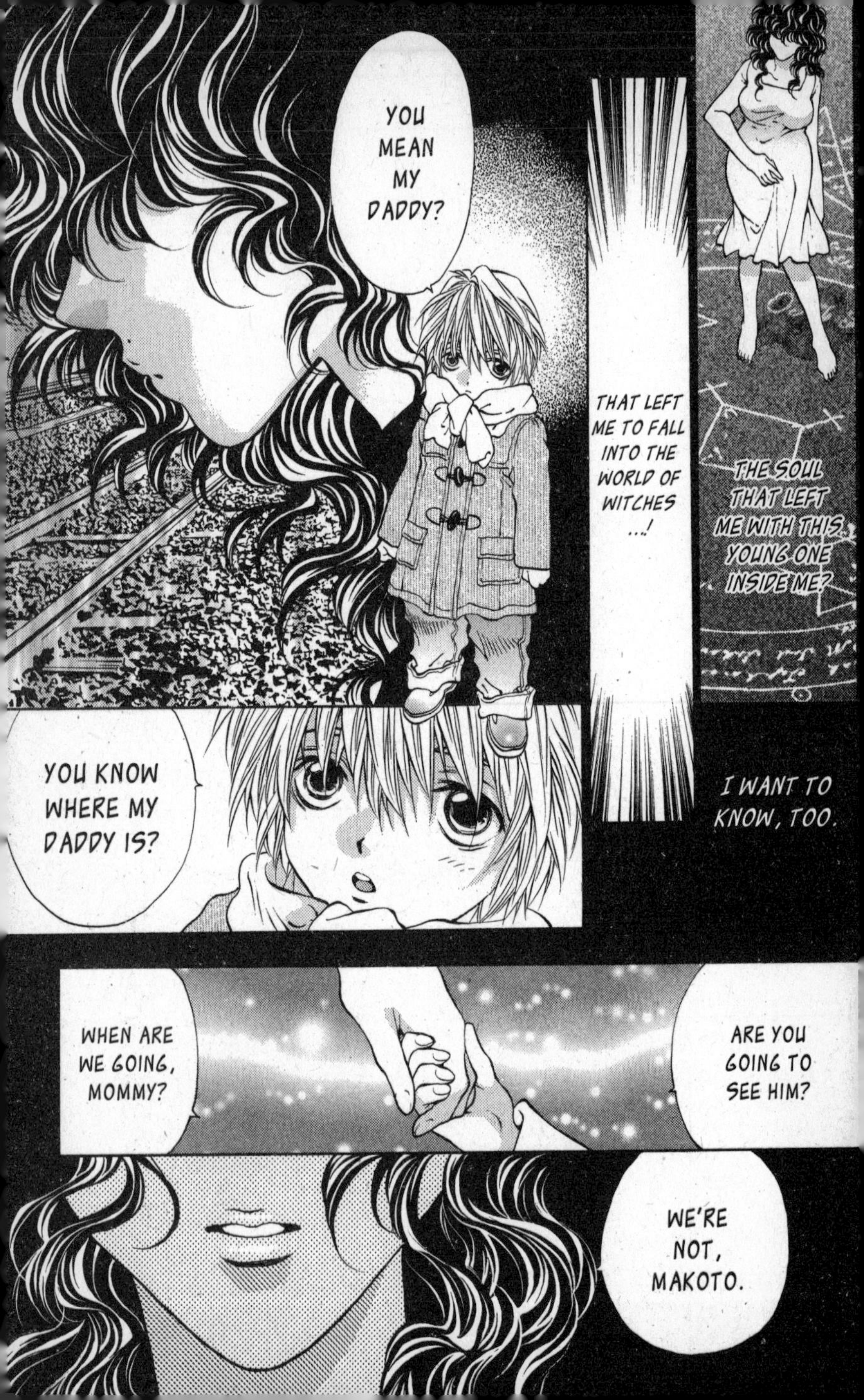
THE SOUL THAT LEFT ME WITH THIS YOUNG ONE INSIDE ME?
THAT LEFT ME TO FALL INTO THE WORLD OF WITCHES ...!
YOU MEAN MY DADDY?
I WANT TO KNOW, TOO.
YOU KNOW WHERE MY DADDY IS?
ARE YOU GOING TO SEE HIM?
WHEN ARE WE GOING, MOMMY?
WE'RE NOT, MAKOTO.

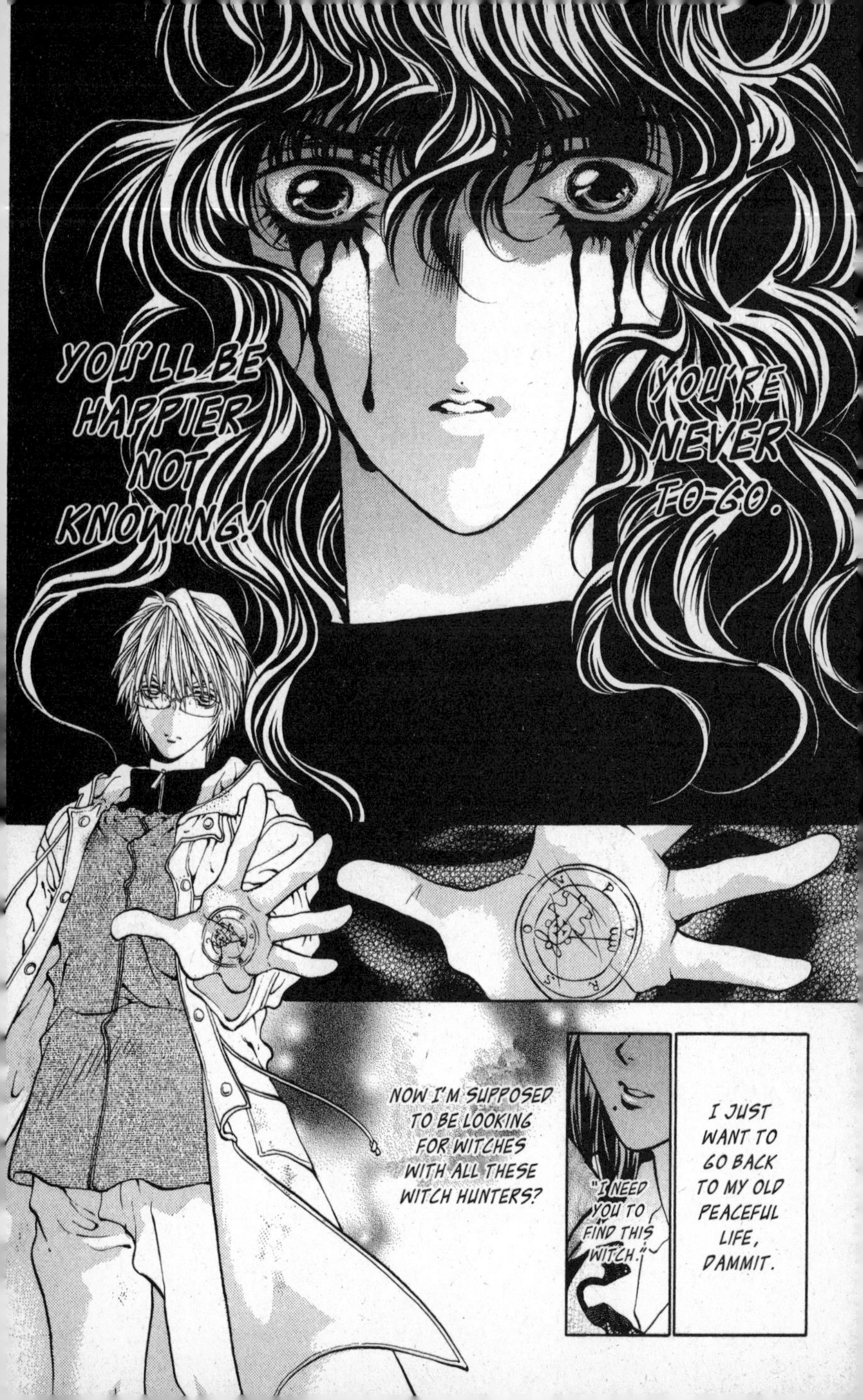
YOU'RE NEVER TO GO.
YOU'LL BE HAPPIER NOT KNOWING!
I JUST WANT TO GO BACK TO MY OLD PEACEFUL LIFE, DAMMIT.
"I NEED YOU TO FIND THIS WITCH."
NOW I'M SUPPOSED TO BE LOOKING FOR WITCHES WITH ALL THESE WITCH HUNTERS?

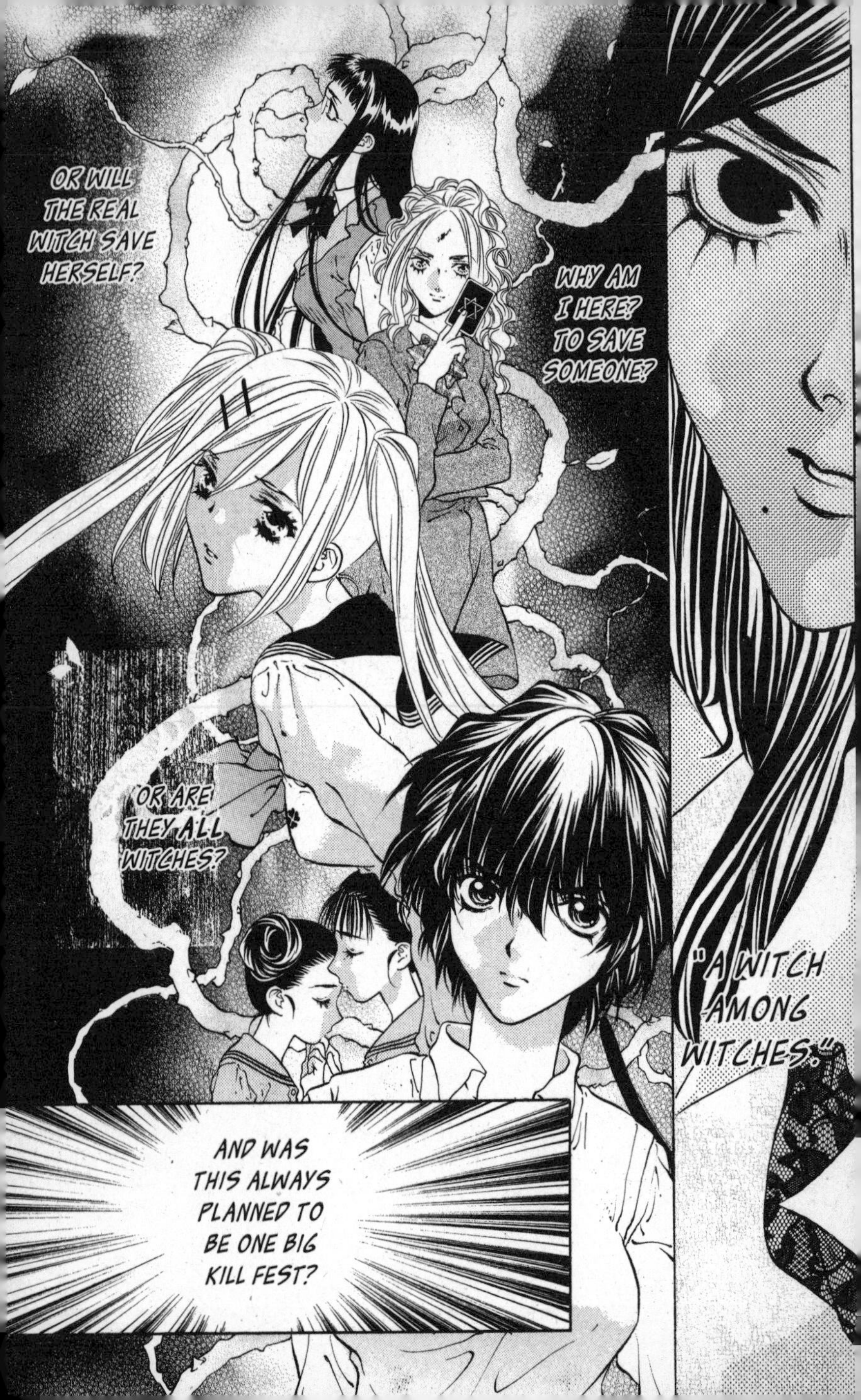
"A WITCH AMONG WITCHES."
WHY AM I HERE? TO SAVE SOMEONE?
OR WILL THE REAL WITCH SAVE HERSELF?
OR ARE THEY ALL WITCHES?
AND WAS THIS ALWAYS PLANNED TO BE ONE BIG KILL FEST?

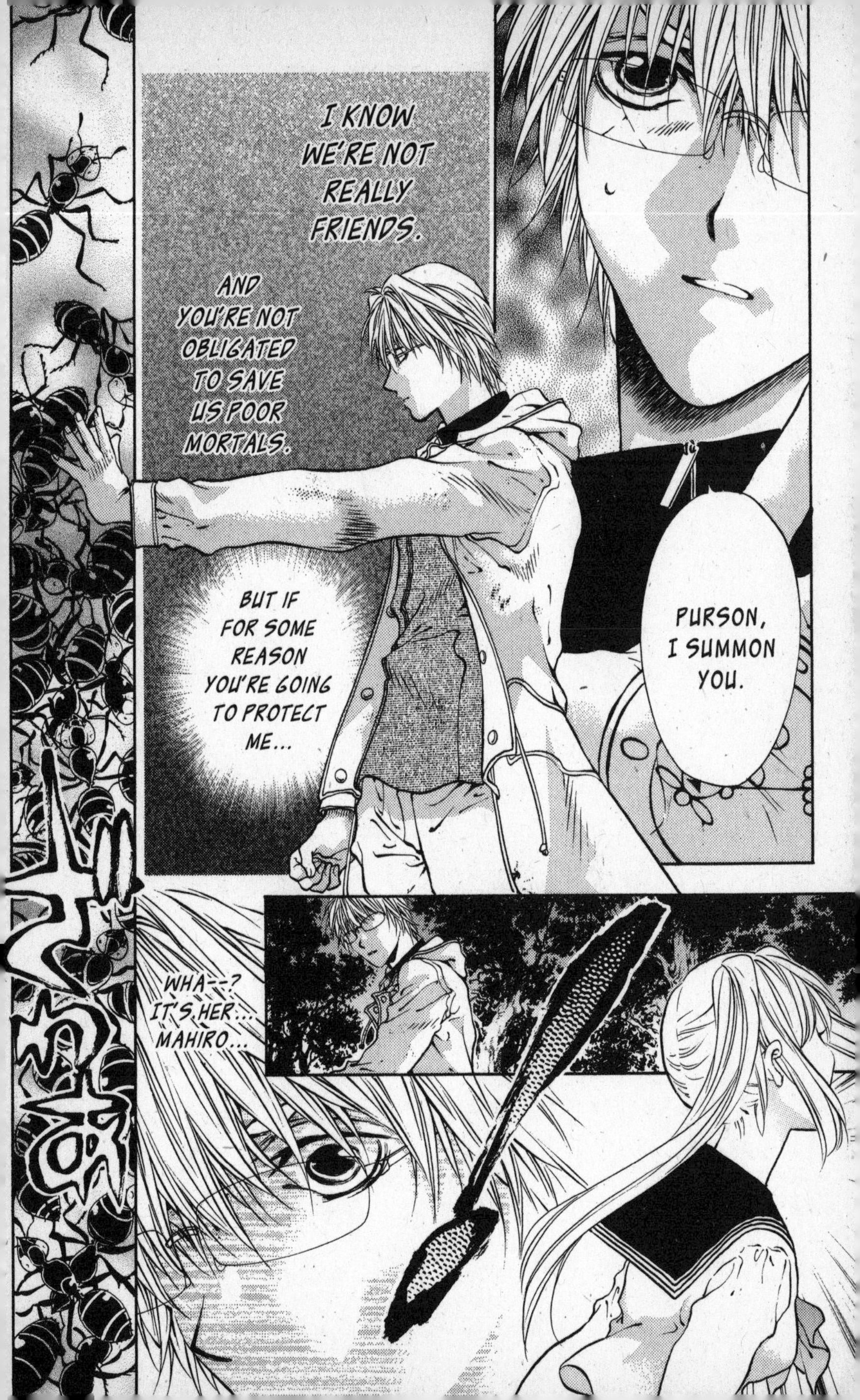
I KNOW WE'RE NOT REALLY FRIENDS.
AND YOU'RE NOT OBLIGATED TO SAVE US POOR MORTALS.
BUT IF FOR SOME REASON YOU'RE GOING TO PROTECT ME...
PURSON, I SUMMON YOU.
WHA--? IT'S HER... MAHIRO...

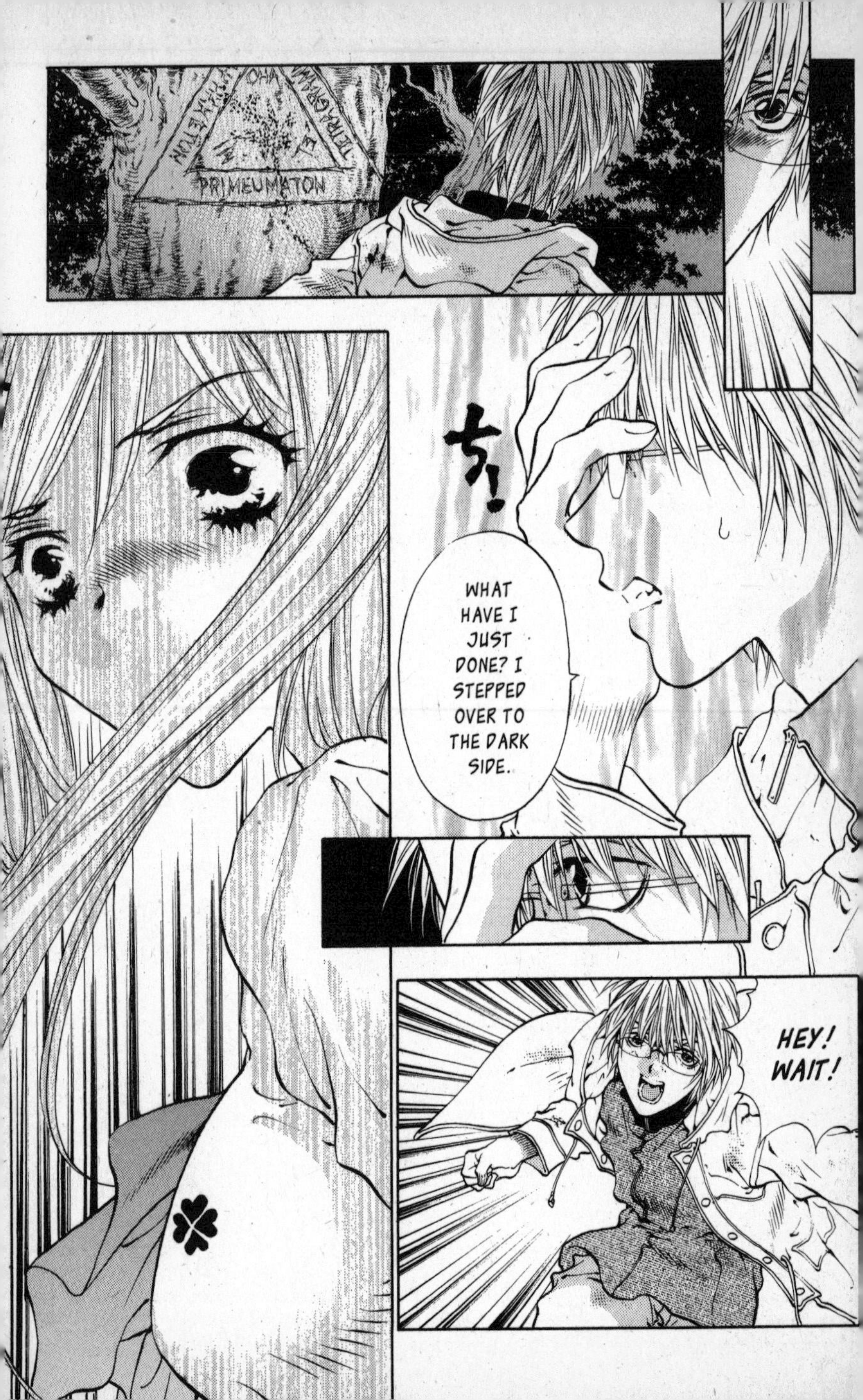
PRIMEUMATON
ち!
WHAT HAVE I JUST DONE? I STEPPED OVER TO THE DARK SIDE.
HEY! WAIT!

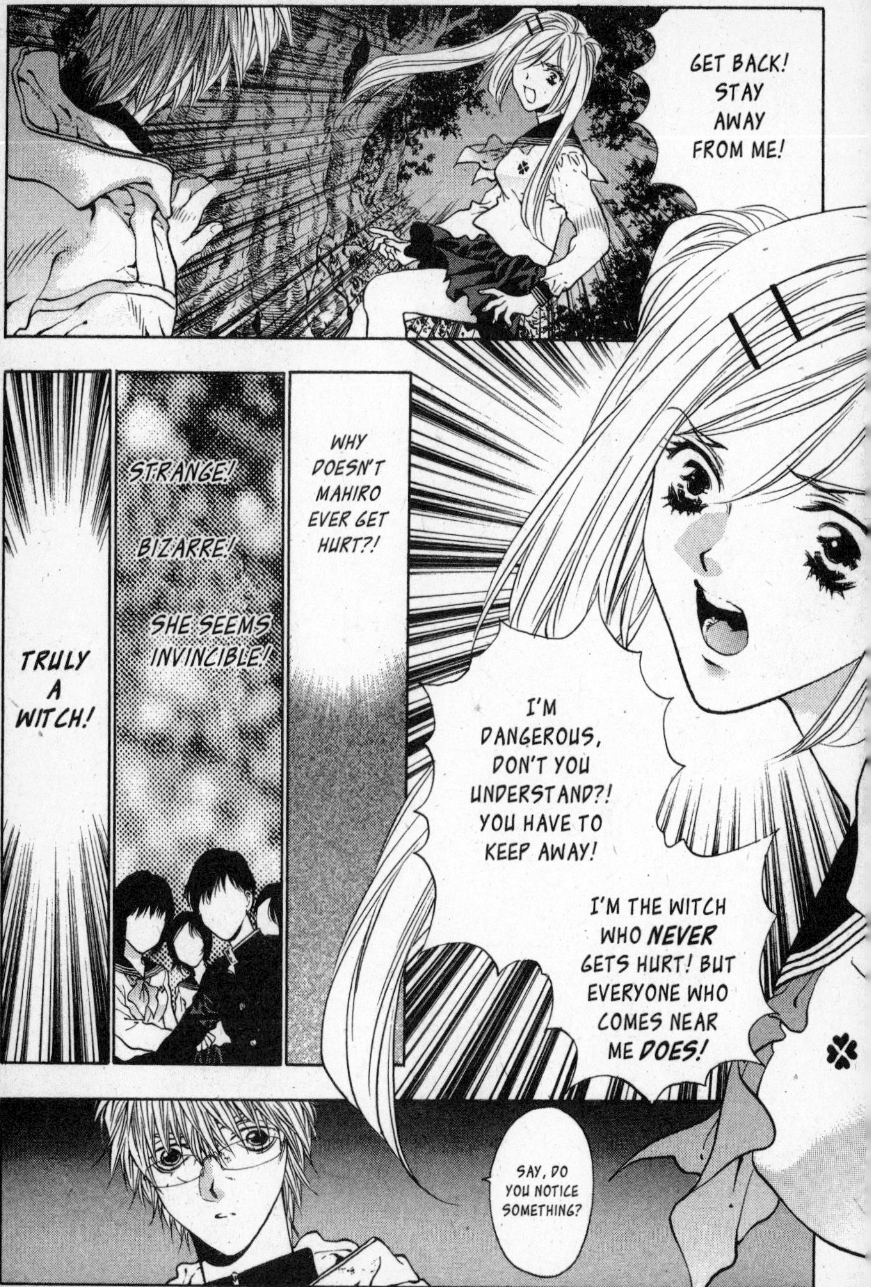
GET BACK! STAY AWAY FROM ME!
I'M DANGEROUS, DON'T YOU UNDERSTAND?! YOU HAVE TO KEEP AWAY!
I'M THE WITCH WHO **NEVER** GETS HURT! BUT EVERYONE WHO COMES NEAR ME ***DOES!***
WHY DOESN'T MAHIRO EVER GET HURT?!
STRANGE!
BIZARRE!
SHE SEEMS INVINCIBLE!
TRULY A WITCH!
SAY, DO YOU NOTICE SOMETHING?

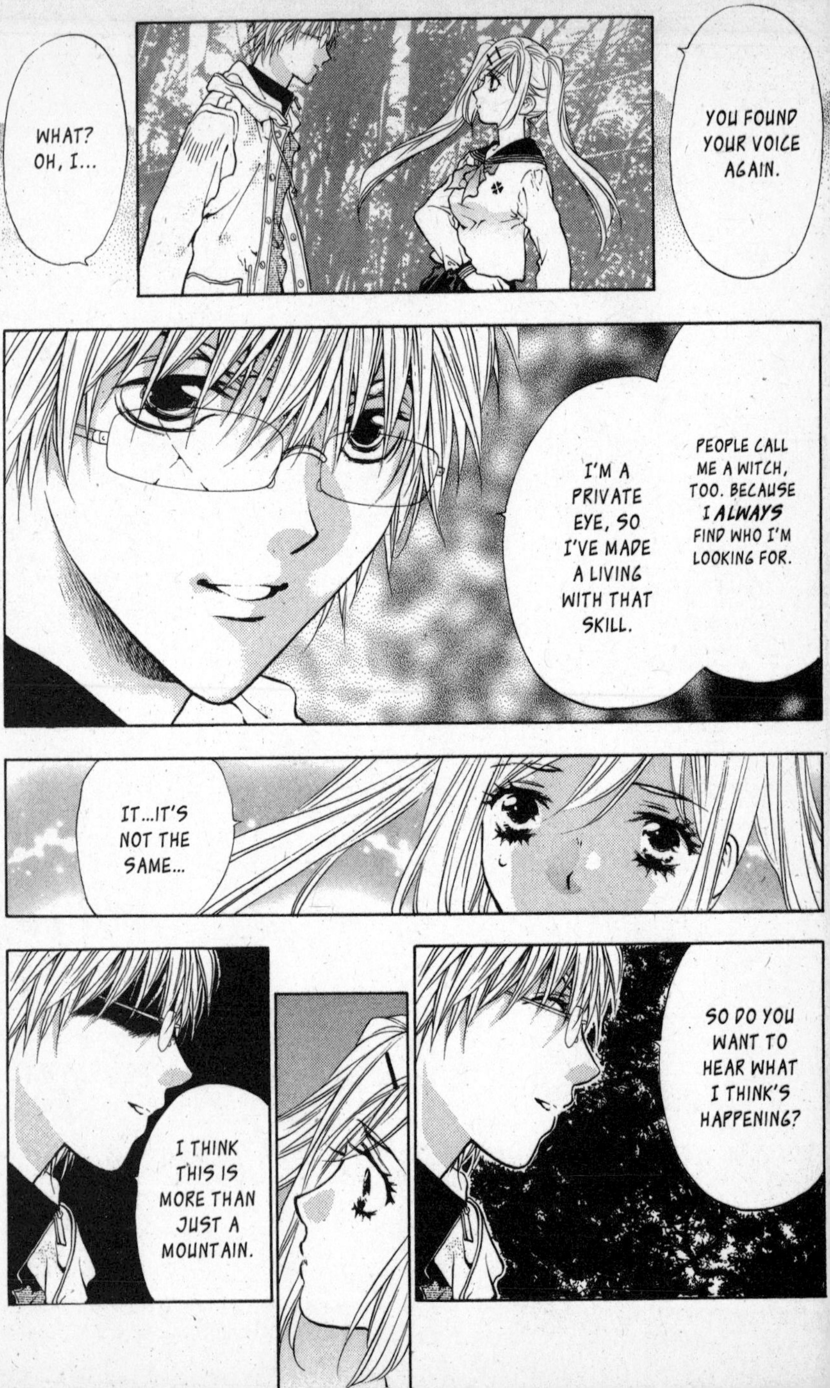
YOU FOUND YOUR VOICE AGAIN.
WHAT? OH, I...
PEOPLE CALL ME A WITCH, TOO. BECAUSE I ***ALWAYS*** FIND WHO I'M LOOKING FOR.
I'M A PRIVATE EYE, SO I'VE MADE A LIVING WITH THAT SKILL.
IT...IT'S NOT THE SAME...
SO DO YOU WANT TO HEAR WHAT I THINK'S HAPPENING?
I THINK THIS IS MORE THAN JUST A MOUNTAIN.

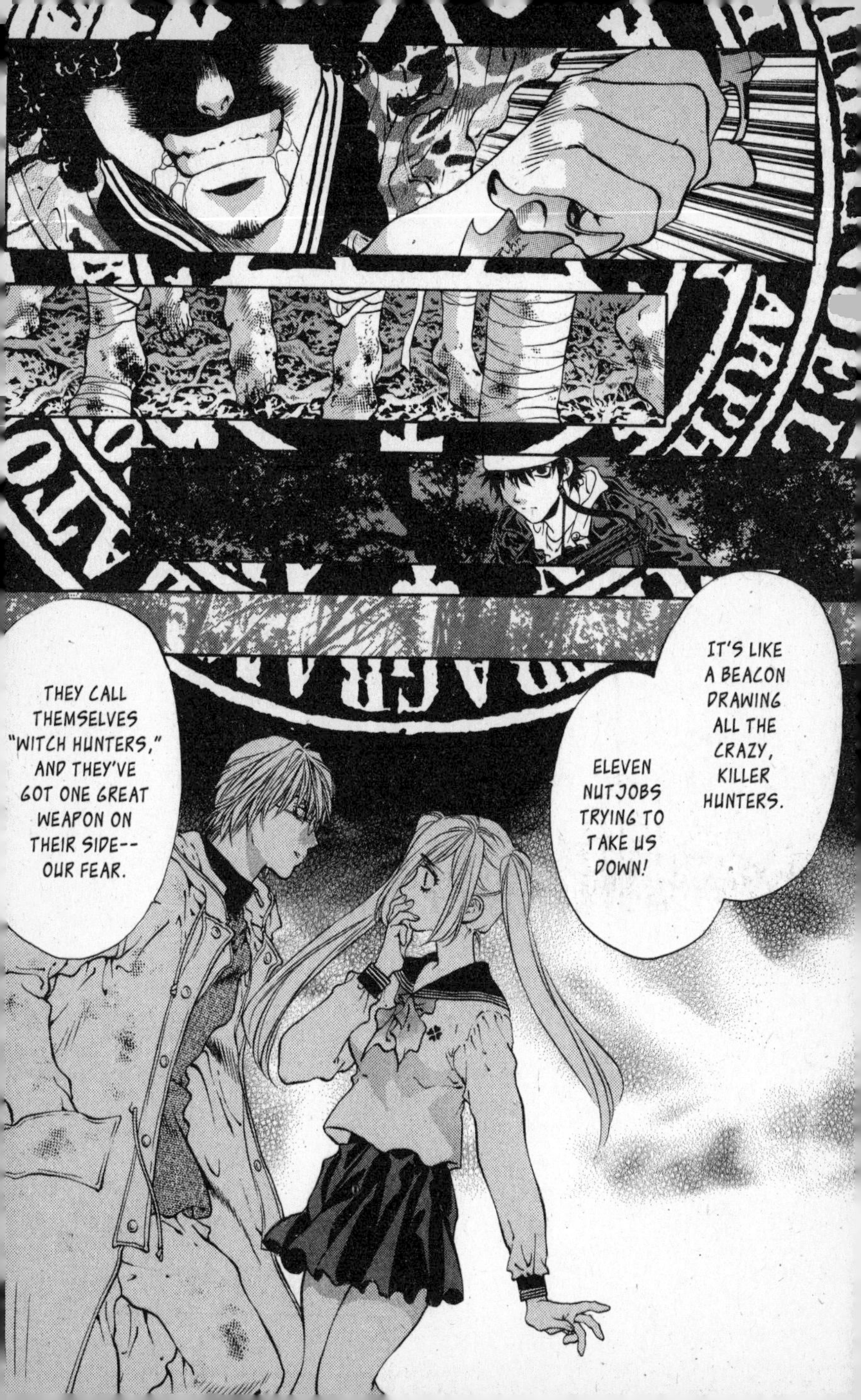
IT'S LIKE A BEACON DRAWING ALL THE CRAZY, KILLER HUNTERS.
ELEVEN NUTJOBS TRYING TO TAKE US DOWN!
THEY CALL THEMSELVES "WITCH HUNTERS," AND THEY'VE GOT ONE GREAT WEAPON ON THEIR SIDE-- OUR FEAR.

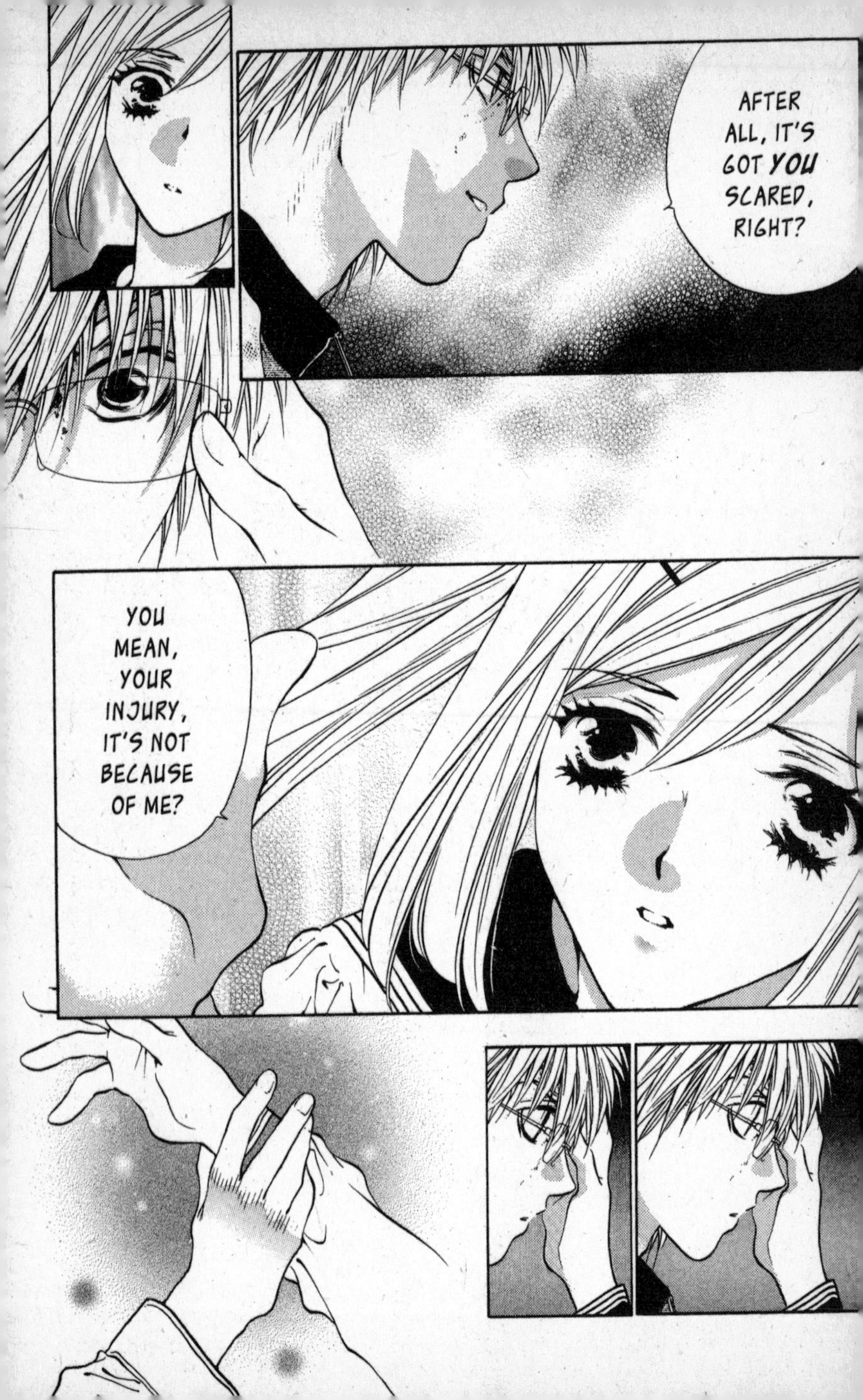
AFTER ALL, IT'S GOT YOU SCARED, RIGHT?
YOU MEAN, YOUR INJURY, IT'S NOT BECAUSE OF ME?

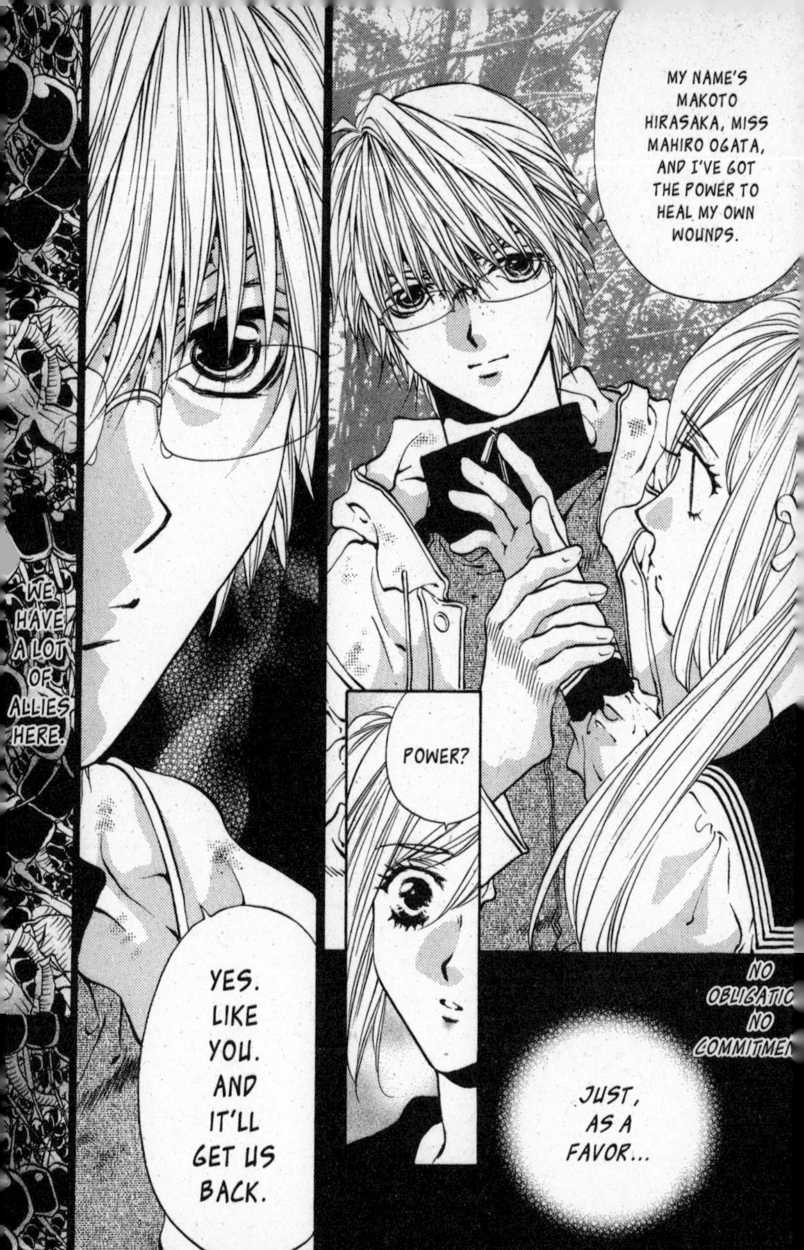
MY NAME'S MAKOTO HIRASAKA, MISS MAHIRO OGATA, AND I'VE GOT THE POWER TO HEAL MY OWN WOUNDS.
POWER?
NO OBLIGATIO NO COMMITMEN
JUST, AS A FAVOR...
YES. LIKE YOU. AND IT'LL GET US BACK.
WE HAVE A LOT OF ALLIES HERE.

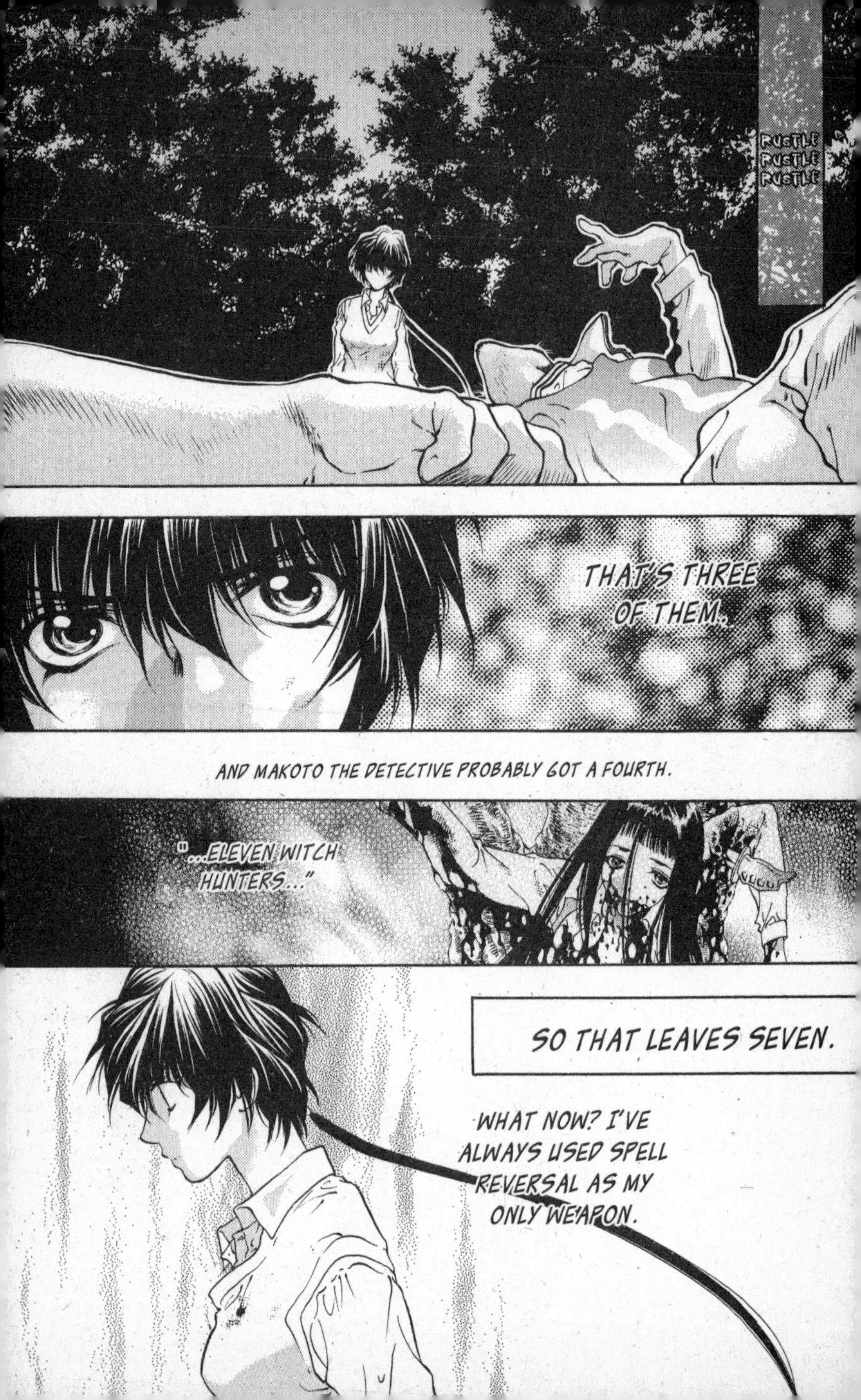
RUSTLE
RUSTLE
RUSTLE
THAT'S THREE OF THEM.
AND MAKOTO THE DETECTIVE PROBABLY GOT A FOURTH.
"...ELEVEN WITCH HUNTERS..."
SO THAT LEAVES SEVEN.
WHAT NOW? I'VE ALWAYS USED SPELL REVERSAL AS MY ONLY WEAPON.

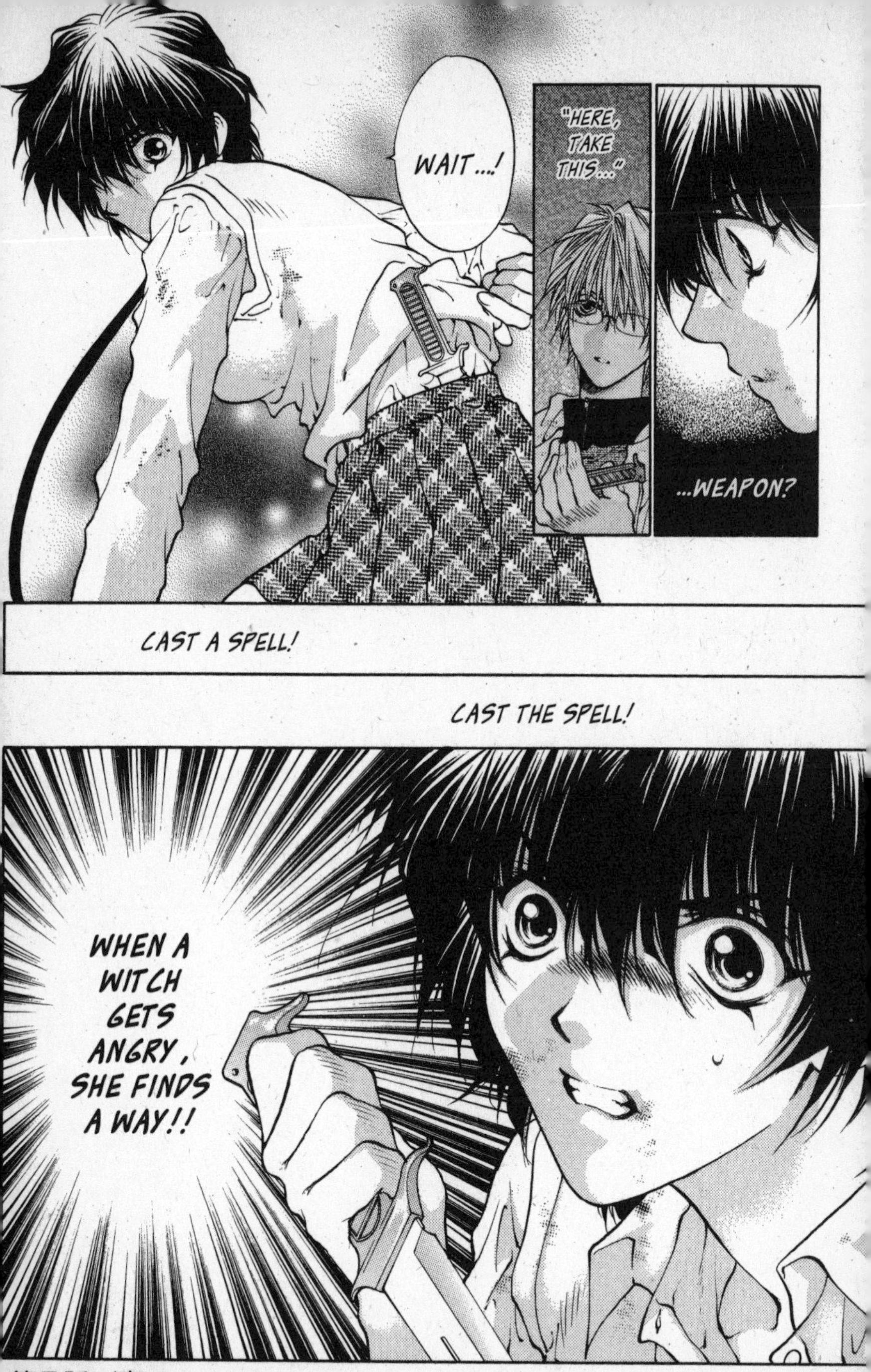
...WEAPON?
"HERE, TAKE THIS..."
WAIT...!
CAST A SPELL!
CAST THE SPELL!
WHEN A WITCH GETS ANGRY, SHE FINDS A WAY!!

第8話／完

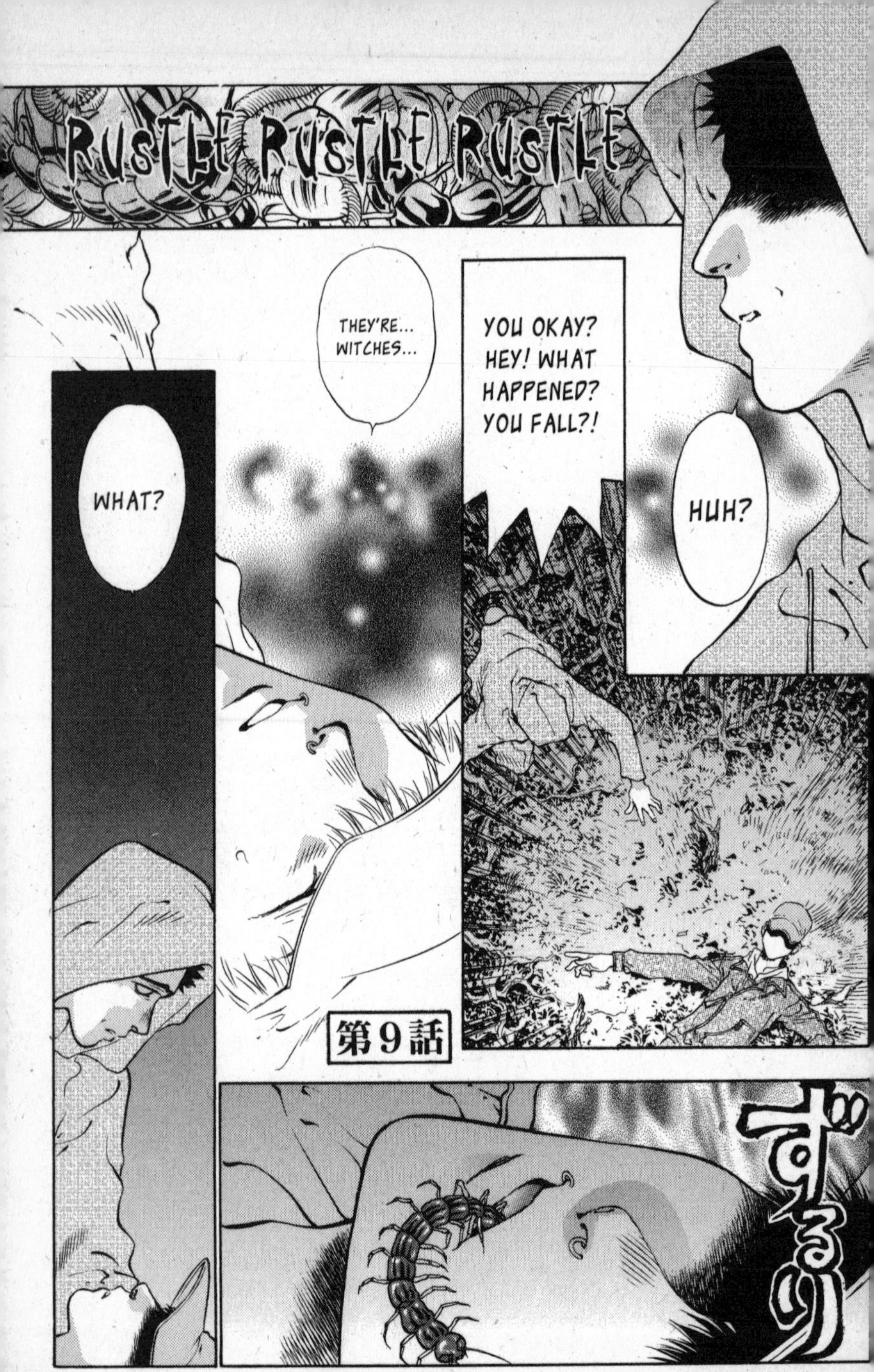
RUSTLE RUSTLE RUSTLE
HUH?
YOU OKAY? HEY! WHAT HAPPENED? YOU FALL?!
THEY'RE... WITCHES...
WHAT?
第9話
ずるり

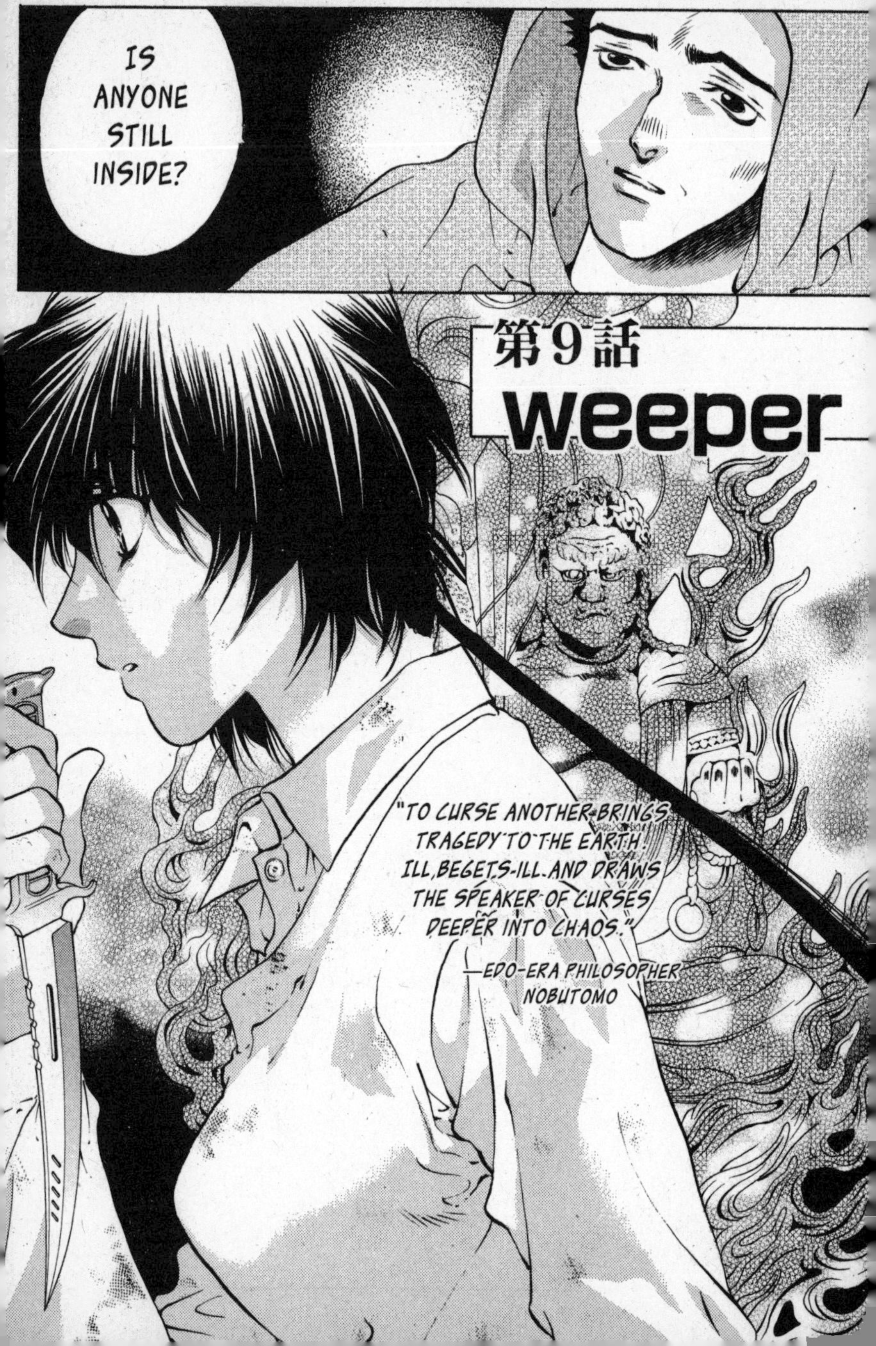
IS ANYONE STILL INSIDE?
第9話
weeper
"TO CURSE ANOTHER BRINGS TRAGEDY TO THE EARTH. ILL BEGETS ILL AND DRAWS THE SPEAKER OF CURSES DEEPER INTO CHAOS."
—EDO-ERA PHILOSOPHER NOBUTOMO

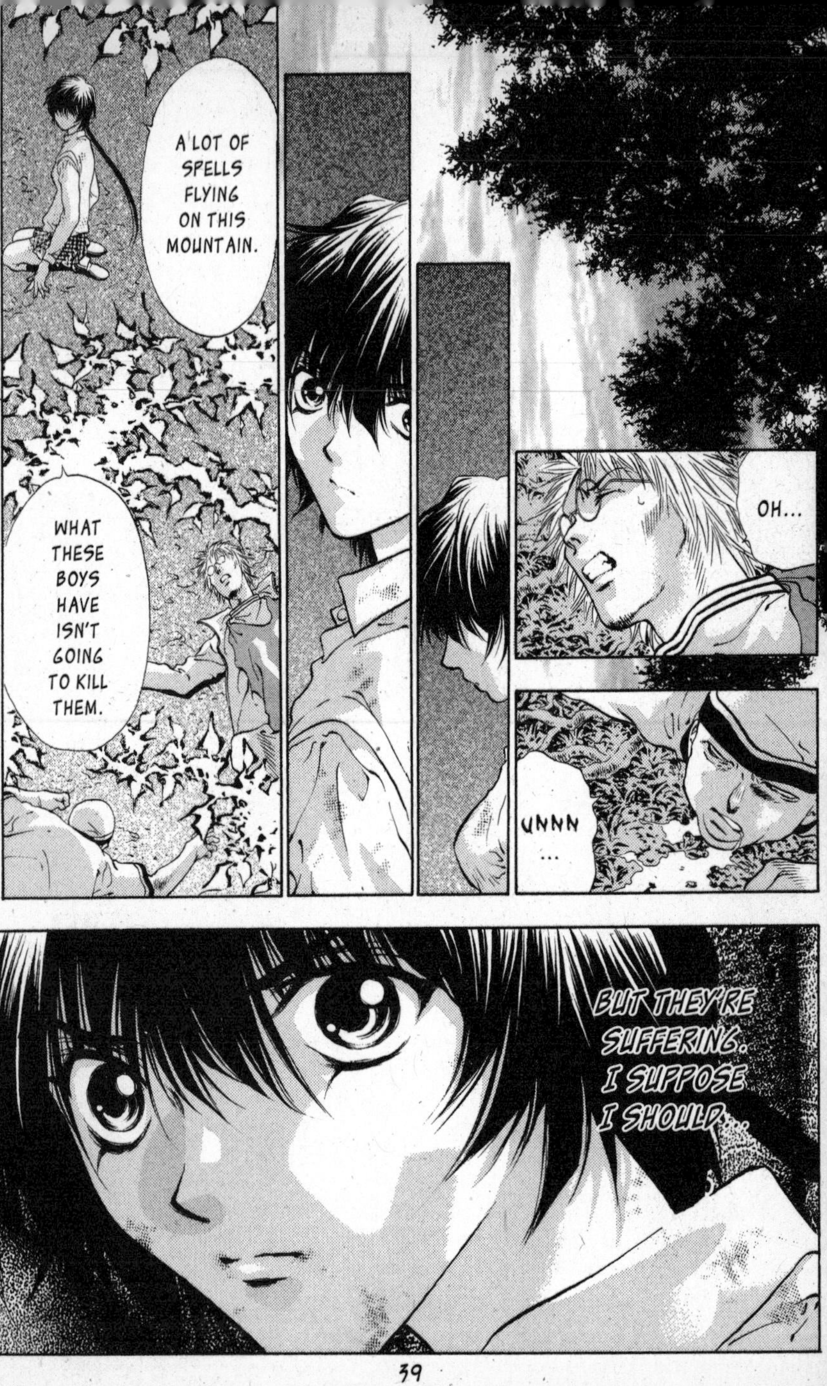
OH...
UNNN ...
A LOT OF SPELLS FLYING ON THIS MOUNTAIN.
WHAT THESE BOYS HAVE ISN'T GOING TO KILL THEM.
BUT THEY'RE SUFFERING. I SUPPOSE I SHOULD...

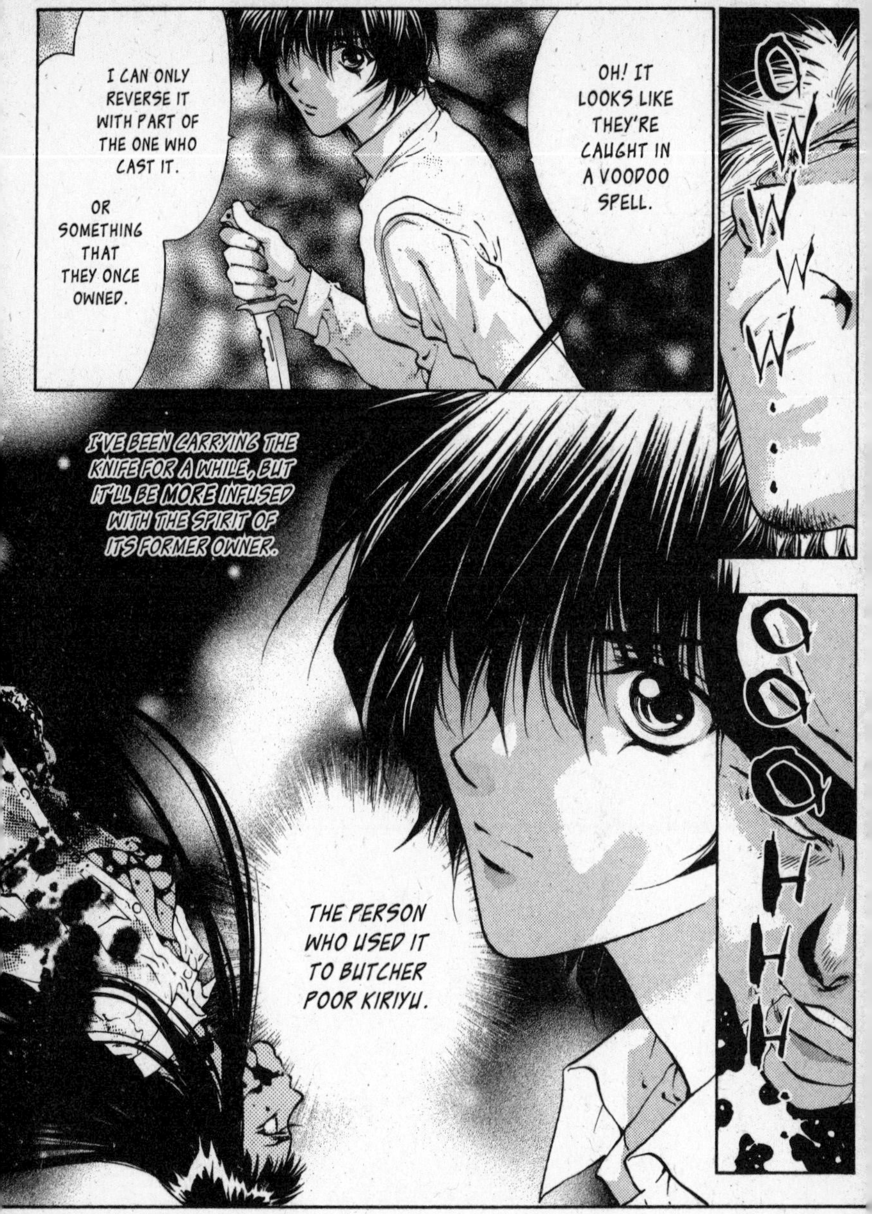
OWWWW...
OH! IT LOOKS LIKE THEY'RE CAUGHT IN A VOODOO SPELL.
I CAN ONLY REVERSE IT WITH PART OF THE ONE WHO CAST IT.
OR SOMETHING THAT THEY ONCE OWNED.
OOOOHH
I'VE BEEN CARRYING THE KNIFE FOR A WHILE, BUT IT'LL BE MORE INFUSED WITH THE SPIRIT OF ITS FORMER OWNER.
THE PERSON WHO USED IT TO BUTCHER POOR KIRIYU.

Ohn Orikirity May-lity May-wayah Shima-lay Sowakah...

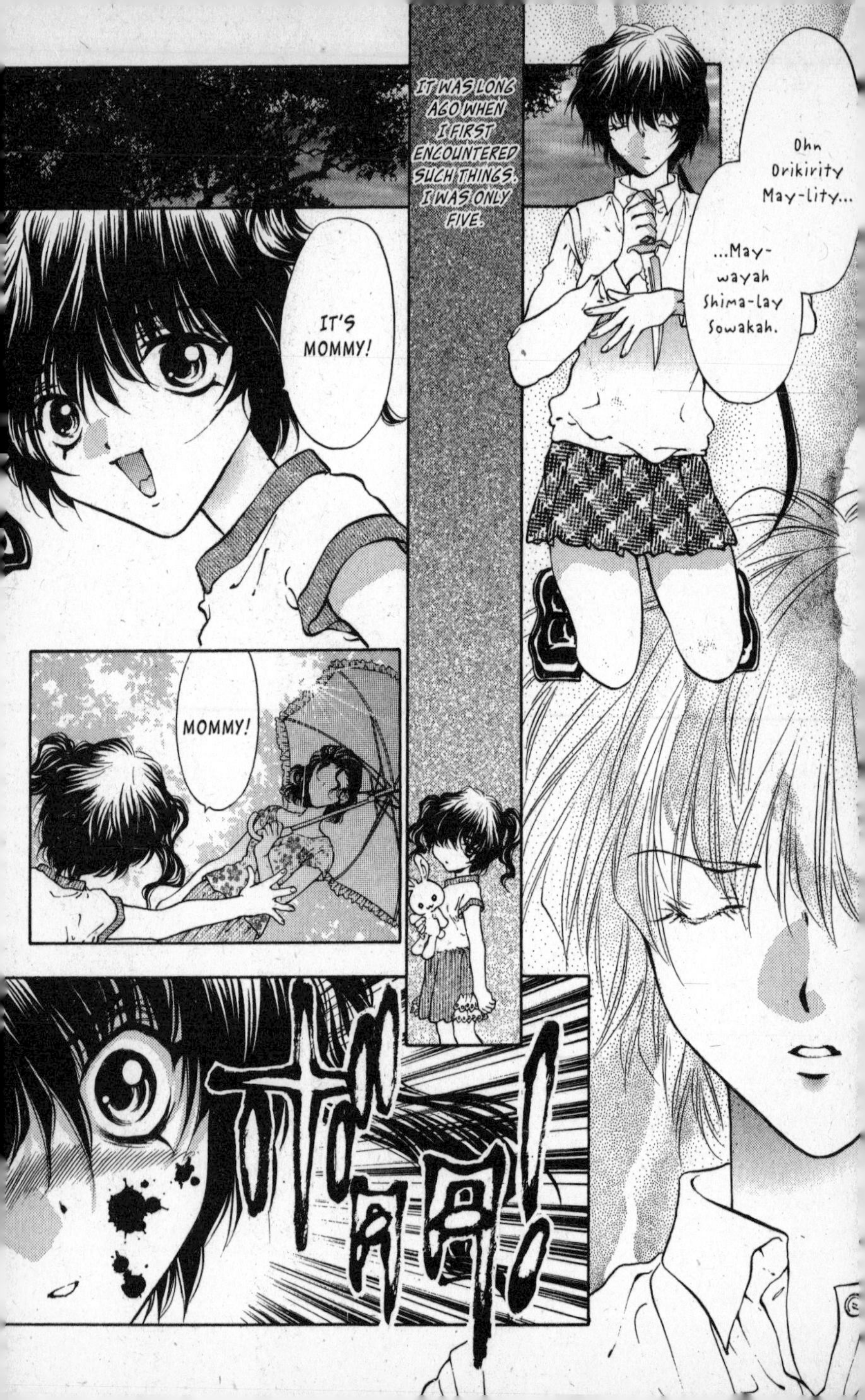
Ohn Orikirity May-Lity...
...May-wayah Shima-lay Sowakah.
IT WAS LONG AGO WHEN I FIRST ENCOUNTERED SUCH THINGS. I WAS ONLY FIVE.
IT'S MOMMY!
MOMMY!

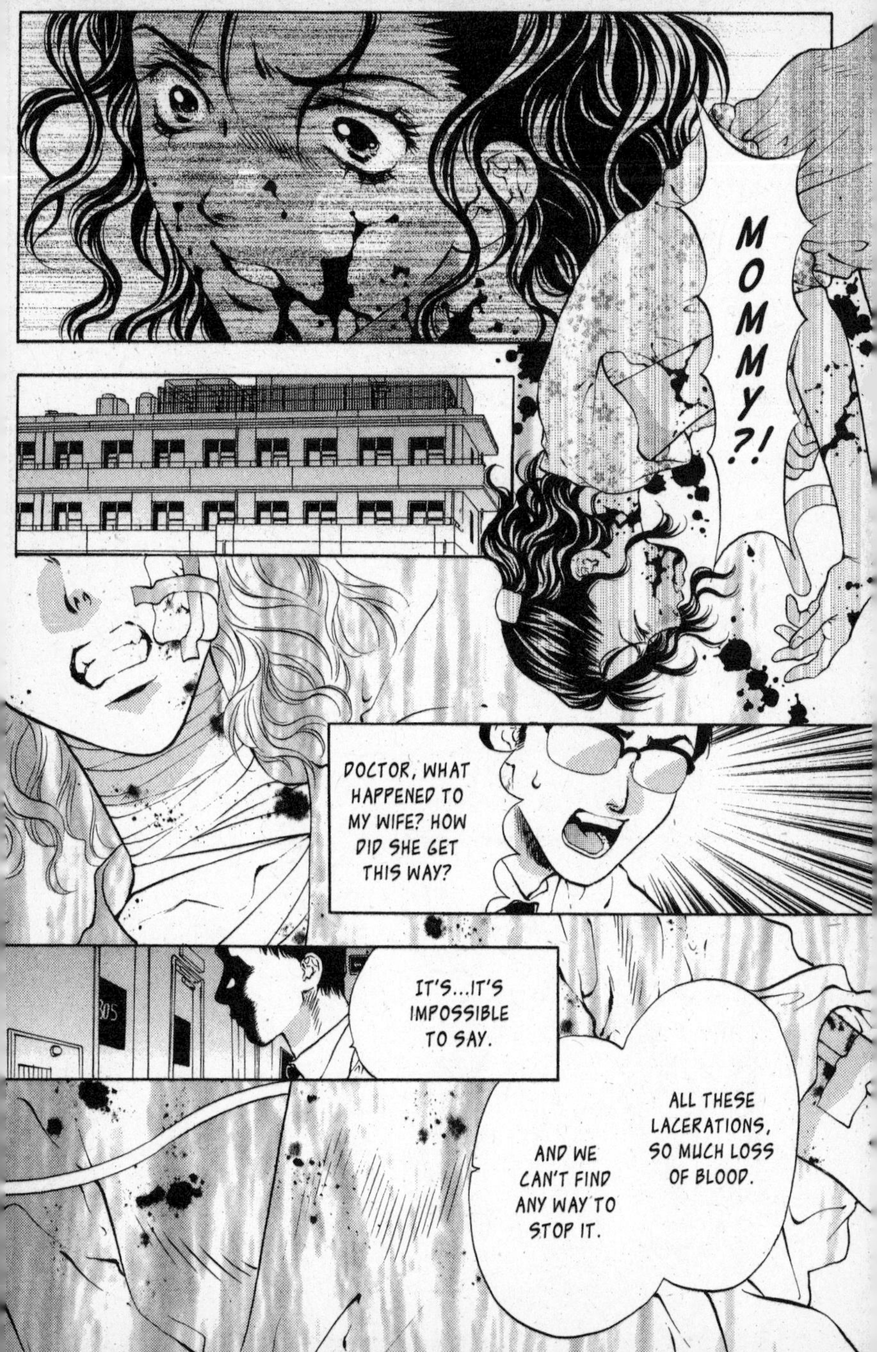
MOMMY?!
DOCTOR, WHAT HAPPENED TO MY WIFE? HOW DID SHE GET THIS WAY?
IT'S...IT'S IMPOSSIBLE TO SAY.
ALL THESE LACERATIONS, SO MUCH LOSS OF BLOOD.
AND WE CAN'T FIND ANY WAY TO STOP IT.

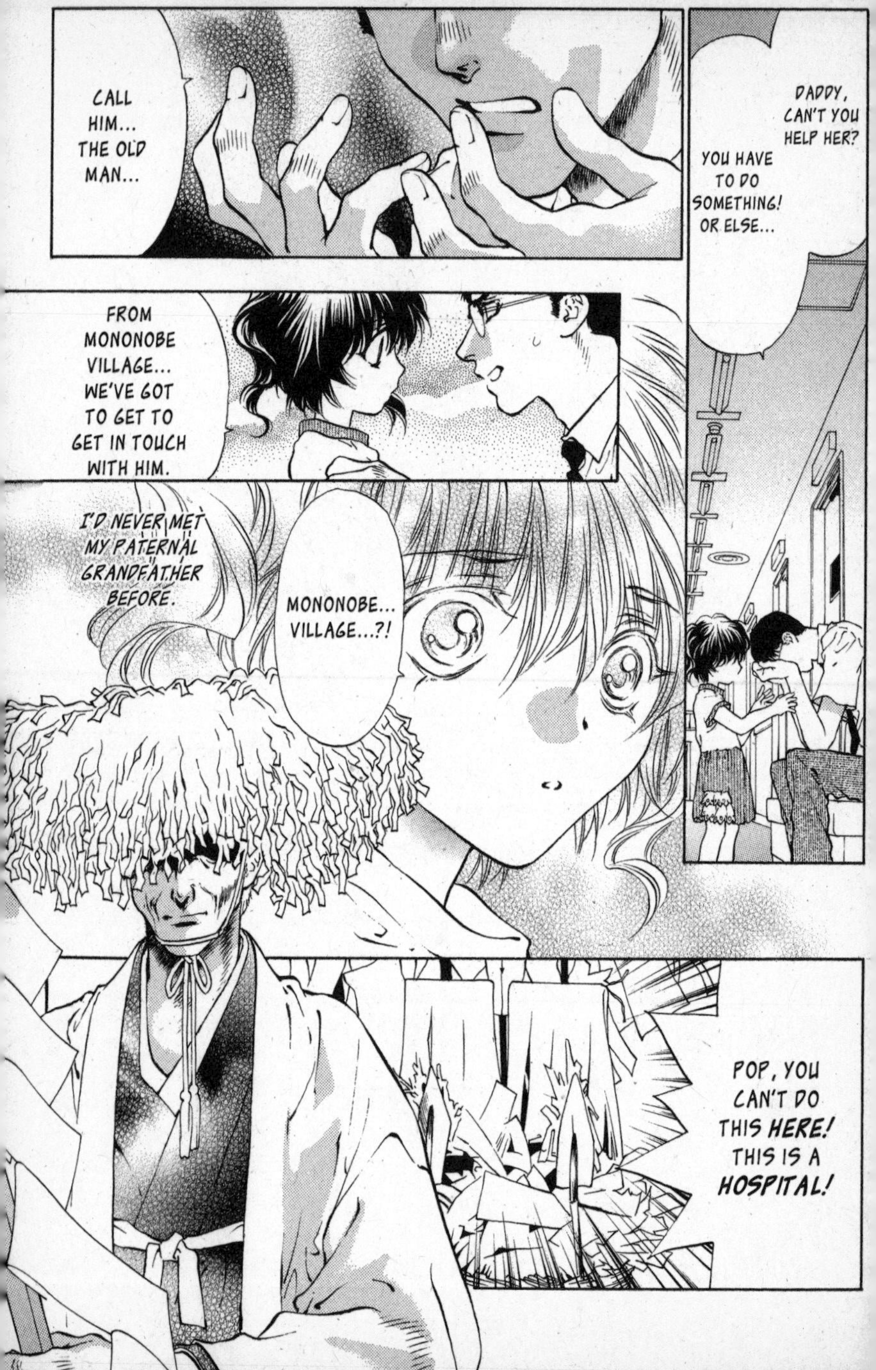
DADDY, CAN'T YOU HELP HER?
YOU HAVE TO DO SOMETHING! OR ELSE...
CALL HIM... THE OLD MAN...
FROM MONONOBE VILLAGE... WE'VE GOT TO GET TO GET IN TOUCH WITH HIM.
MONONOBE... VILLAGE...?!
I'D NEVER MET MY PATERNAL GRANDFATHER BEFORE.
POP, YOU CAN'T DO THIS HERE! THIS IS A HOSPITAL!

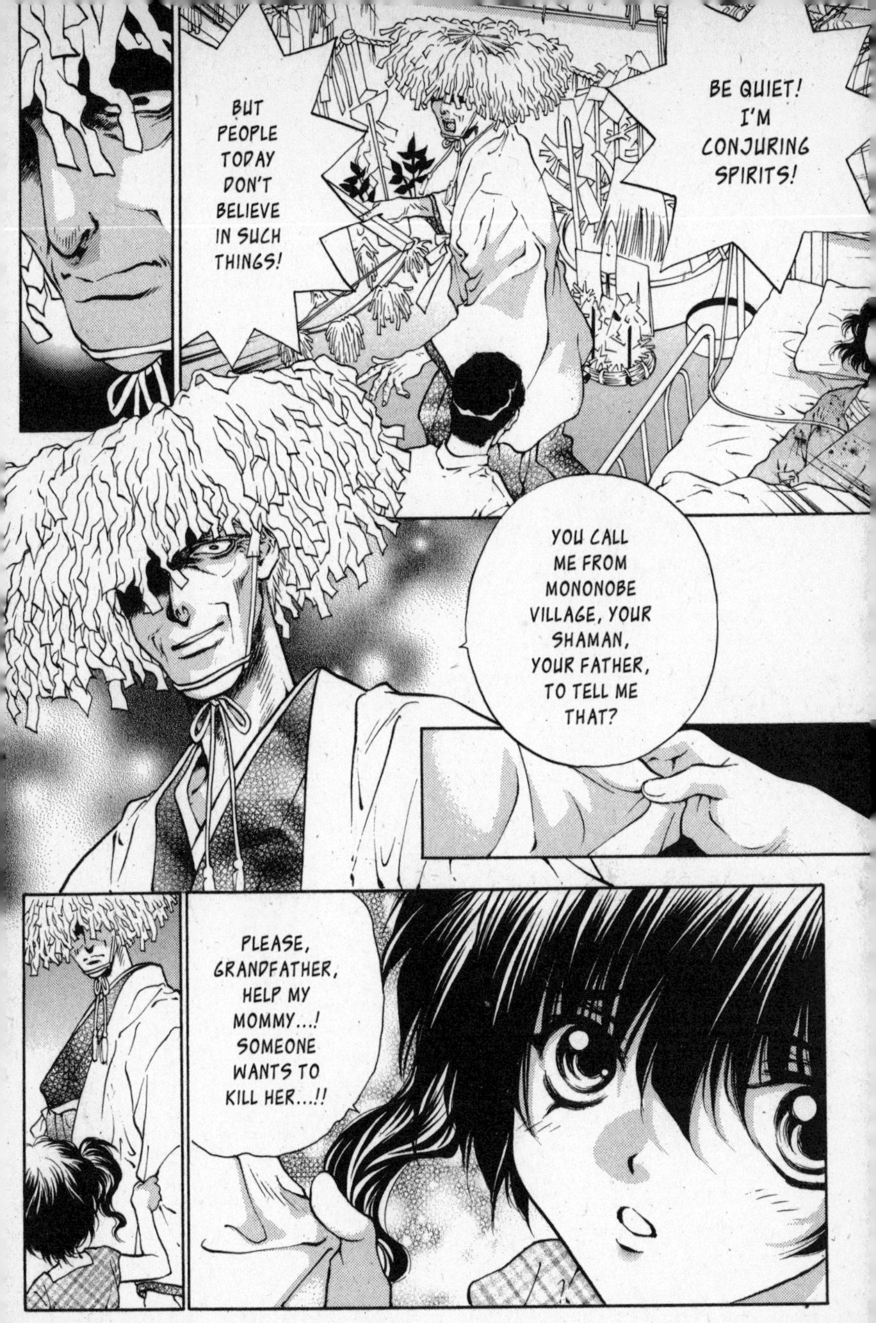
BE QUIET! I'M CONJURING SPIRITS!
BUT PEOPLE TODAY DON'T BELIEVE IN SUCH THINGS!
YOU CALL ME FROM MONONOBE VILLAGE, YOUR SHAMAN, YOUR FATHER, TO TELL ME THAT?
PLEASE, GRANDFATHER, HELP MY MOMMY...! SOMEONE WANTS TO KILL HER...!!

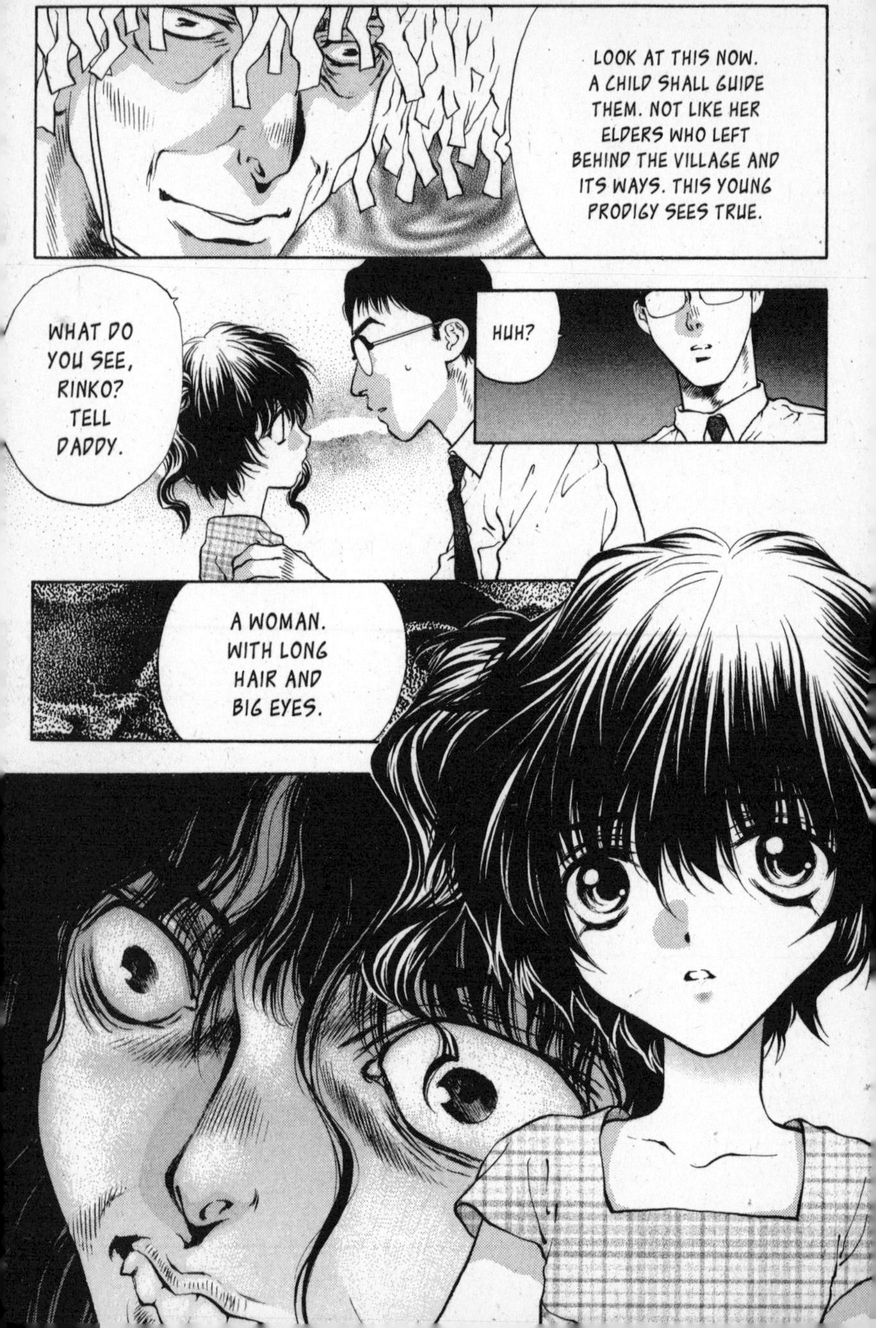
LOOK AT THIS NOW. A CHILD SHALL GUIDE THEM. NOT LIKE HER ELDERS WHO LEFT BEHIND THE VILLAGE AND ITS WAYS. THIS YOUNG PRODIGY SEES TRUE.
HUH?
WHAT DO YOU SEE, RINKO? TELL DADDY.
A WOMAN. WITH LONG HAIR AND BIG EYES.

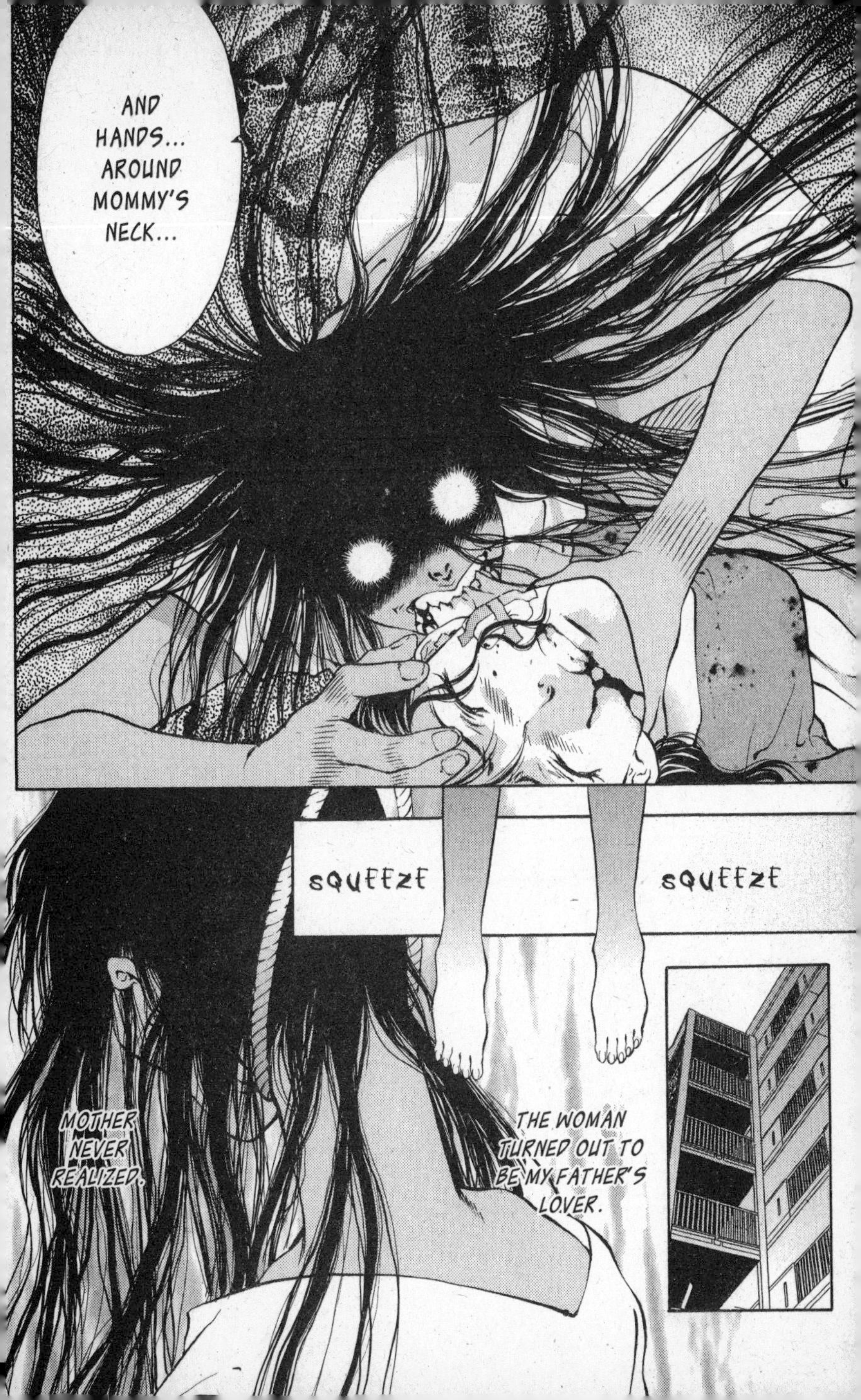
AND HANDS... AROUND MOMMY'S NECK...
SQUEEZE
SQUEEZE
THE WOMAN TURNED OUT TO BE MY FATHER'S LOVER.
MOTHER NEVER REALIZED.

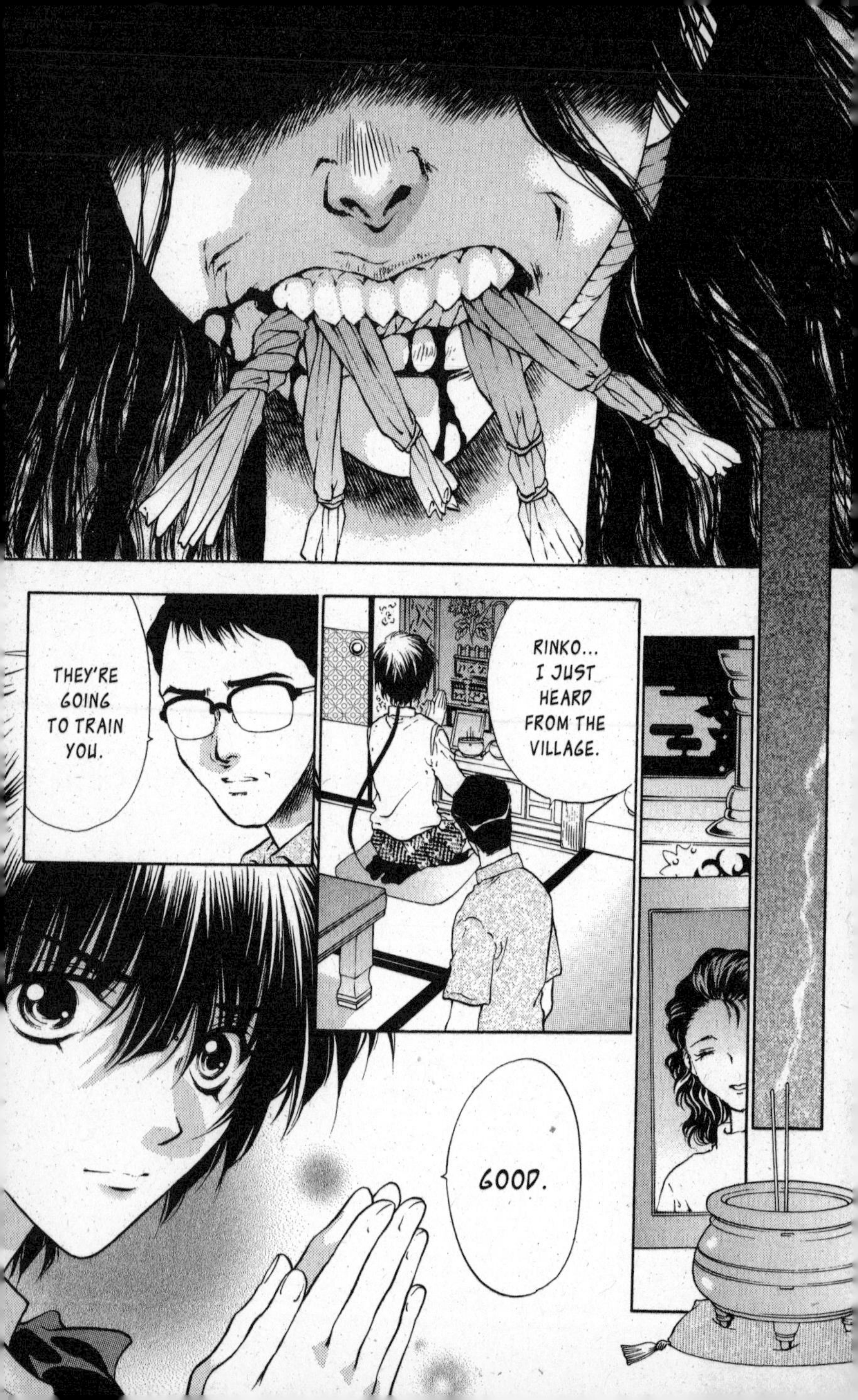
RINKO... I JUST HEARD FROM THE VILLAGE.
THEY'RE GOING TO TRAIN YOU.
GOOD.

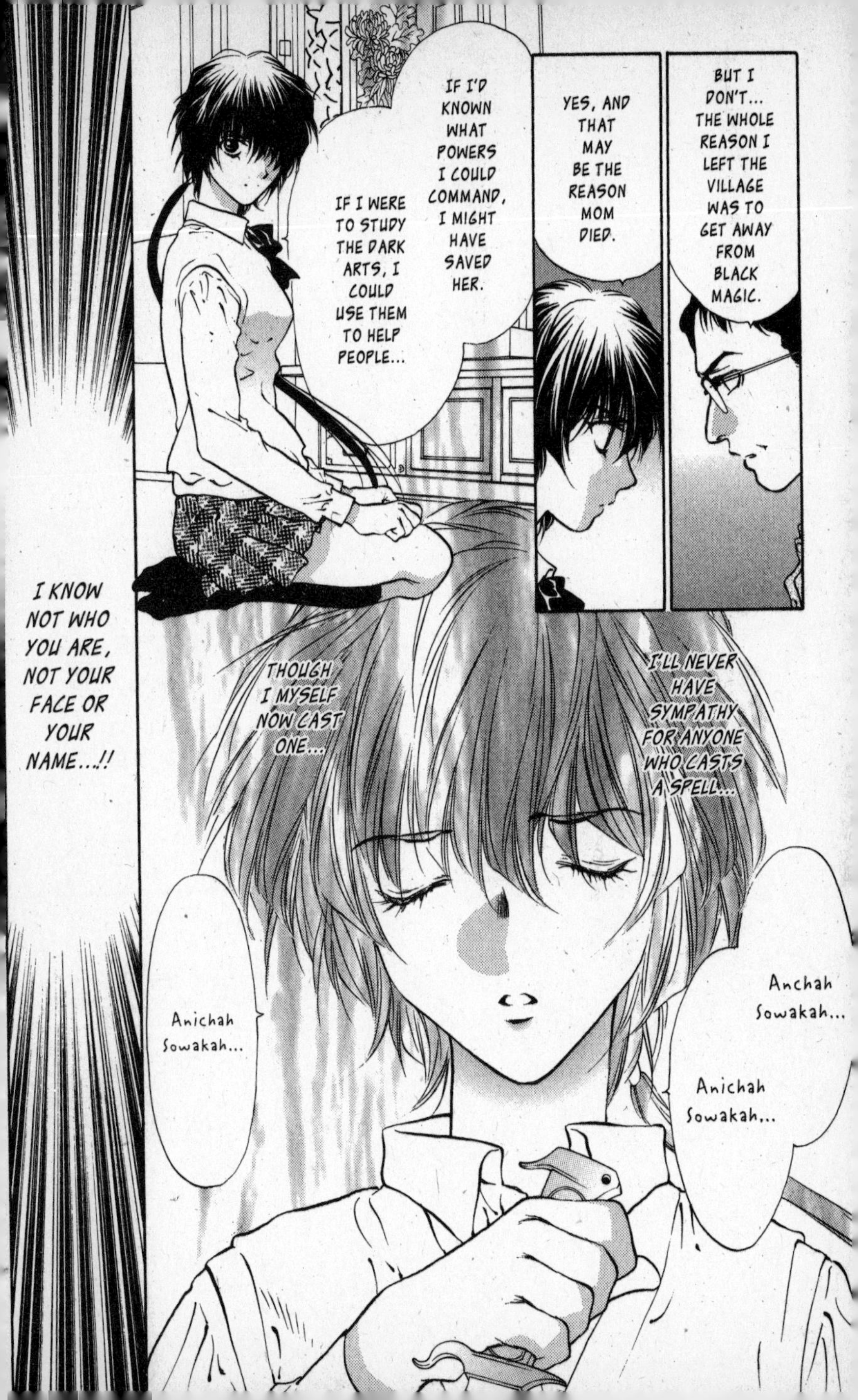
BUT I DON'T... THE WHOLE REASON I LEFT THE VILLAGE WAS TO GET AWAY FROM BLACK MAGIC.
YES, AND THAT MAY BE THE REASON MOM DIED.
IF I'D KNOWN WHAT POWERS I COULD COMMAND, I MIGHT HAVE SAVED HER.
IF I WERE TO STUDY THE DARK ARTS, I COULD USE THEM TO HELP PEOPLE...
I'LL NEVER HAVE SYMPATHY FOR ANYONE WHO CASTS A SPELL...
THOUGH I MYSELF NOW CAST ONE...
Anchah Sowakah...
Anichah Sowakah...
Anichah Sowakah...
I KNOW NOT WHO YOU ARE, NOT YOUR FACE OR YOUR NAME...!!

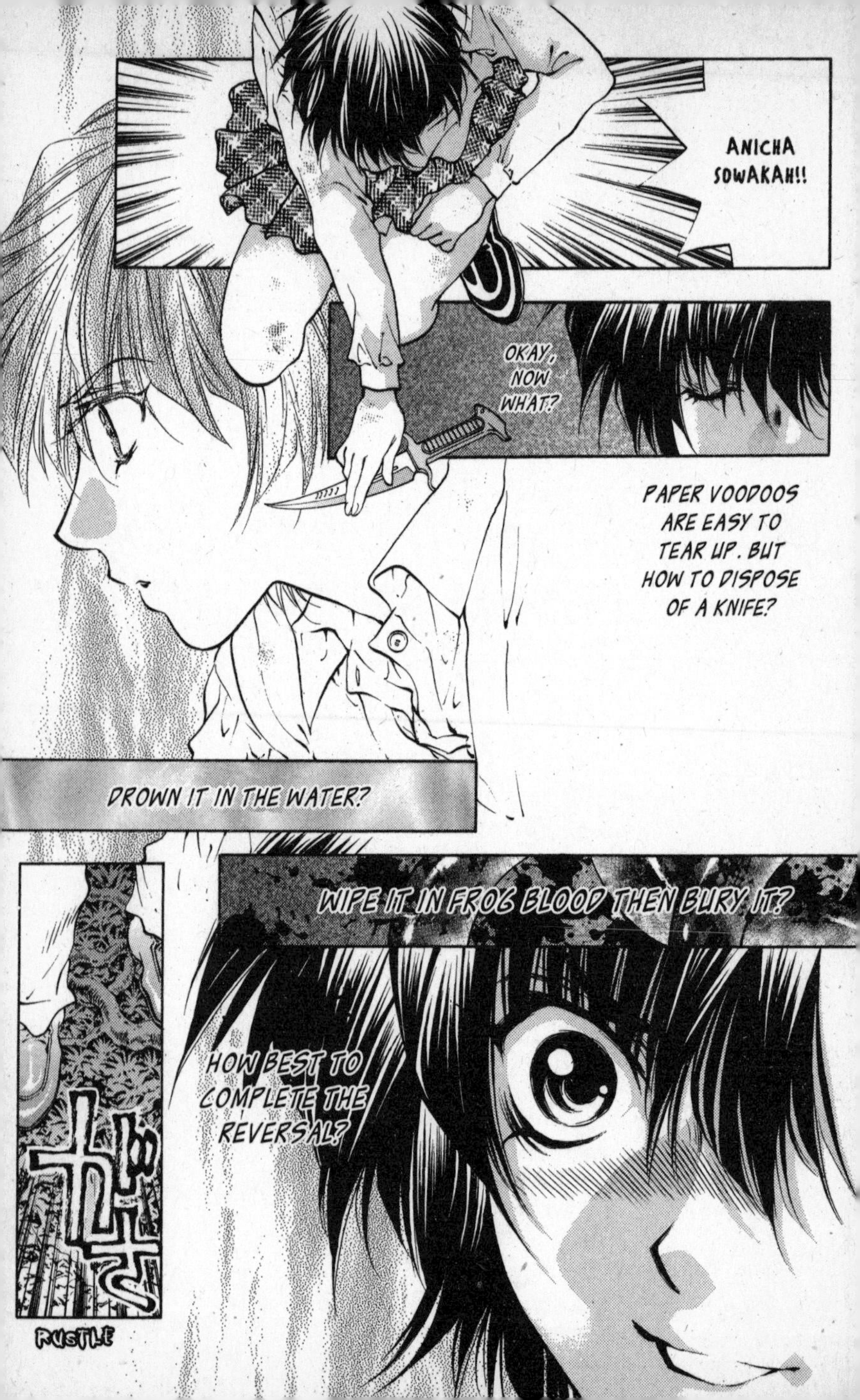
ANICHA SOWAKAH!!
OKAY, NOW WHAT?
PAPER VOODOOS ARE EASY TO TEAR UP. BUT HOW TO DISPOSE OF A KNIFE?
DROWN IT IN THE WATER?
WIPE IT IN FROG BLOOD THEN BURY IT?
HOW BEST TO COMPLETE THE REVERSAL?
RUSTLE

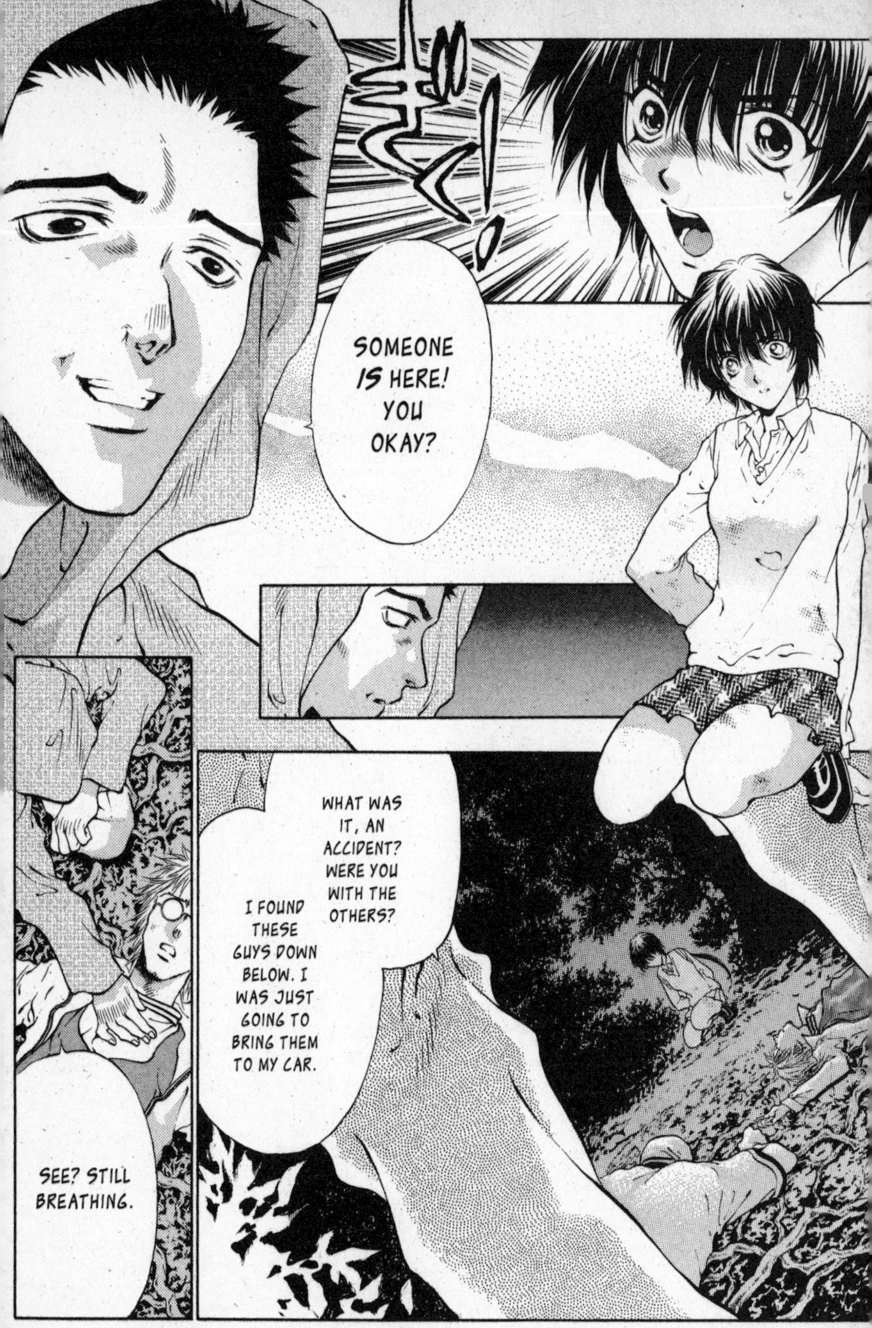
SOMEONE IS HERE! YOU OKAY?
WHAT WAS IT, AN ACCIDENT? WERE YOU WITH THE OTHERS?
I FOUND THESE GUYS DOWN BELOW. I WAS JUST GOING TO BRING THEM TO MY CAR.
SEE? STILL BREATHING.

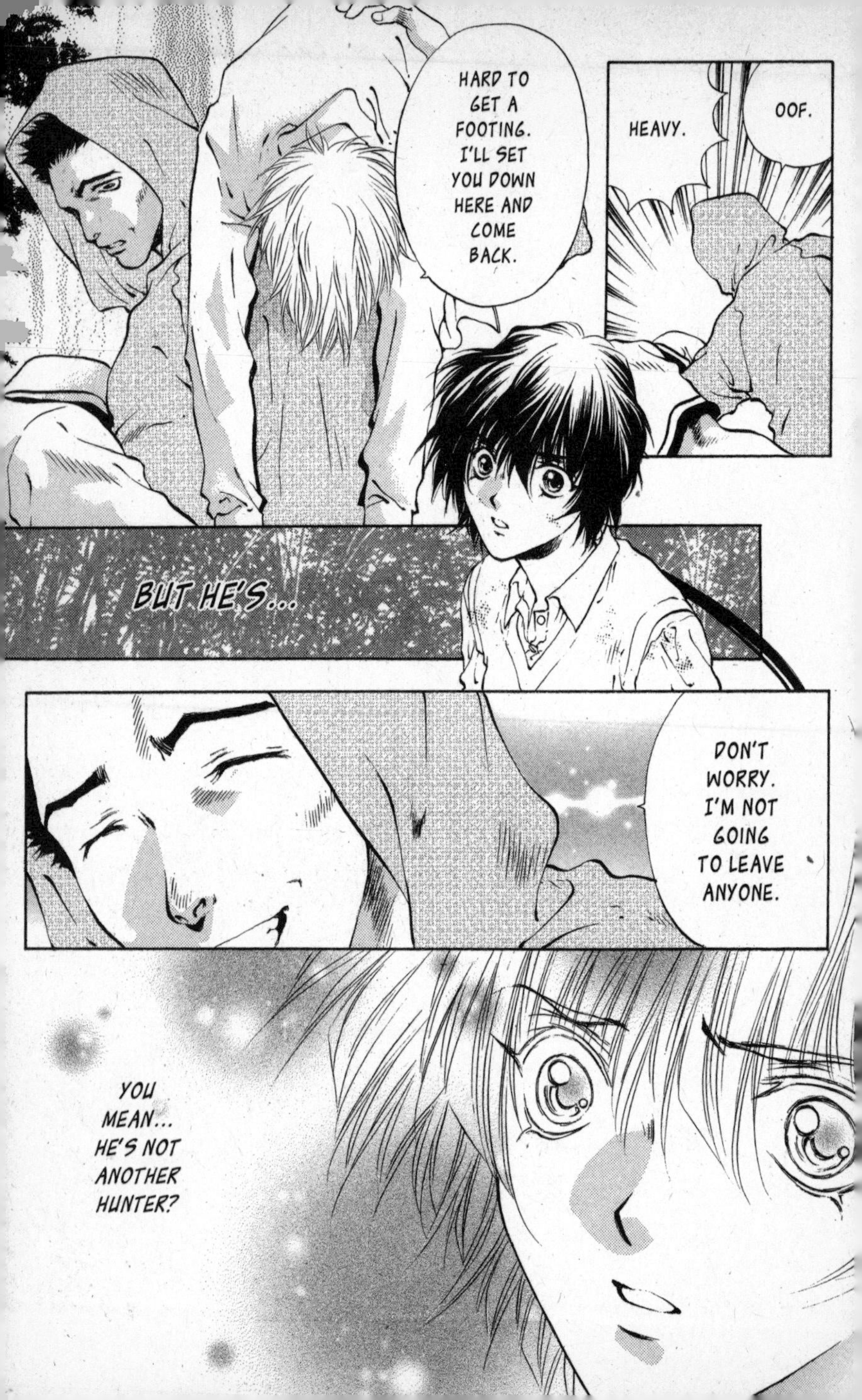
OOF.
HEAVY.
HARD TO GET A FOOTING. I'LL SET YOU DOWN HERE AND COME BACK.
BUT HE'S...
DON'T WORRY. I'M NOT GOING TO LEAVE ANYONE.
YOU MEAN... HE'S NOT ANOTHER HUNTER?

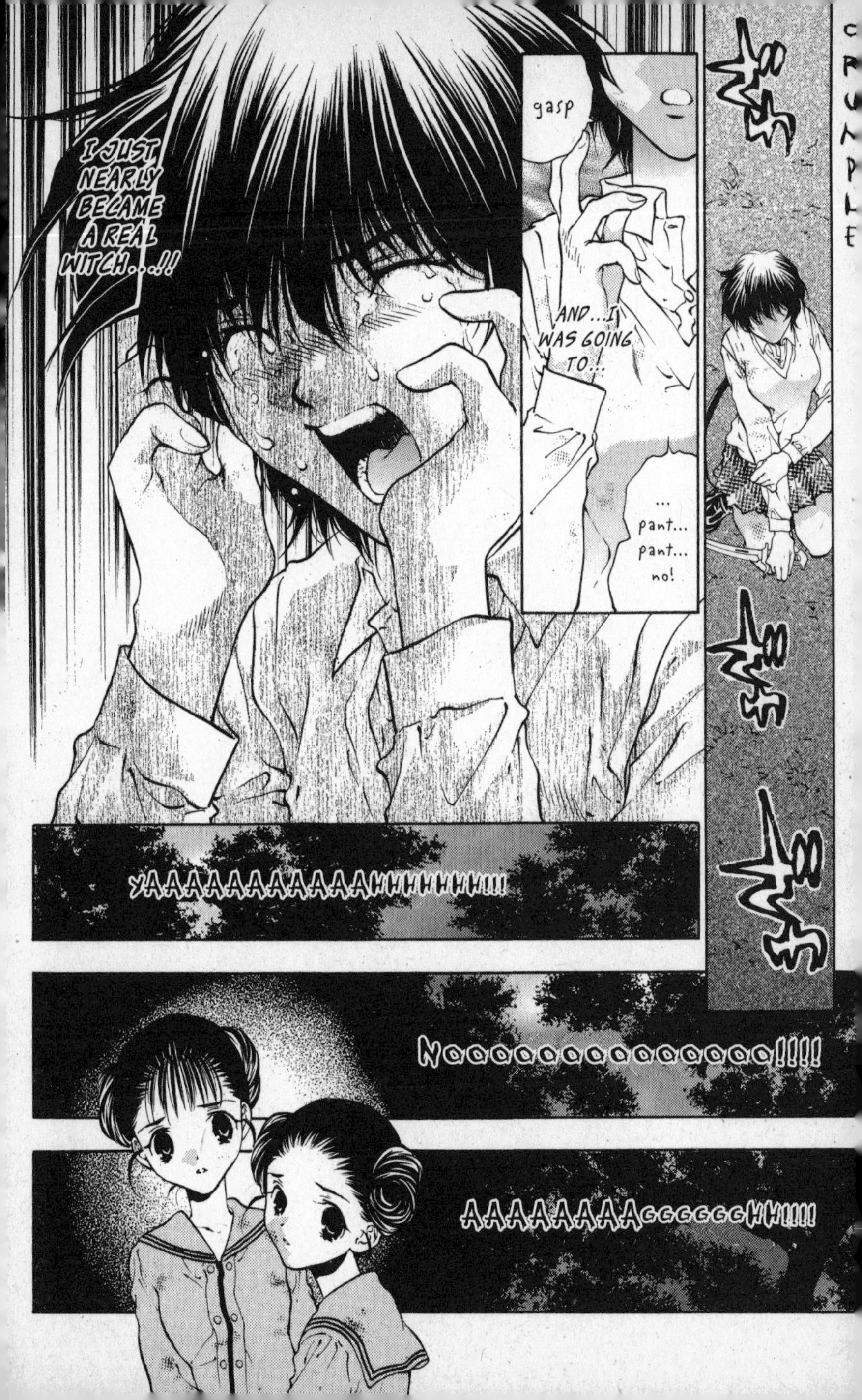
CRUMPLE
gasp
AND...I WAS GOING TO...
...
pant...
pant...
no!
I JUST NEARLY BECAME A REAL WITCH...!!
YAAAAAAAAAAAAAHHHHHHHH!!!
Naaaaaaaaaaaaaaaa!!!!
AAAAAAAAAAeeeeeeHH!!!!

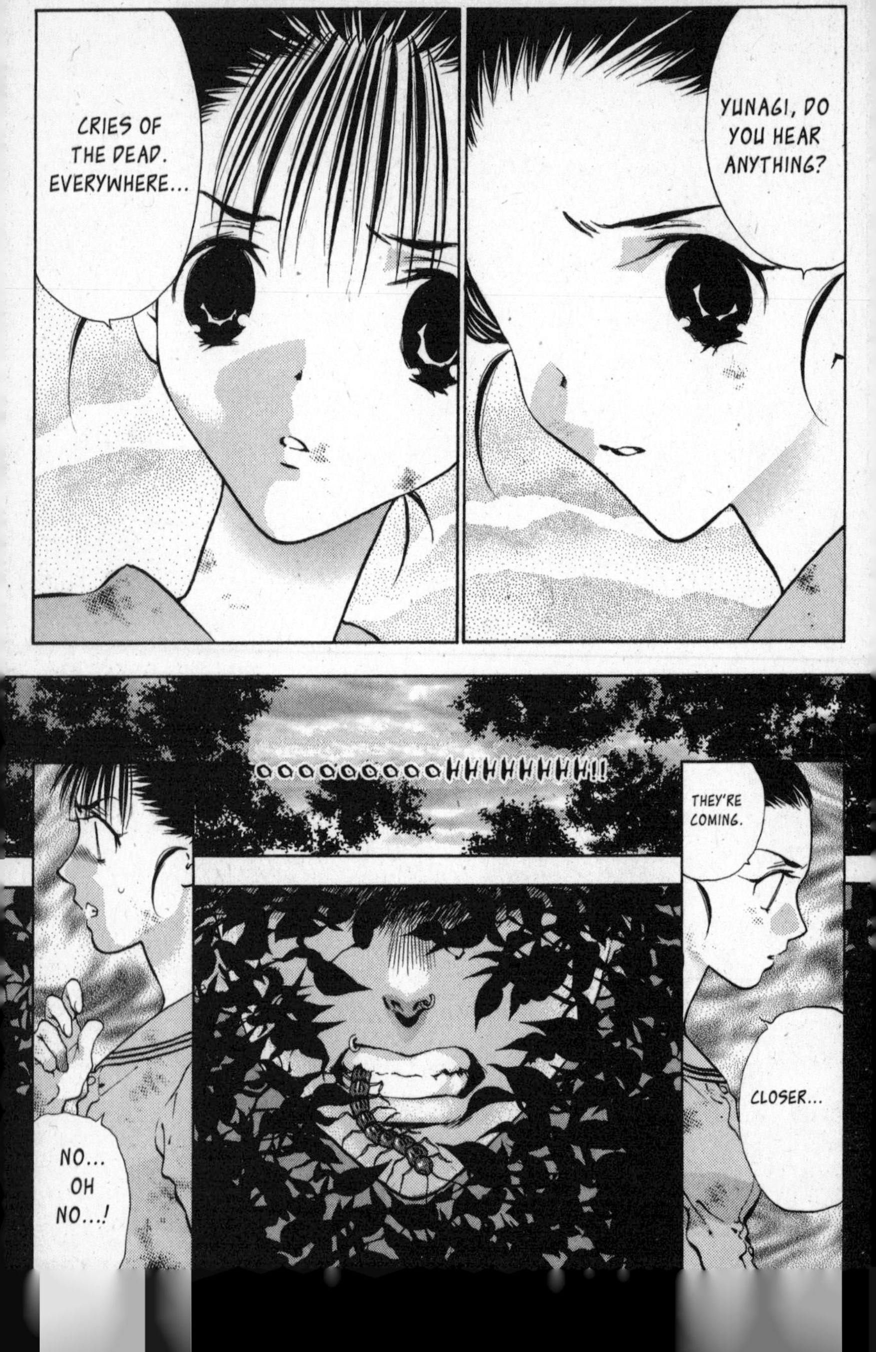
YUNAGI, DO YOU HEAR ANYTHING?
CRIES OF THE DEAD. EVERYWHERE...
aaaaaaaaaaaHHHHHHHHH!!
THEY'RE COMING.
CLOSER...
NO... OH NO...!

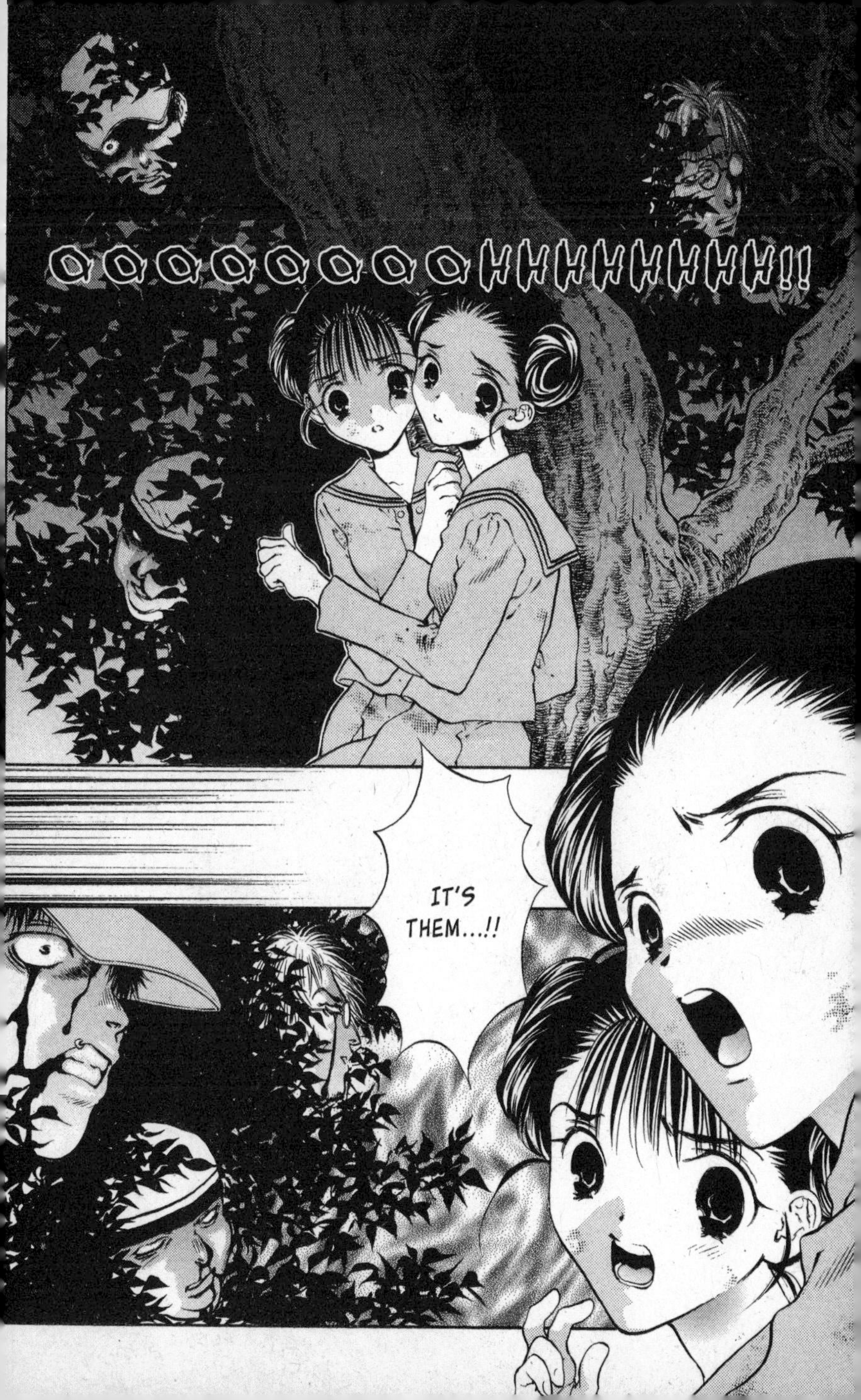
AAAAAAAAHHHHHHHHH!!
IT'S THEM...!!

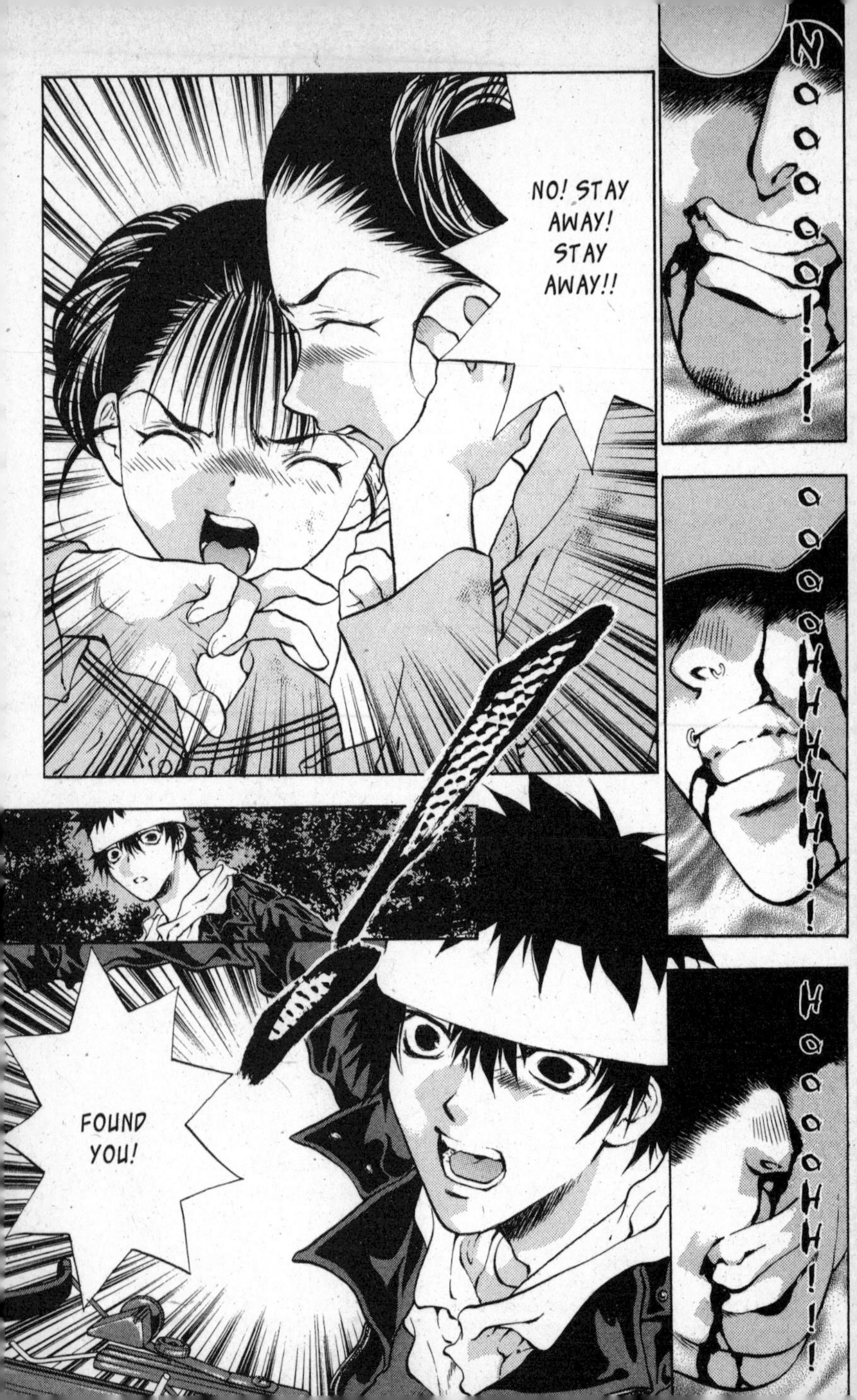
NOOOOOO!!!!!
OOOOOHHHHHH!!!
HOOOOOHH!!!!
NO! STAY AWAY! STAY AWAY!!
FOUND YOU!

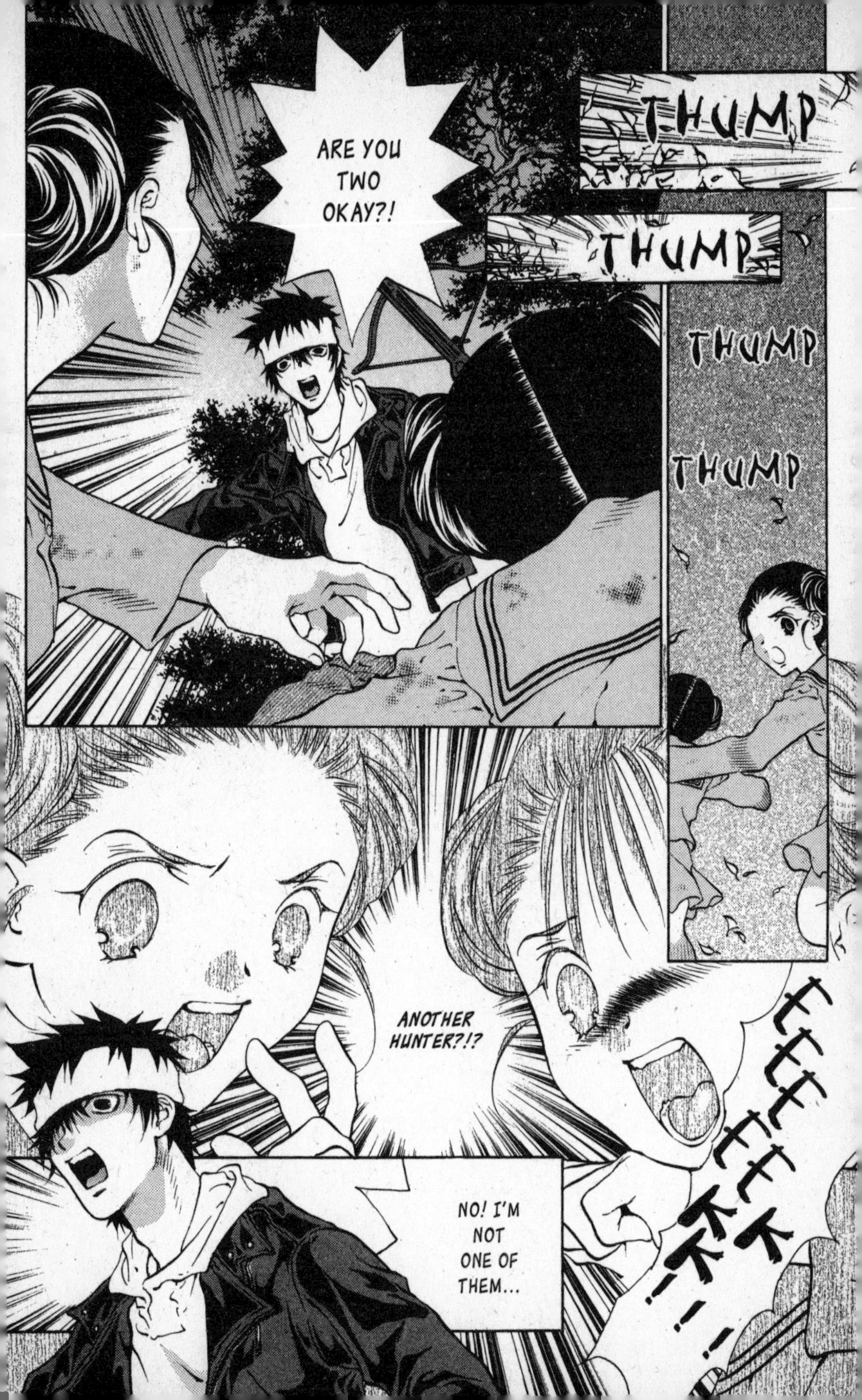
THUMP
THUMP
THUMP
THUMP
ARE YOU TWO OKAY?!
EEEEEEKK!!!
ANOTHER HUNTER?!?
NO! I'M NOT ONE OF THEM...

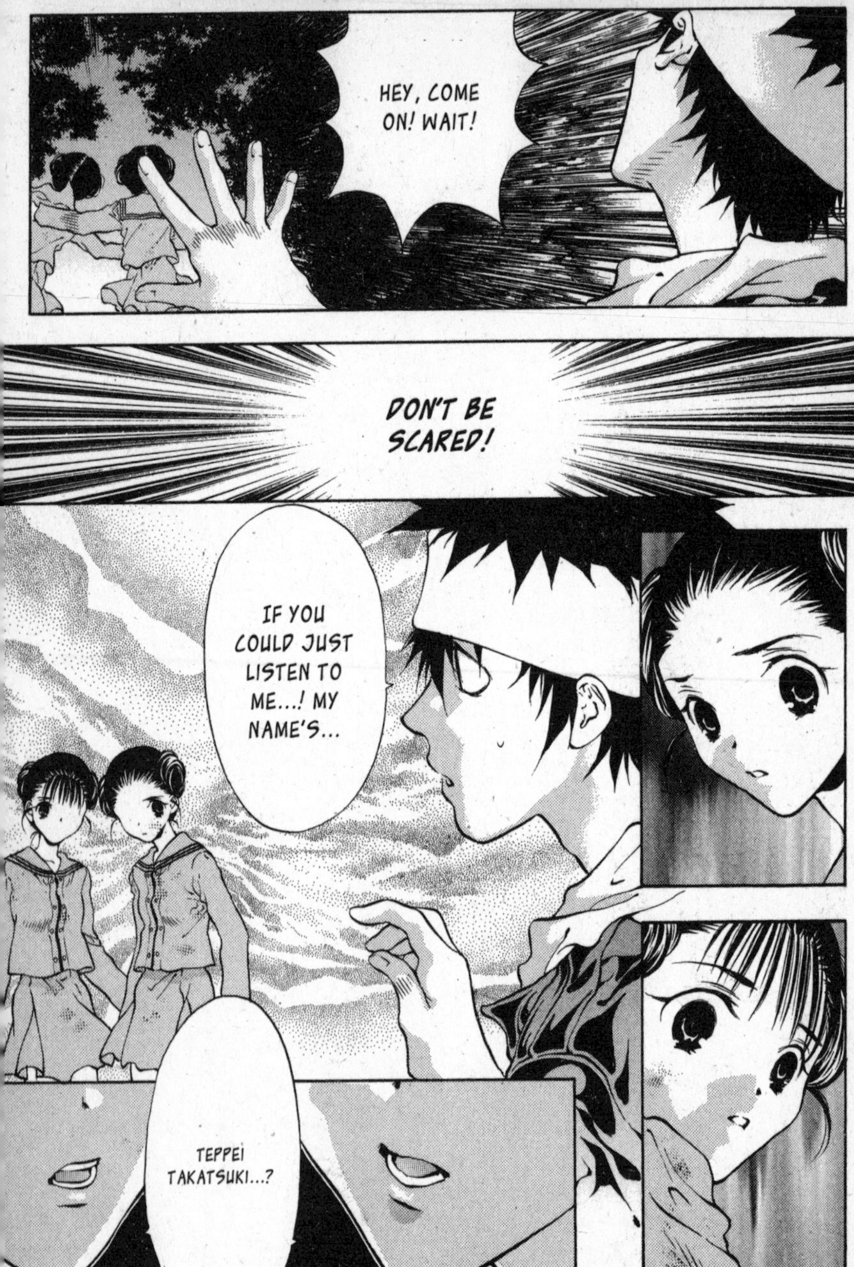
HEY, COME ON! WAIT!
DON'T BE SCARED!
IF YOU COULD JUST LISTEN TO ME...! MY NAME'S...
TEPPEI TAKATSUKI...?

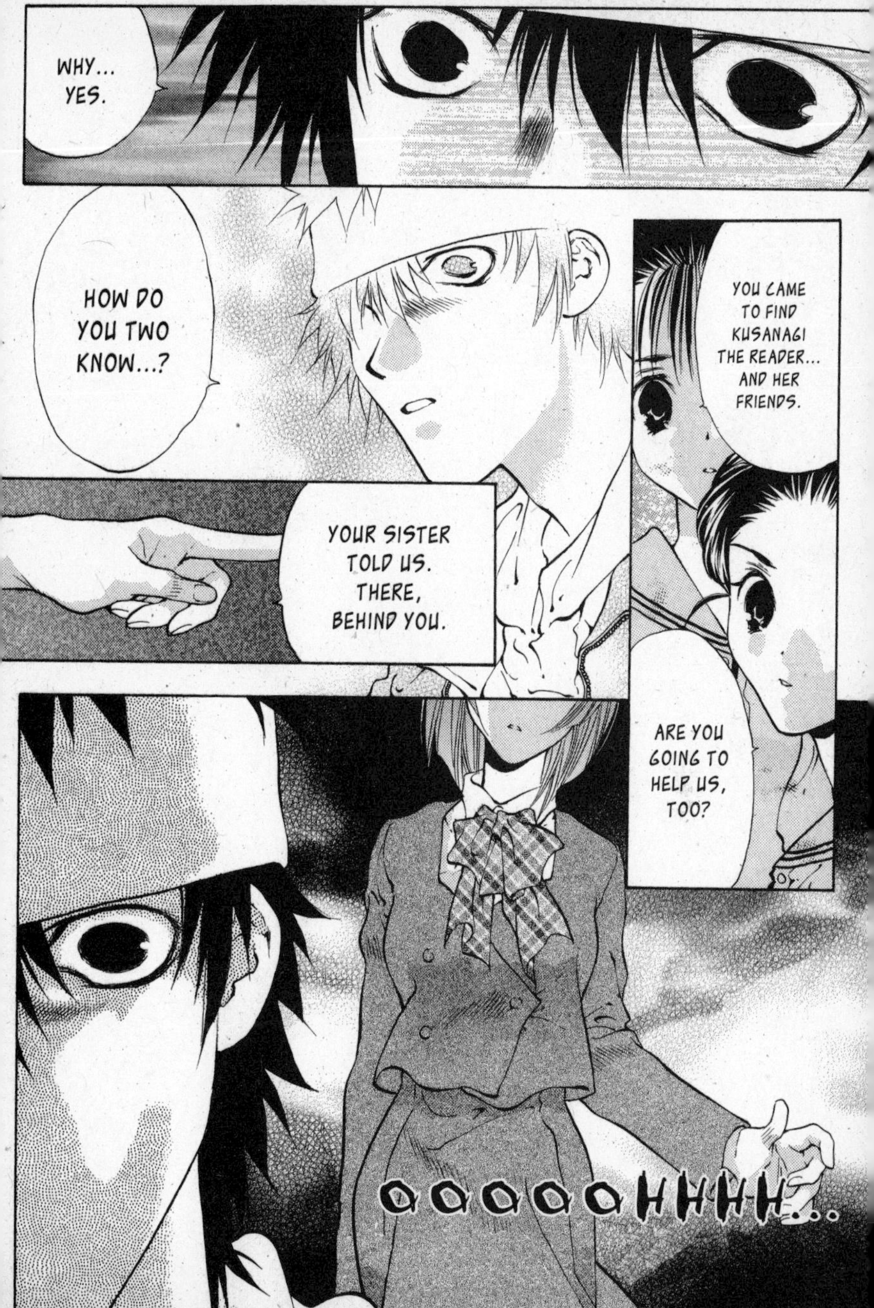
WHY... YES.
YOU CAME TO FIND KUSANAGI THE READER... AND HER FRIENDS.
ARE YOU GOING TO HELP US, TOO?
HOW DO YOU TWO KNOW...?
YOUR SISTER TOLD US. THERE, BEHIND YOU.
OOOOOHHHH...

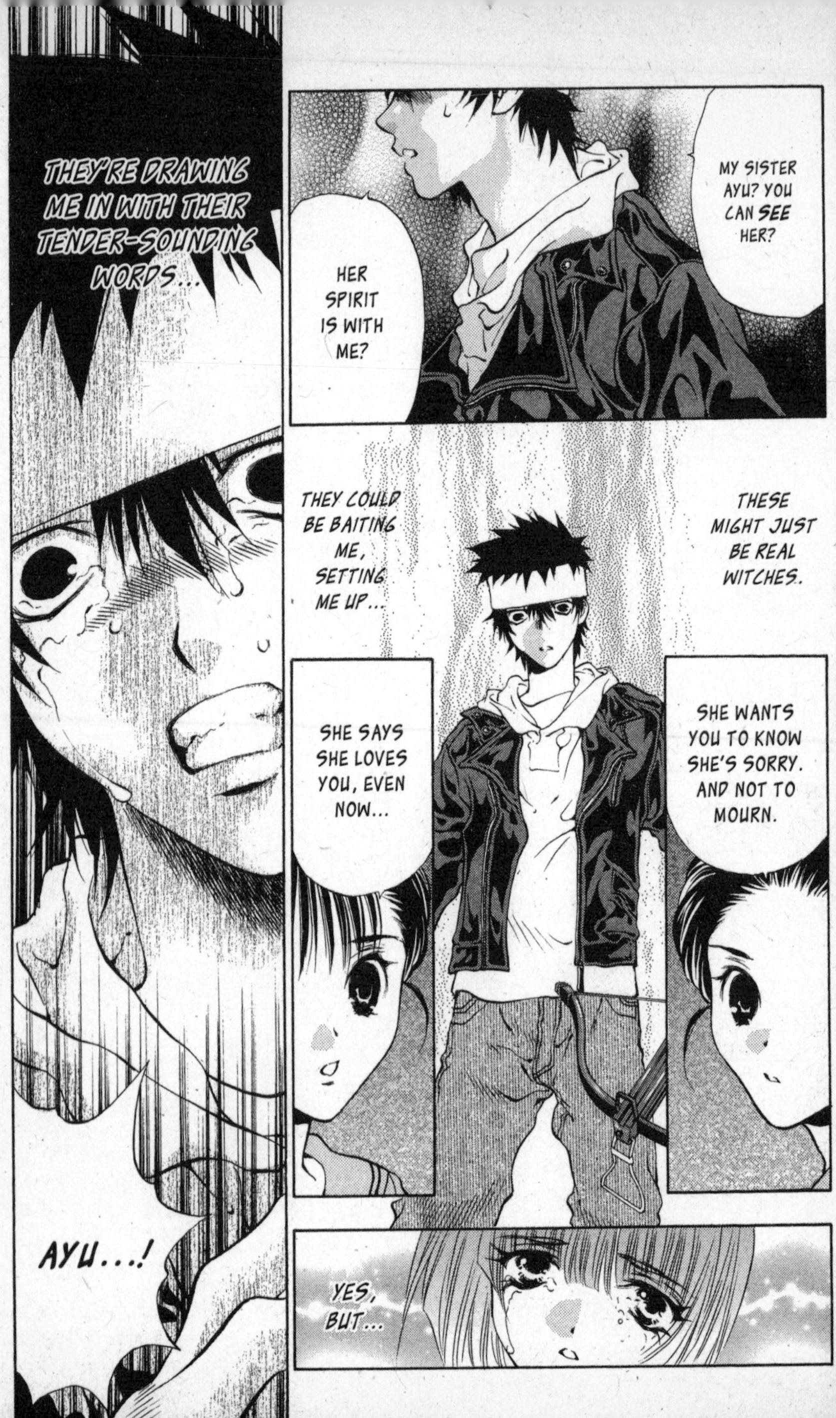
MY SISTER AYU? YOU CAN SEE HER?
HER SPIRIT IS WITH ME?
THESE MIGHT JUST BE REAL WITCHES.
THEY COULD BE BAITING ME, SETTING ME UP...
SHE WANTS YOU TO KNOW SHE'S SORRY. AND NOT TO MOURN.
SHE SAYS SHE LOVES YOU, EVEN NOW...
YES, BUT...
THEY'RE DRAWING ME IN WITH THEIR TENDER-SOUNDING WORDS...
AYU...!

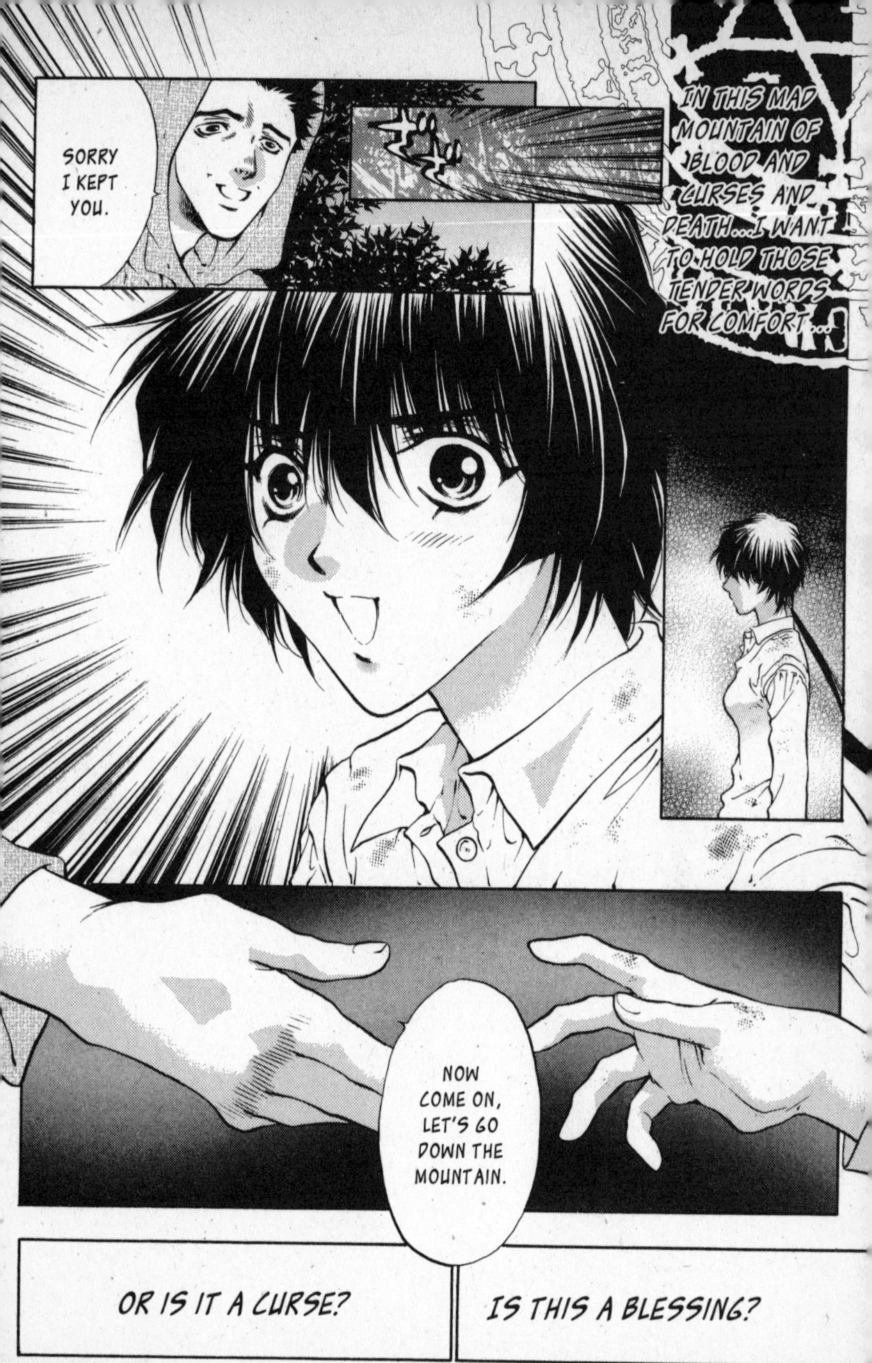
IN THIS MAD MOUNTAIN OF BLOOD AND CURSES AND DEATH...I WANT TO HOLD THOSE TENDER WORDS FOR COMFORT...
SORRY I KEPT YOU.
NOW COME ON, LET'S GO DOWN THE MOUNTAIN.
IS THIS A BLESSING?
OR IS IT A CURSE?

第9話／完

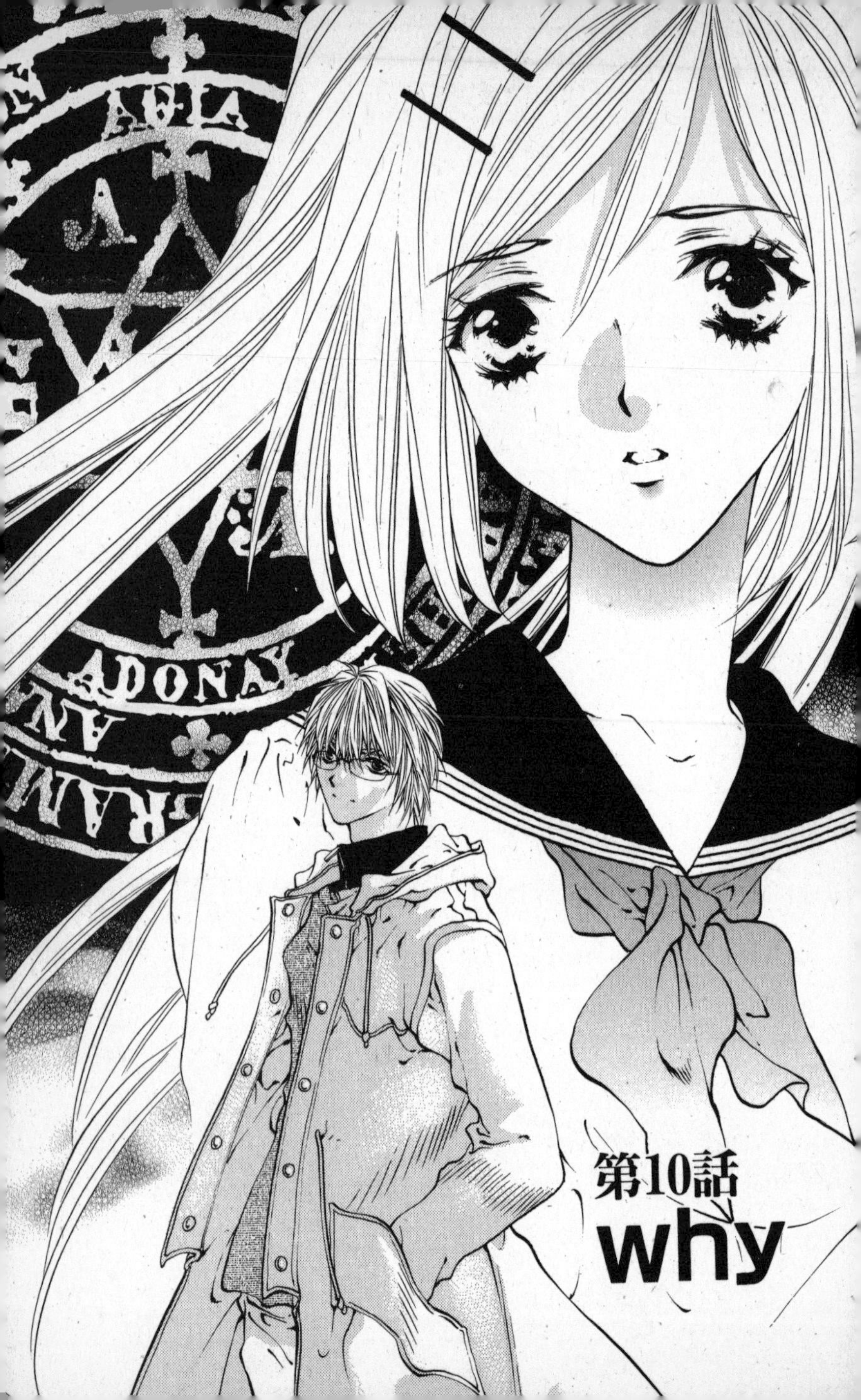
ADONAY
第10話
why

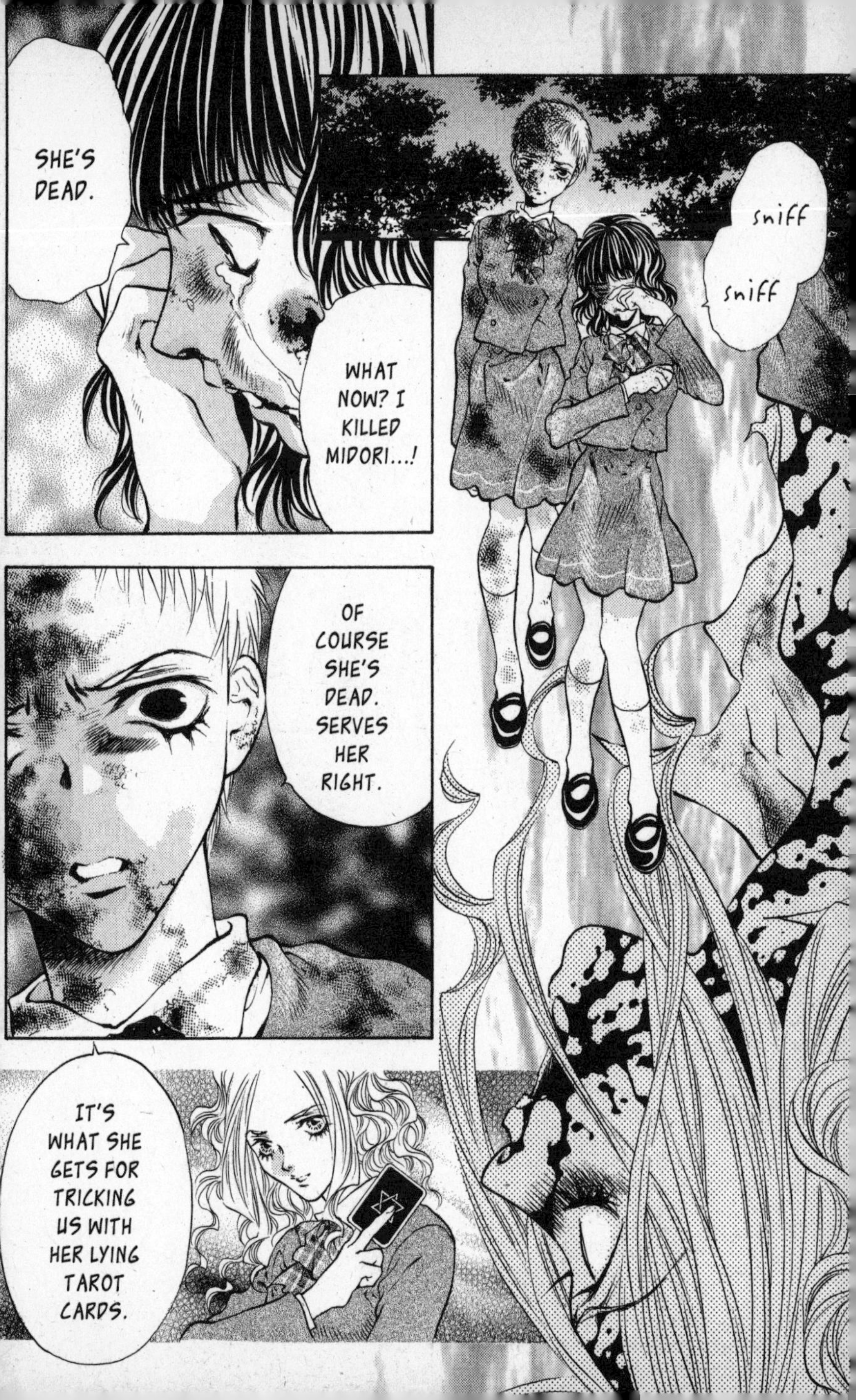
sniff
sniff
SHE'S DEAD.
WHAT NOW? I KILLED MIDORI...!
OF COURSE SHE'S DEAD. SERVES HER RIGHT.
IT'S WHAT SHE GETS FOR TRICKING US WITH HER LYING TAROT CARDS.

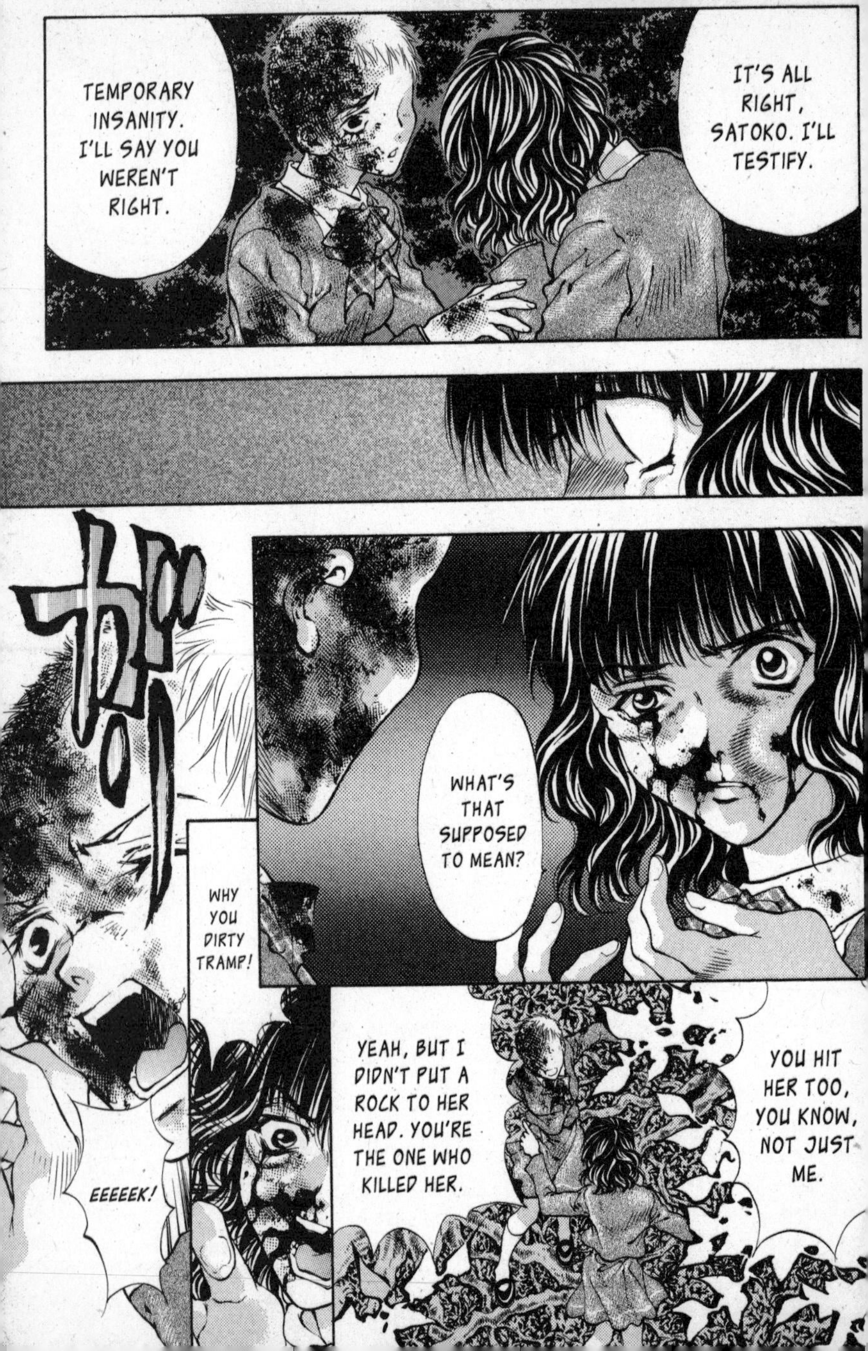
IT'S ALL RIGHT, SATOKO. I'LL TESTIFY.
TEMPORARY INSANITY. I'LL SAY YOU WEREN'T RIGHT.
WHAT'S THAT SUPPOSED TO MEAN?
WHY YOU DIRTY TRAMP!
YOU HIT HER TOO, YOU KNOW, NOT JUST ME.
YEAH, BUT I DIDN'T PUT A ROCK TO HER HEAD. YOU'RE THE ONE WHO KILLED HER.
EEEEEK!

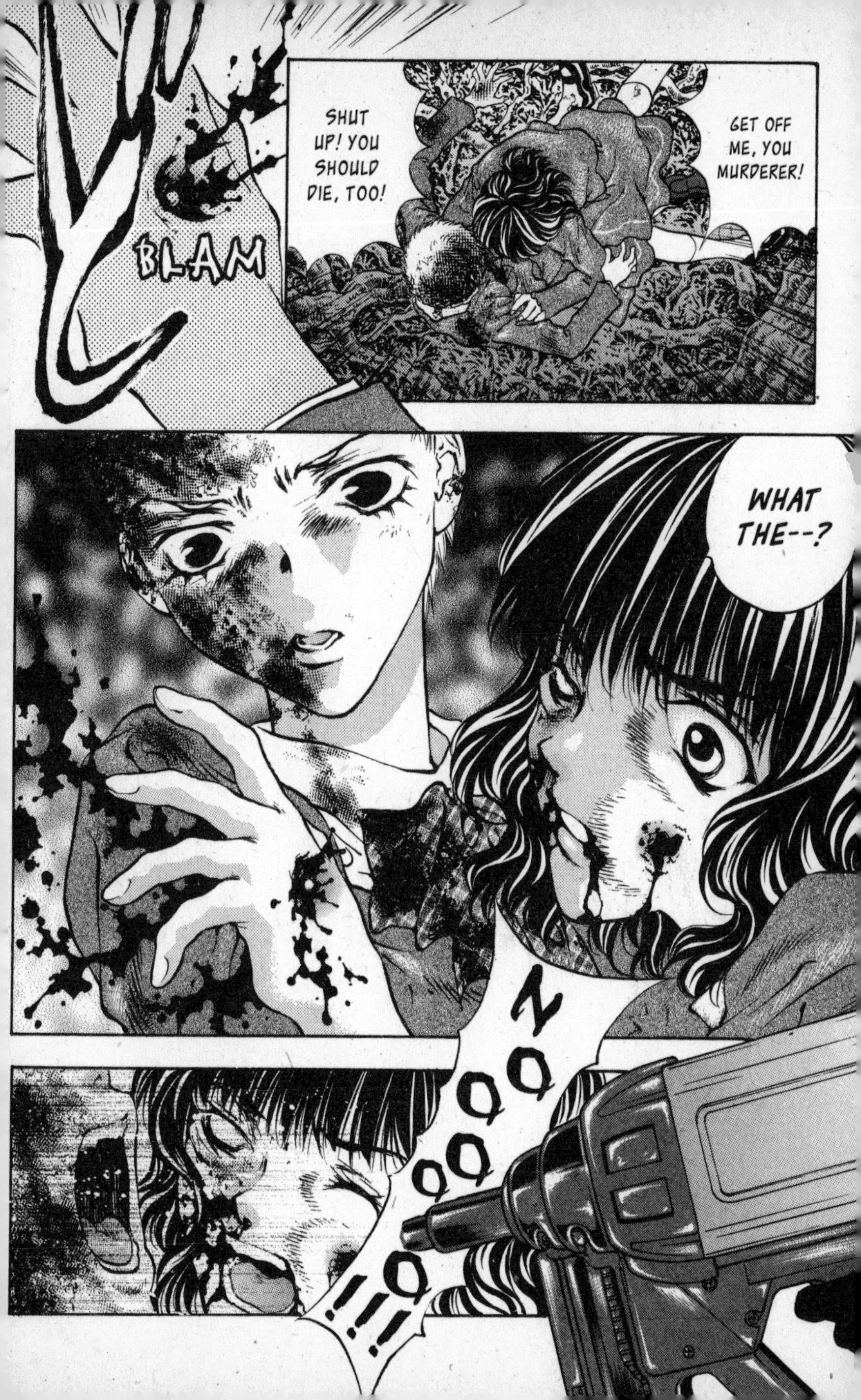
GET OFF ME, YOU MURDERER!
SHUT UP! YOU SHOULD DIE, TOO!
BLAM
WHAT THE--?
NOOOOOOO!!!

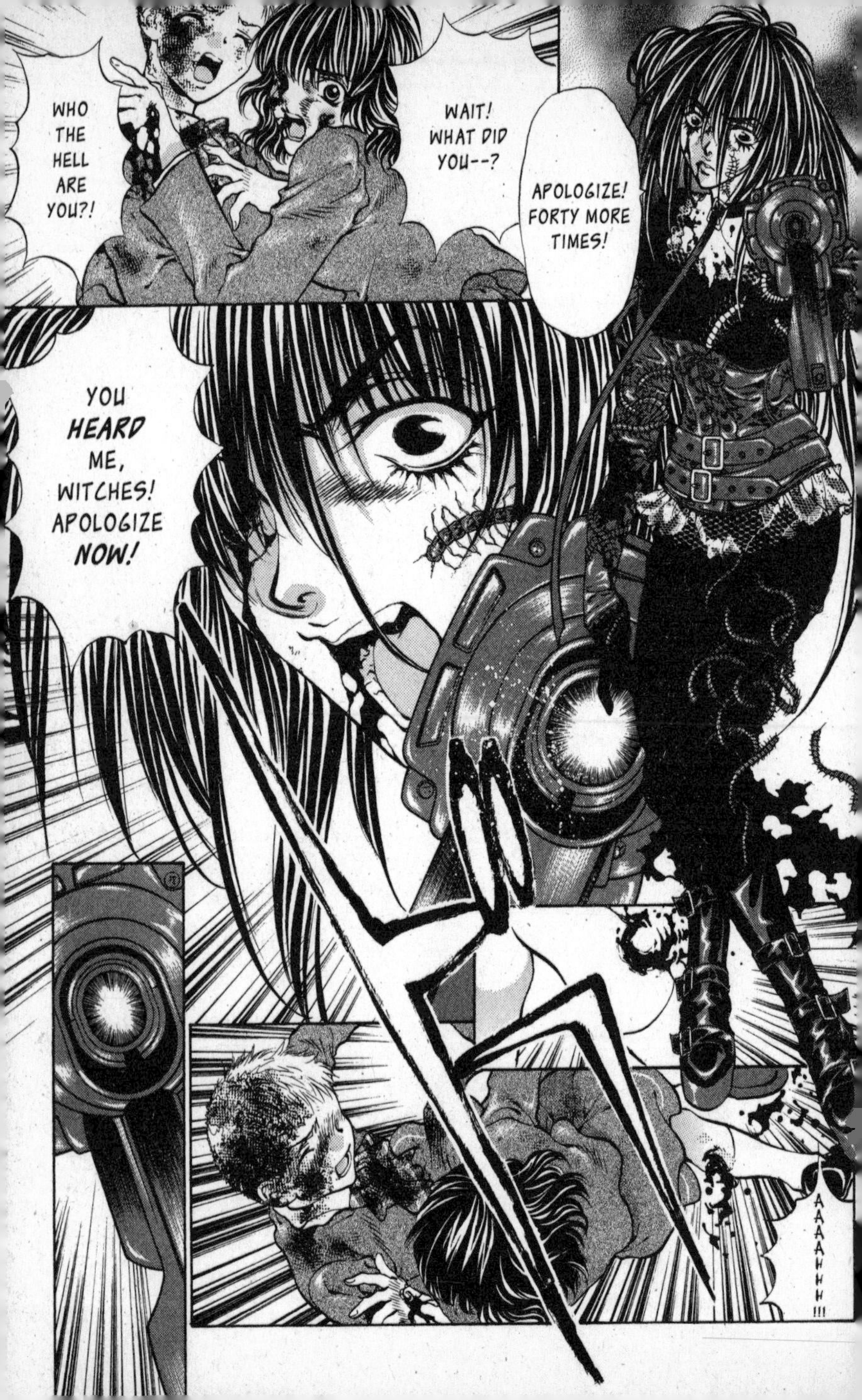
APOLOGIZE! FORTY MORE TIMES!
WAIT! WHAT DID YOU--?
WHO THE HELL ARE YOU?!
YOU **HEARD** ME, WITCHES! APOLOGIZE **NOW!**
AAAAAHHH!!!

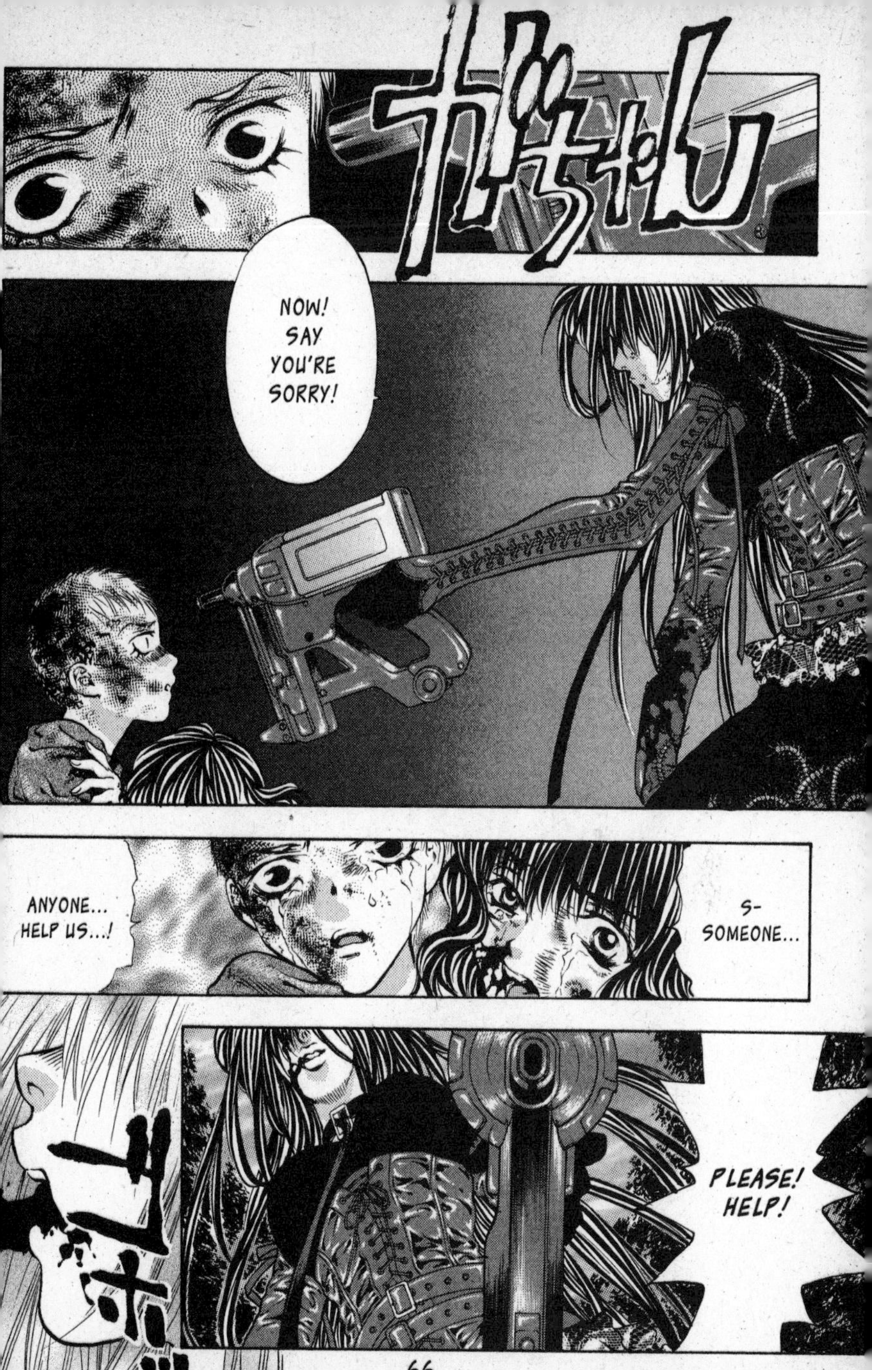
NOW! SAY YOU'RE SORRY!
S- SOMEONE...
ANYONE... HELP US...!
PLEASE! HELP!

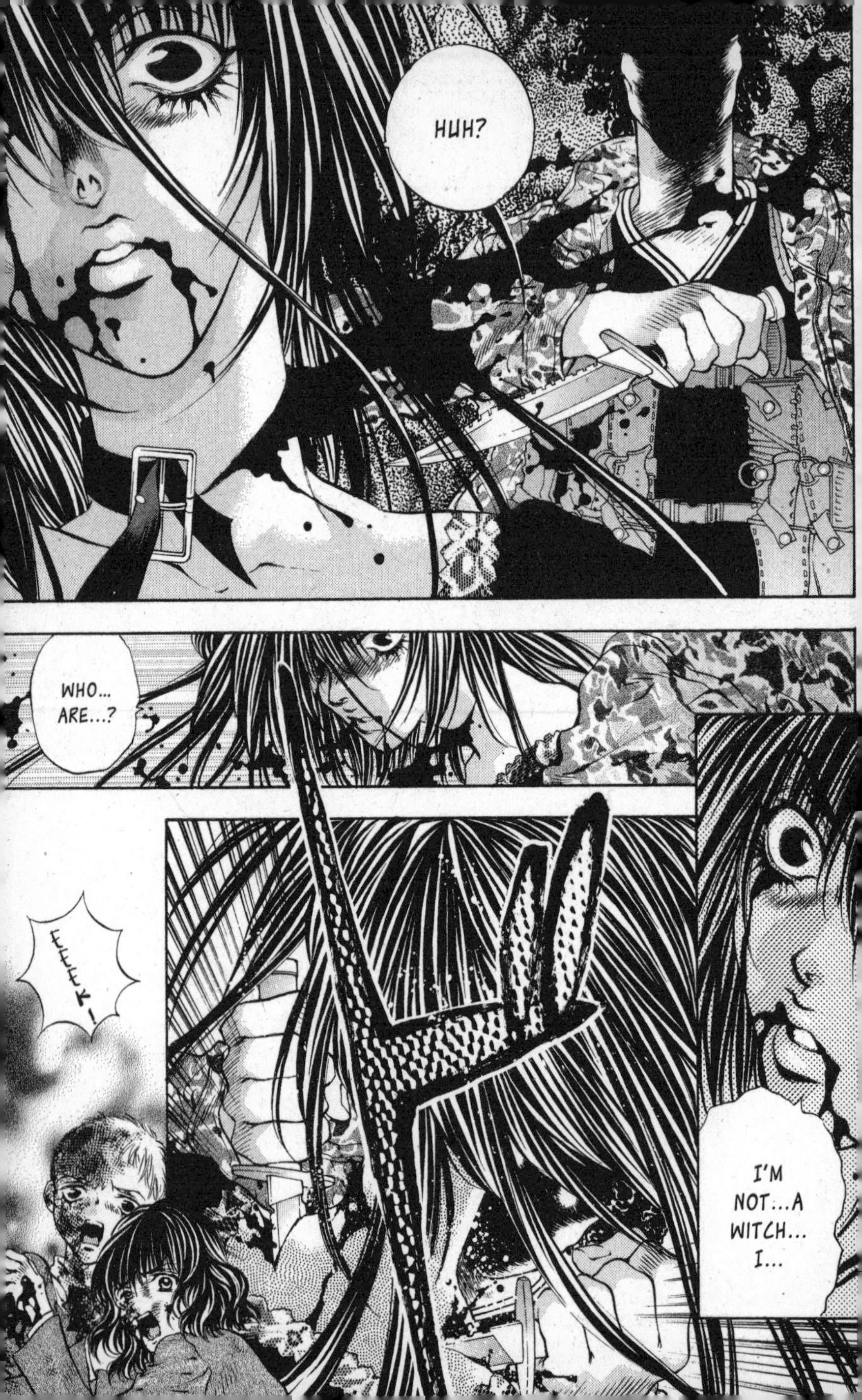
HUH?
WHO... ARE...?
I'M NOT...A WITCH... I...
EEEEK!

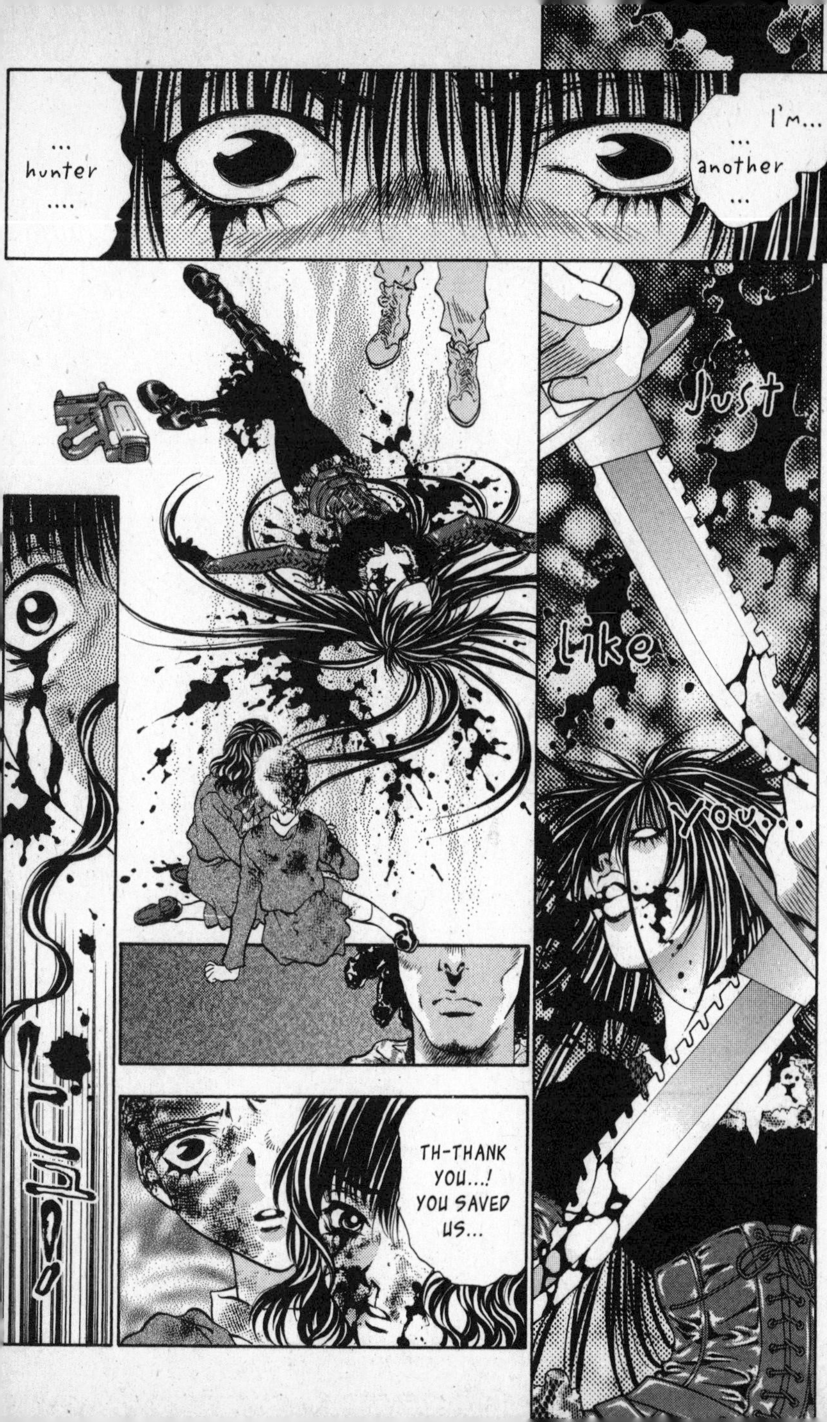
I'm... ... another ...
... hunter ....
Just like you...
TH-THANK YOU...! YOU SAVED US...

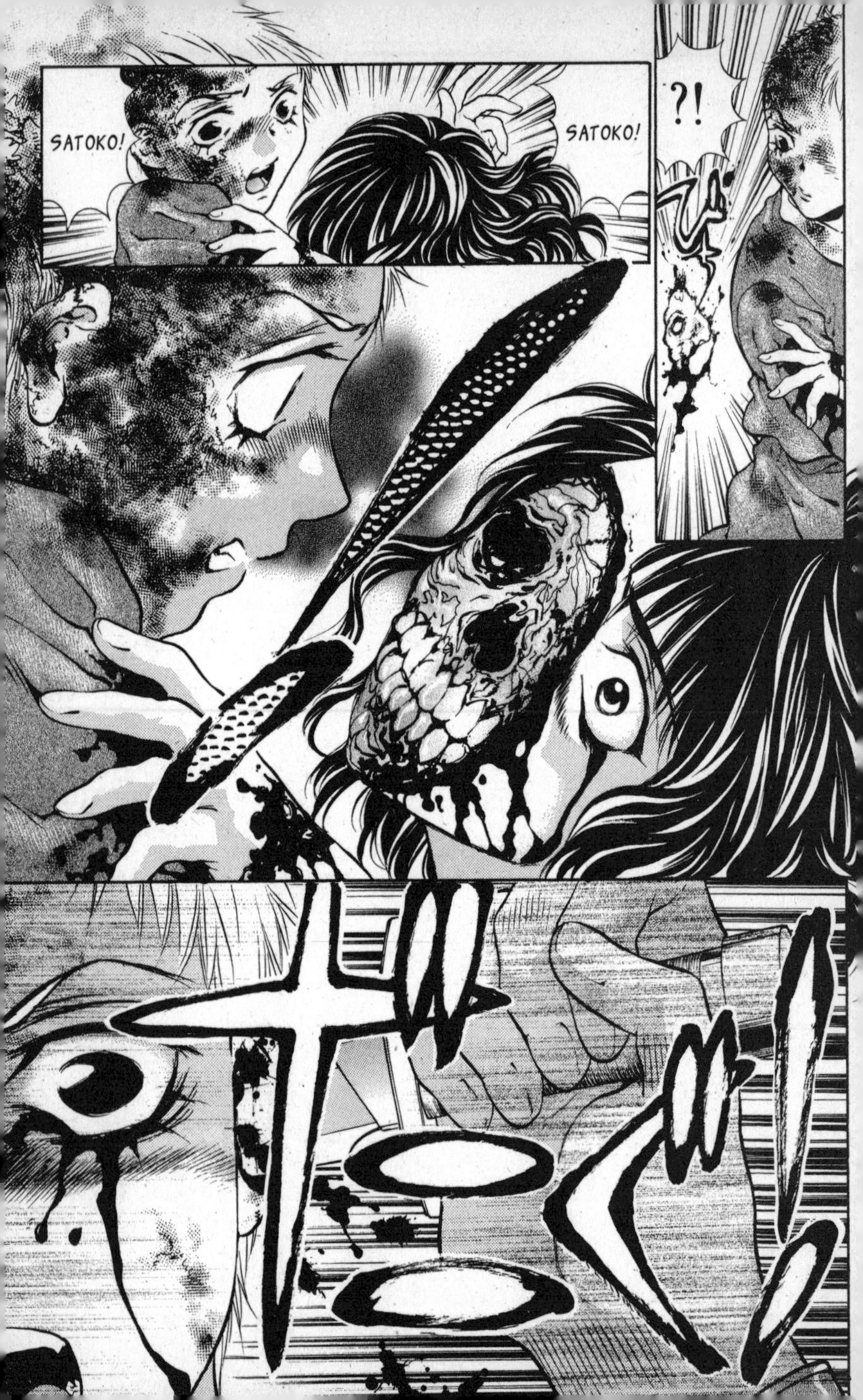
?!
SATOKO!
SATOKO!

NO!
PLEEEEEASE!
どん
どん
どん
どん
stab

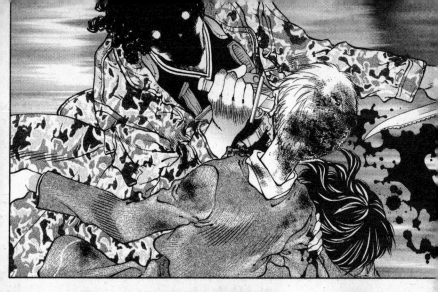

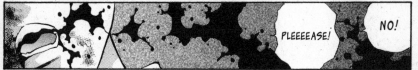

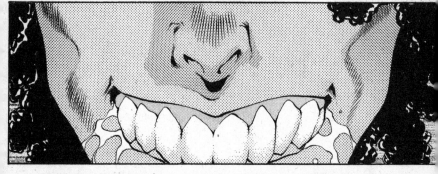

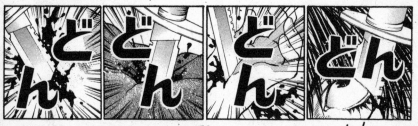

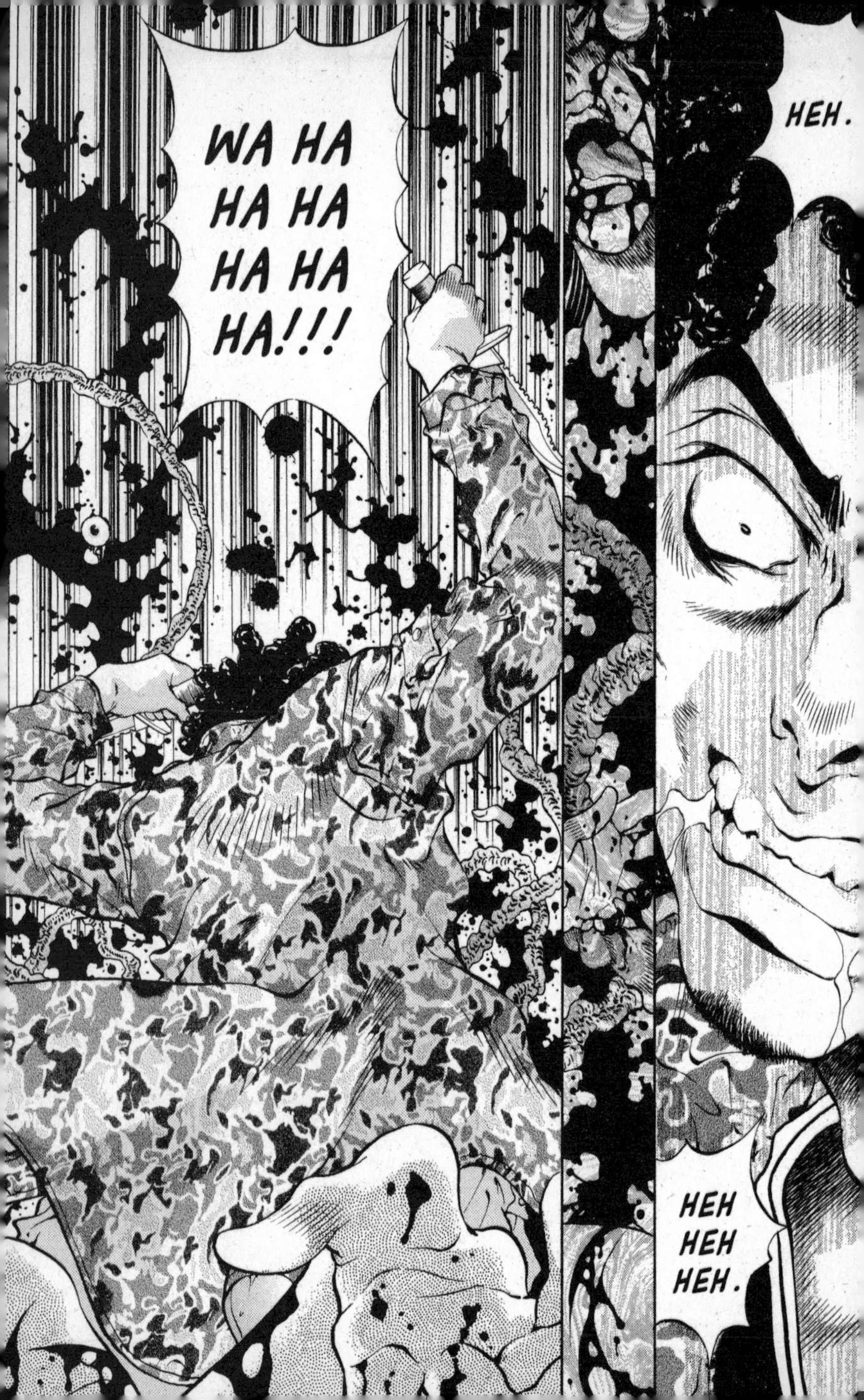
HEH.
HEH HEH HEH.
WA HA HA HA HA HA HA!!!

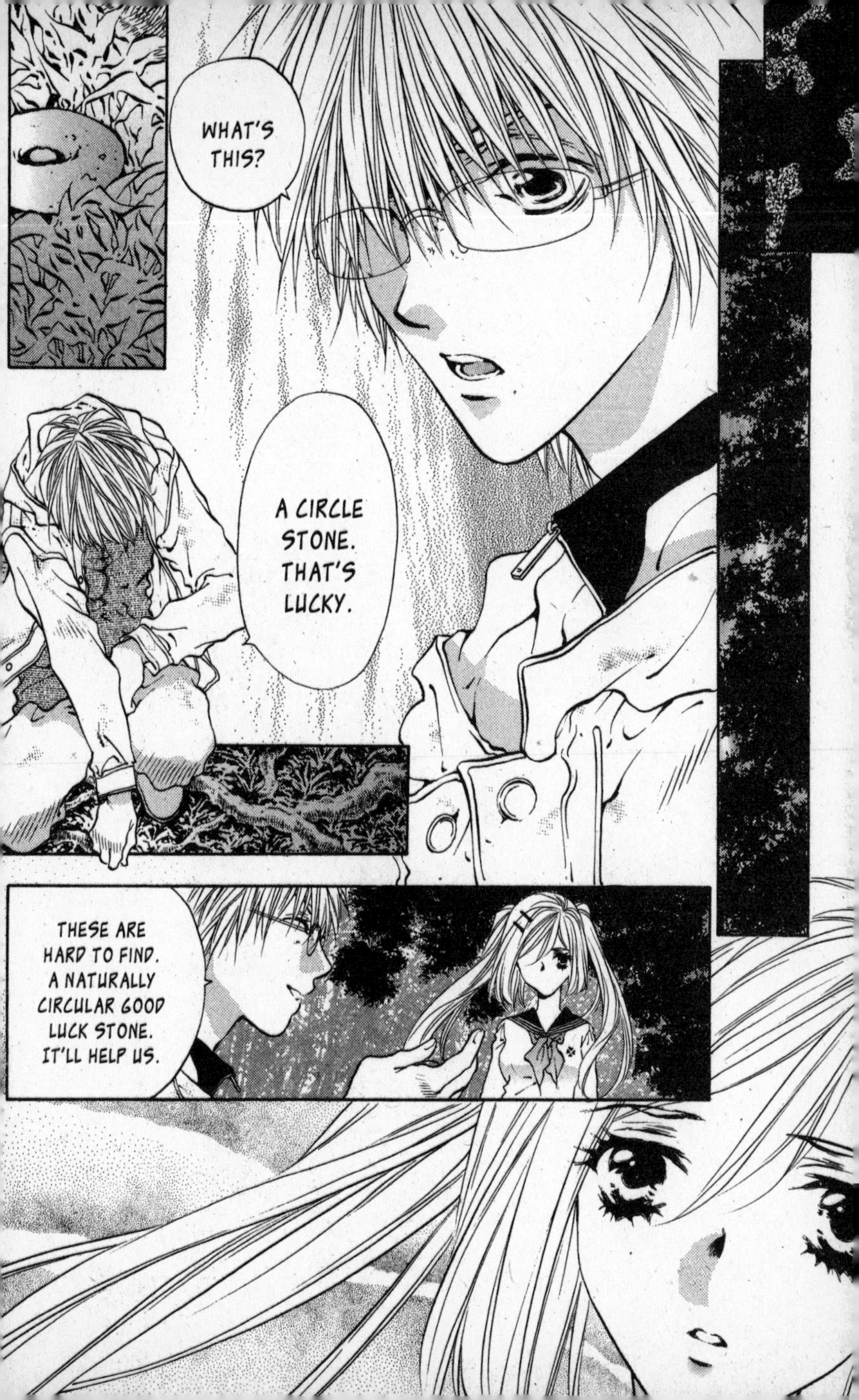
WHAT'S THIS?
A CIRCLE STONE. THAT'S LUCKY.
THESE ARE HARD TO FIND. A NATURALLY CIRCULAR GOOD LUCK STONE. IT'LL HELP US.

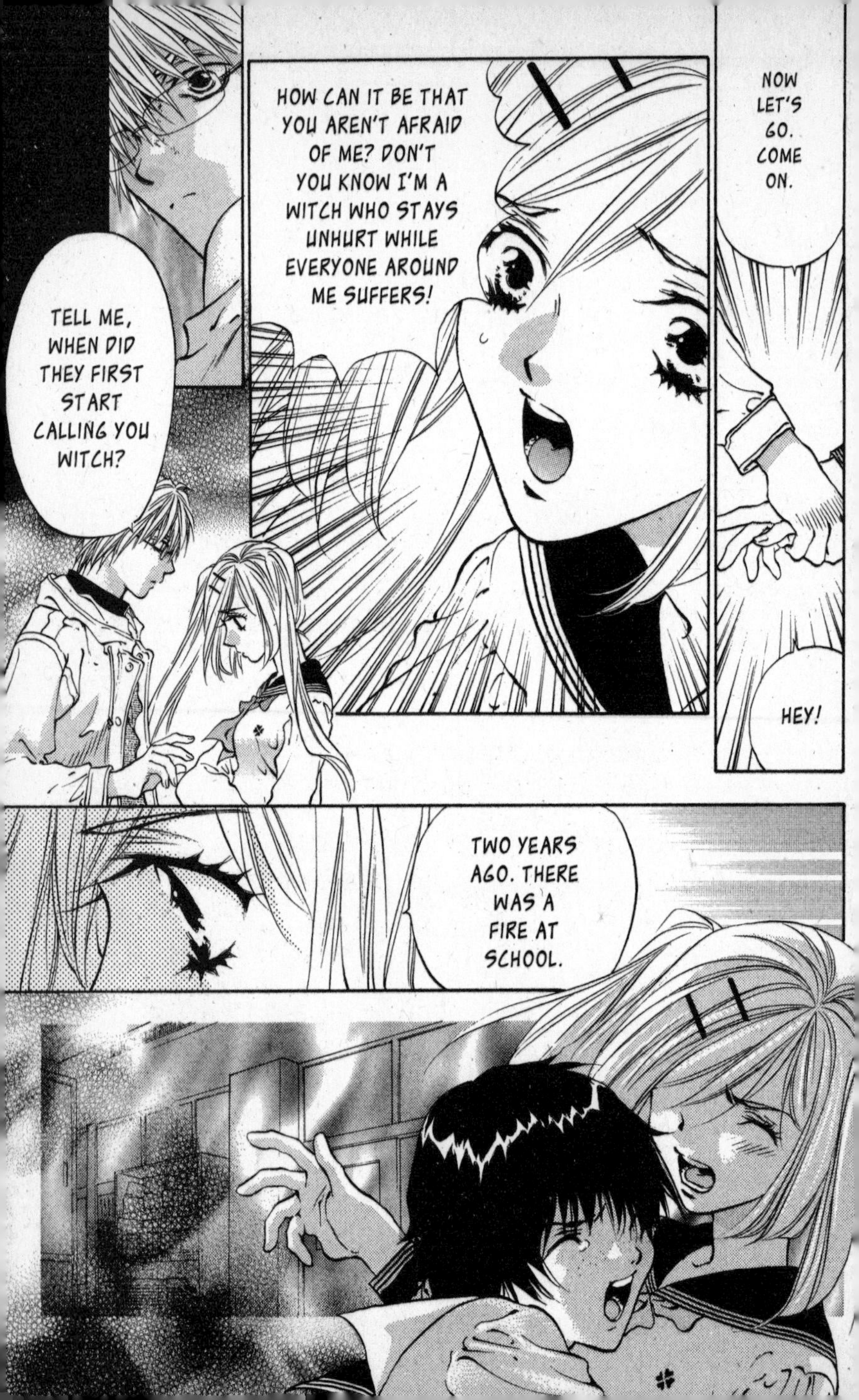
NOW LET'S GO. COME ON.
HEY!
HOW CAN IT BE THAT YOU AREN'T AFRAID OF ME? DON'T YOU KNOW I'M A WITCH WHO STAYS UNHURT WHILE EVERYONE AROUND ME SUFFERS!
TELL ME, WHEN DID THEY FIRST START CALLING YOU WITCH?
TWO YEARS AGO. THERE WAS A FIRE AT SCHOOL.

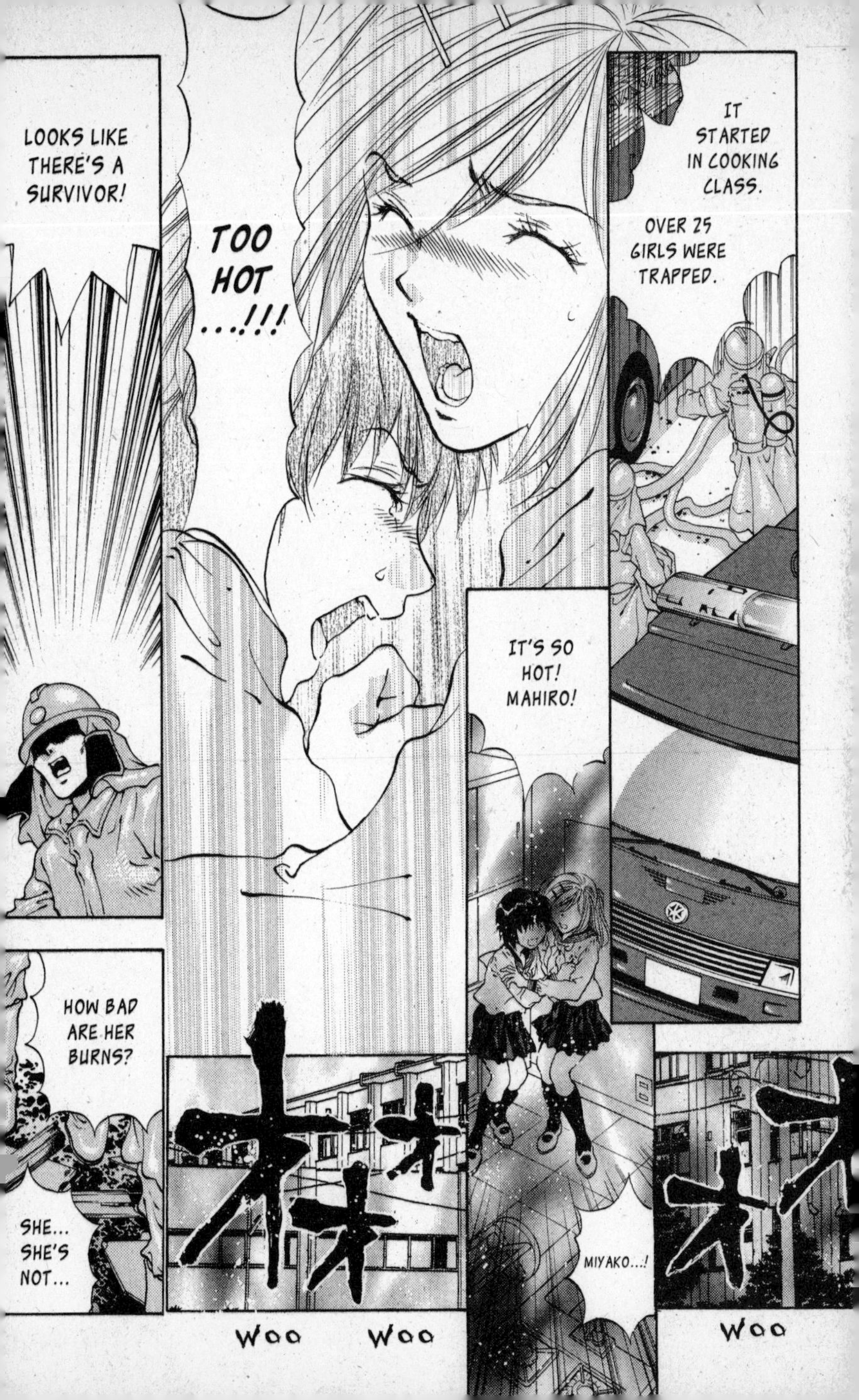

IT STARTED IN COOKING CLASS.
OVER 25 GIRLS WERE TRAPPED.
TOO HOT ...!!!
LOOKS LIKE THERE'S A SURVIVOR!
IT'S SO HOT! MAHIRO!
MIYAKO...!
Woo
Woo Woo
HOW BAD ARE HER BURNS?
SHE... SHE'S NOT...

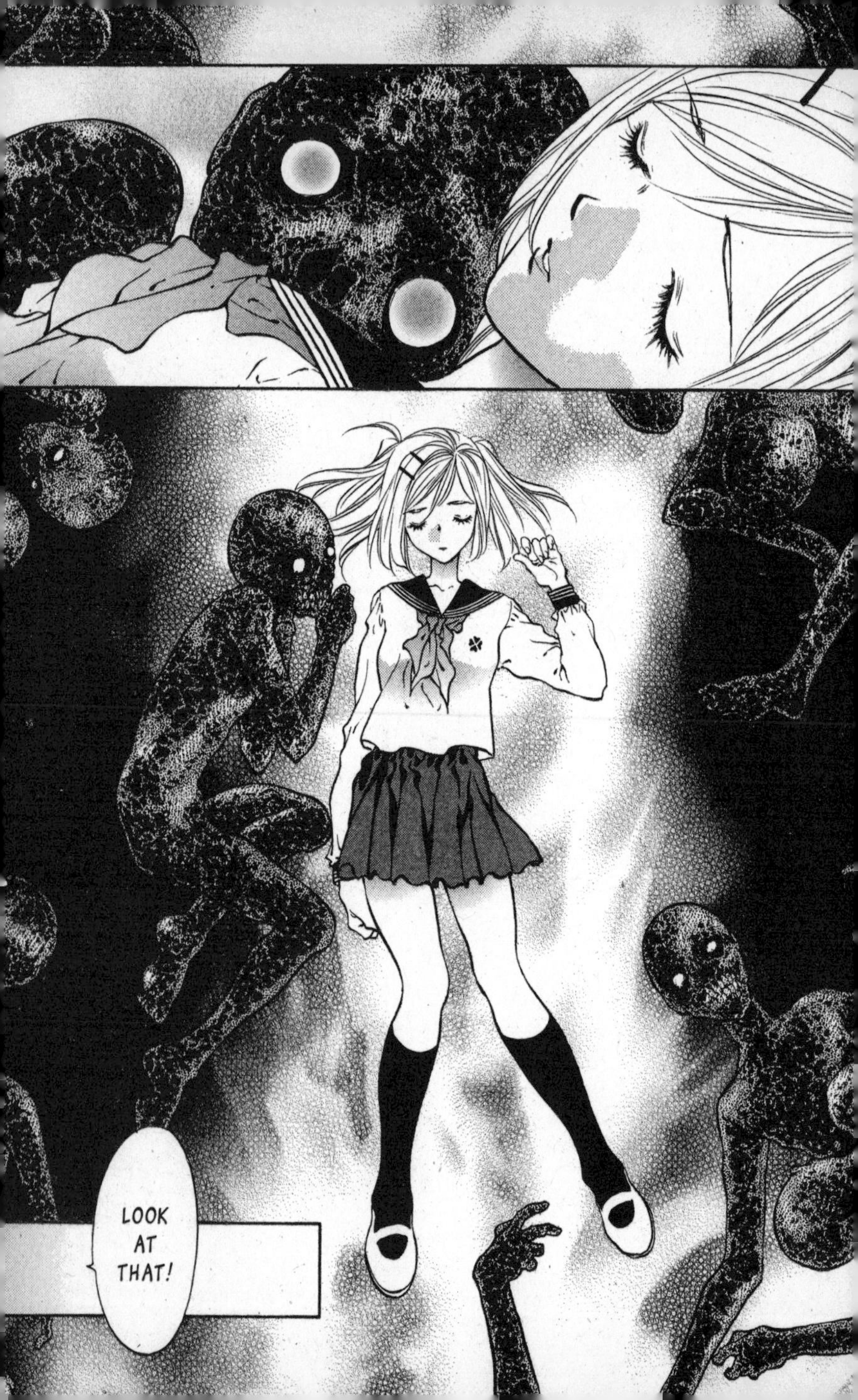
LOOK AT THAT!

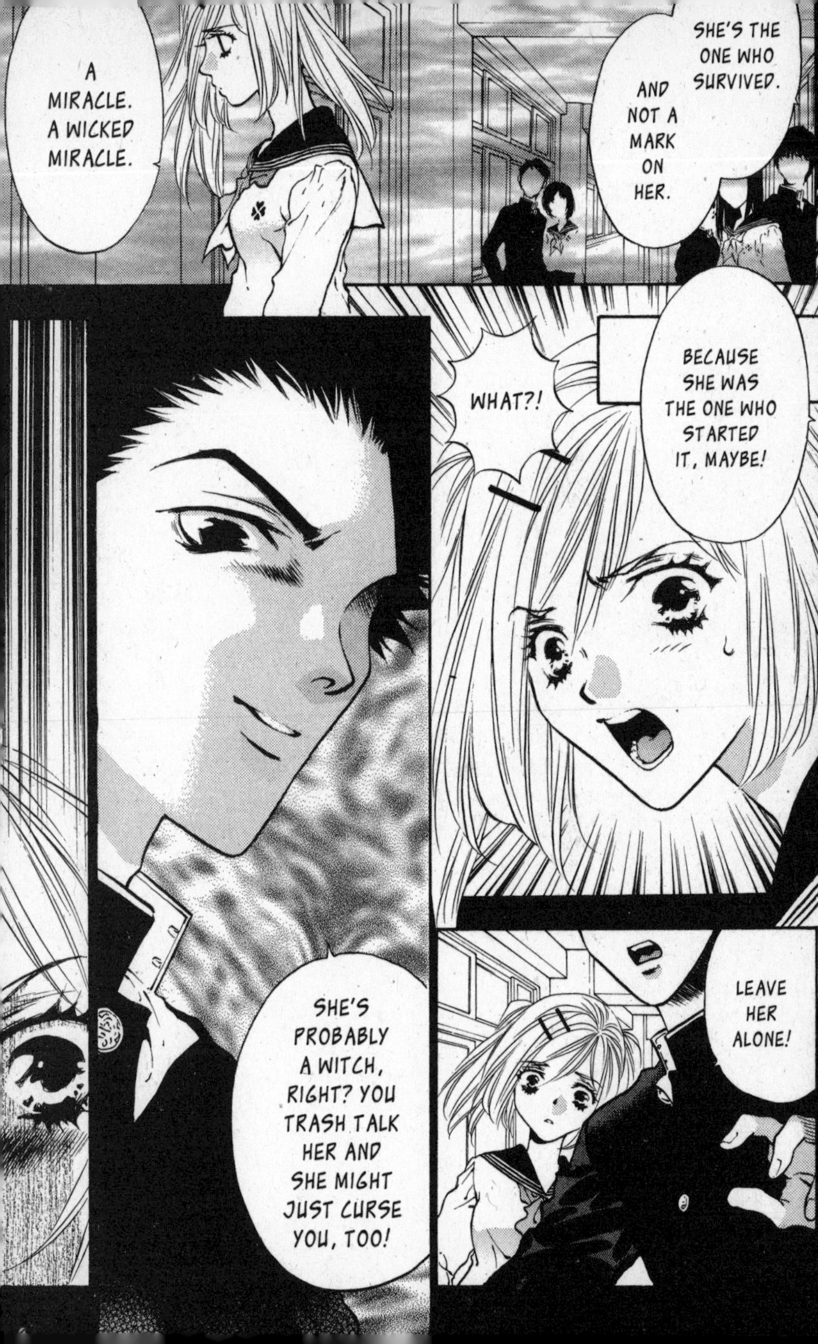
SHE'S THE ONE WHO SURVIVED.
AND NOT A MARK ON HER.
A MIRACLE. A WICKED MIRACLE.
BECAUSE SHE WAS THE ONE WHO STARTED IT, MAYBE!
WHAT?!
LEAVE HER ALONE!
SHE'S PROBABLY A WITCH, RIGHT? YOU TRASH TALK HER AND SHE MIGHT JUST CURSE YOU, TOO!

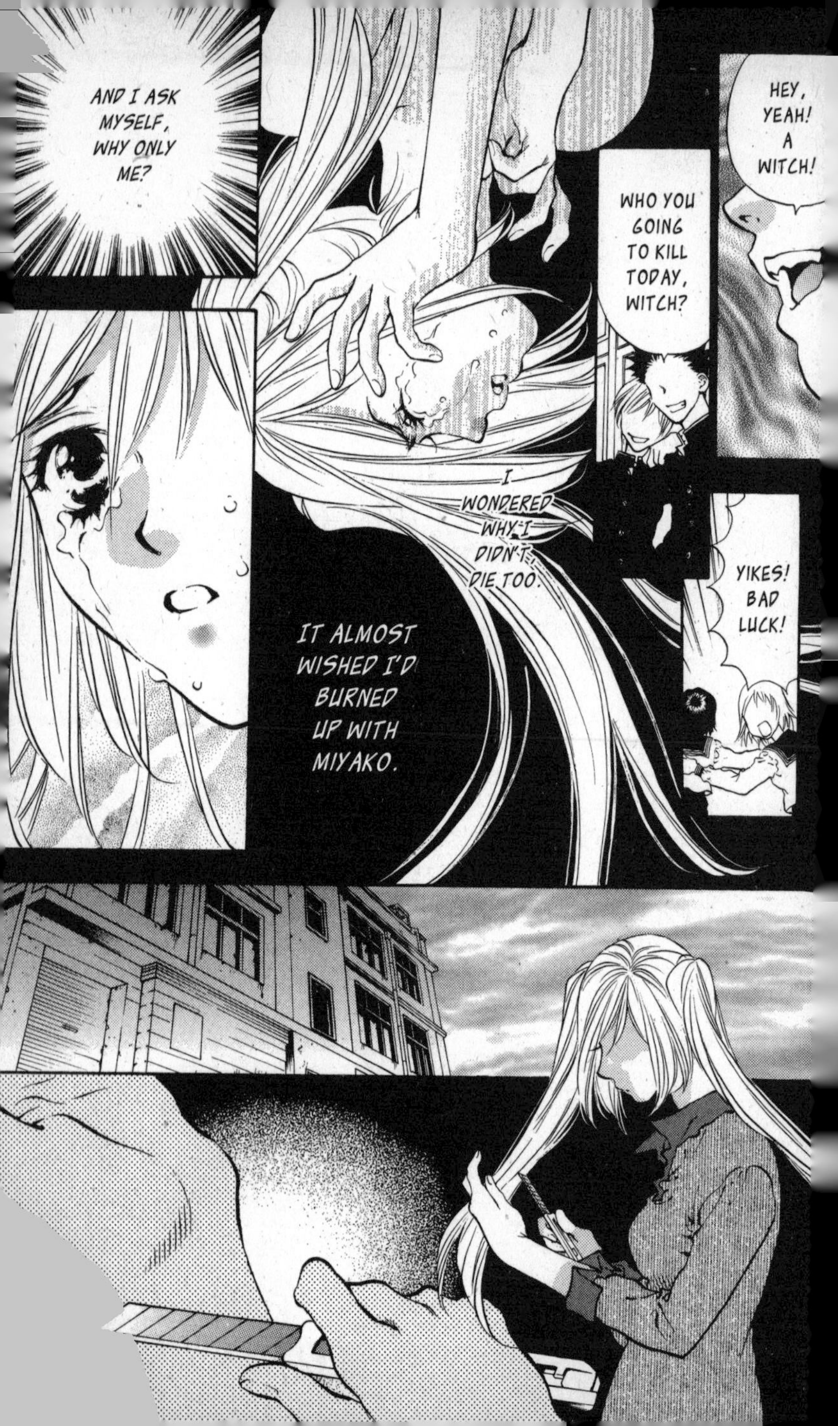
HEY, YEAH! A WITCH!
WHO YOU GOING TO KILL TODAY, WITCH?
YIKES! BAD LUCK!
I WONDERED WHY I DIDN'T DIE TOO.
IT ALMOST WISHED I'D BURNED UP WITH MIYAKO.
AND I ASK MYSELF, WHY ONLY ME?

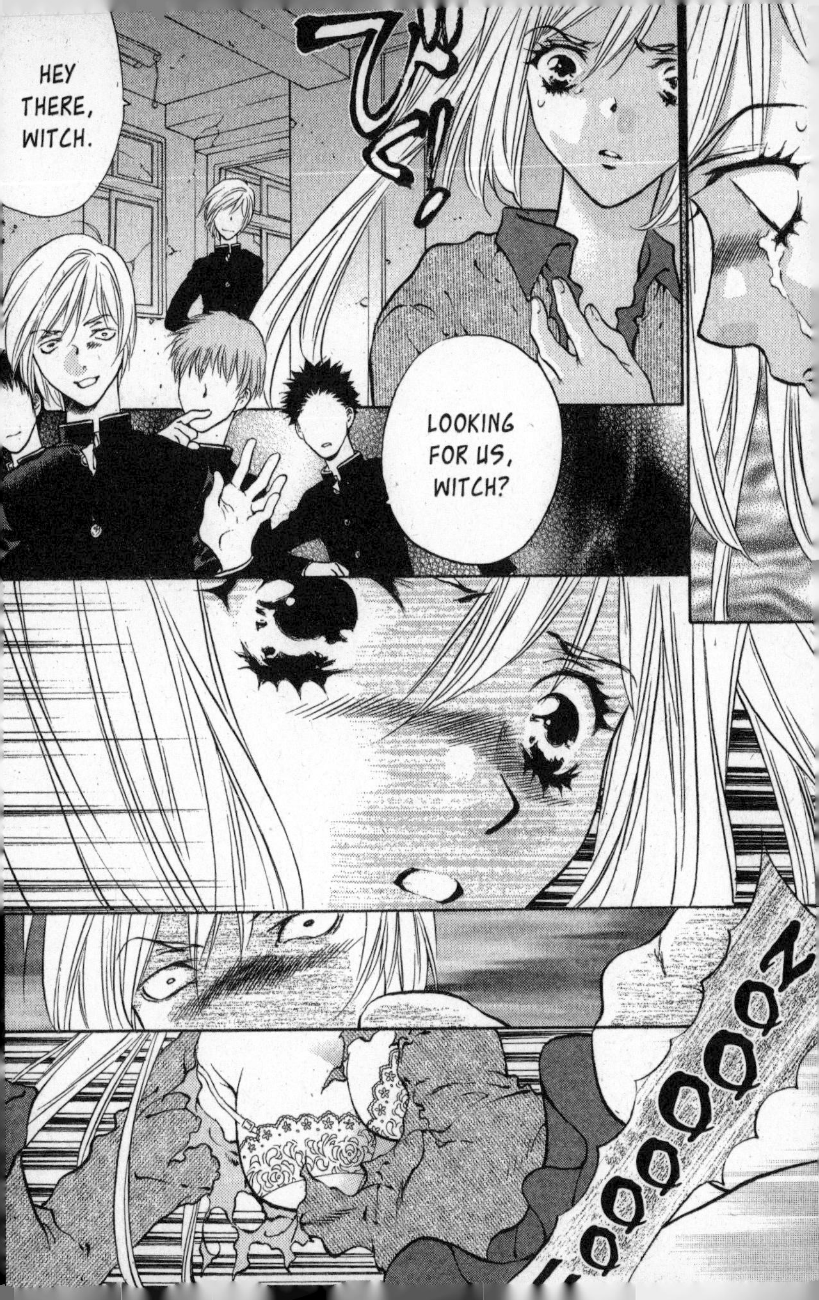
HEY THERE, WITCH.
LOOKING FOR US, WITCH?
NOOOOOOO

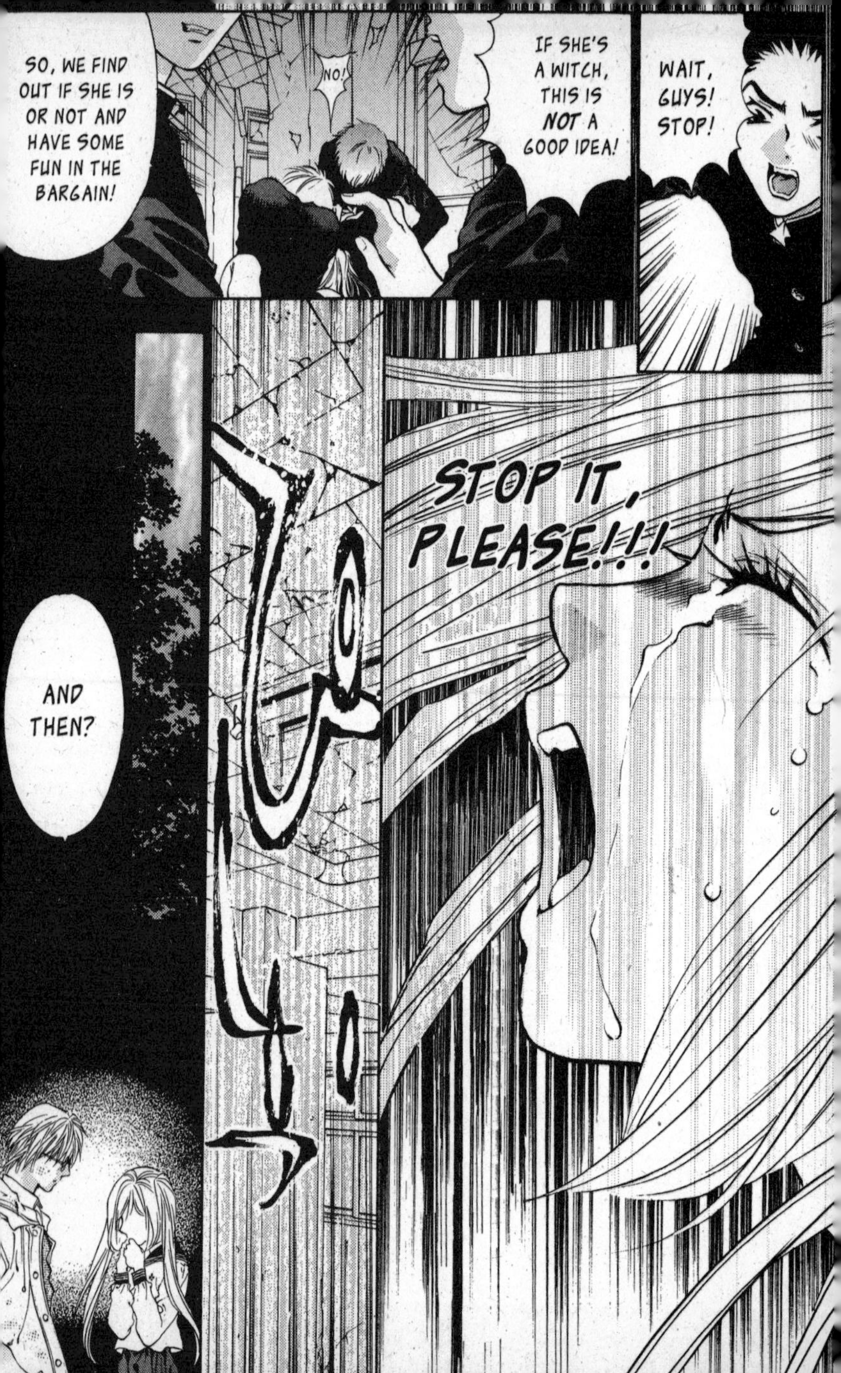
WAIT, GUYS! STOP!
IF SHE'S A WITCH, THIS IS *NOT* A GOOD IDEA!
NO!
SO, WE FIND OUT IF SHE IS OR NOT AND HAVE SOME FUN IN THE BARGAIN!
STOP IT, PLEASE!!!
AND THEN?

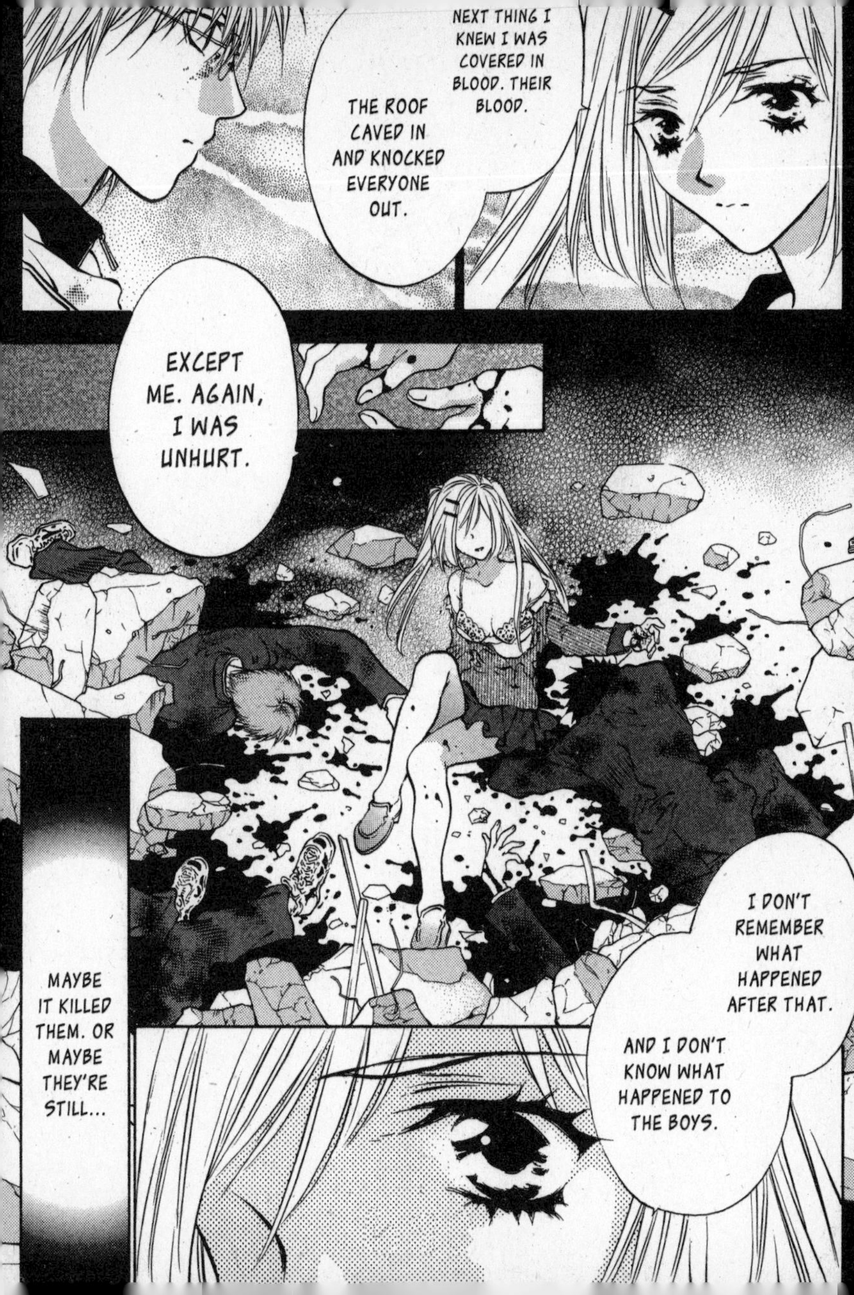
THE ROOF CAVED IN AND KNOCKED EVERYONE OUT.
EXCEPT ME. AGAIN, I WAS UNHURT.
NEXT THING I KNEW I WAS COVERED IN BLOOD. THEIR BLOOD.
I DON'T REMEMBER WHAT HAPPENED AFTER THAT.
AND I DON'T KNOW WHAT HAPPENED TO THE BOYS.
MAYBE IT KILLED THEM. OR MAYBE THEY'RE STILL...

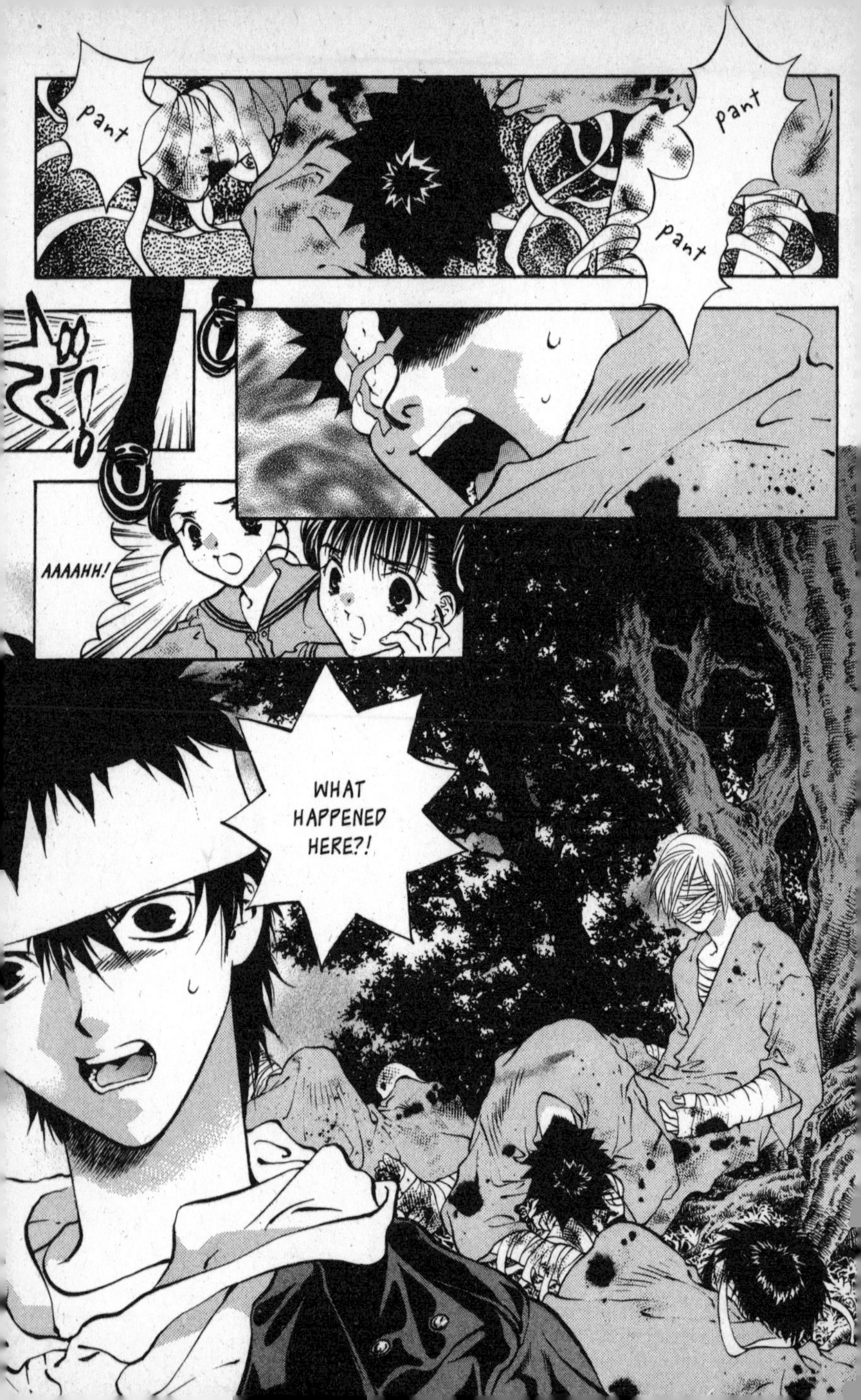
pant
pant
pant
AAAAHH!
WHAT HAPPENED HERE?!

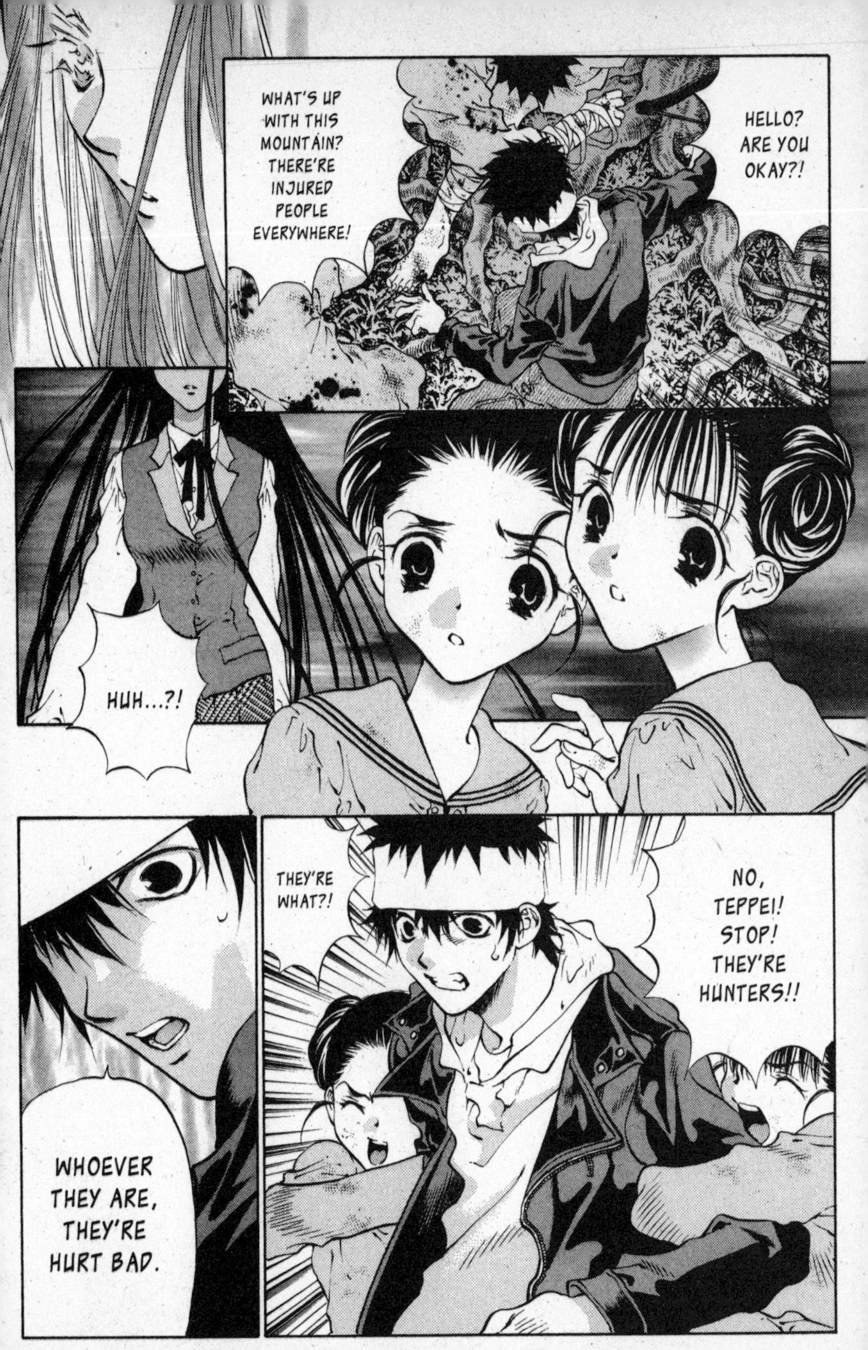
HELLO? ARE YOU OKAY?!
WHAT'S UP WITH THIS MOUNTAIN? THERE'RE INJURED PEOPLE EVERYWHERE!
HUH...?!
NO, TEPPEI! STOP! THEY'RE HUNTERS!!
THEY'RE WHAT?!
WHOEVER THEY ARE, THEY'RE HURT BAD.

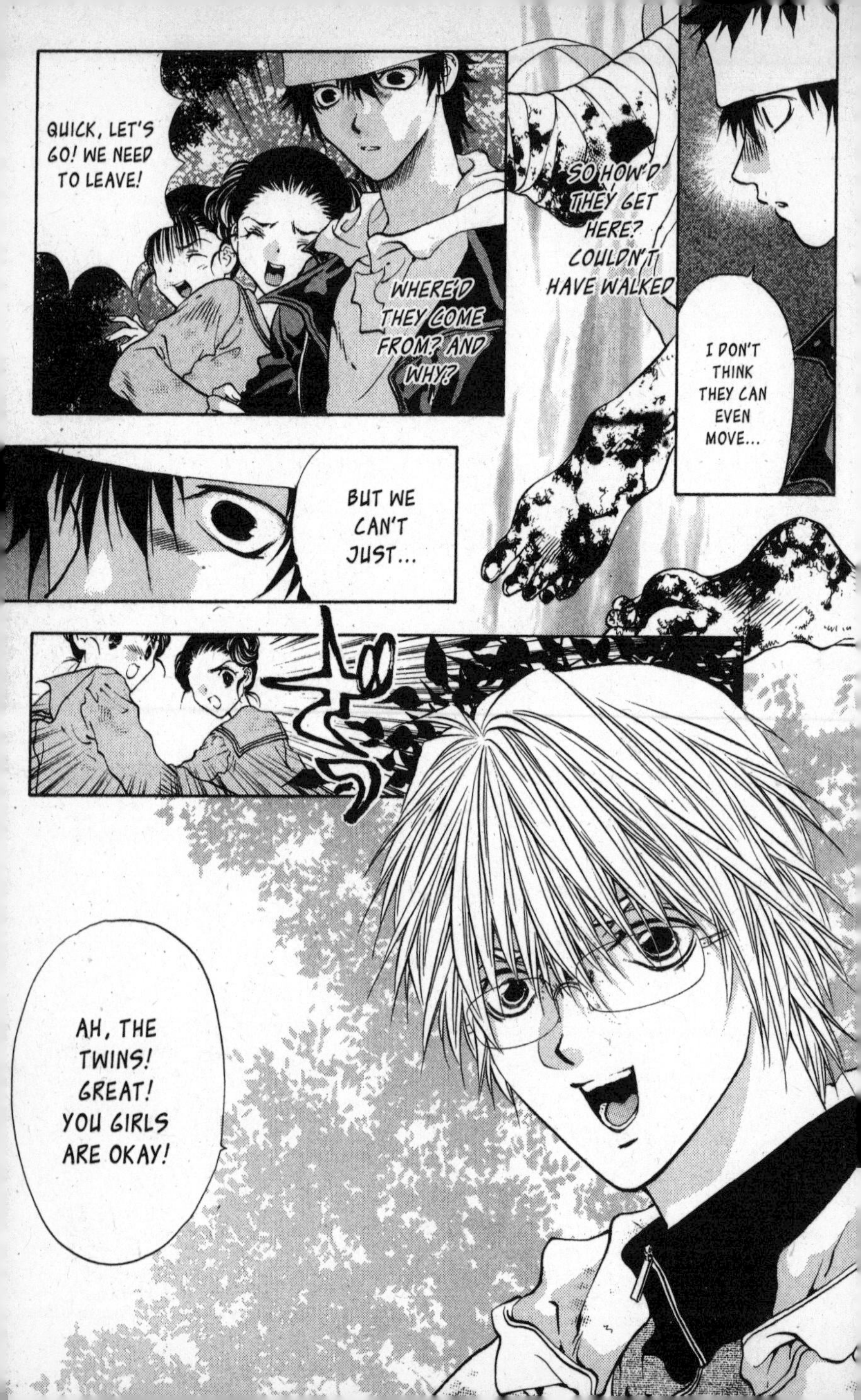
SO HOW'D THEY GET HERE? COULDN'T HAVE WALKED
I DON'T THINK THEY CAN EVEN MOVE...
WHERE'D THEY COME FROM? AND WHY?
QUICK, LET'S GO! WE NEED TO LEAVE!
BUT WE CAN'T JUST...
AH, THE TWINS! GREAT! YOU GIRLS ARE OKAY!

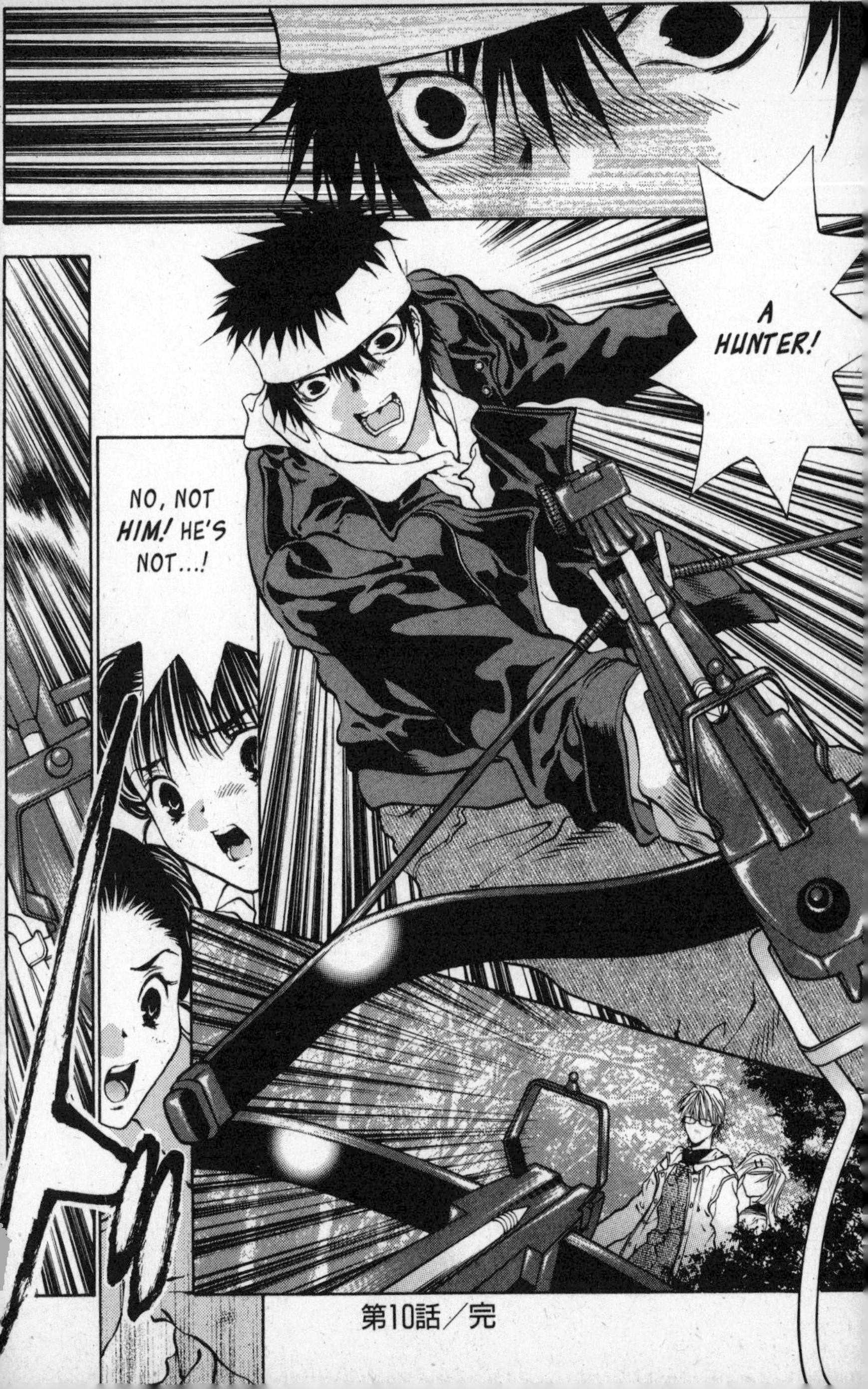
A HUNTER!
NO, NOT *HIM!* HE'S NOT...!
第10話／完

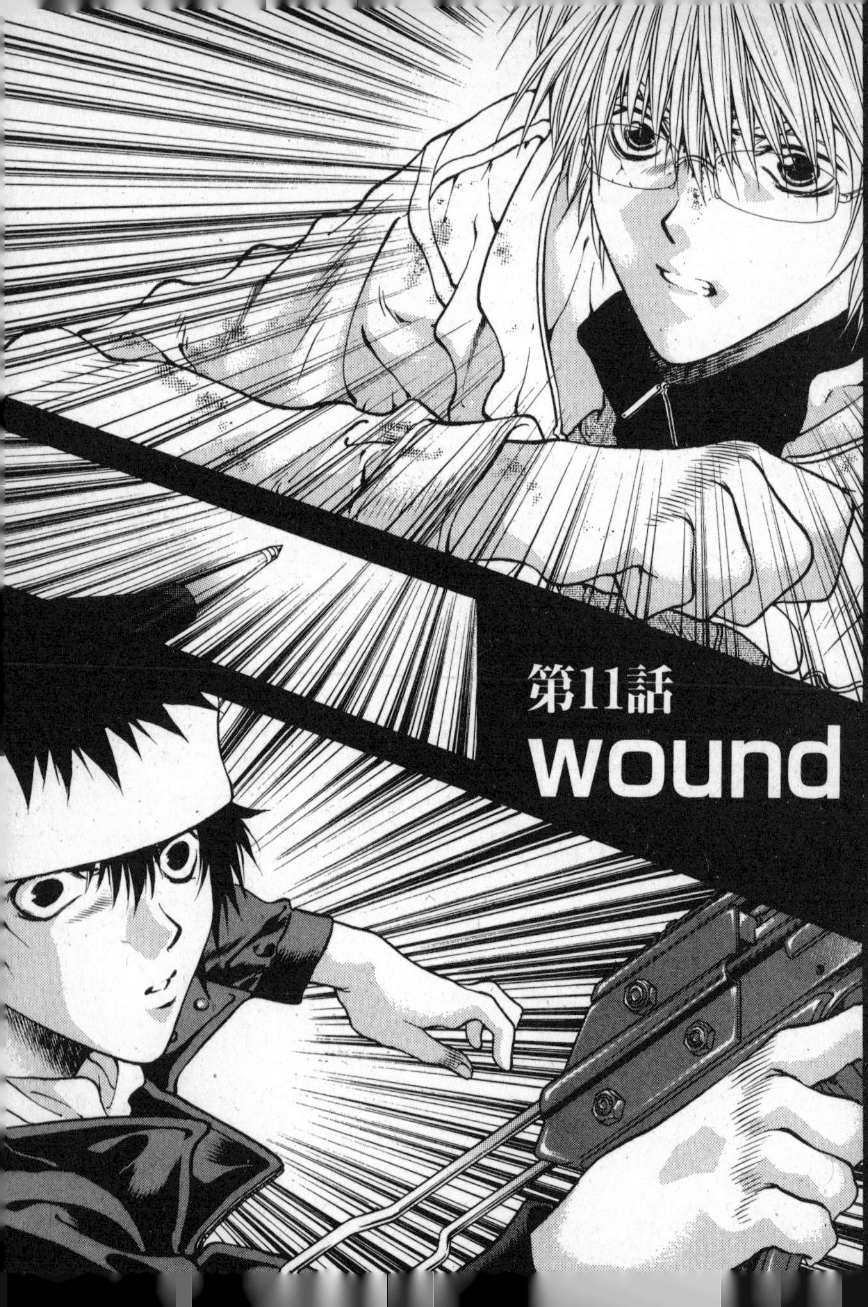
第11話
wound

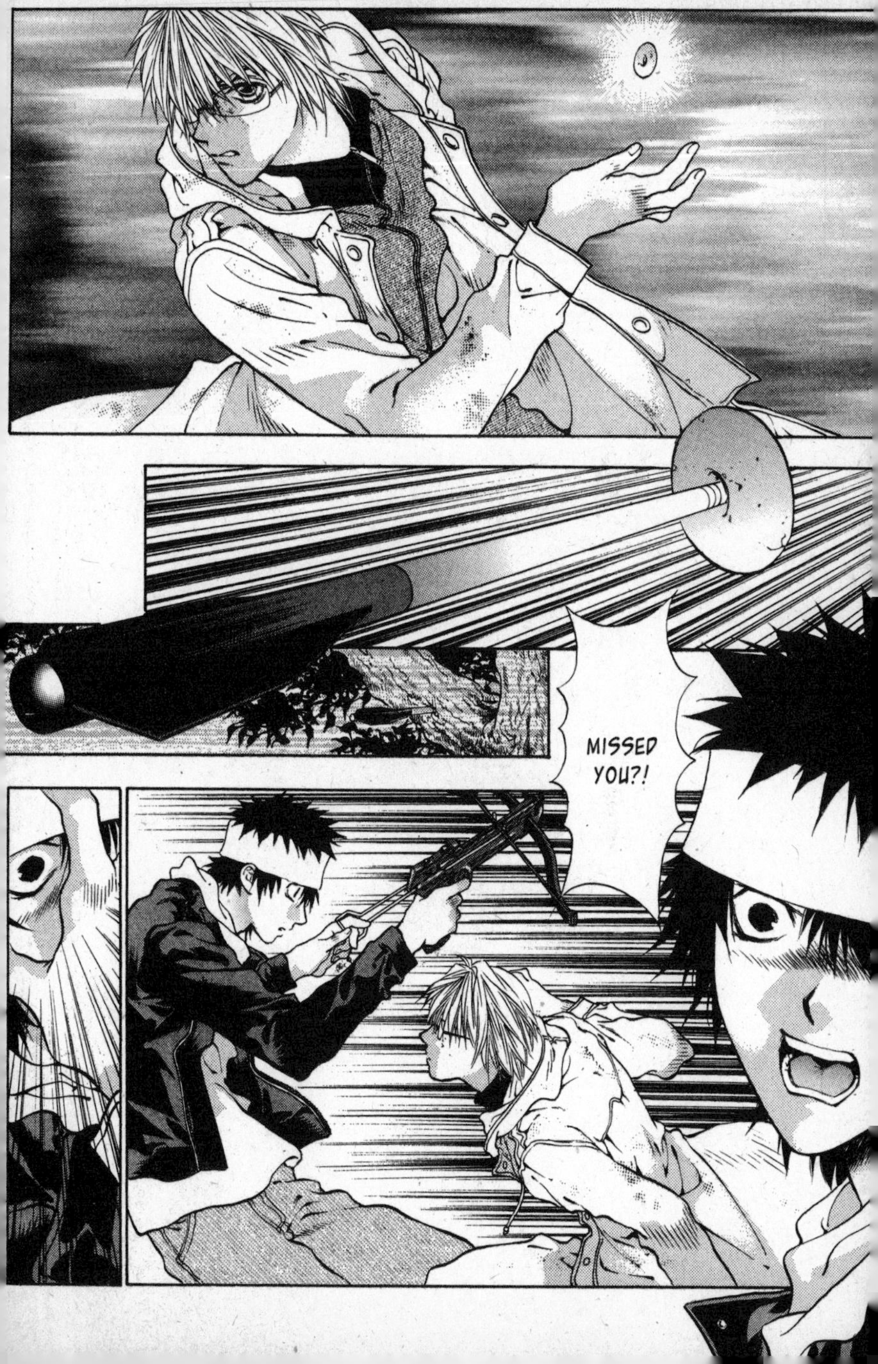
MISSED YOU?!

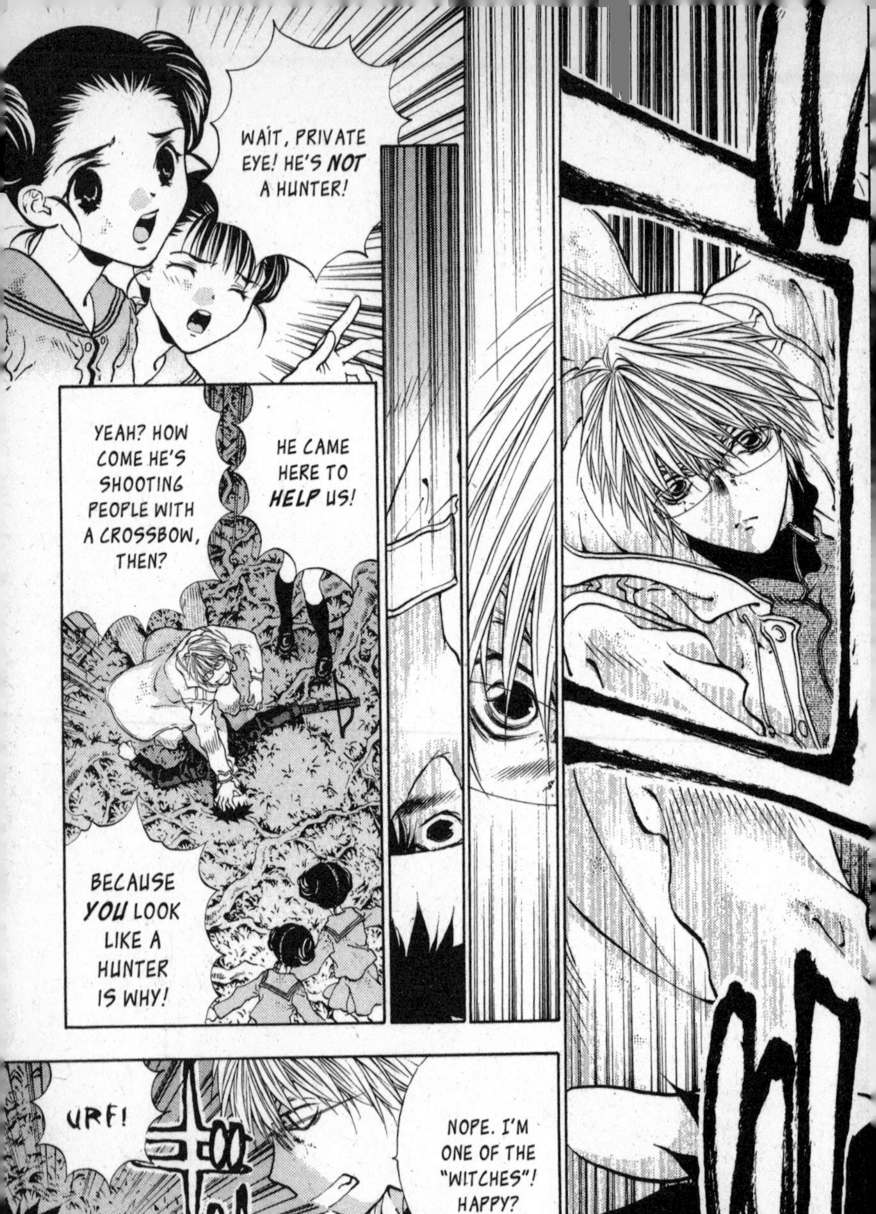
WAIT, PRIVATE EYE! HE'S NOT A HUNTER!
HE CAME HERE TO HELP US!
YEAH? HOW COME HE'S SHOOTING PEOPLE WITH A CROSSBOW, THEN?
BECAUSE YOU LOOK LIKE A HUNTER IS WHY!
NOPE. I'M ONE OF THE "WITCHES"! HAPPY?
URF!

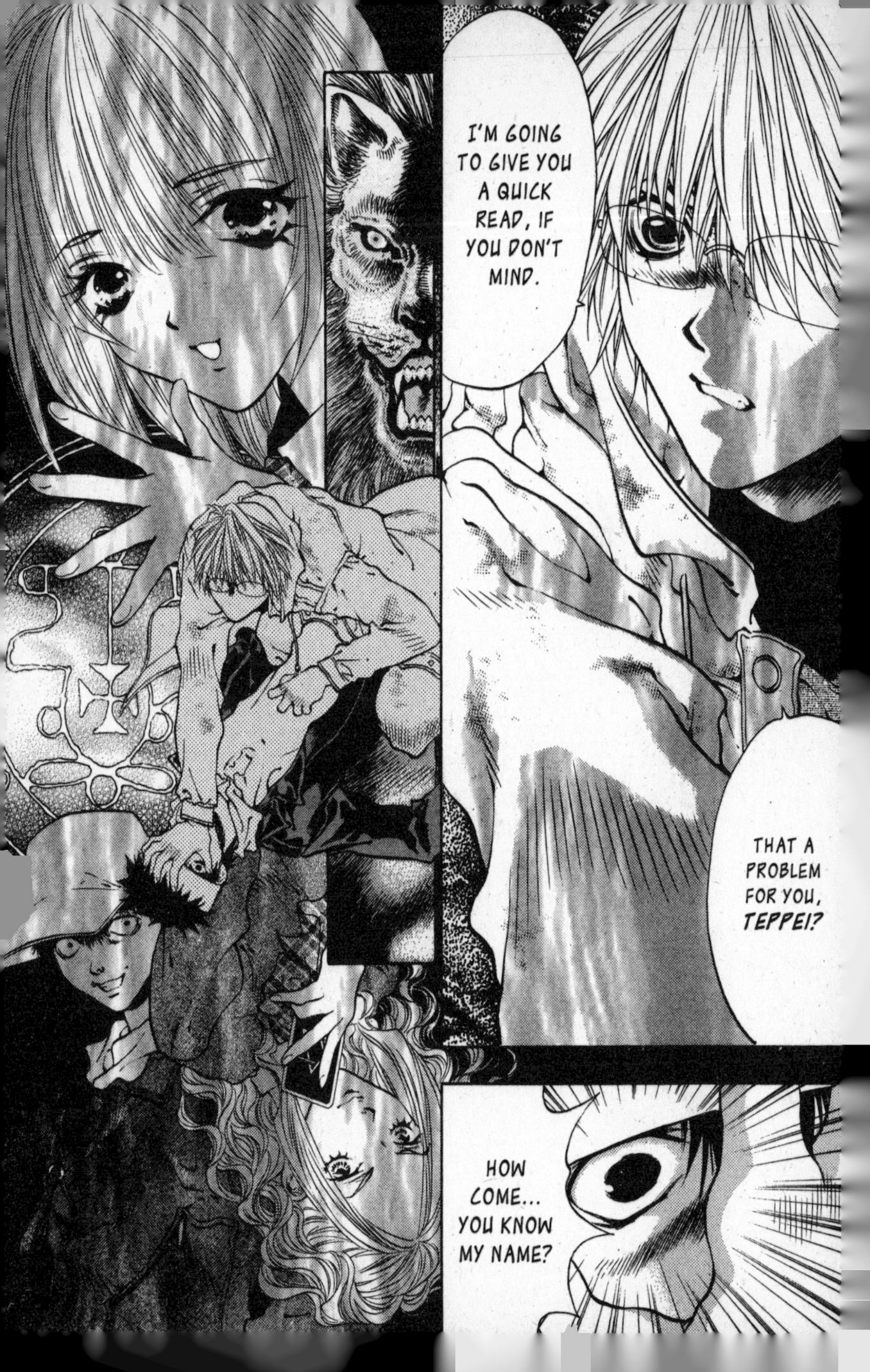
I'M GOING TO GIVE YOU A QUICK READ, IF YOU DON'T MIND.
THAT A PROBLEM FOR YOU, *TEPPEI?*
HOW COME... YOU KNOW MY NAME?

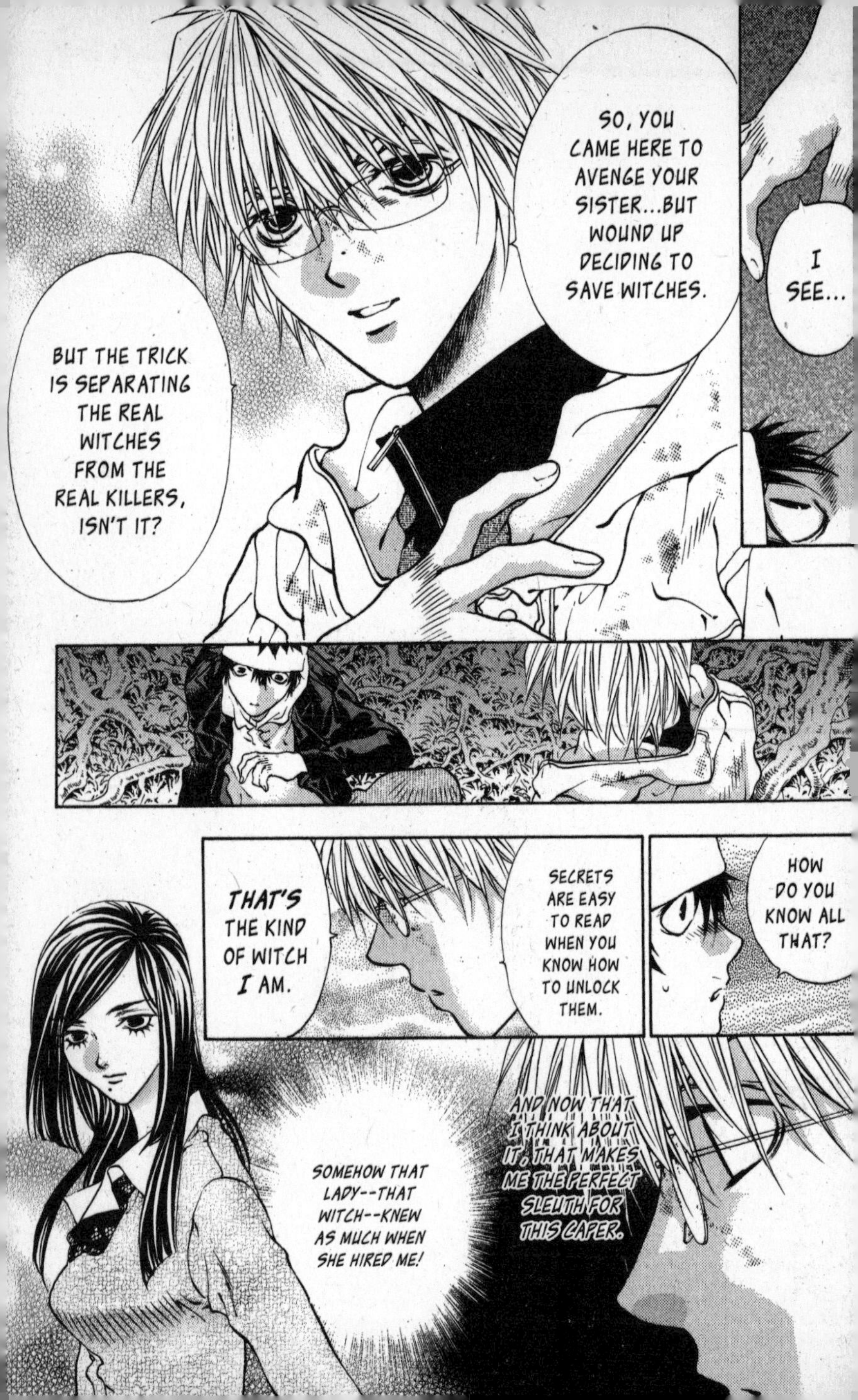
I SEE...
SO, YOU CAME HERE TO AVENGE YOUR SISTER...BUT WOUND UP DECIDING TO SAVE WITCHES.
BUT THE TRICK IS SEPARATING THE REAL WITCHES FROM THE REAL KILLERS, ISN'T IT?
HOW DO YOU KNOW ALL THAT?
SECRETS ARE EASY TO READ WHEN YOU KNOW HOW TO UNLOCK THEM.
THAT'S THE KIND OF WITCH I AM.
AND NOW THAT I THINK ABOUT IT, THAT MAKES ME THE PERFECT SLEUTH FOR THIS CAPER.
SOMEHOW THAT LADY--THAT WITCH--KNEW AS MUCH WHEN SHE HIRED ME!

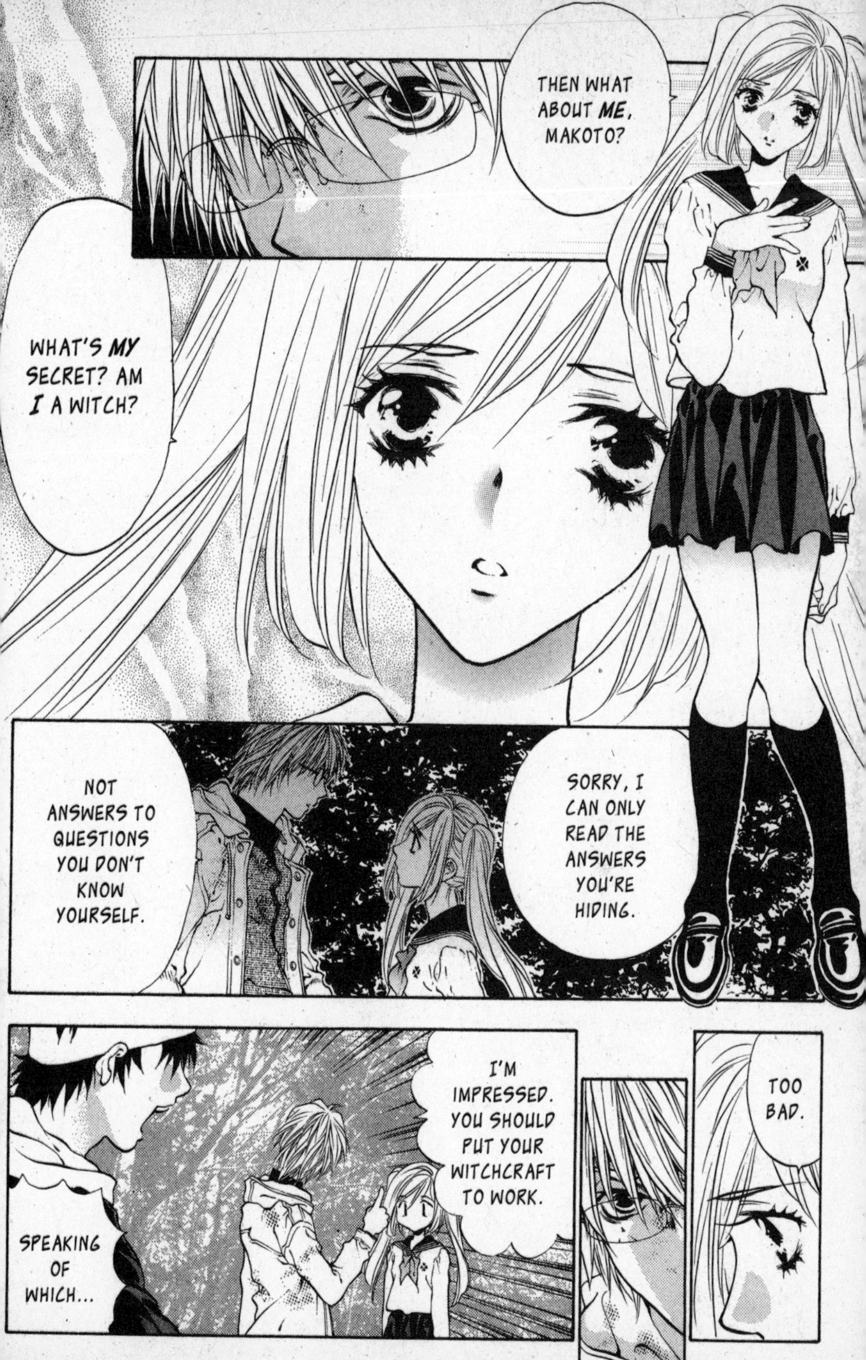
THEN WHAT ABOUT *ME*, MAKOTO?
WHAT'S *MY* SECRET? AM *I* A WITCH?
SORRY, I CAN ONLY READ THE ANSWERS YOU'RE HIDING.
NOT ANSWERS TO QUESTIONS YOU DON'T KNOW YOURSELF.
TOO BAD.
I'M IMPRESSED. YOU SHOULD PUT YOUR WITCHCRAFT TO WORK.
SPEAKING OF WHICH...

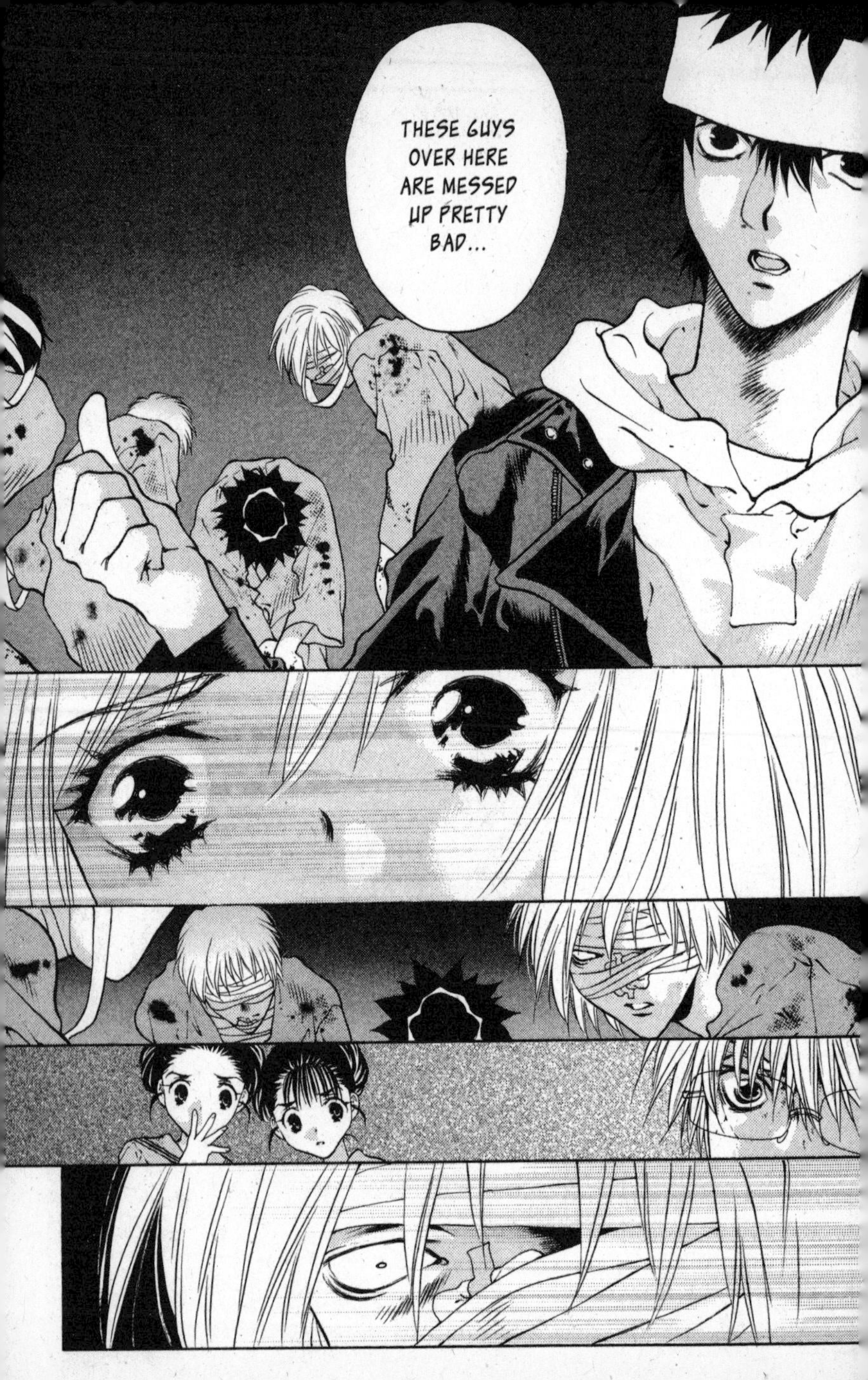
THESE GUYS OVER HERE ARE MESSED UP PRETTY BAD...

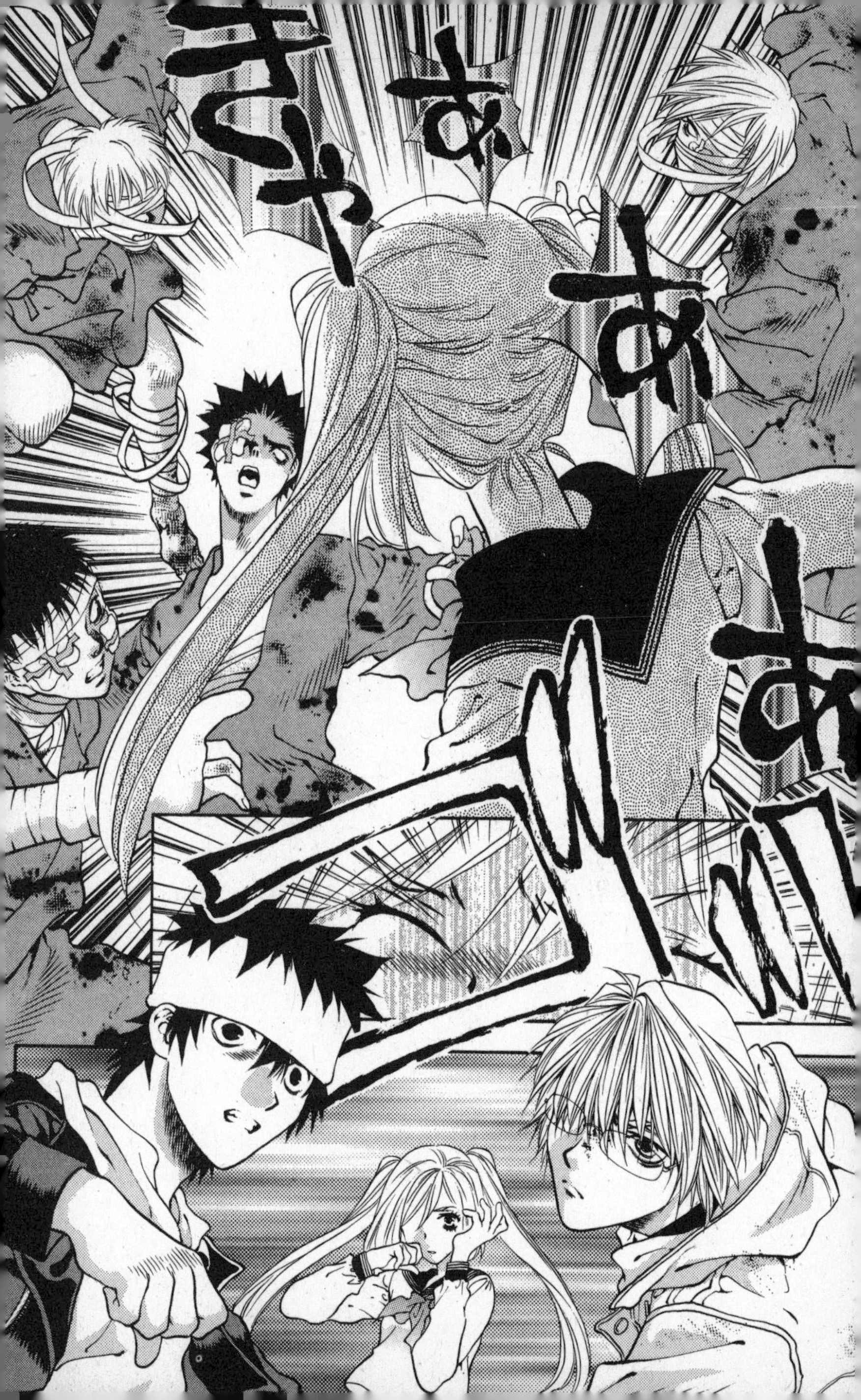
きゃあああッ

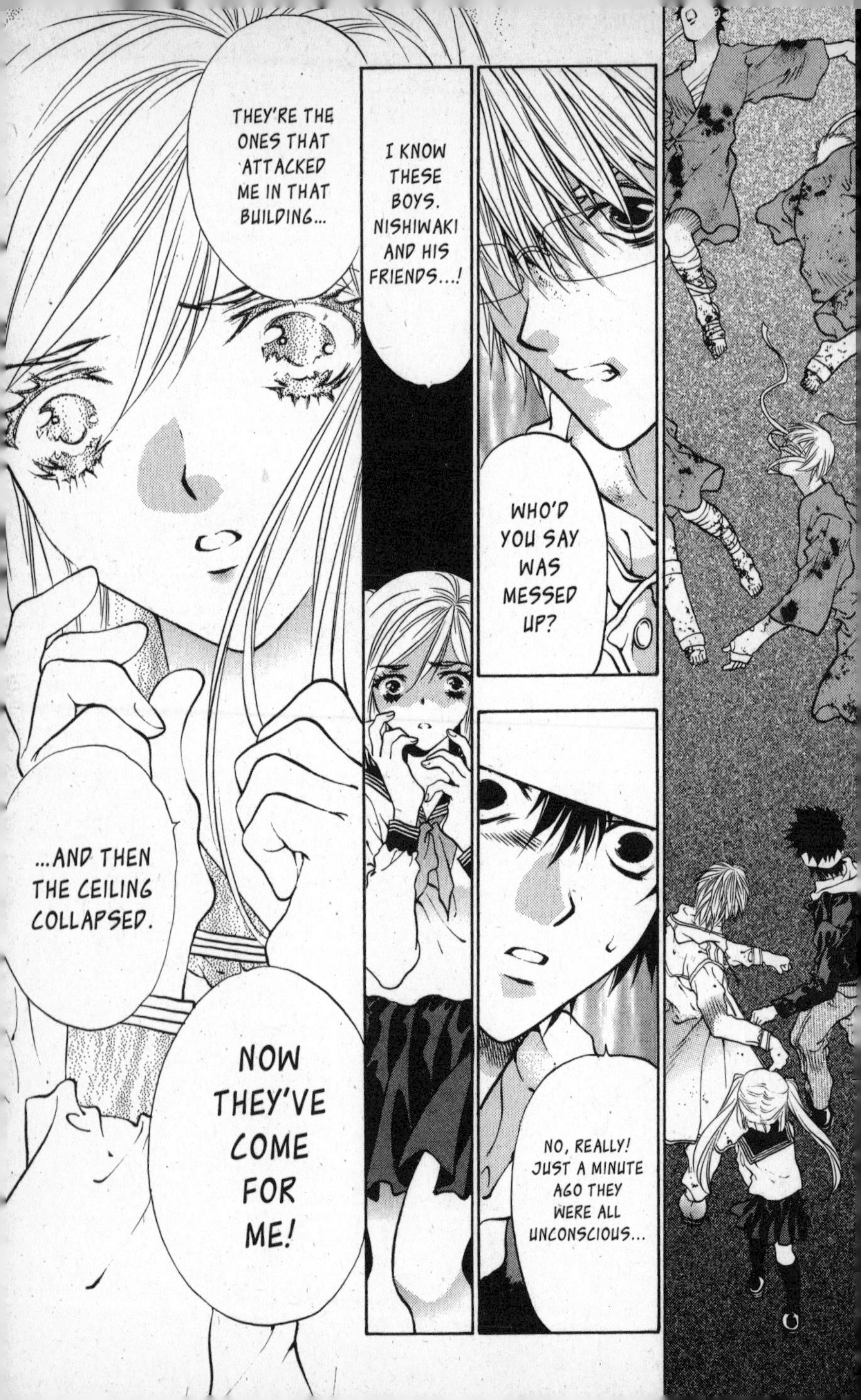
WHO'D YOU SAY WAS MESSED UP?
NO, REALLY! JUST A MINUTE AGO THEY WERE ALL UNCONSCIOUS...
I KNOW THESE BOYS. NISHIWAKI AND HIS FRIENDS...!
THEY'RE THE ONES THAT ATTACKED ME IN THAT BUILDING...
...AND THEN THE CEILING COLLAPSED.
NOW THEY'VE COME FOR ME!

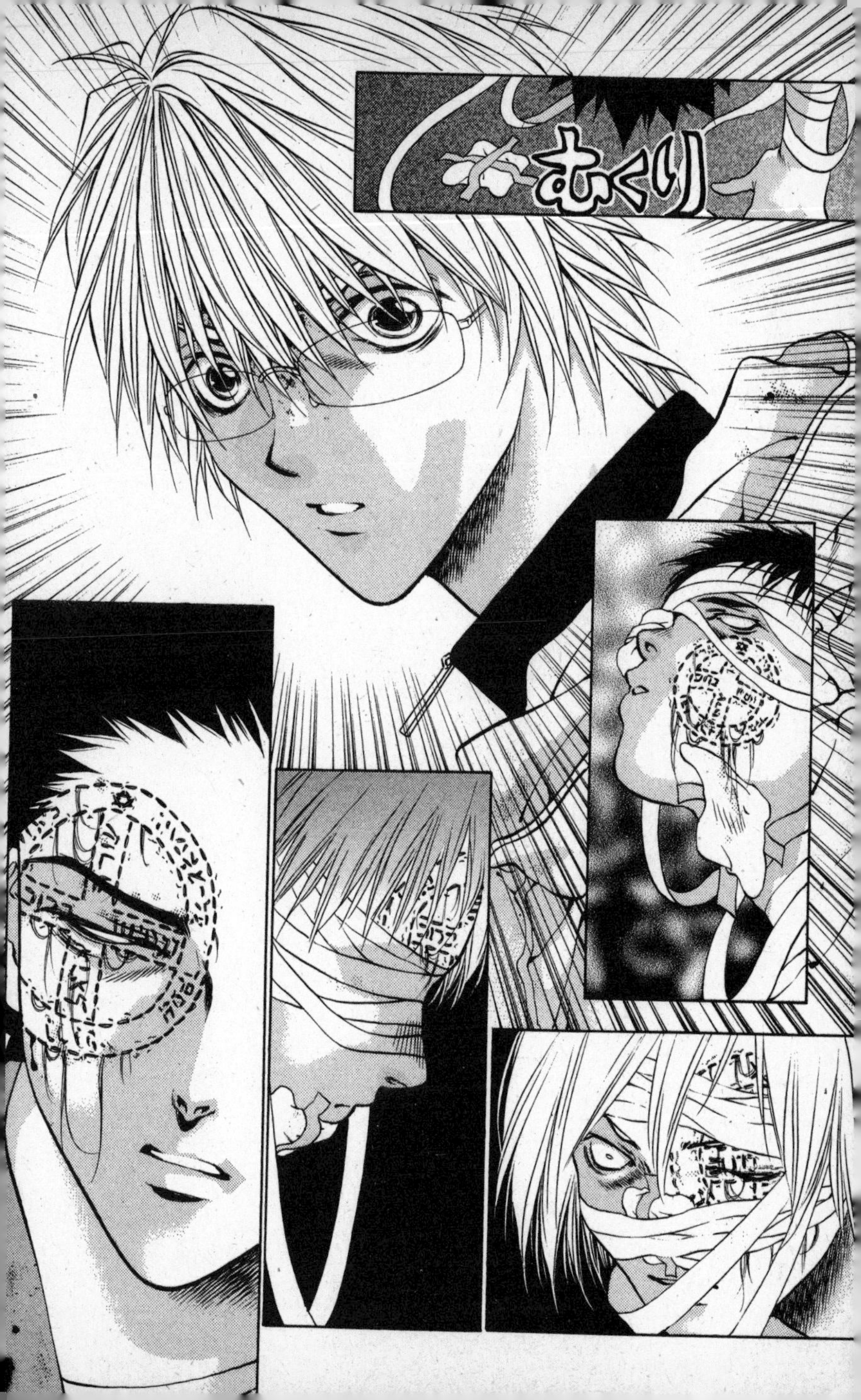
むくり

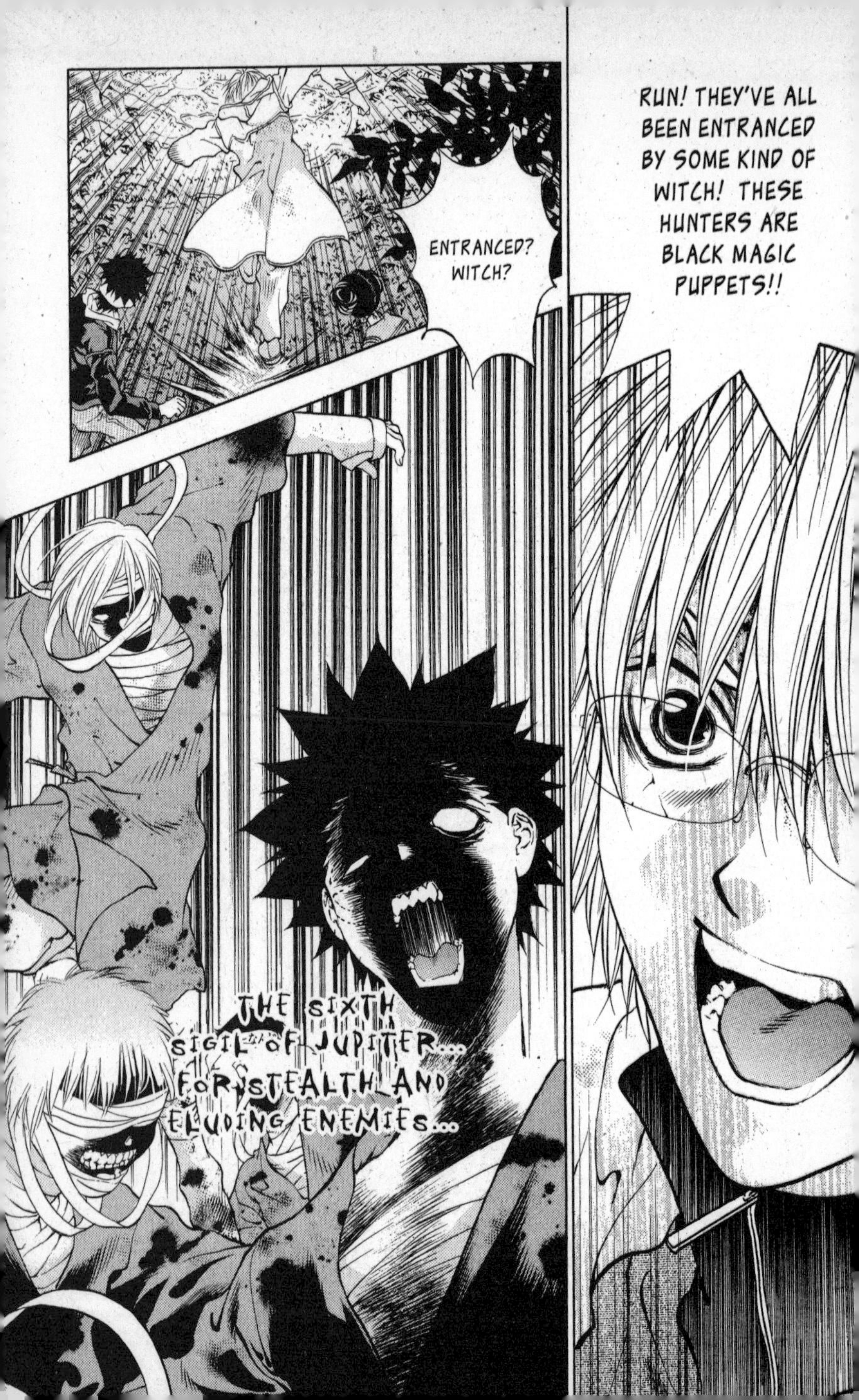
RUN! THEY'VE ALL BEEN ENTRANCED BY SOME KIND OF WITCH! THESE HUNTERS ARE BLACK MAGIC PUPPETS!!
ENTRANCED? WITCH?
THE SIXTH SIGIL OF JUPITER... FOR STEALTH AND ELUDING ENEMIES...

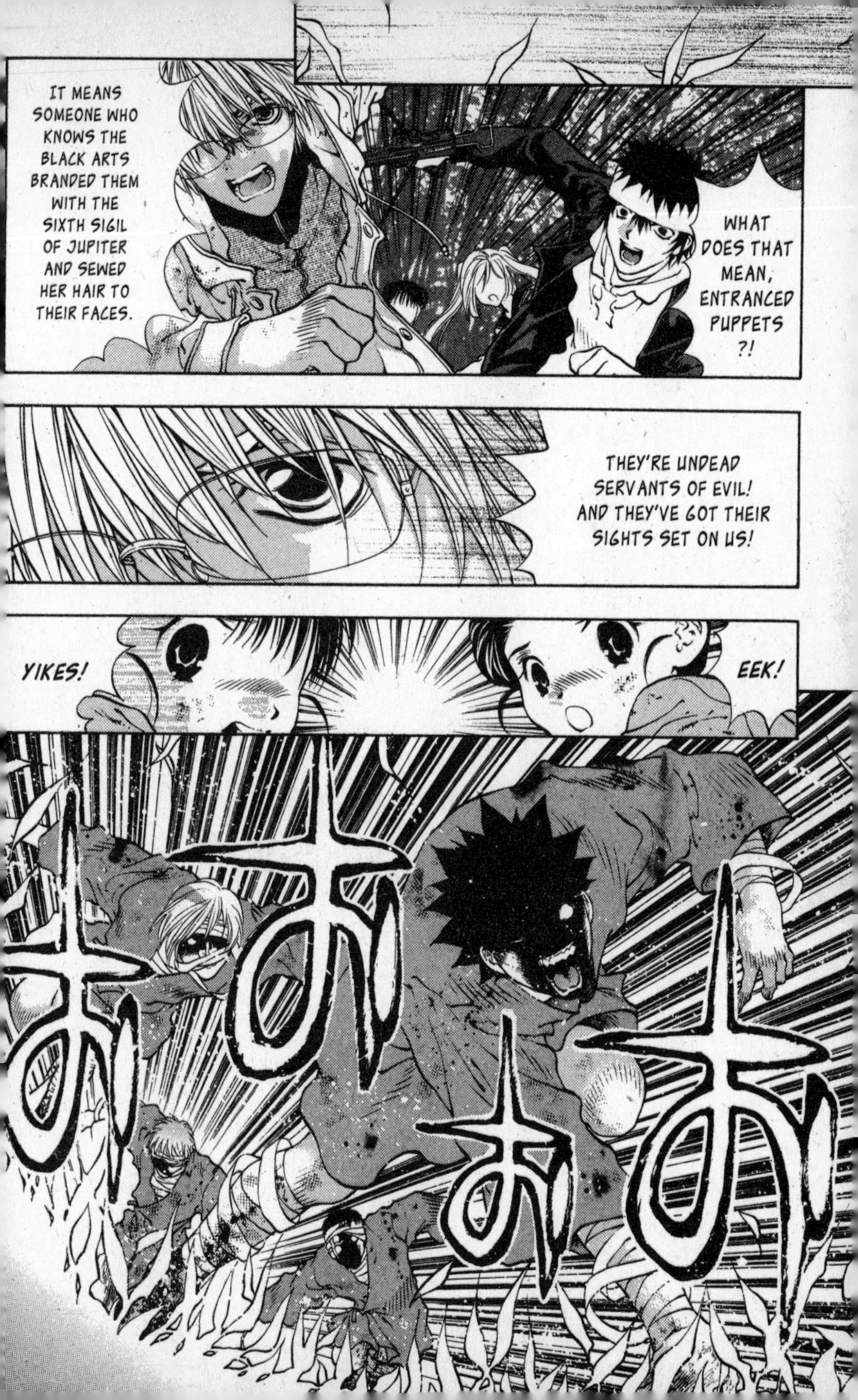
WHAT DOES THAT MEAN, ENTRANCED PUPPETS ?!
IT MEANS SOMEONE WHO KNOWS THE BLACK ARTS BRANDED THEM WITH THE SIXTH SIGIL OF JUPITER AND SEWED HER HAIR TO THEIR FACES.
THEY'RE UNDEAD SERVANTS OF EVIL! AND THEY'VE GOT THEIR SIGHTS SET ON US!
EEK!
YIKES!
おおおお

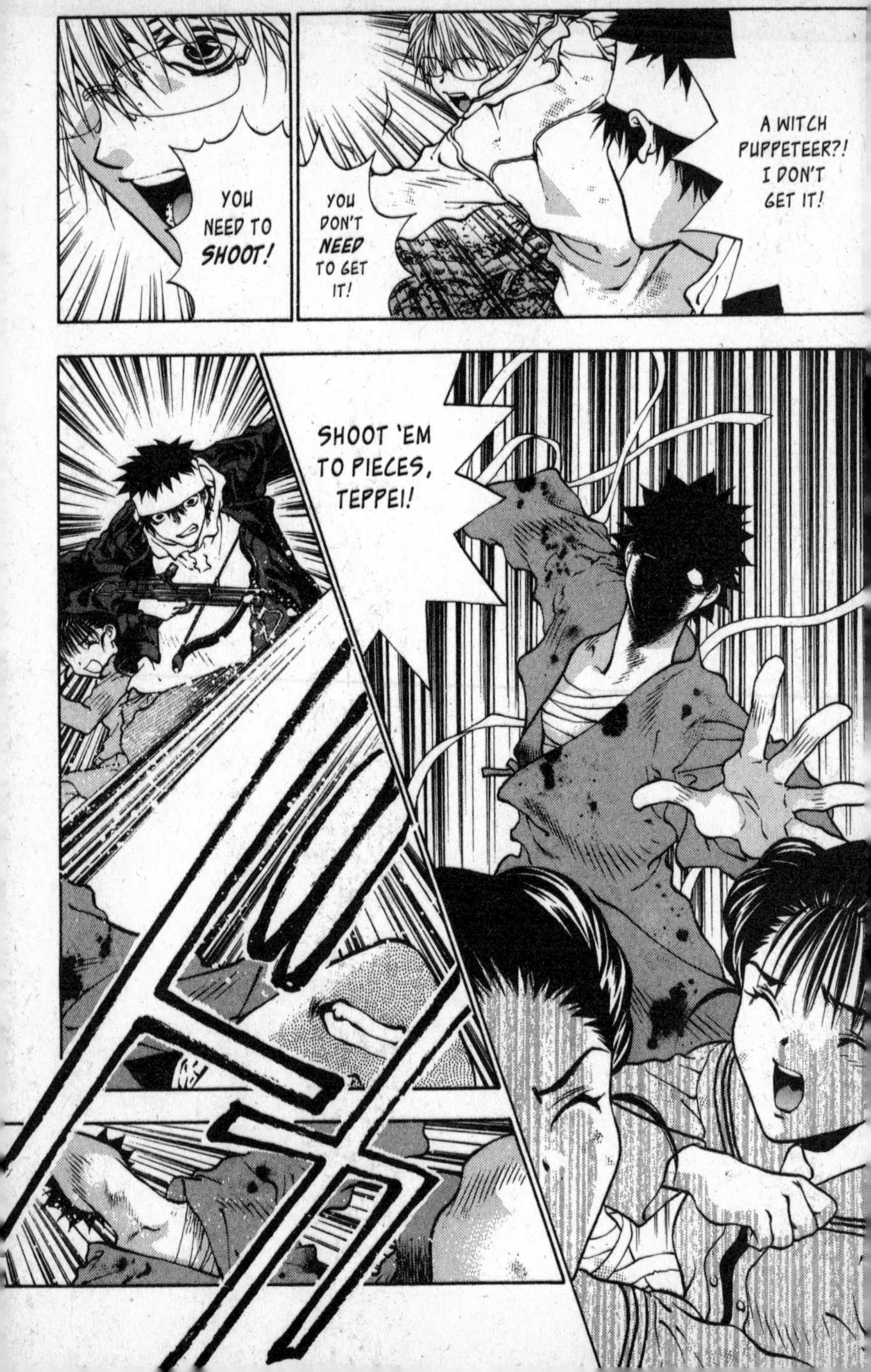
A WITCH PUPPETEER?! I DON'T GET IT!
YOU DON'T NEED TO GET IT!
YOU NEED TO SHOOT!
SHOOT 'EM TO PIECES, TEPPEI!

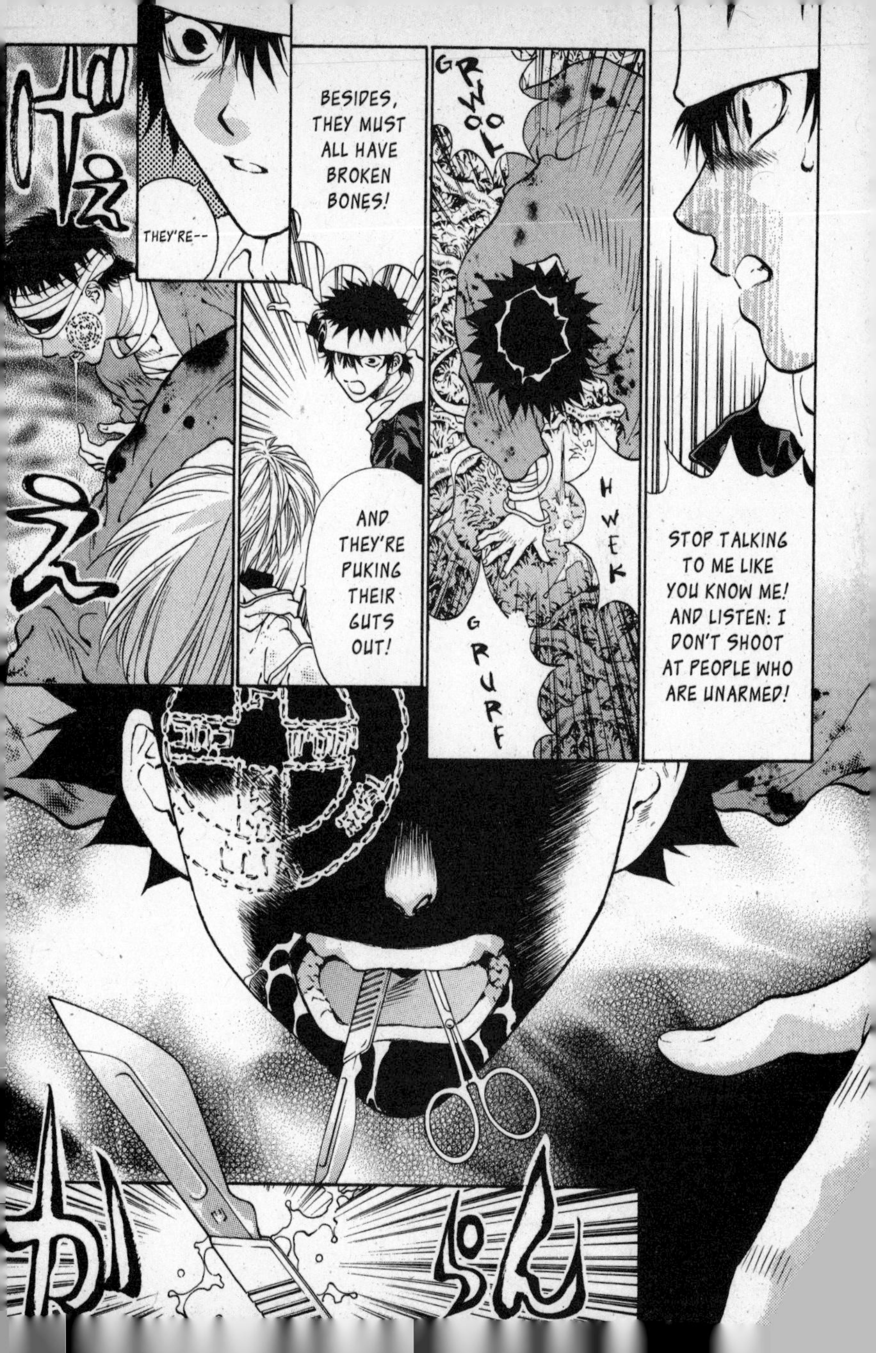
STOP TALKING TO ME LIKE YOU KNOW ME! AND LISTEN: I DON'T SHOOT AT PEOPLE WHO ARE UNARMED!
GRWOOL
HWEK
GRURF
BESIDES, THEY MUST ALL HAVE BROKEN BONES!
AND THEY'RE PUKING THEIR GUTS OUT!
THEY'RE--

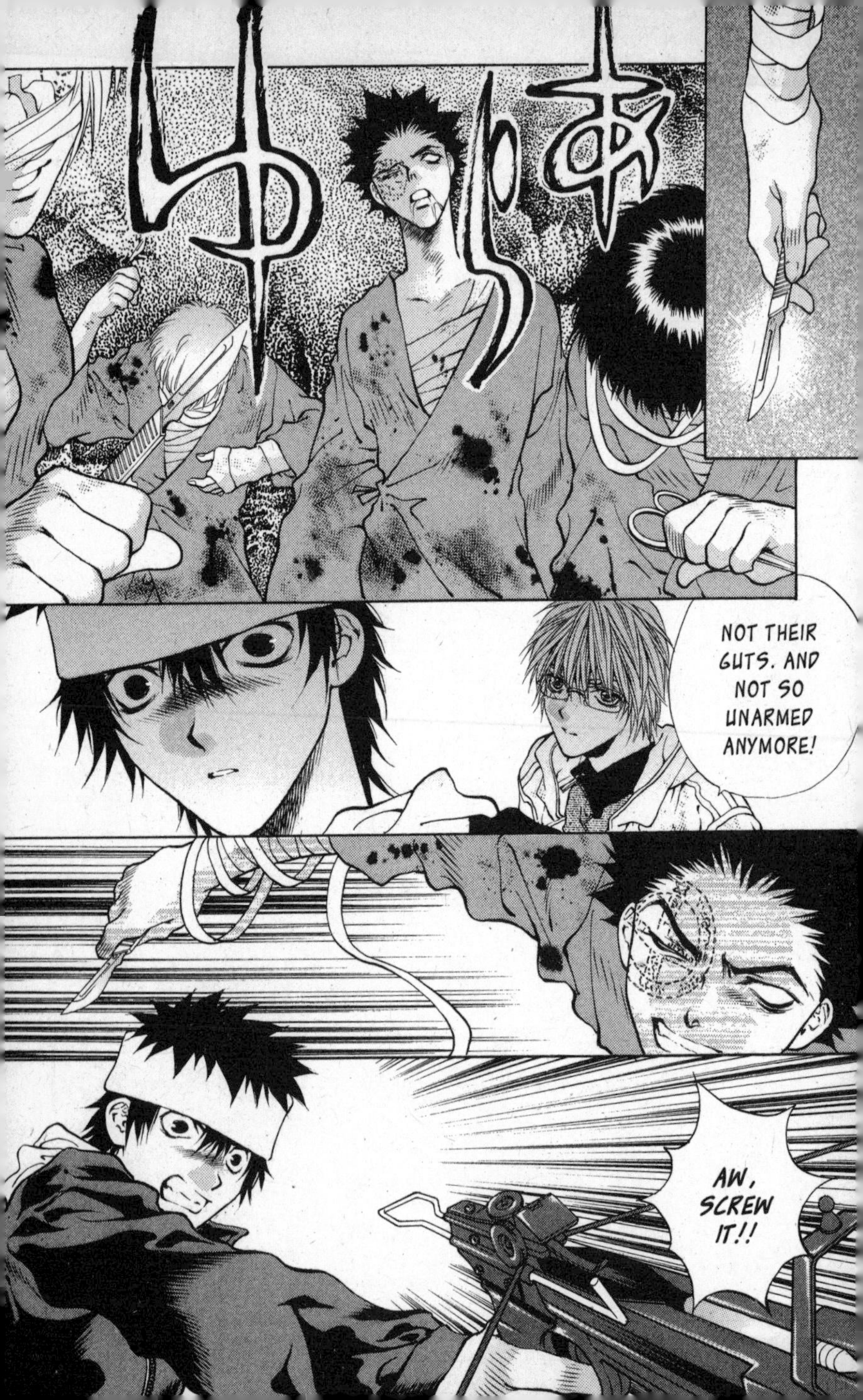
NOT THEIR GUTS. AND NOT SO UNARMED ANYMORE!
AW, SCREW IT!!

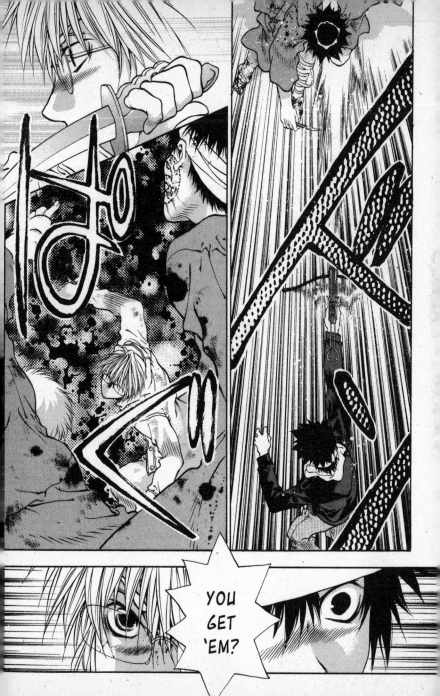

YOU
GET
'EM?

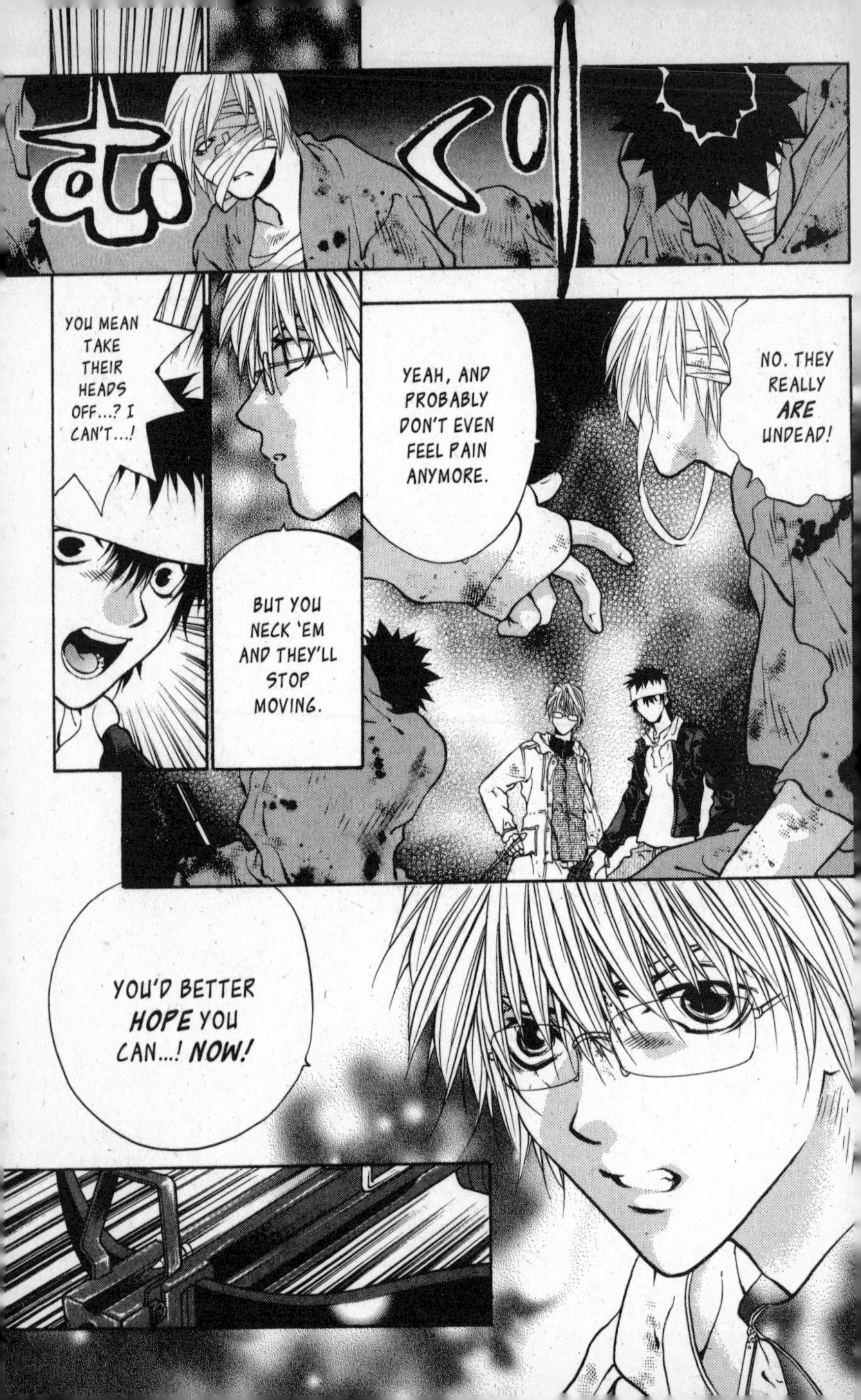
NO. THEY REALLY ARE UNDEAD!
YEAH, AND PROBABLY DON'T EVEN FEEL PAIN ANYMORE.
BUT YOU NECK 'EM AND THEY'LL STOP MOVING.
YOU MEAN TAKE THEIR HEADS OFF...? I CAN'T...!
YOU'D BETTER HOPE YOU CAN...! NOW!

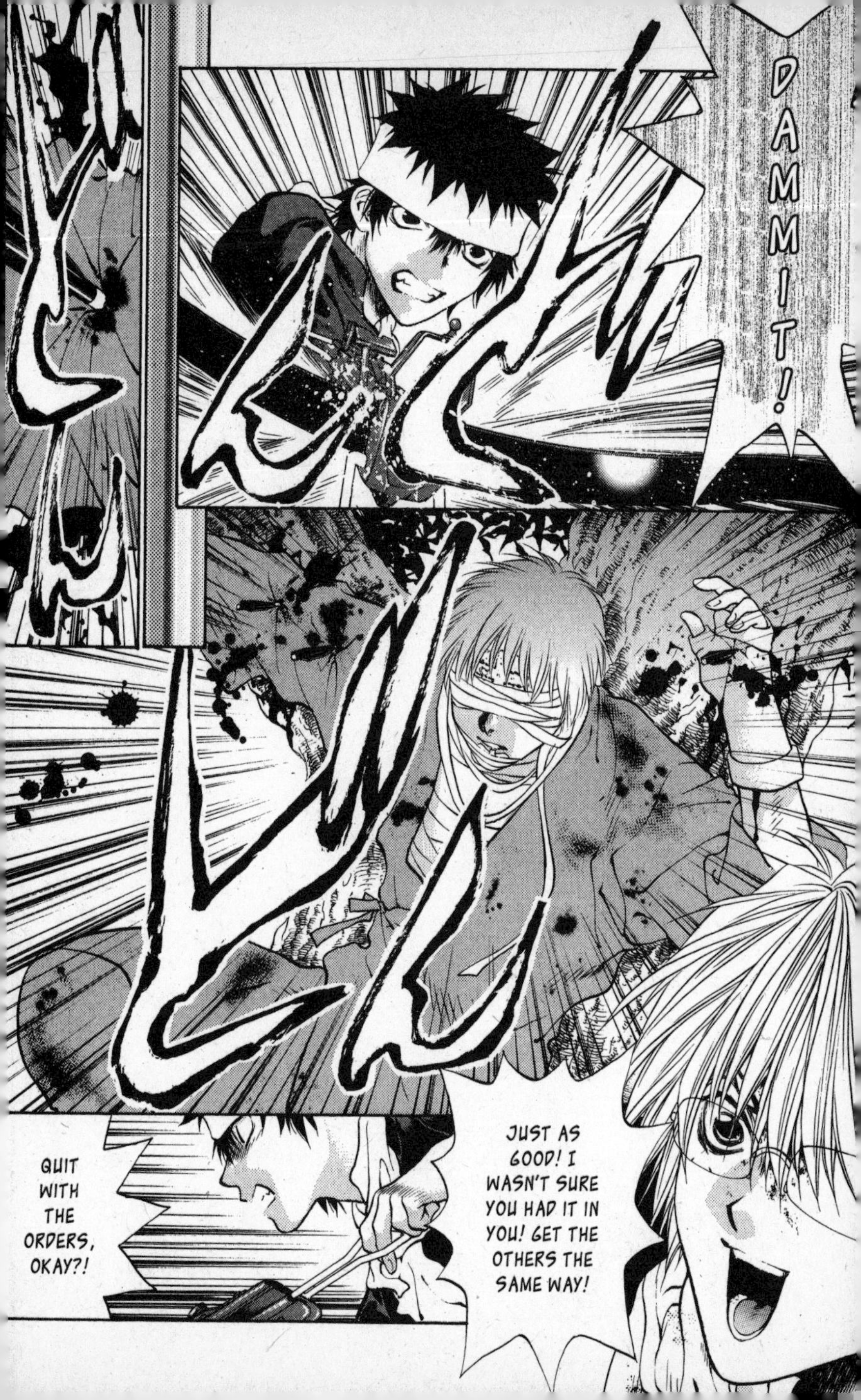
DAMMIT!
JUST AS GOOD! I WASN'T SURE YOU HAD IT IN YOU! GET THE OTHERS THE SAME WAY!
QUIT WITH THE ORDERS, OKAY?!

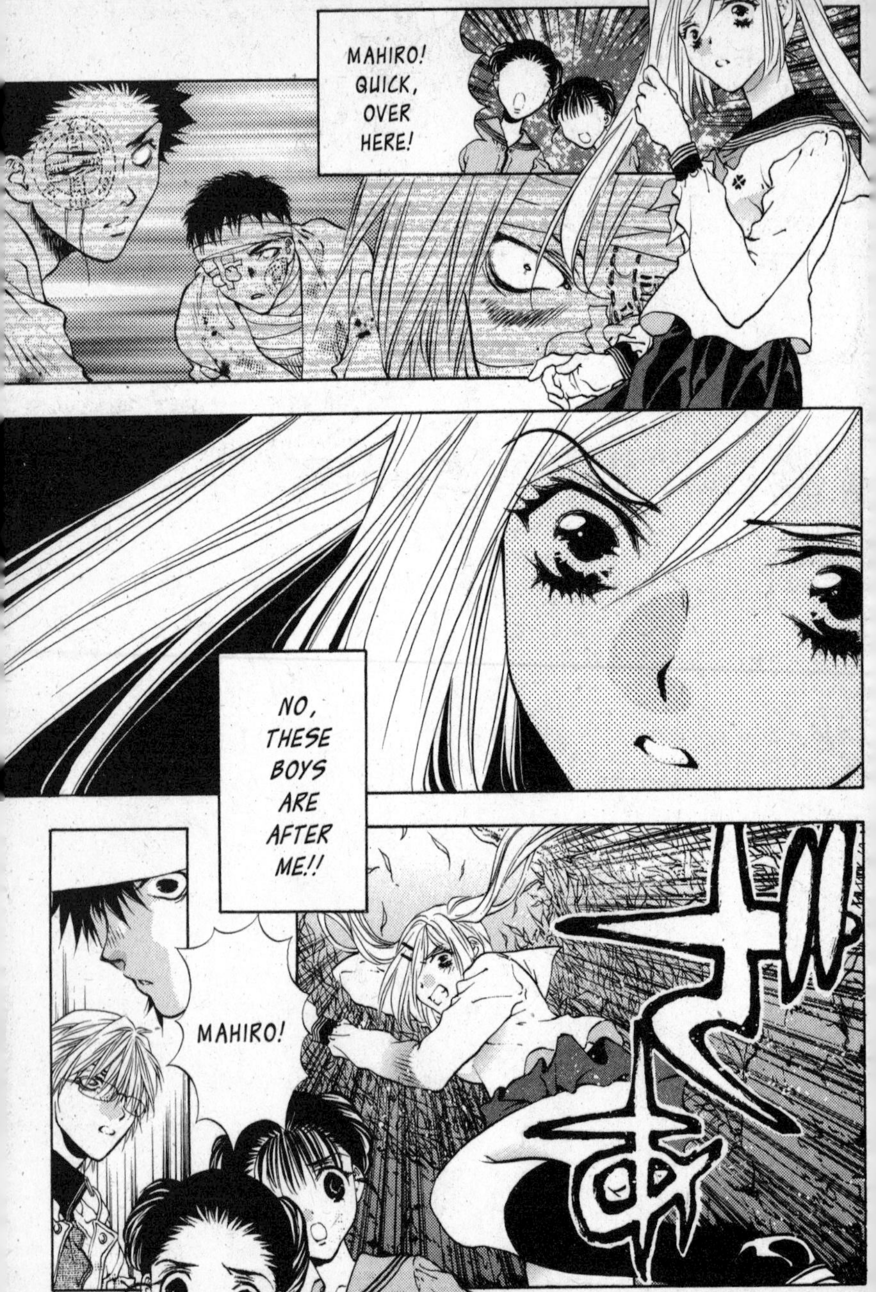
MAHIRO! QUICK, OVER HERE!
NO, THESE BOYS ARE AFTER ME!!
MAHIRO!

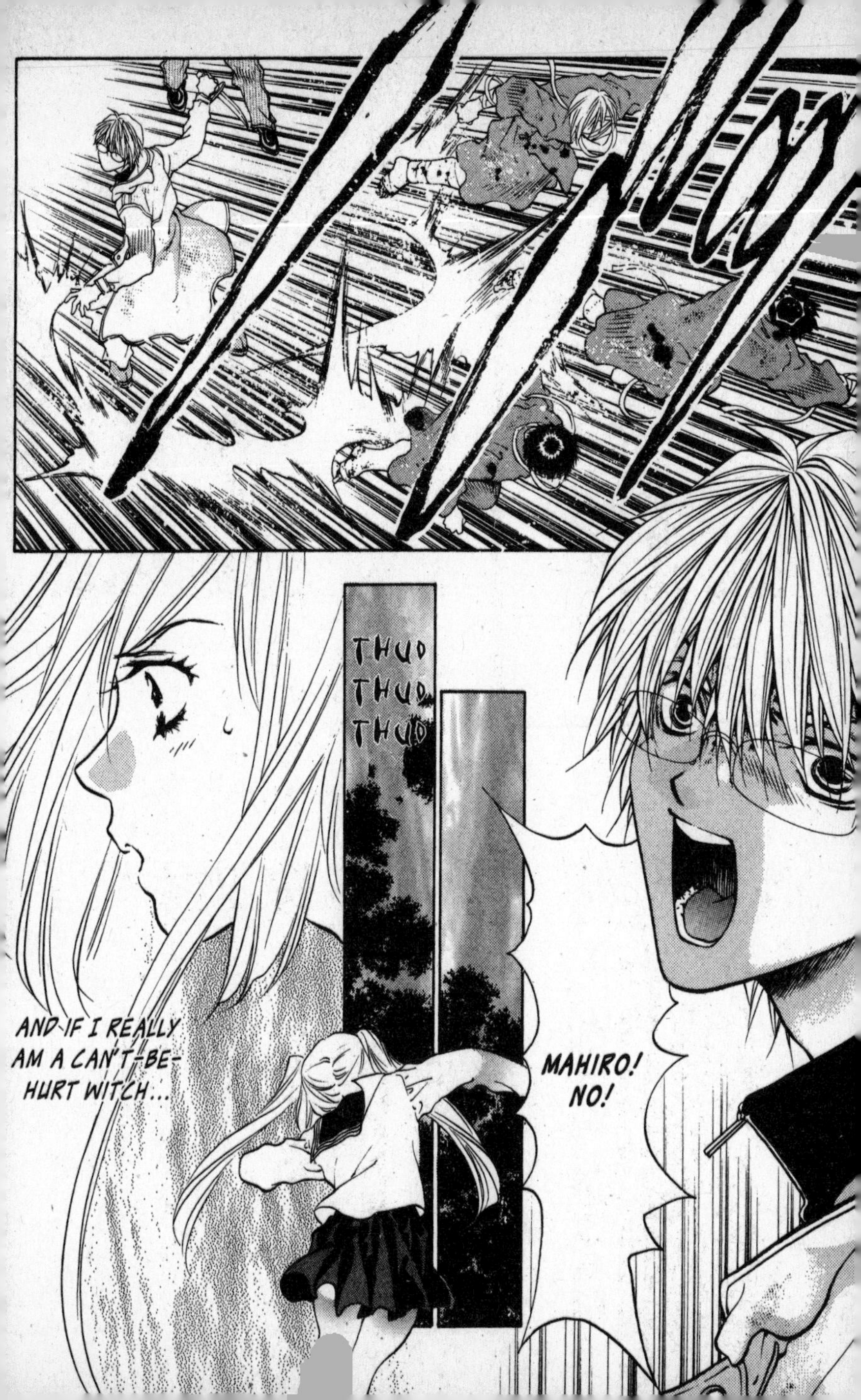
MAHIRO! NO!
THUD THUD THUD
AND IF I REALLY AM A CAN'T-BE-HURT WITCH...

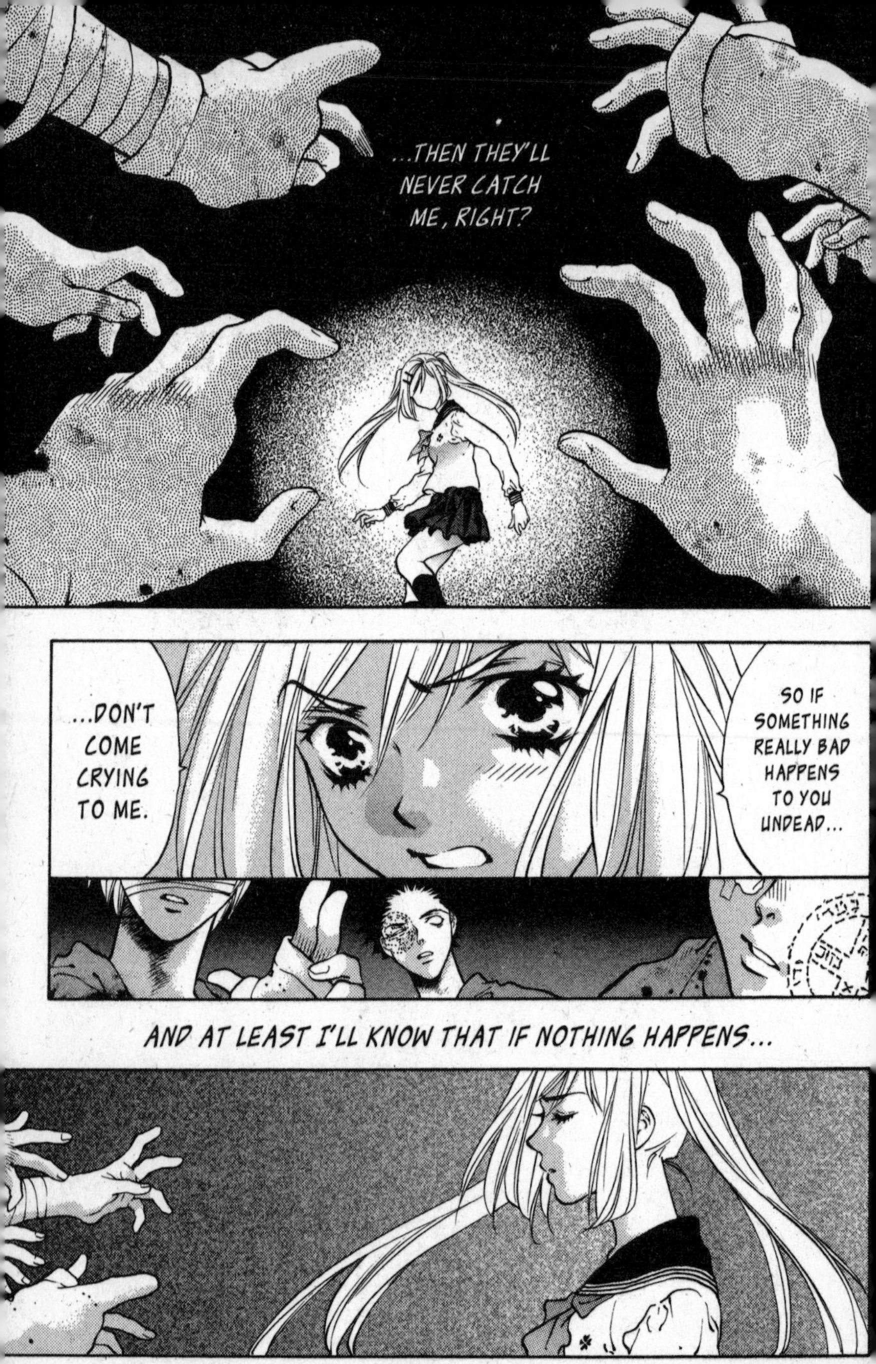
...THEN THEY'LL NEVER CATCH ME, RIGHT?
SO IF SOMETHING REALLY BAD HAPPENS TO YOU UNDEAD...
...DON'T COME CRYING TO ME.
AND AT LEAST I'LL KNOW THAT IF NOTHING HAPPENS...

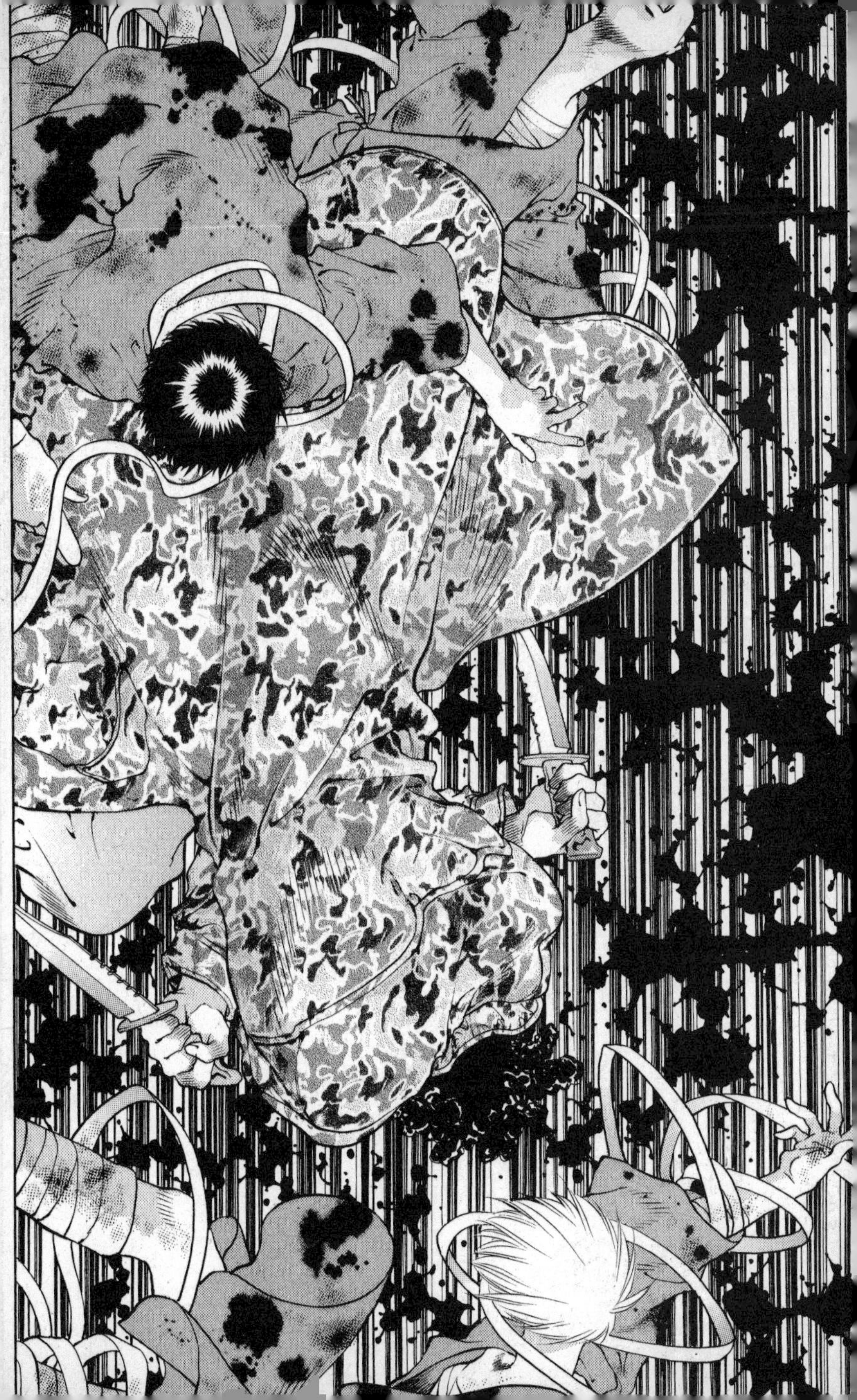

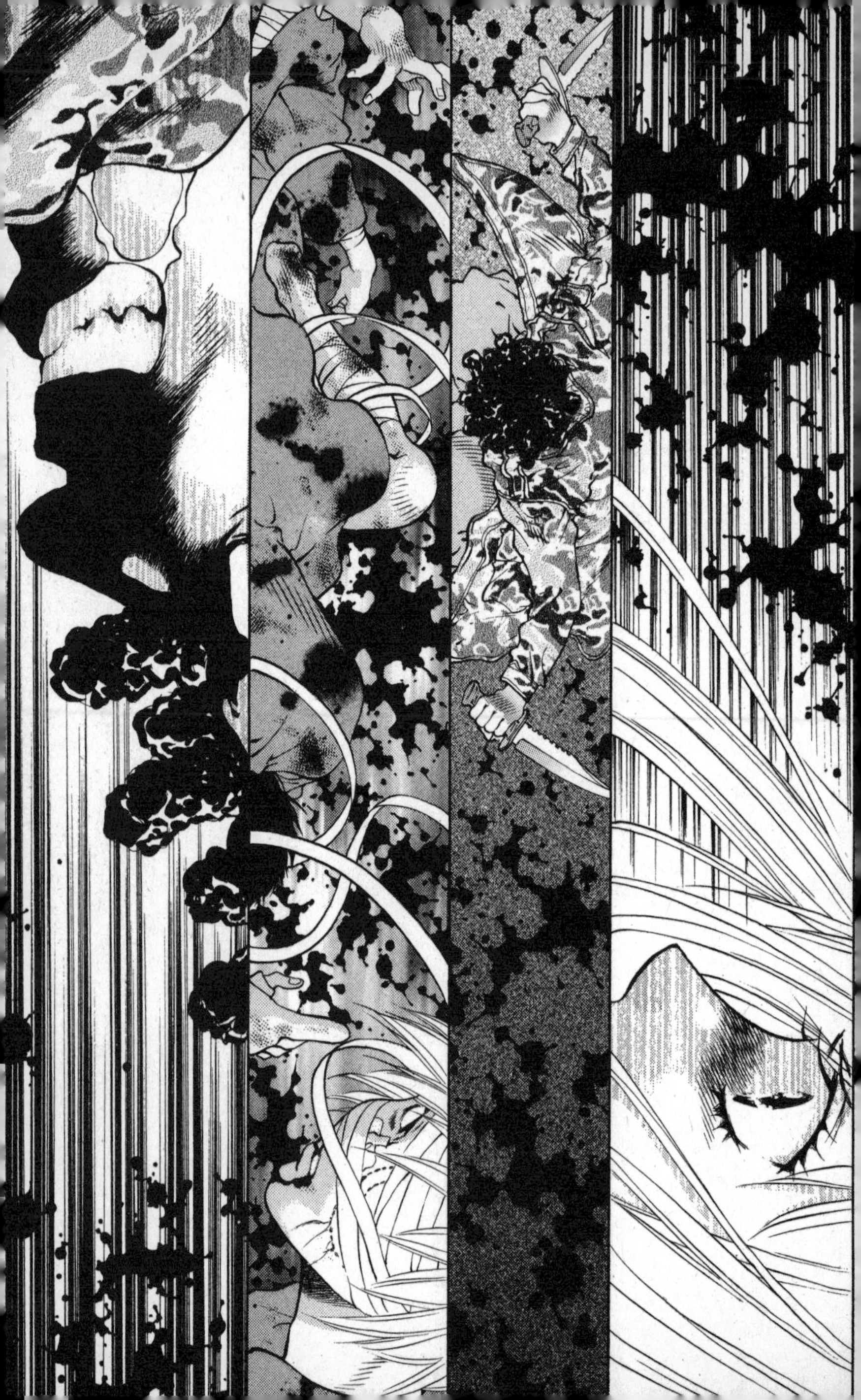

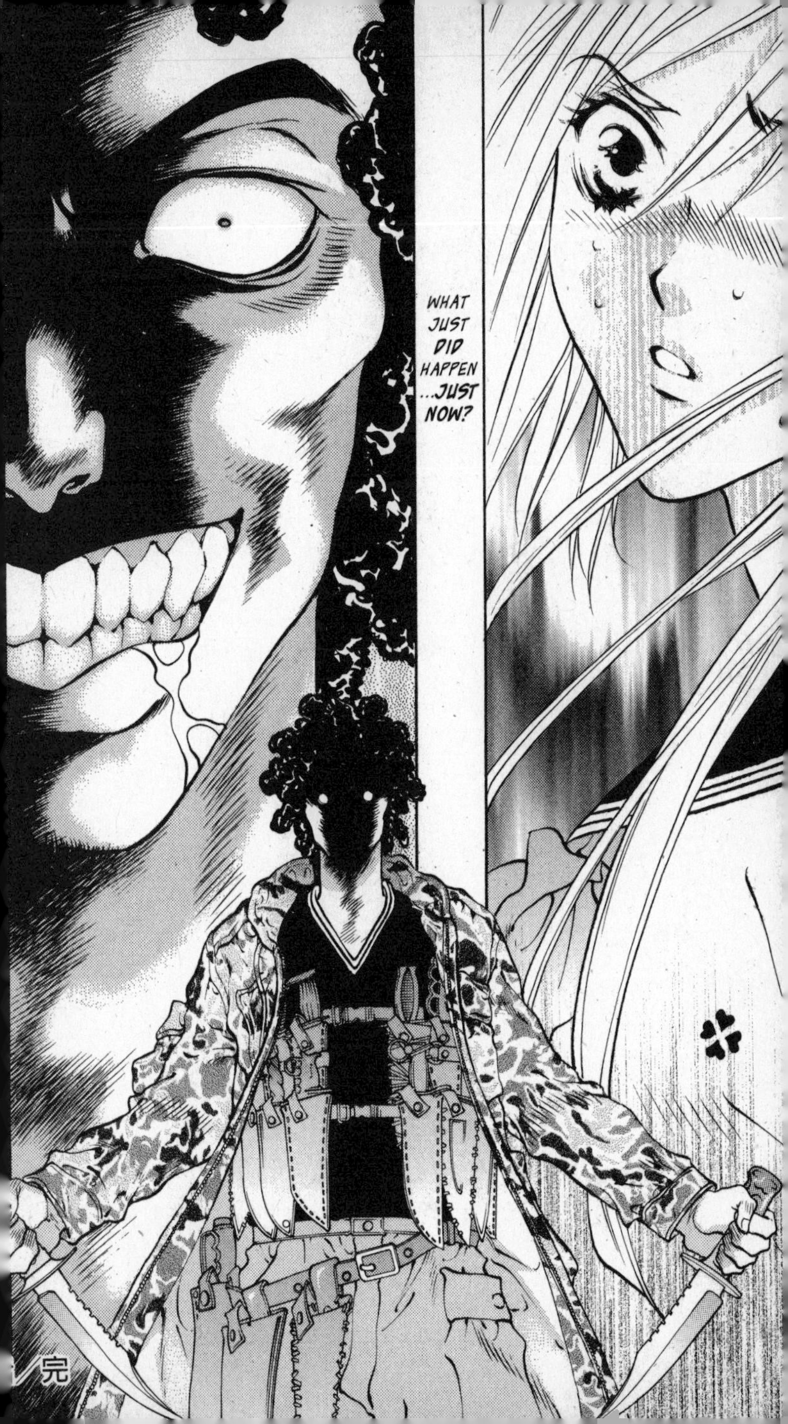
WHAT JUST DID HAPPEN ...JUST NOW?
完

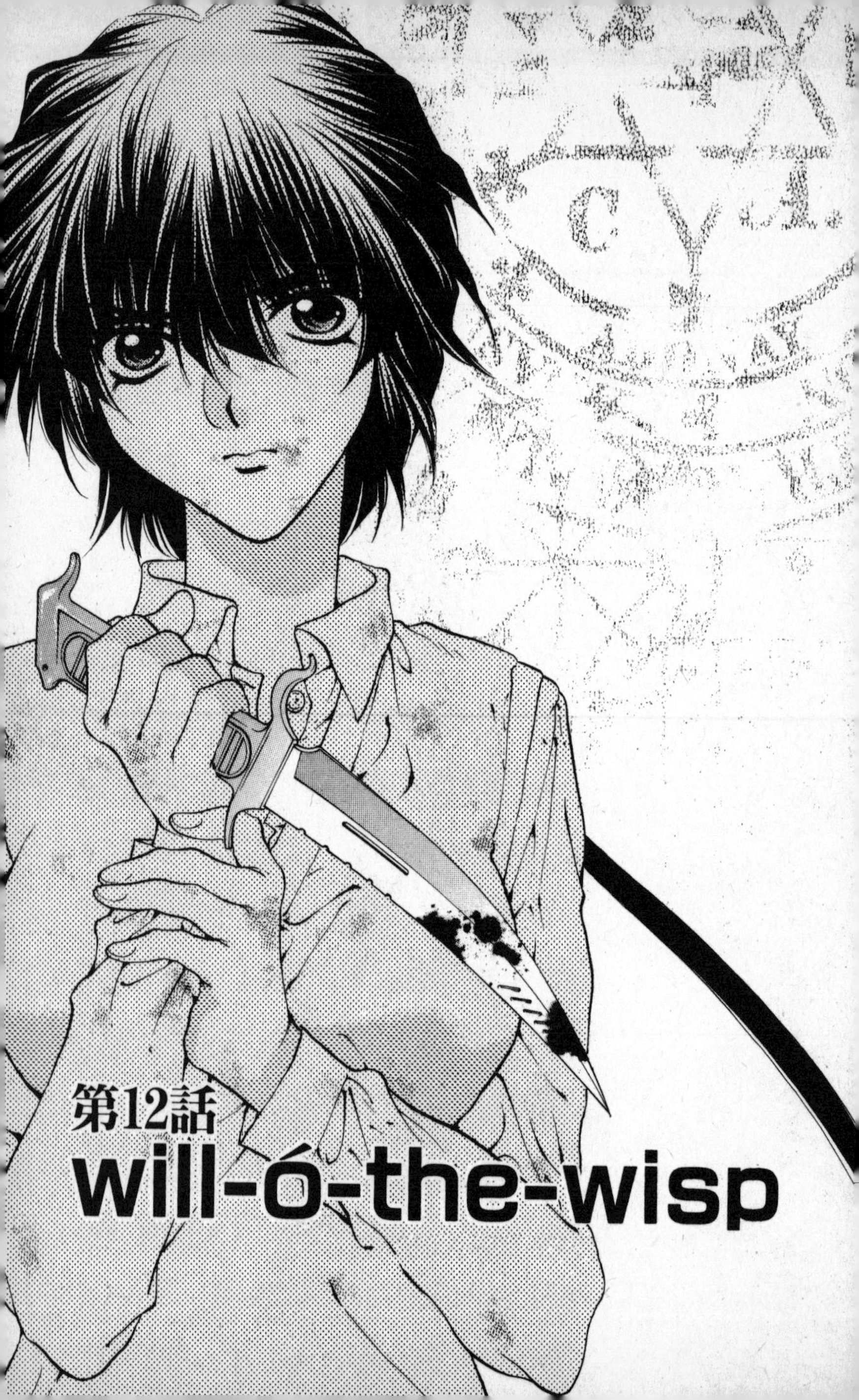
第12話
will-ó-the-wisp

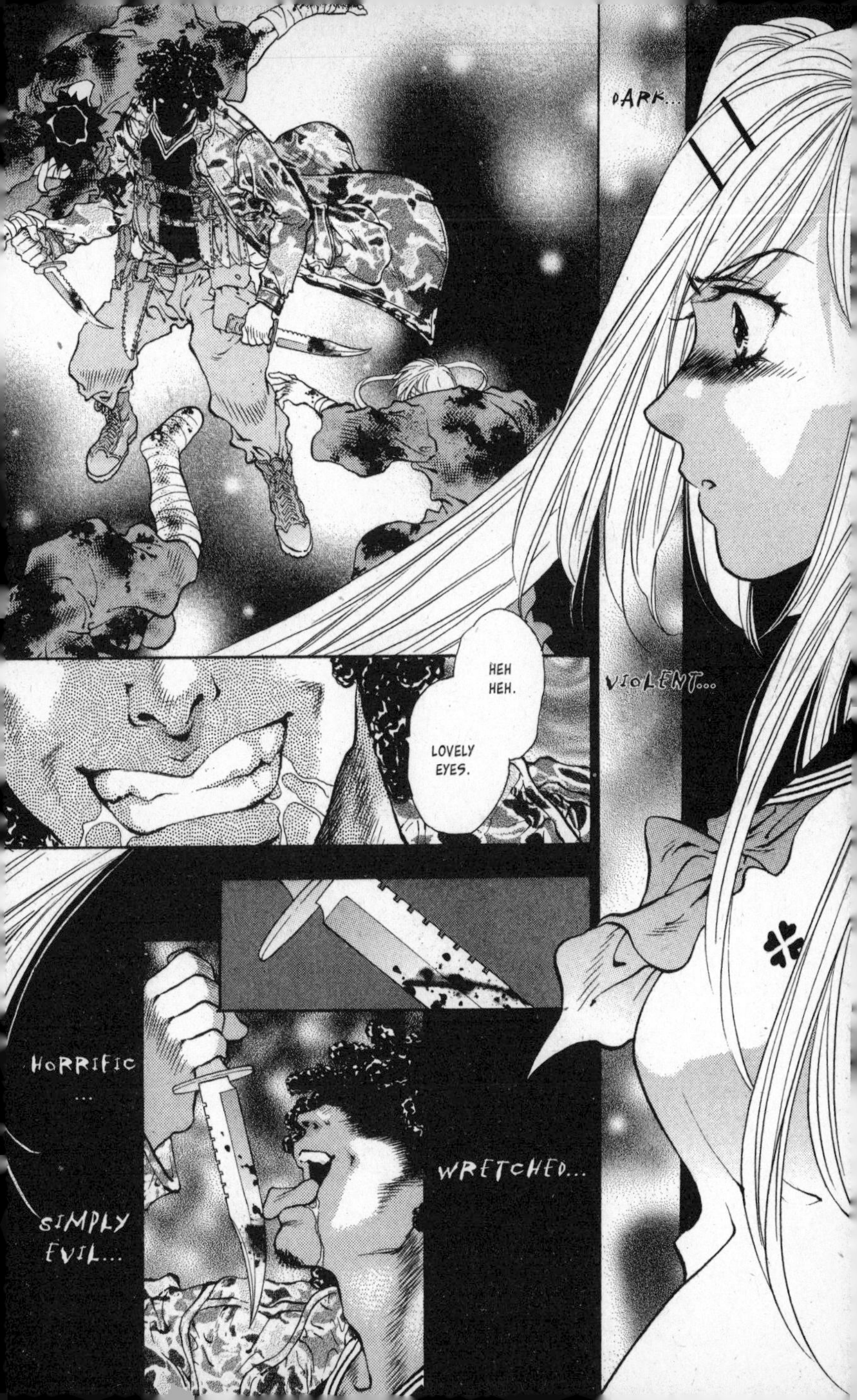
DARK...
VIOLENT...
HEH HEH.
LOVELY EYES.
WRETCHED...
HORRIFIC...
SIMPLY EVIL...

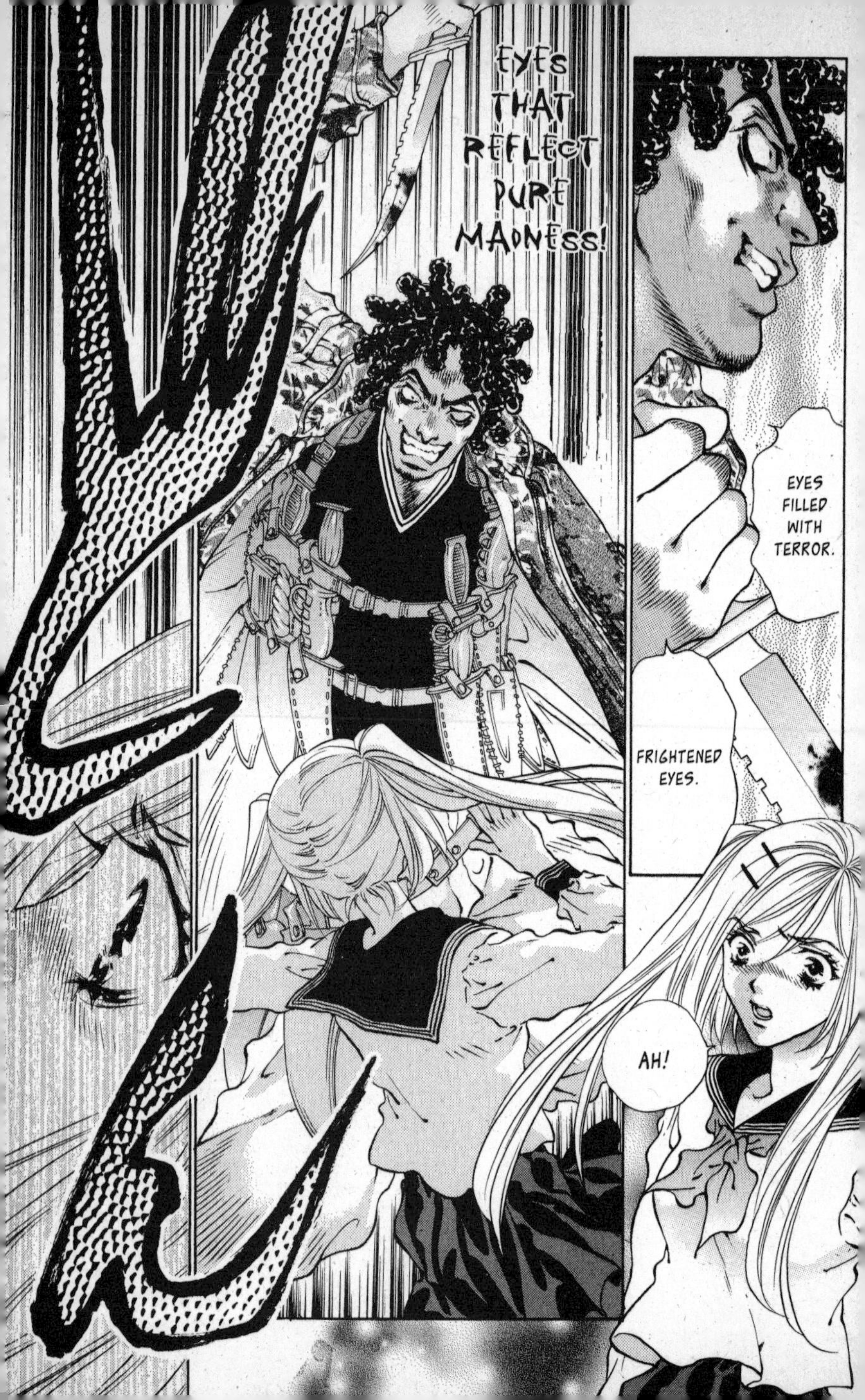
EYES FILLED WITH TERROR.
FRIGHTENED EYES.
AH!
EYES THAT REFLECT PURE MADNESS!

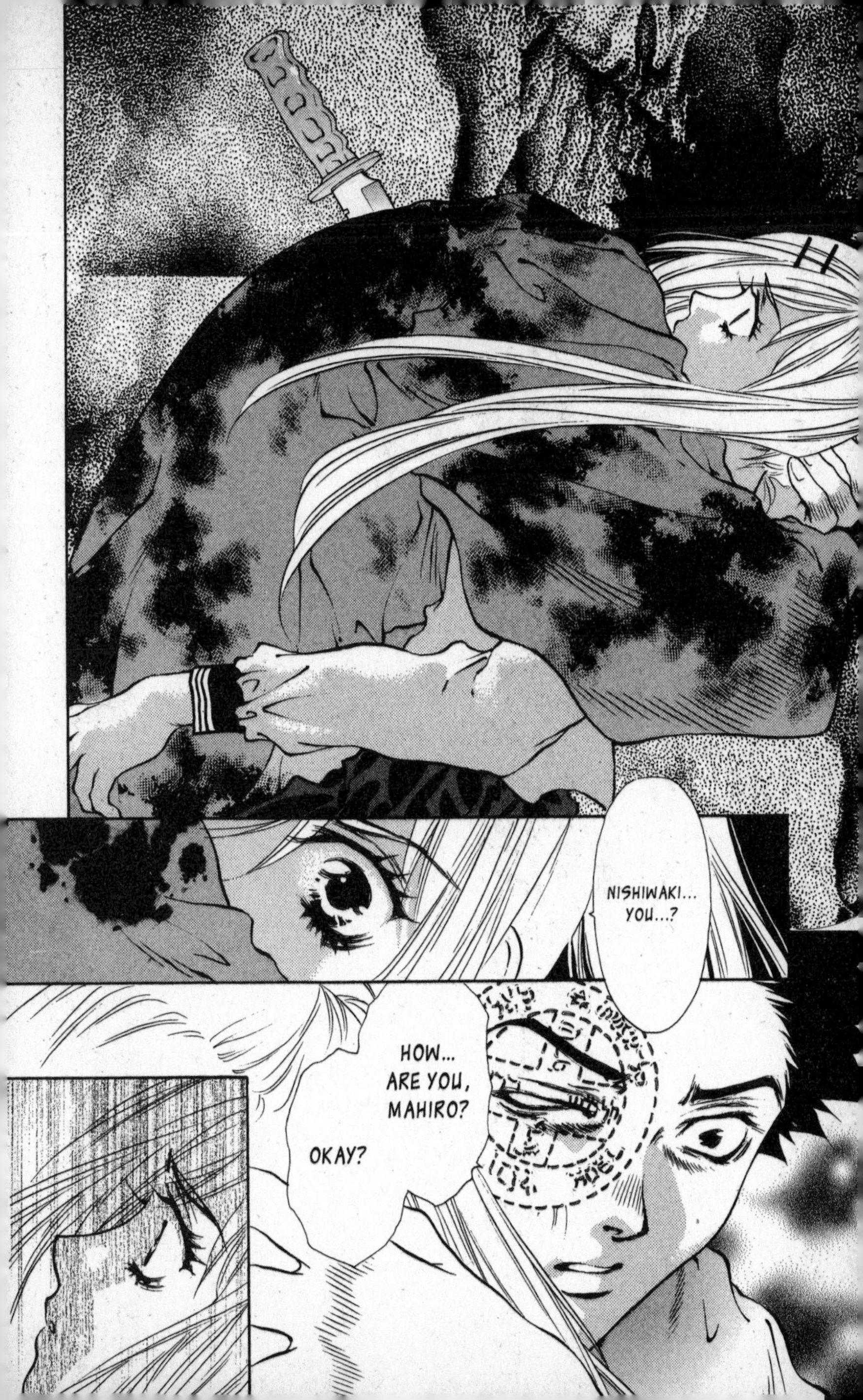
NISHIWAKI... YOU...?
HOW... ARE YOU, MAHIRO?
OKAY?

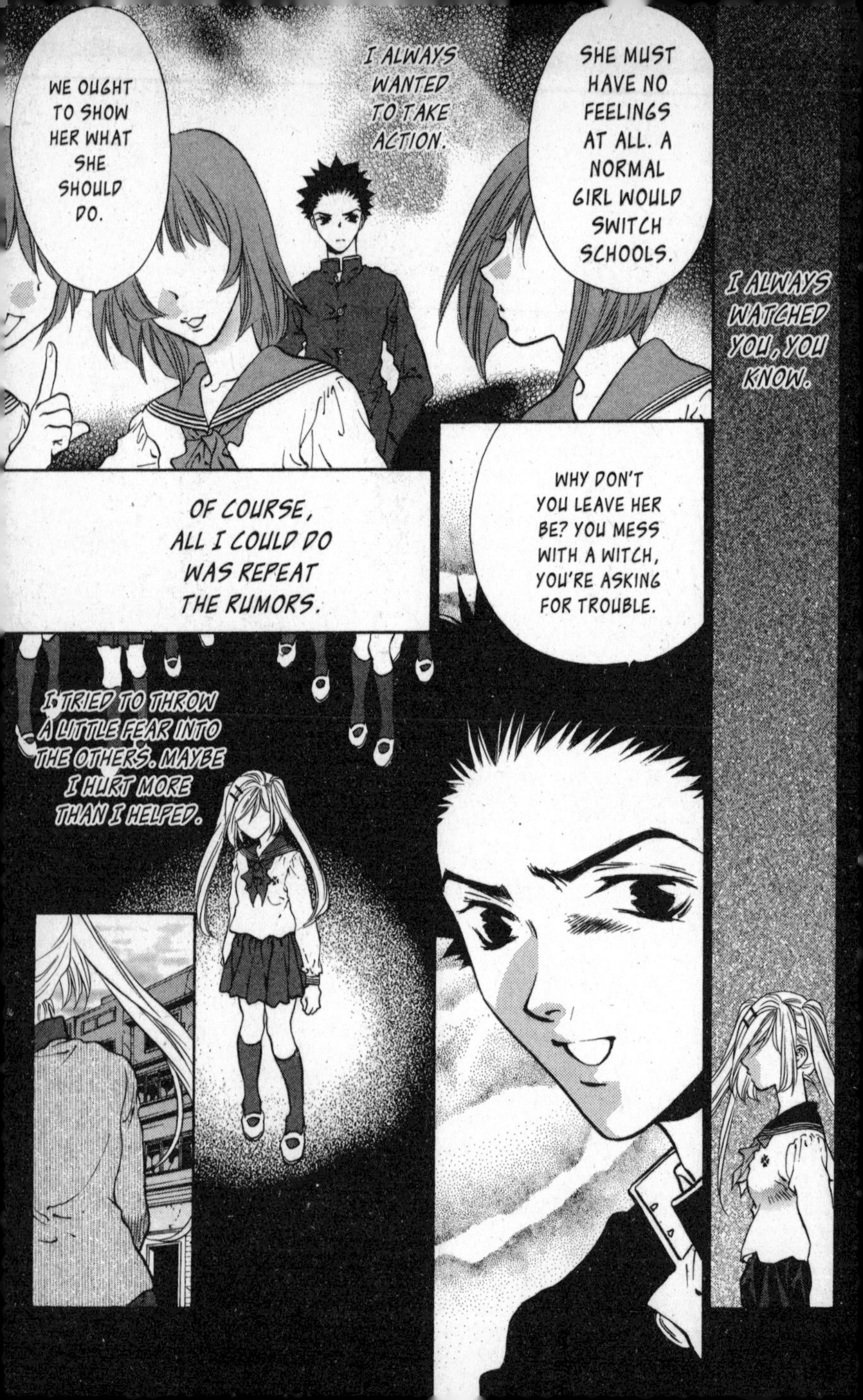
I ALWAYS WATCHED YOU, YOU KNOW.
SHE MUST HAVE NO FEELINGS AT ALL. A NORMAL GIRL WOULD SWITCH SCHOOLS.
I ALWAYS WANTED TO TAKE ACTION.
WE OUGHT TO SHOW HER WHAT SHE SHOULD DO.
WHY DON'T YOU LEAVE HER BE? YOU MESS WITH A WITCH, YOU'RE ASKING FOR TROUBLE.
OF COURSE, ALL I COULD DO WAS REPEAT THE RUMORS.
I TRIED TO THROW A LITTLE FEAR INTO THE OTHERS. MAYBE I HURT MORE THAN I HELPED.

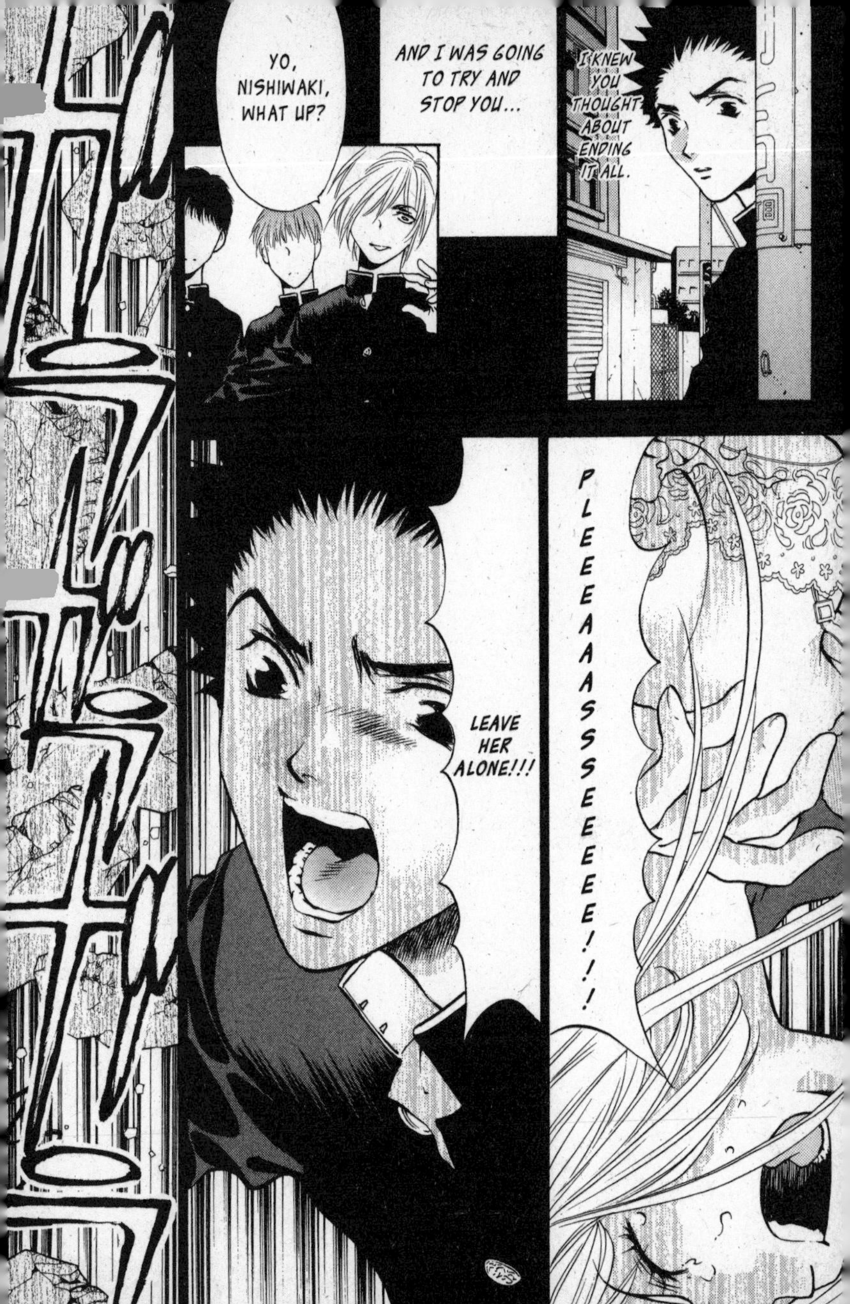
I KNEW YOU THOUGHT ABOUT ENDING IT ALL.
AND I WAS GOING TO TRY AND STOP YOU...
YO, NISHIWAKI, WHAT UP?
PLEEEAAASSEEEE!!!
LEAVE HER ALONE!!!

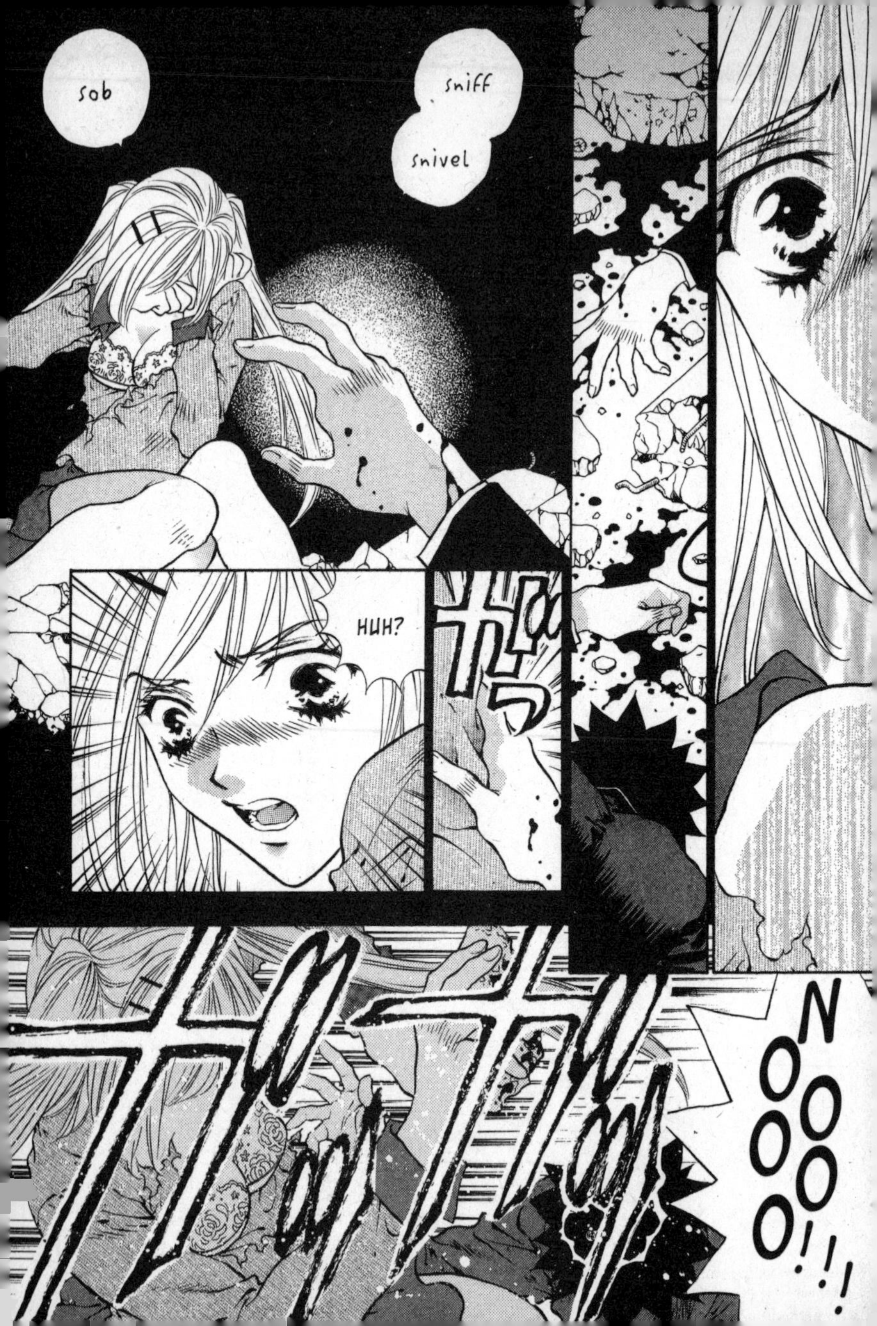
sob
sniff
snivel
HUH?
NOOOOO!!!

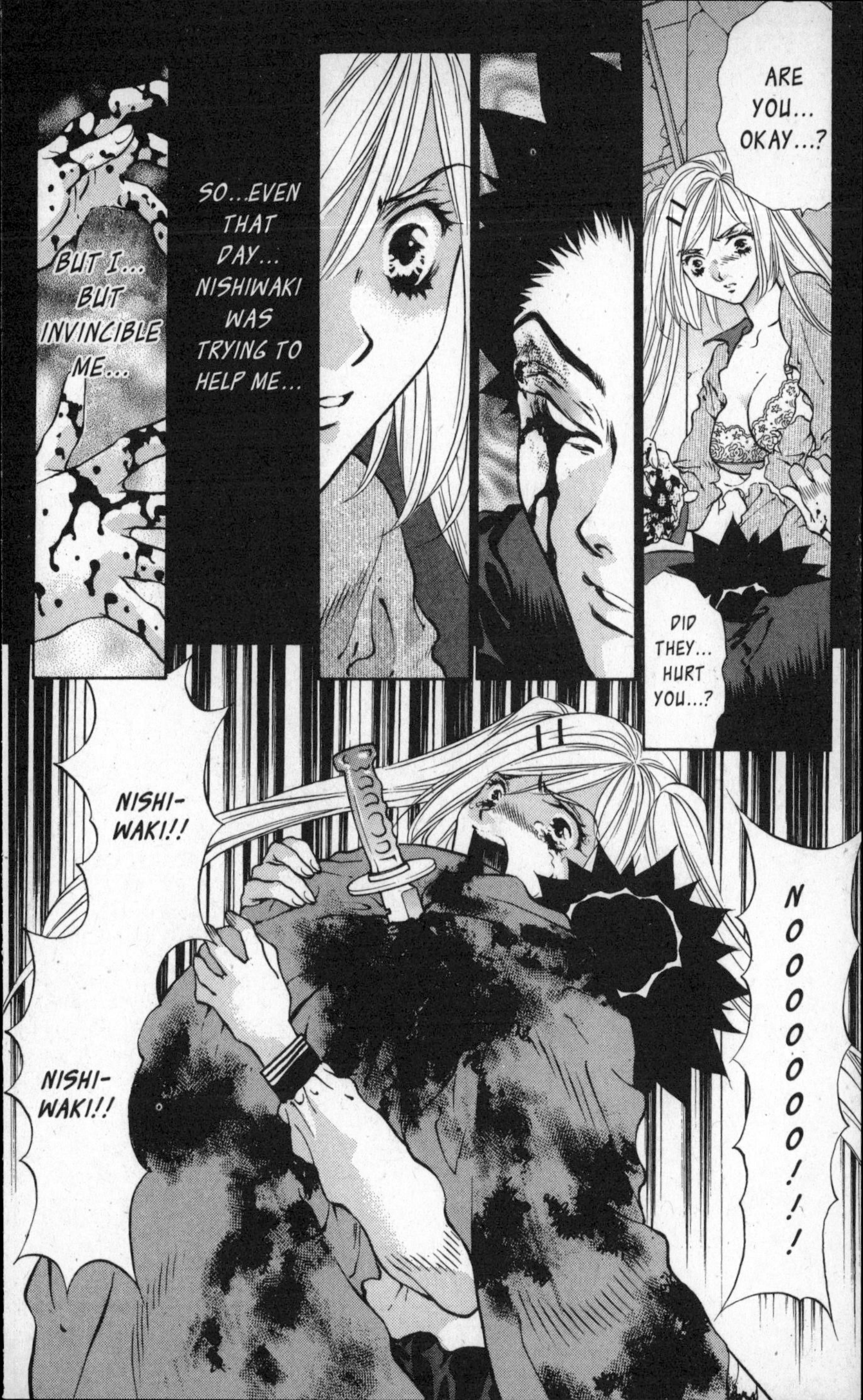

ARE YOU... OKAY...?
DID THEY... HURT YOU...?
SO...EVEN THAT DAY... NISHIWAKI WAS TRYING TO HELP ME...
BUT I... BUT INVINCIBLE ME...
NOOOOOOOOO!!!
NISHI-WAKI!!
NISHI-WAKI!!

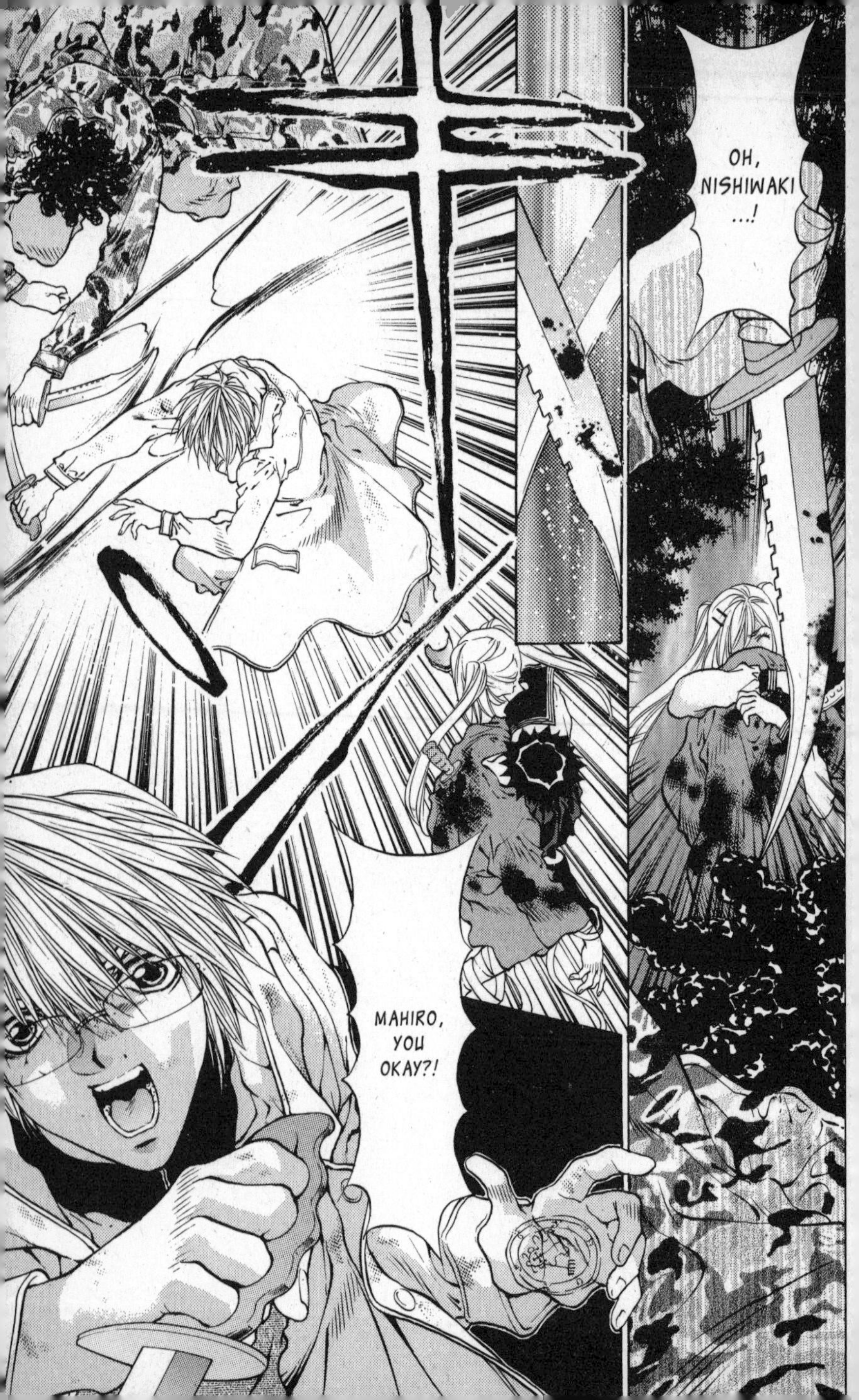
OH, NISHIWAKI ...!
MAHIRO, YOU OKAY?!

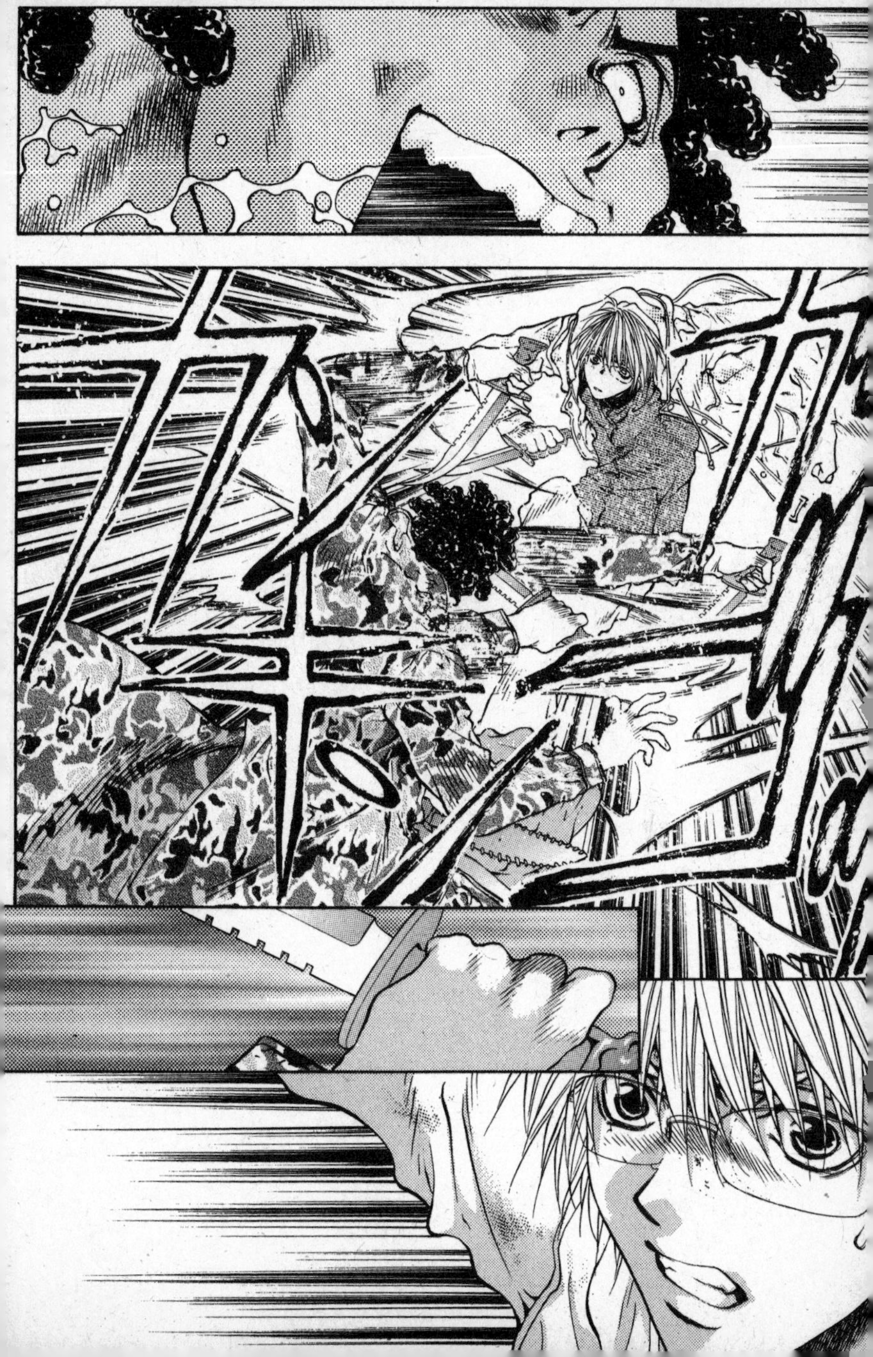

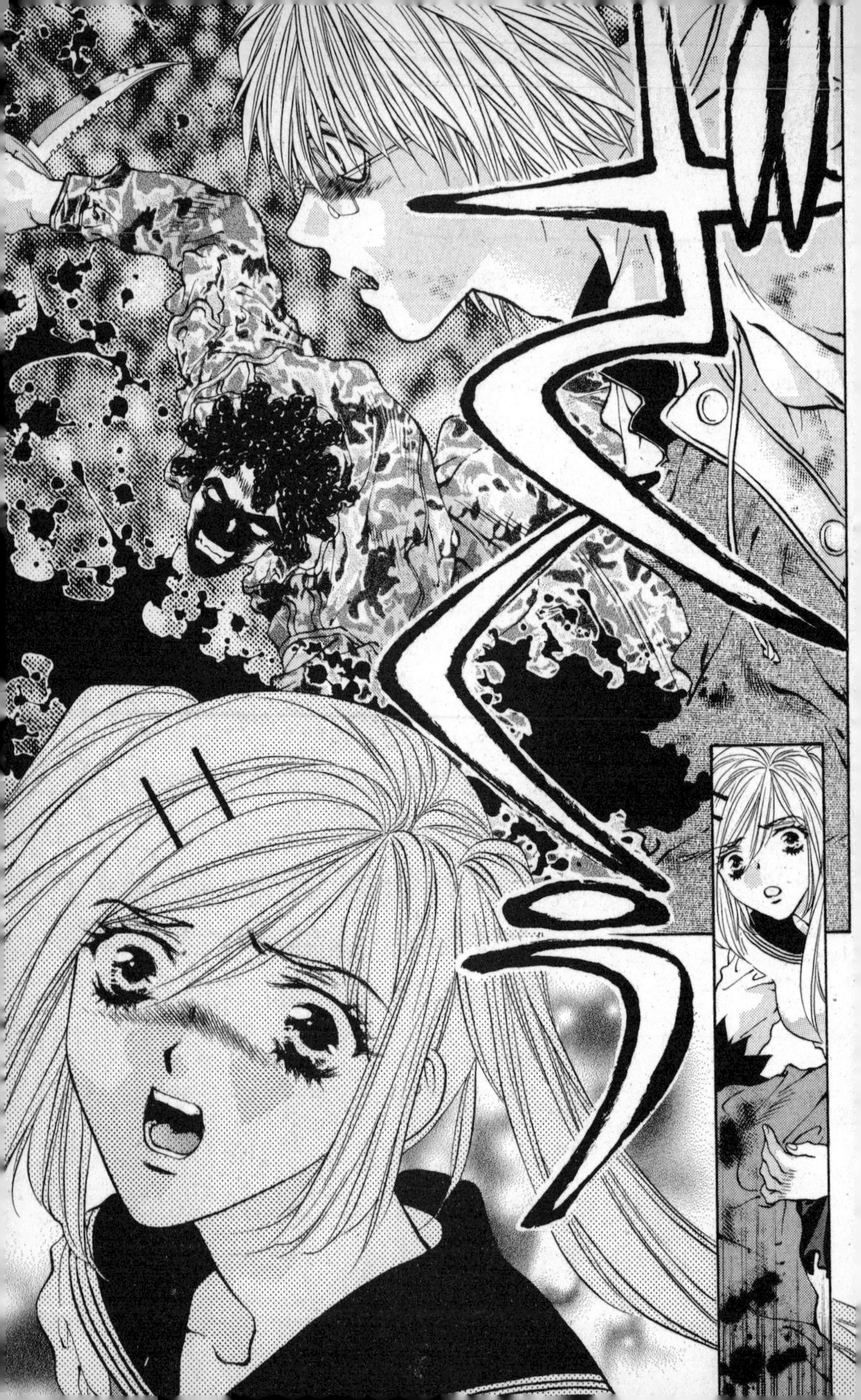

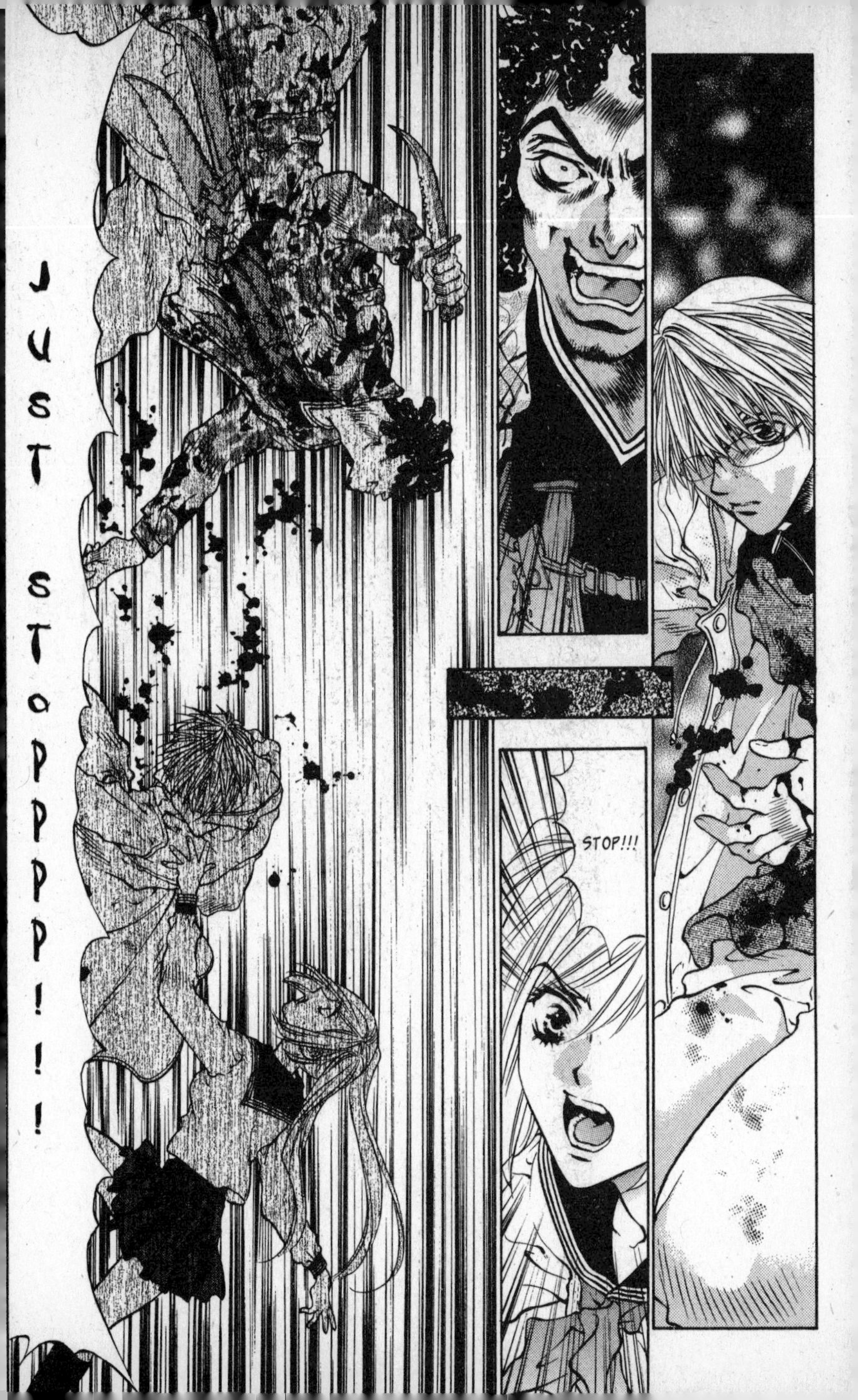
STOP!!!
JUST STOPPPP!!!

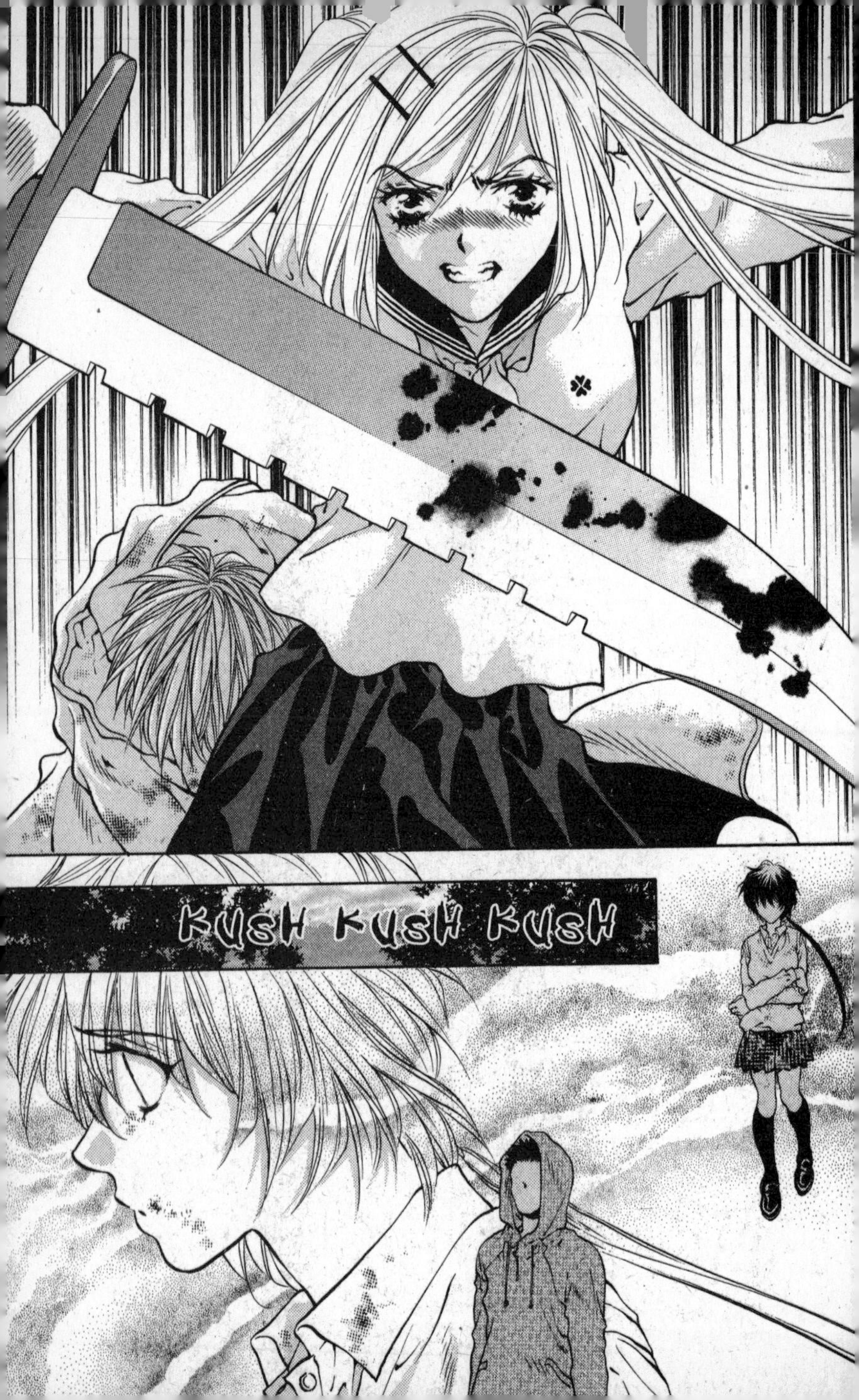
KUSH KUSH KUSH

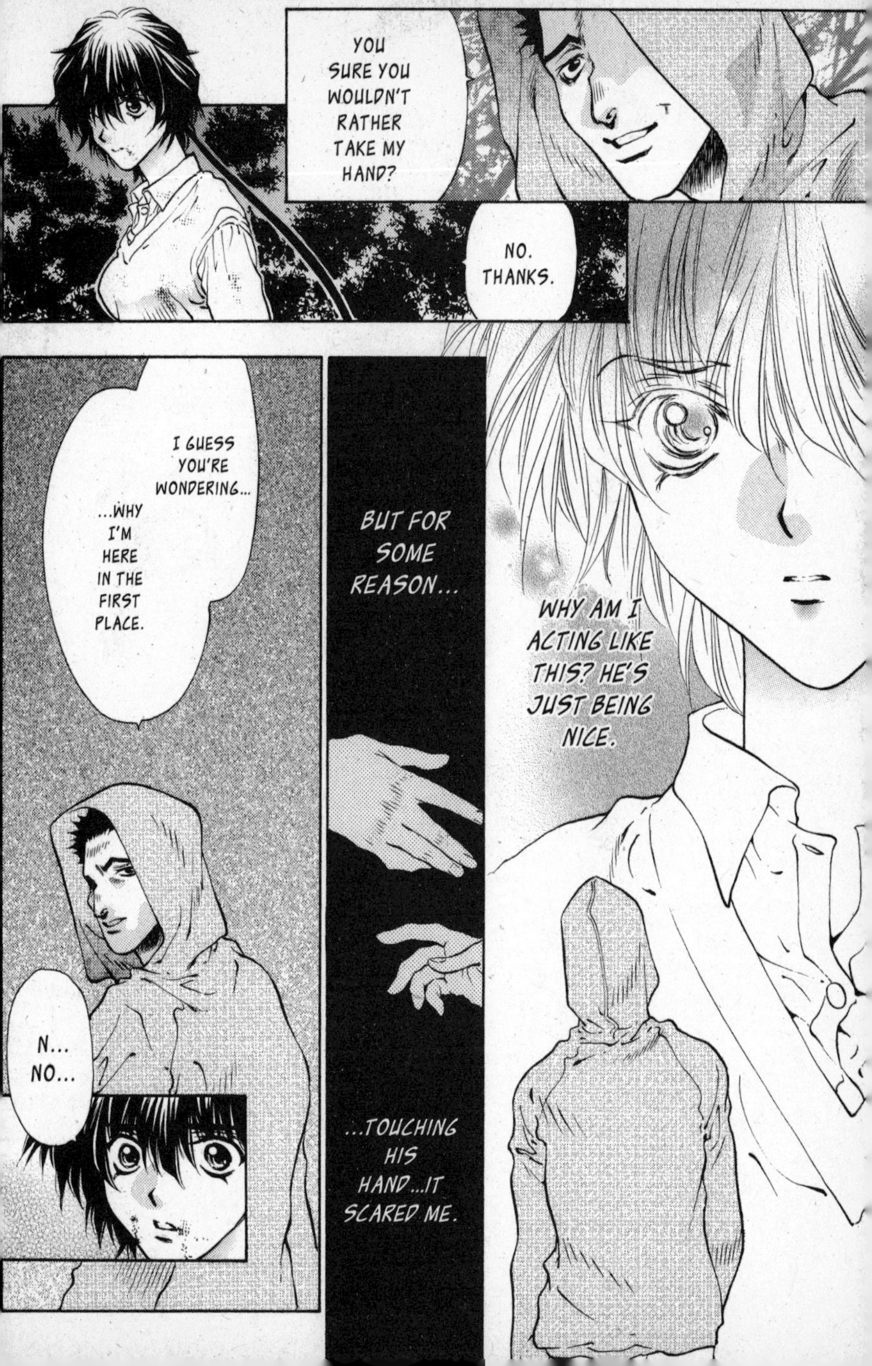
YOU SURE YOU WOULDN'T RATHER TAKE MY HAND?
NO. THANKS.
WHY AM I ACTING LIKE THIS? HE'S JUST BEING NICE.
BUT FOR SOME REASON...
...TOUCHING HIS HAND...IT SCARED ME.
I GUESS YOU'RE WONDERING...
...WHY I'M HERE IN THE FIRST PLACE.
N... NO...

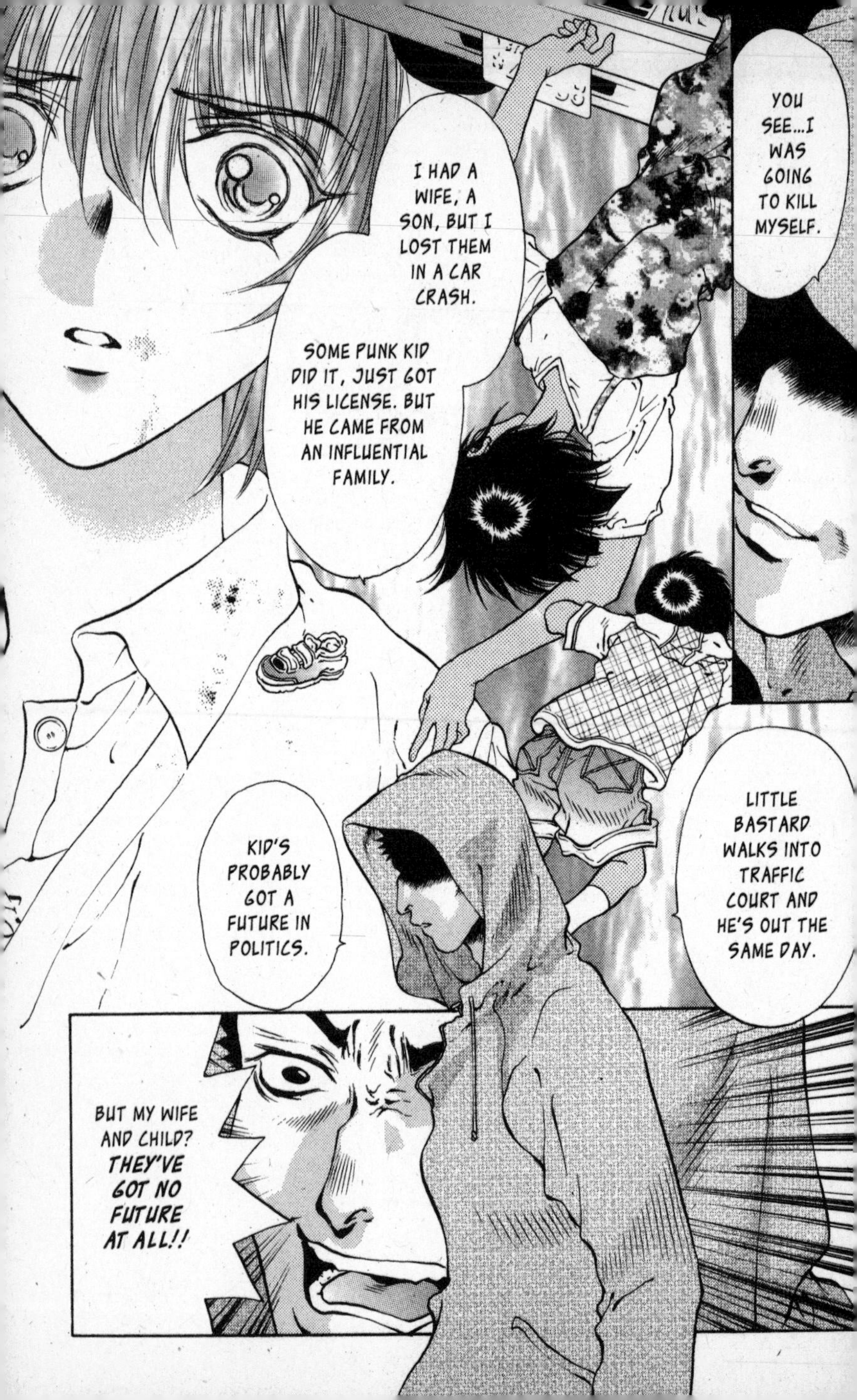
YOU SEE...I WAS GOING TO KILL MYSELF.
I HAD A WIFE, A SON, BUT I LOST THEM IN A CAR CRASH.
SOME PUNK KID DID IT, JUST GOT HIS LICENSE. BUT HE CAME FROM AN INFLUENTIAL FAMILY.
LITTLE BASTARD WALKS INTO TRAFFIC COURT AND HE'S OUT THE SAME DAY.
KID'S PROBABLY GOT A FUTURE IN POLITICS.
BUT MY WIFE AND CHILD? THEY'VE GOT NO FUTURE AT ALL!!

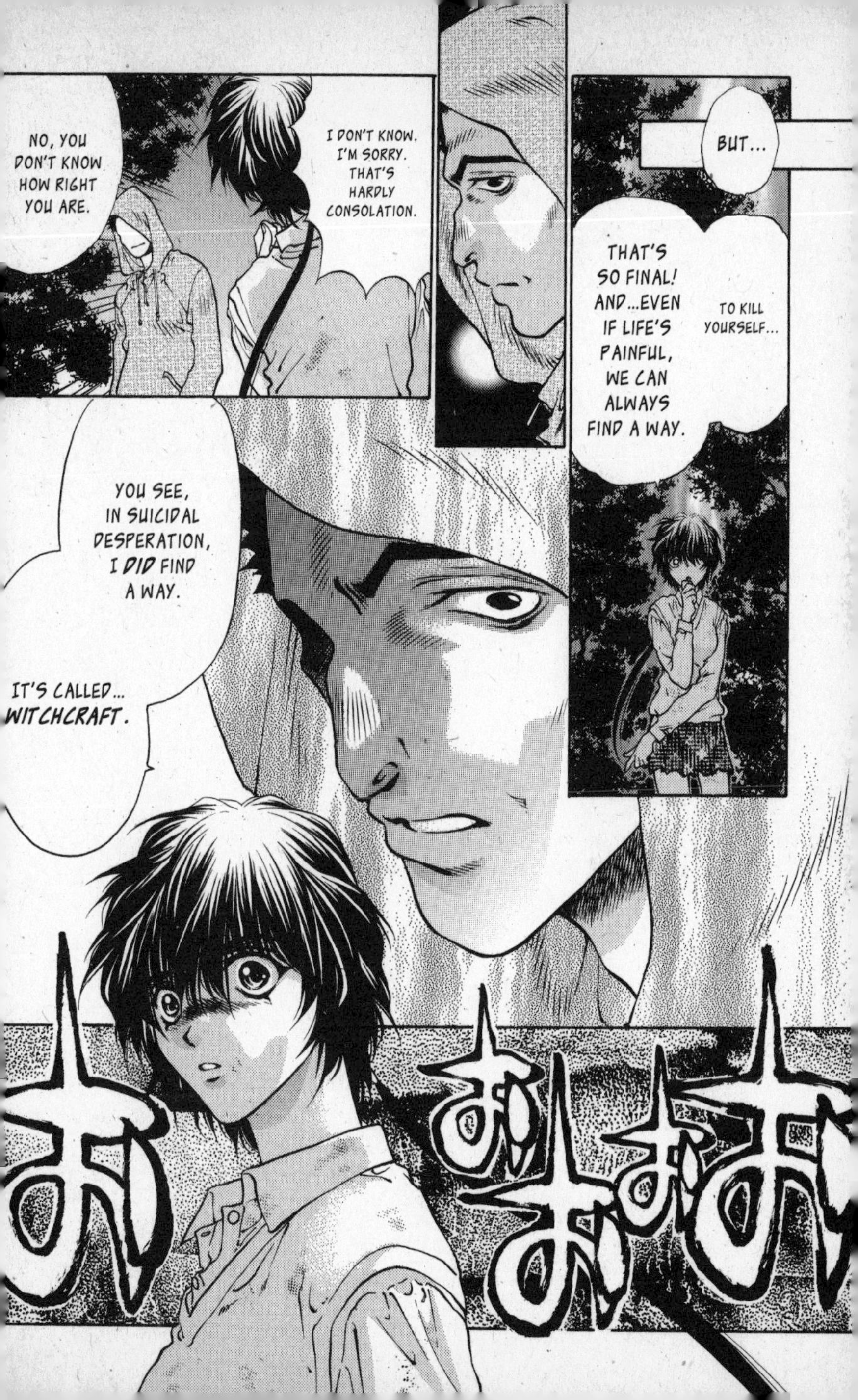
BUT...
TO KILL YOURSELF...
THAT'S SO FINAL! AND...EVEN IF LIFE'S PAINFUL, WE CAN ALWAYS FIND A WAY.
I DON'T KNOW. I'M SORRY. THAT'S HARDLY CONSOLATION.
NO, YOU DON'T KNOW HOW RIGHT YOU ARE.
YOU SEE, IN SUICIDAL DESPERATION, I *DID* FIND A WAY.
IT'S CALLED... **WITCHCRAFT**.

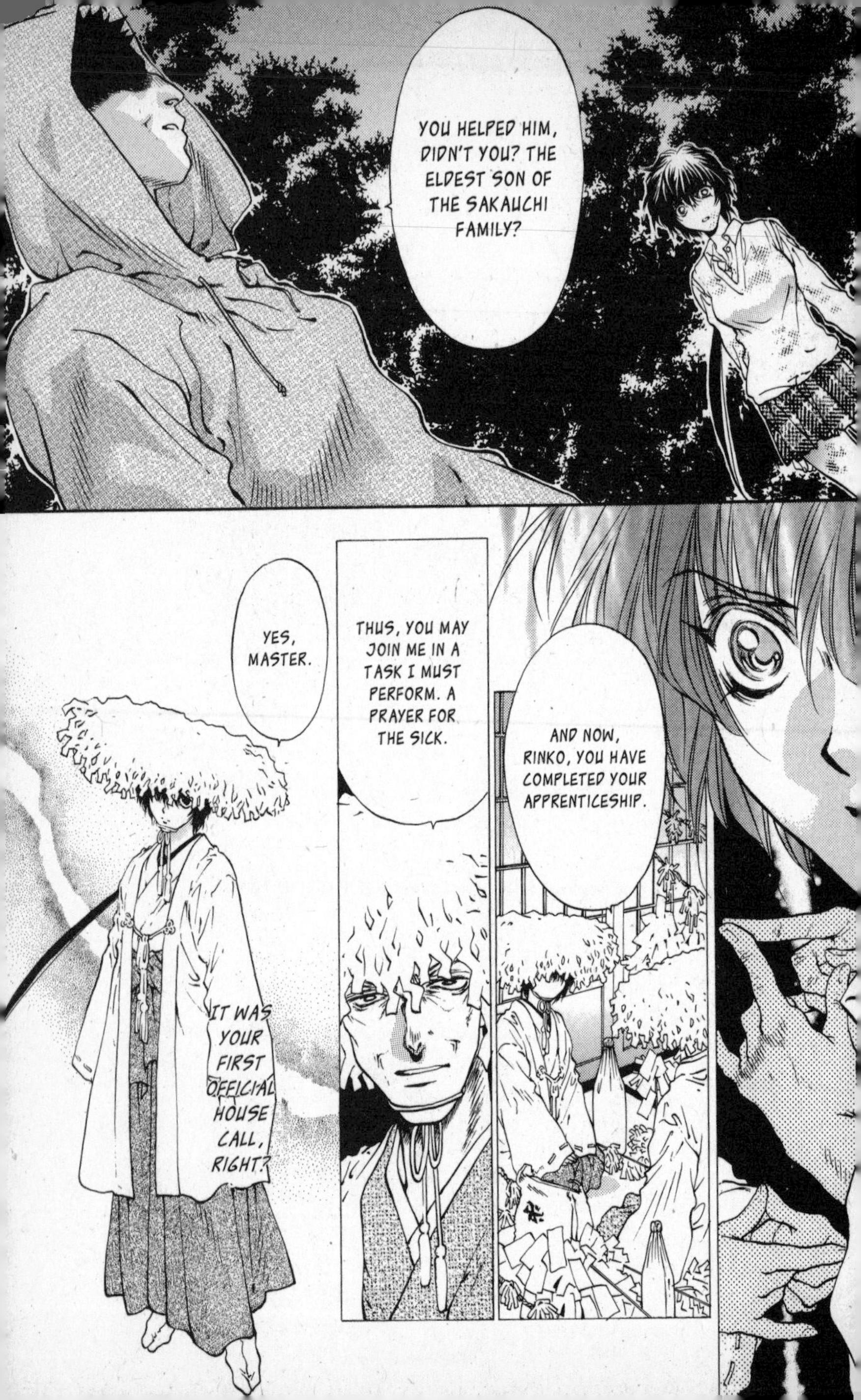
YOU HELPED HIM, DIDN'T YOU? THE ELDEST SON OF THE SAKAUCHI FAMILY?
AND NOW, RINKO, YOU HAVE COMPLETED YOUR APPRENTICESHIP.
THUS, YOU MAY JOIN ME IN A TASK I MUST PERFORM. A PRAYER FOR THE SICK.
YES, MASTER.
IT WAS YOUR FIRST OFFICIAL HOUSE CALL, RIGHT?

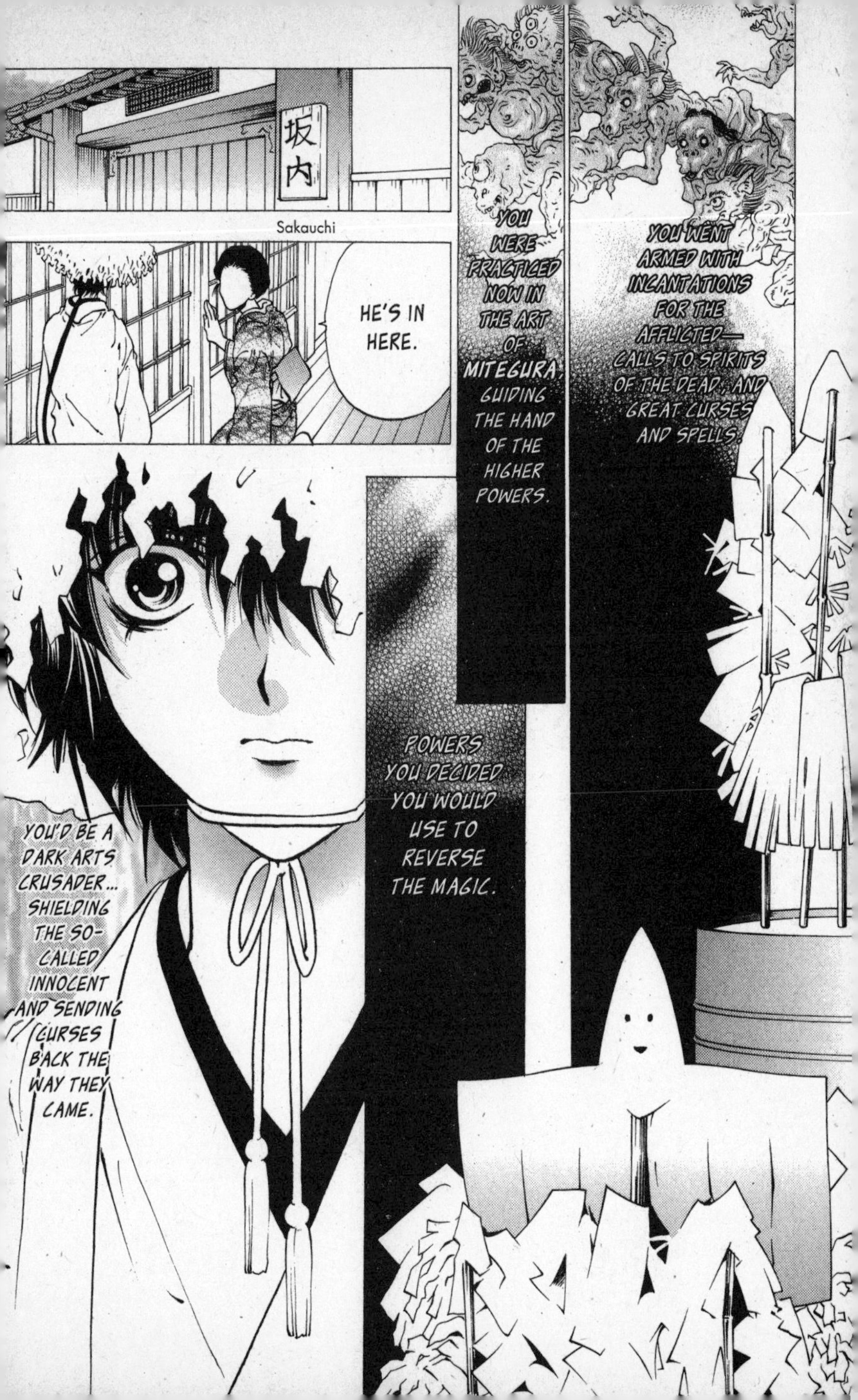

YOU WENT ARMED WITH INCANTATIONS FOR THE AFFLICTED— CALLS TO SPIRITS OF THE DEAD, AND GREAT CURSES AND SPELLS.
YOU WERE PRACTICED NOW IN THE ART OF MITEGURA, GUIDING THE HAND OF THE HIGHER POWERS.
坂内
Sakauchi
HE'S IN HERE.
POWERS YOU DECIDED YOU WOULD USE TO REVERSE THE MAGIC.
YOU'D BE A DARK ARTS CRUSADER... SHIELDING THE SO-CALLED INNOCENT AND SENDING CURSES BACK THE WAY THEY CAME.

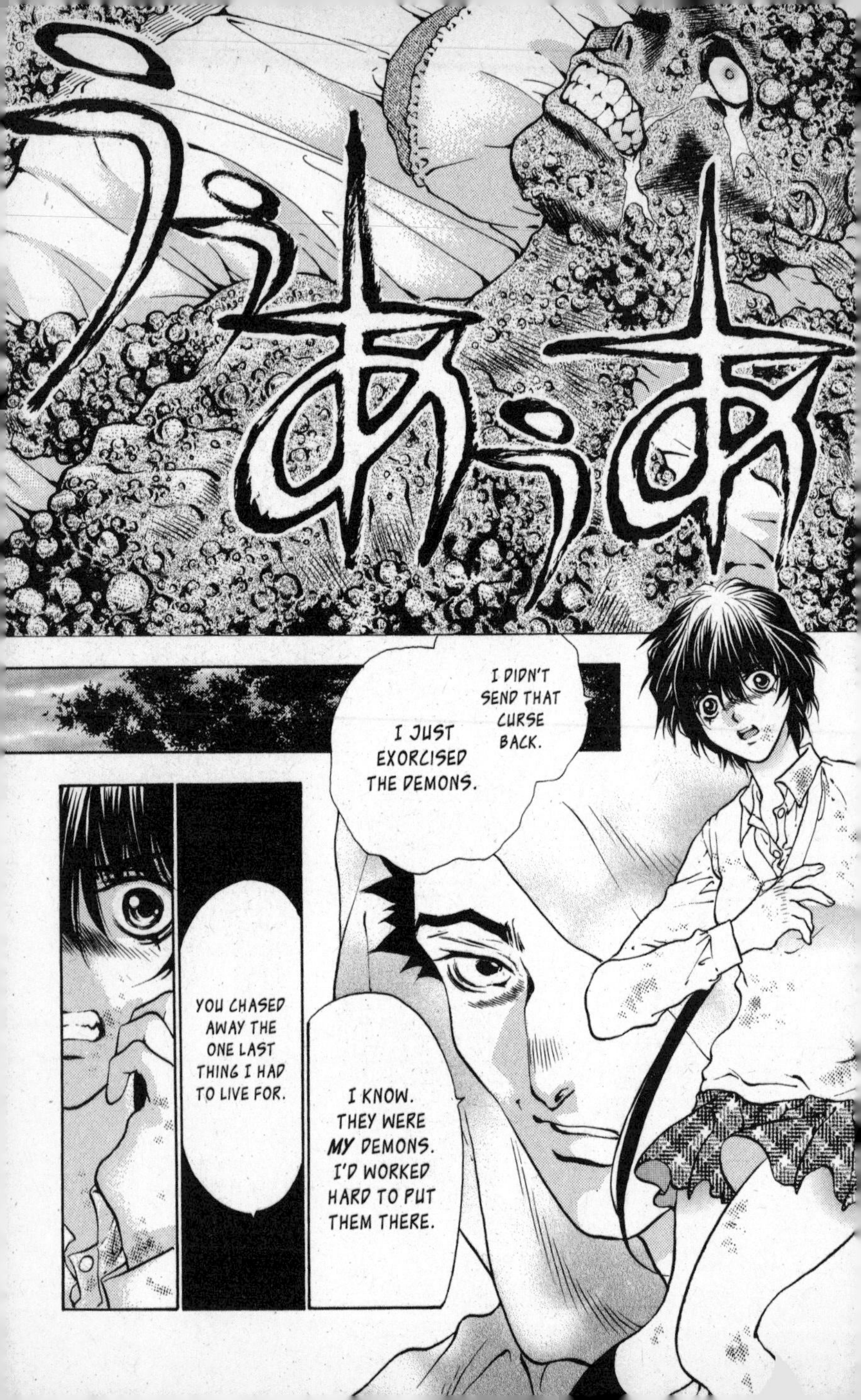
I DIDN'T SEND THAT CURSE BACK.
I JUST EXORCISED THE DEMONS.
I KNOW. THEY WERE MY DEMONS. I'D WORKED HARD TO PUT THEM THERE.
YOU CHASED AWAY THE ONE LAST THING I HAD TO LIVE FOR.

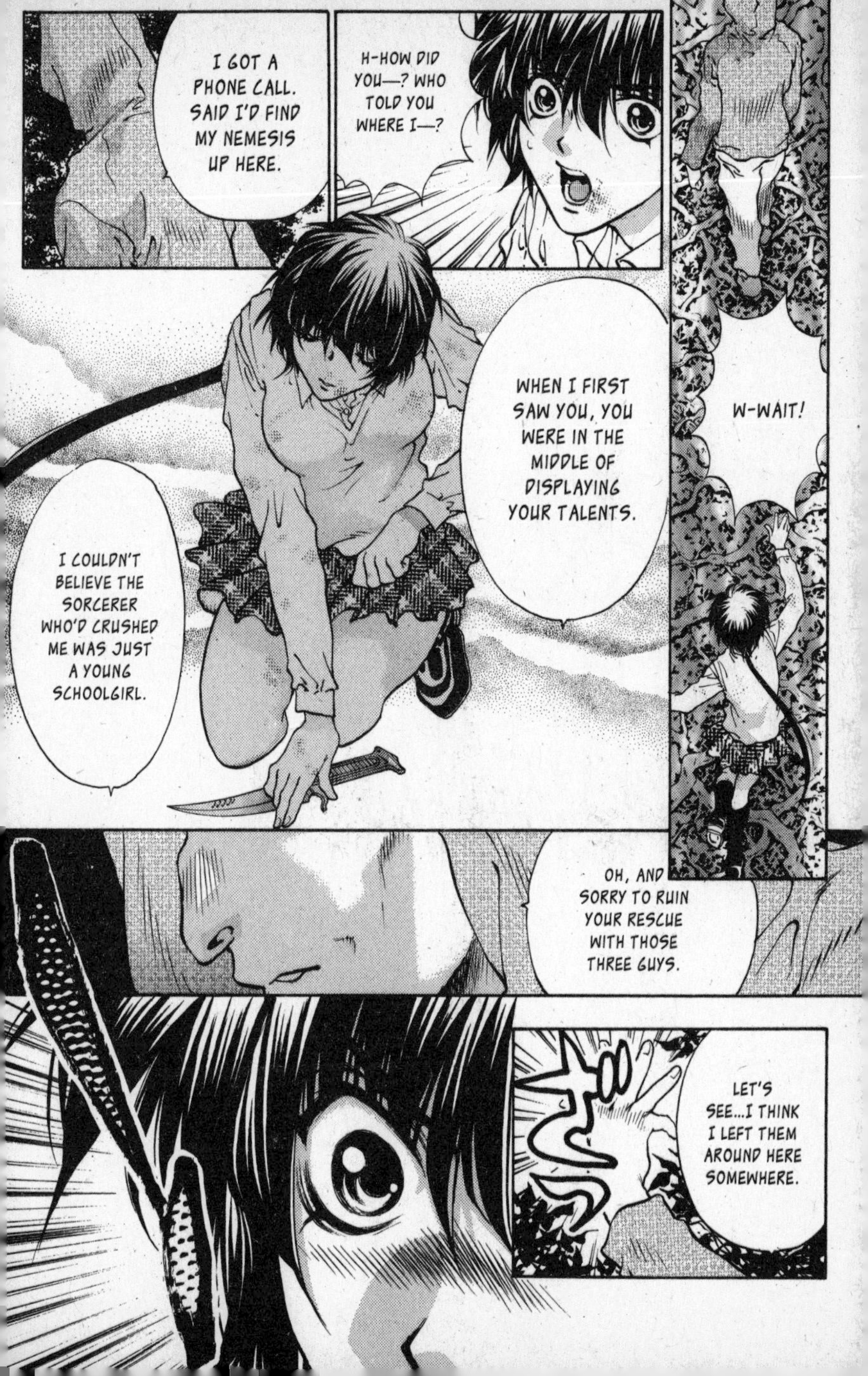
W-WAIT!
H-HOW DID YOU—? WHO TOLD YOU WHERE I—?
I GOT A PHONE CALL. SAID I'D FIND MY NEMESIS UP HERE.
WHEN I FIRST SAW YOU, YOU WERE IN THE MIDDLE OF DISPLAYING YOUR TALENTS.
I COULDN'T BELIEVE THE SORCERER WHO'D CRUSHED ME WAS JUST A YOUNG SCHOOLGIRL.
OH, AND SORRY TO RUIN YOUR RESCUE WITH THOSE THREE GUYS.
LET'S SEE...I THINK I LEFT THEM AROUND HERE SOMEWHERE.

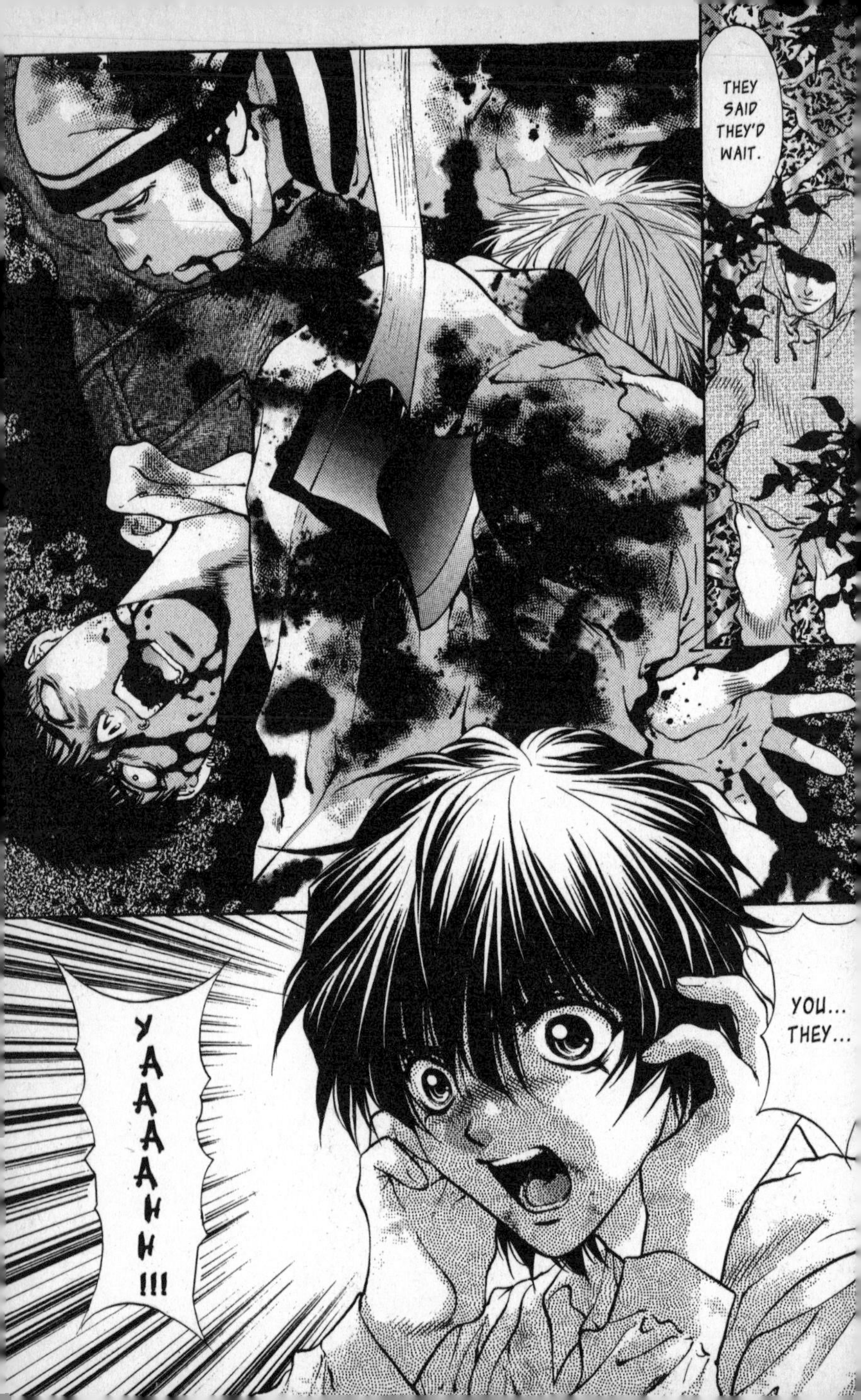
THEY SAID THEY'D WAIT.
YOU... THEY...
YAAAAHH!!!

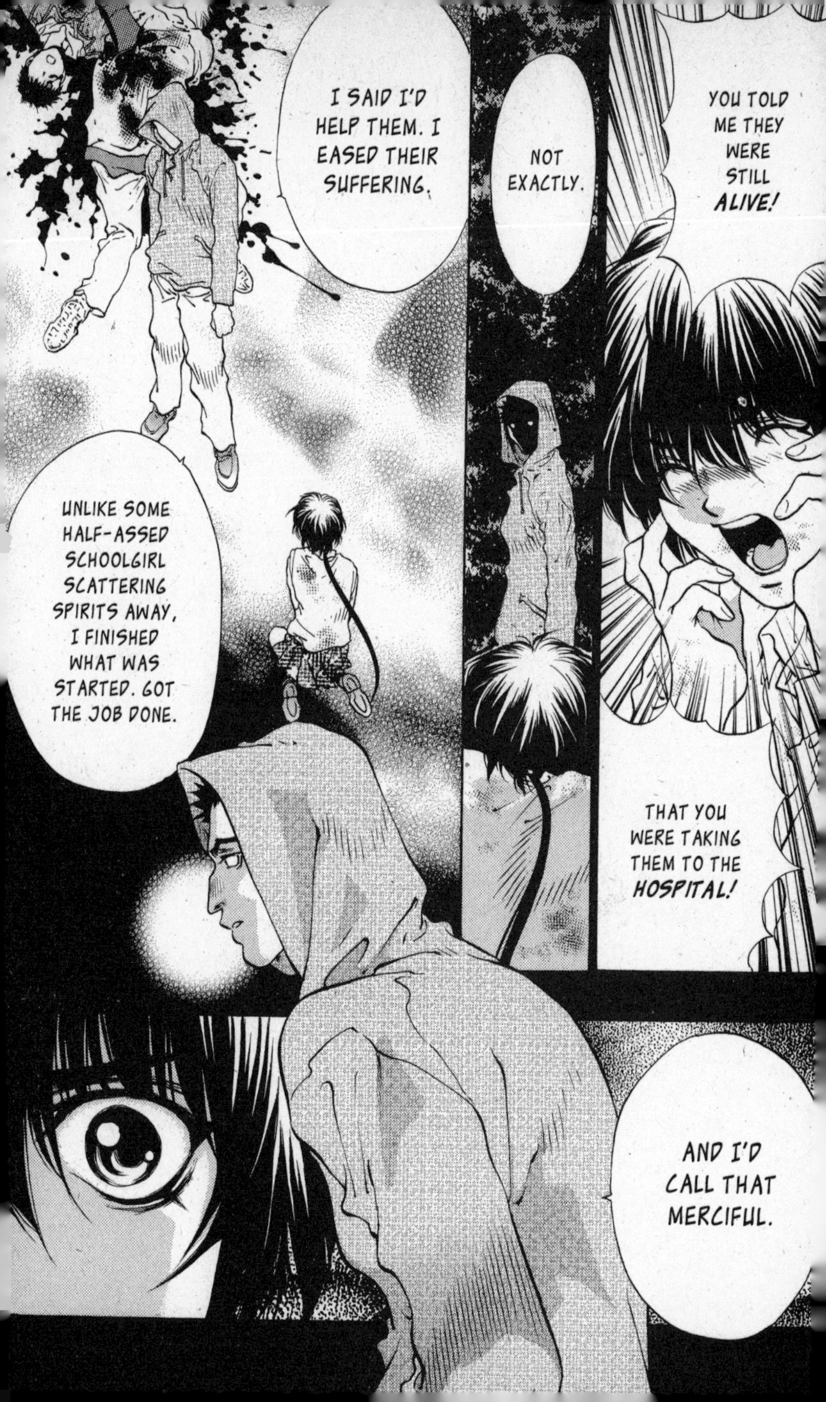
YOU TOLD ME THEY WERE STILL ALIVE!
THAT YOU WERE TAKING THEM TO THE HOSPITAL!
NOT EXACTLY.
I SAID I'D HELP THEM. I EASED THEIR SUFFERING.
UNLIKE SOME HALF-ASSED SCHOOLGIRL SCATTERING SPIRITS AWAY, I FINISHED WHAT WAS STARTED. GOT THE JOB DONE.
AND I'D CALL THAT MERCIFUL.

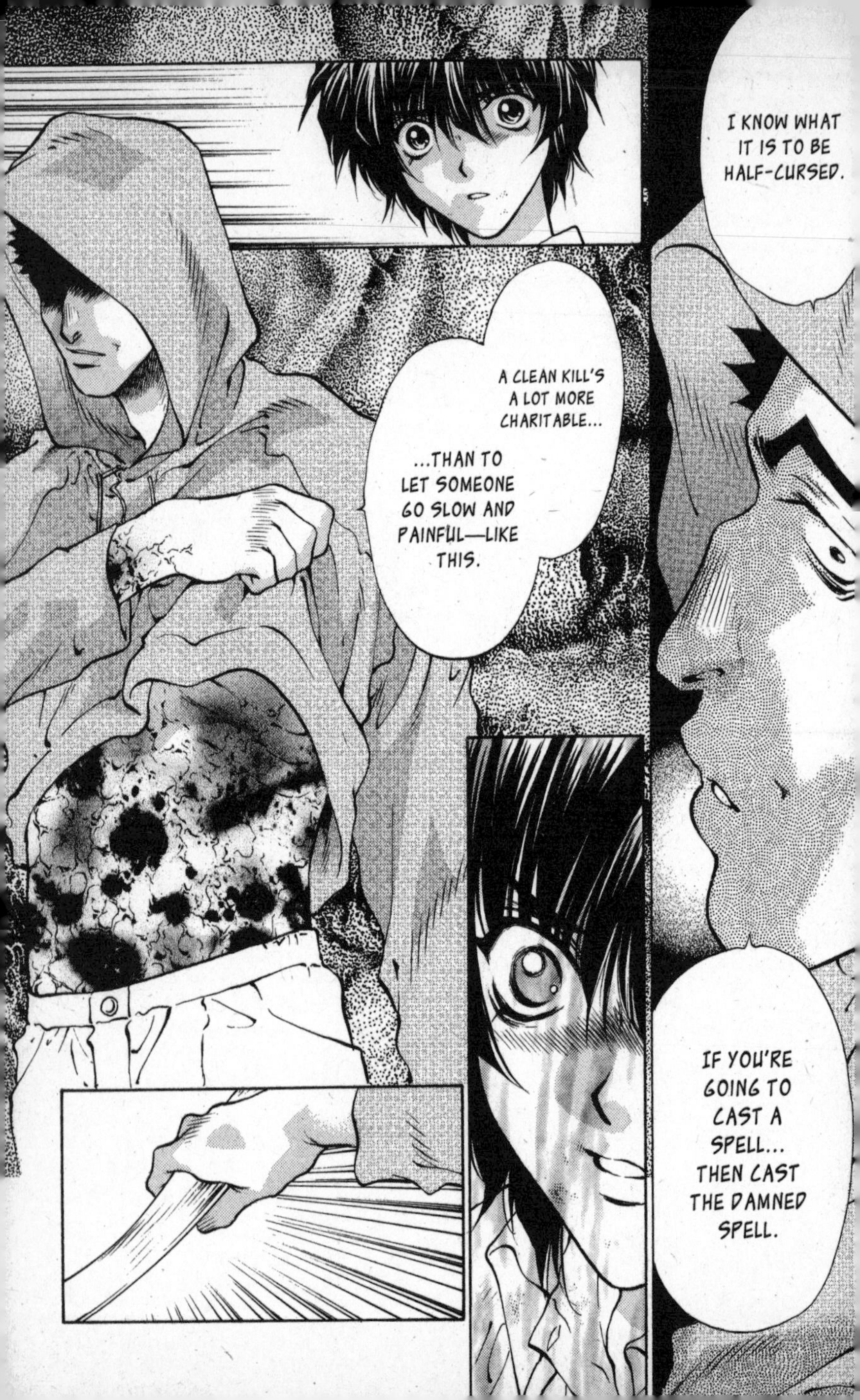
I KNOW WHAT IT IS TO BE HALF-CURSED.
A CLEAN KILL'S A LOT MORE CHARITABLE...
...THAN TO LET SOMEONE GO SLOW AND PAINFUL—LIKE THIS.
IF YOU'RE GOING TO CAST A SPELL... THEN CAST THE DAMNED SPELL.

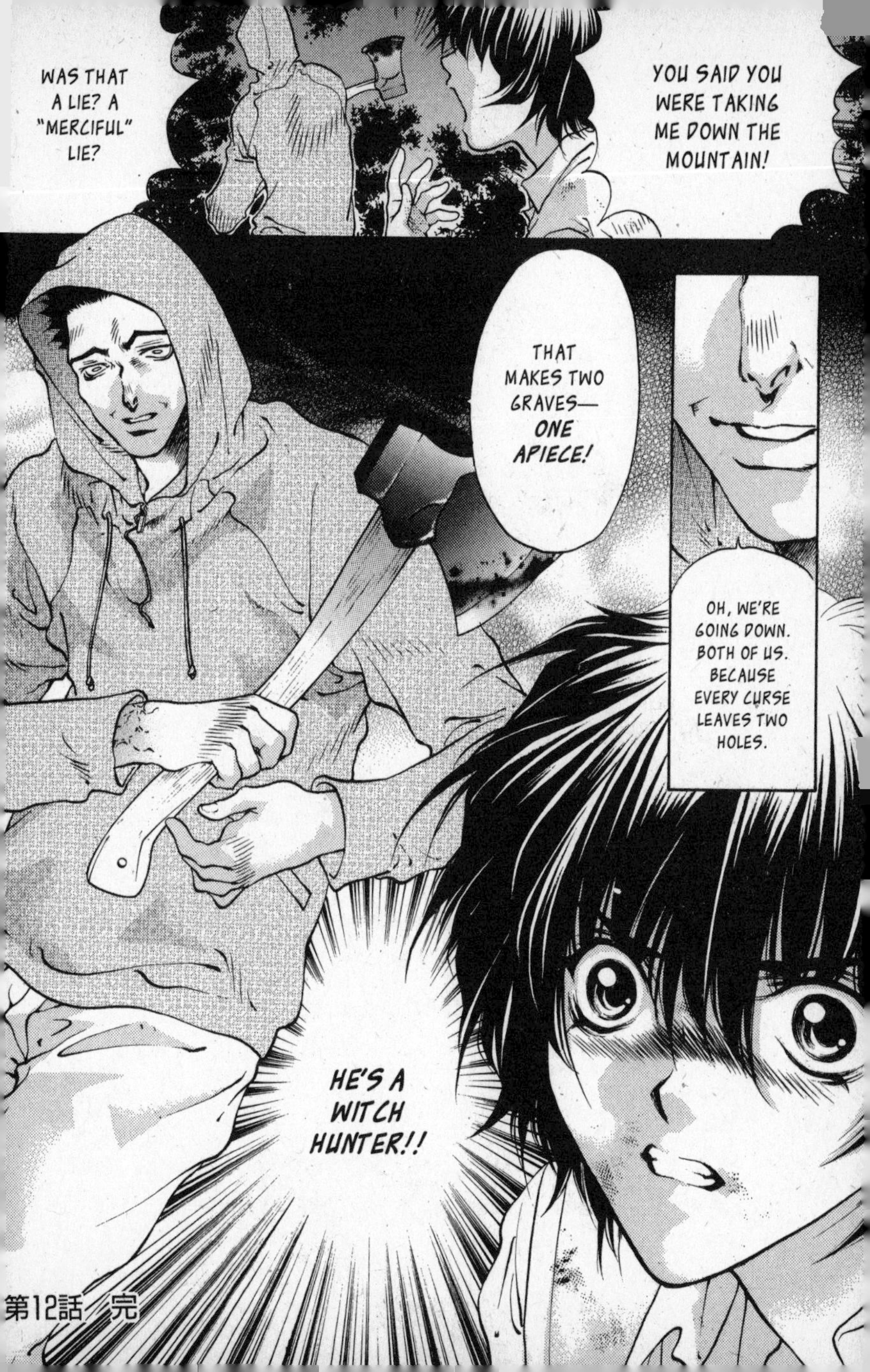
YOU SAID YOU WERE TAKING ME DOWN THE MOUNTAIN!
WAS THAT A LIE? A "MERCIFUL" LIE?
OH, WE'RE GOING DOWN. BOTH OF US. BECAUSE EVERY CURSE LEAVES TWO HOLES.
THAT MAKES TWO GRAVES—ONE APIECE!
HE'S A WITCH HUNTER!!
第12話 完

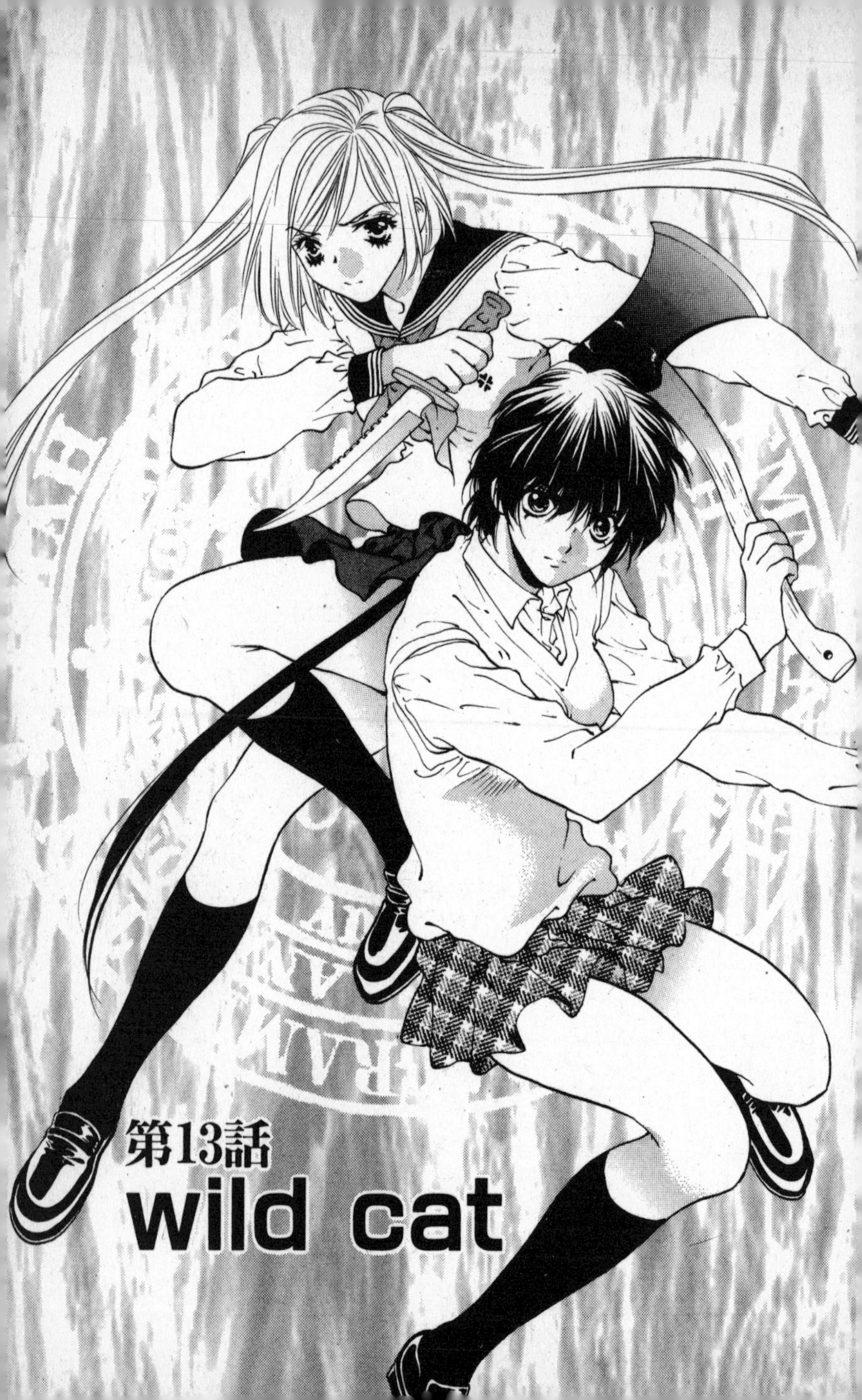
第13話
wild cat

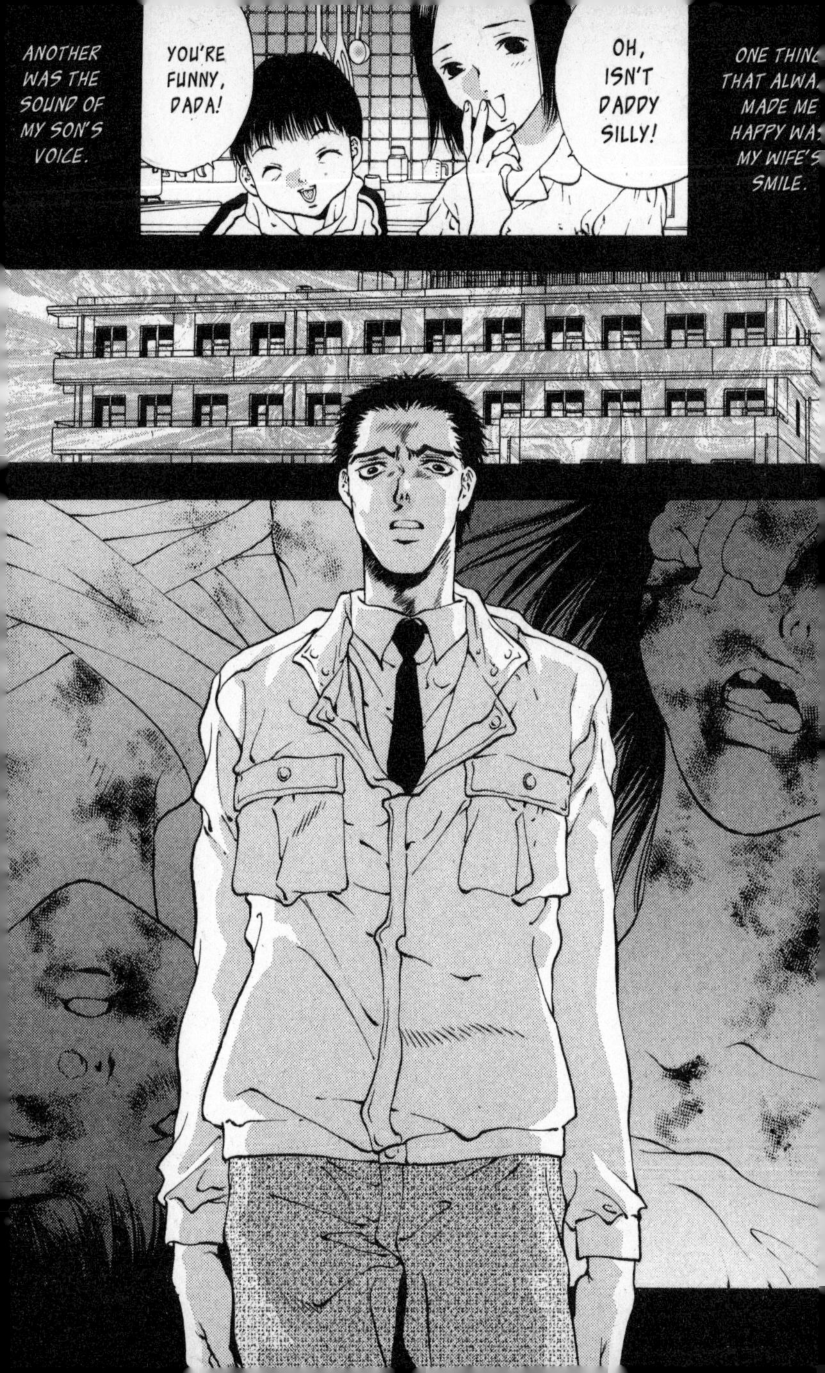
ONE THIN THAT ALWA MADE ME HAPPY WA MY WIFE'S SMILE.
OH, ISN'T DADDY SILLY!
YOU'RE FUNNY, DADA!
ANOTHER WAS THE SOUND OF MY SON'S VOICE.

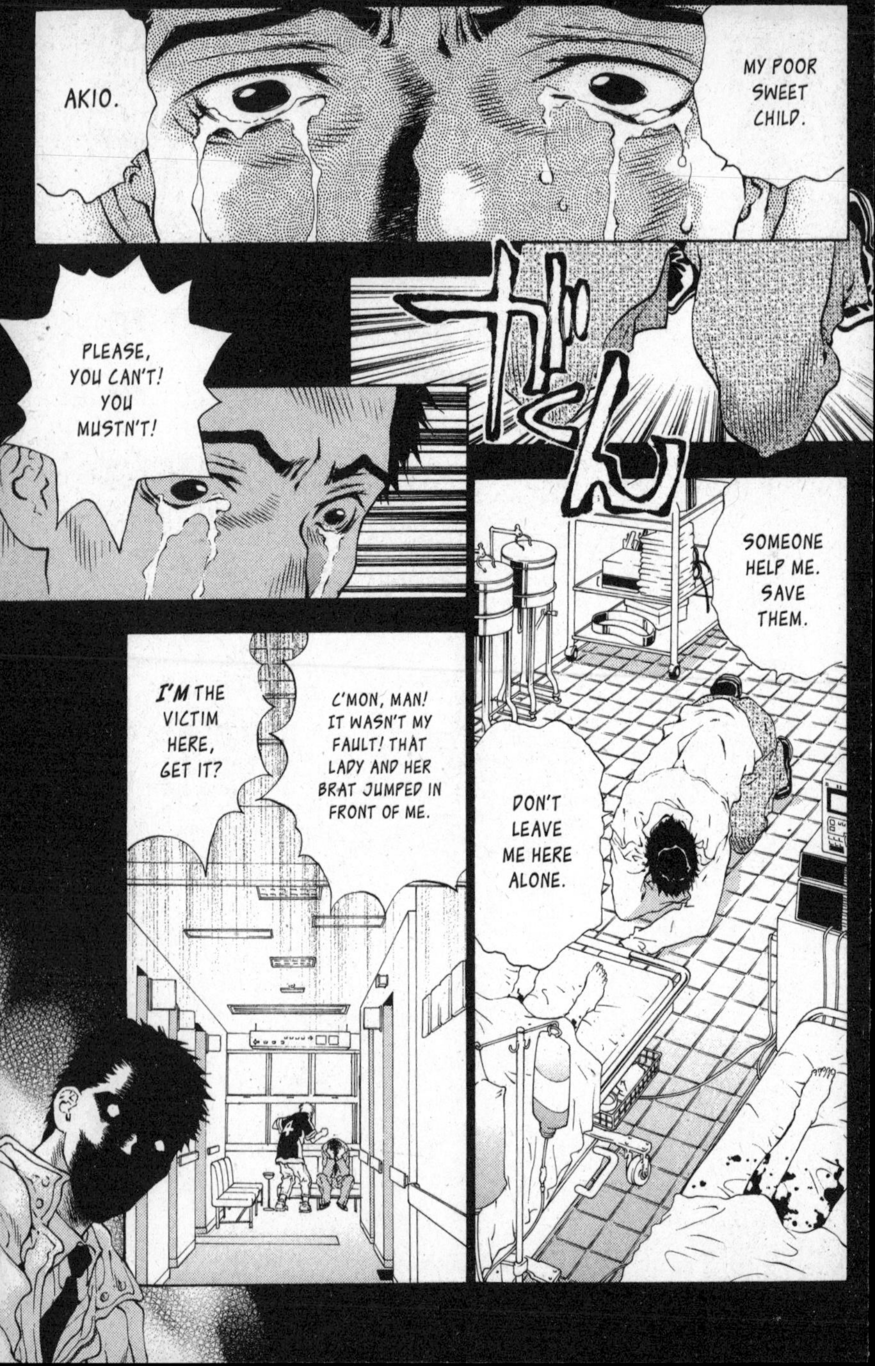
MY POOR SWEET CHILD.
AKIO.
がくん
PLEASE, YOU CAN'T! YOU MUSTN'T!
SOMEONE HELP ME. SAVE THEM.
DON'T LEAVE ME HERE ALONE.
C'MON, MAN! IT WASN'T MY FAULT! THAT LADY AND HER BRAT JUMPED IN FRONT OF ME.
I'M THE VICTIM HERE, GET IT?

I MEAN...
I HATE YOU I HATE YOU I HATE YOU I HATE YOU I HATE YOU!
NOOOOOO!!!

THEN CAME THE RESTRAINING ORDER.

I HATE YOU I HATE YOU I HATE YOU I HATE YOU I HATE YOU!

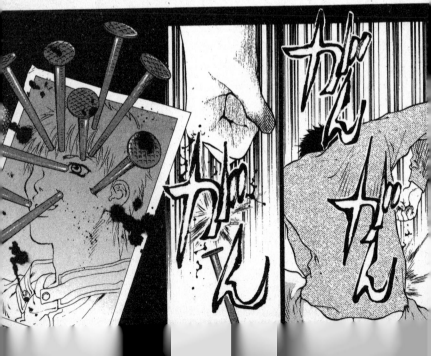

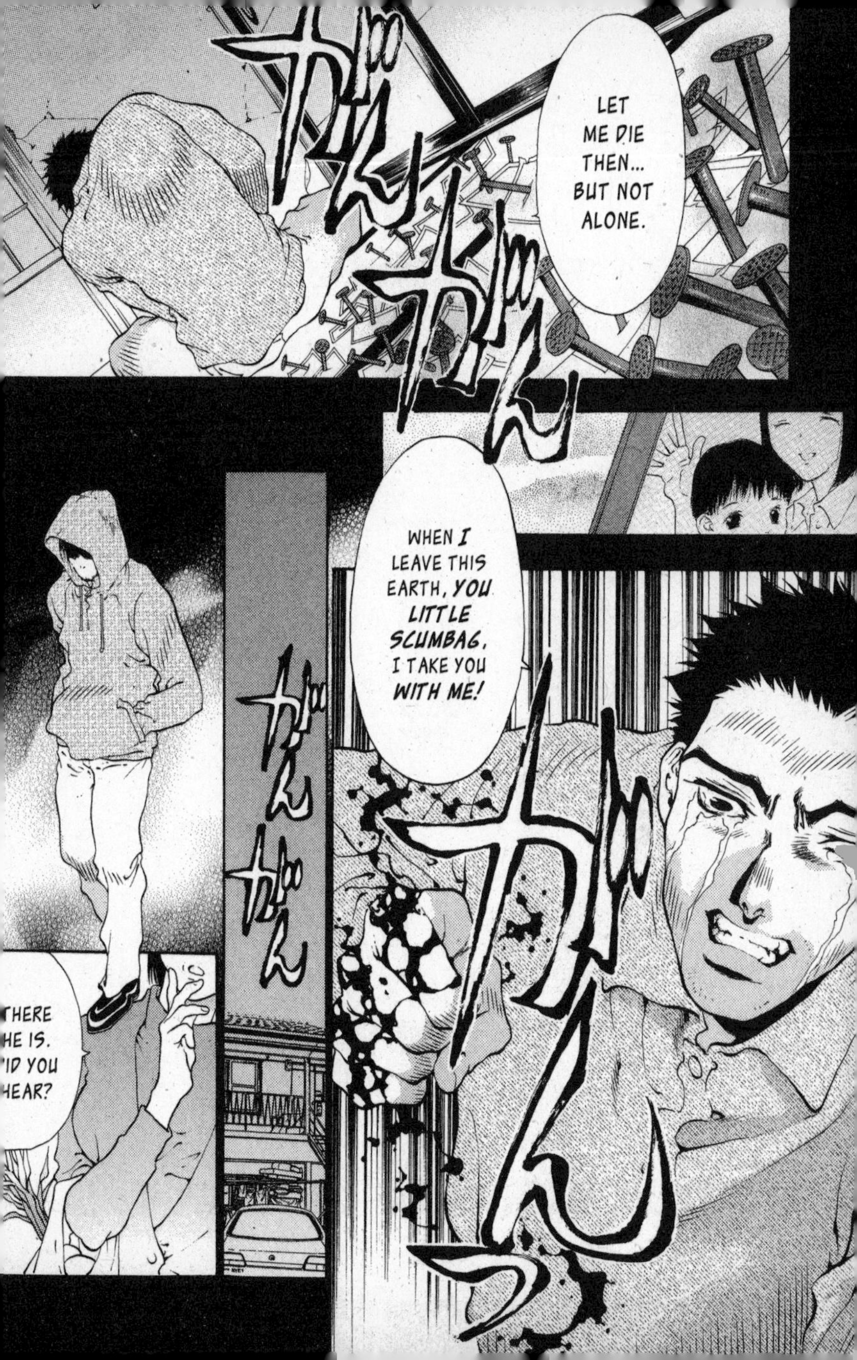
LET ME DIE THEN... BUT NOT ALONE.
WHEN I LEAVE THIS EARTH, YOU LITTLE SCUMBAG, I TAKE YOU WITH ME!
THERE HE IS. ID YOU HEAR?

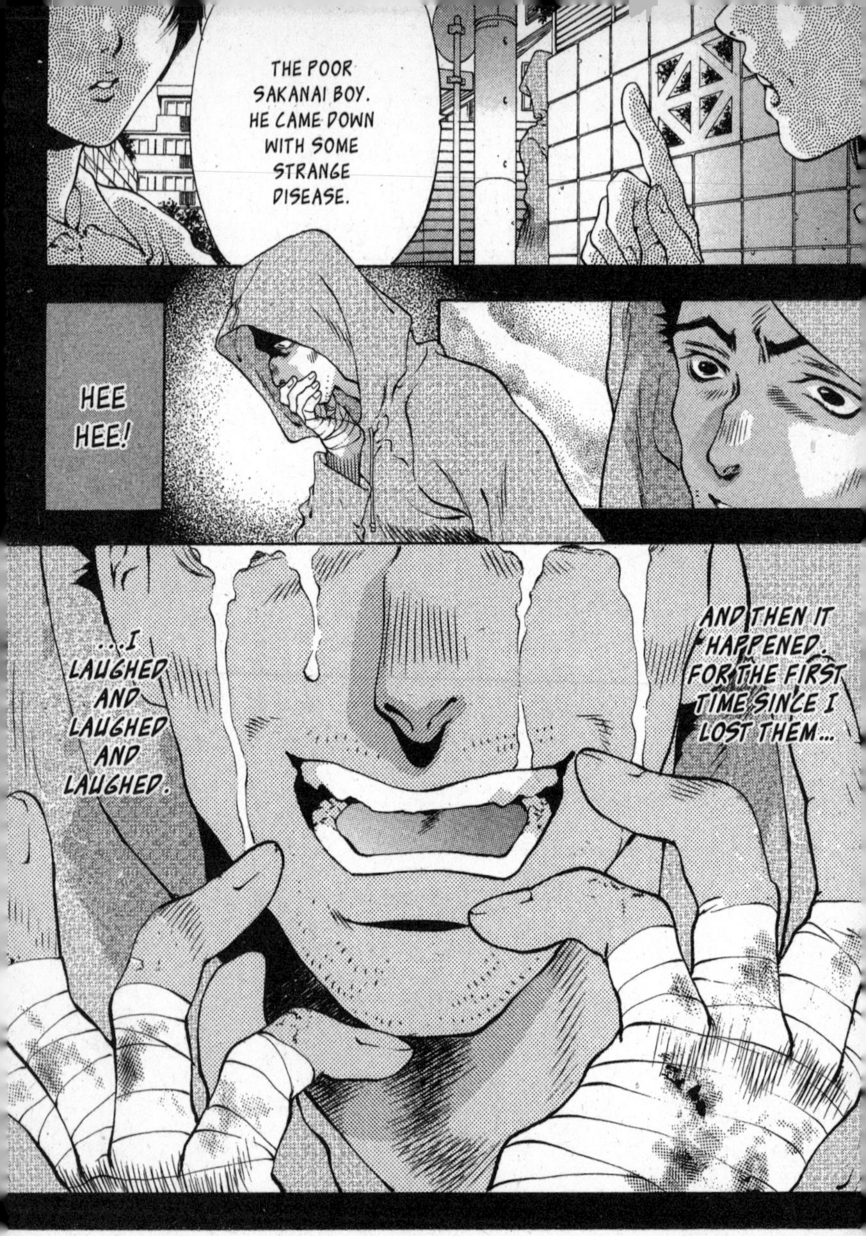
THE POOR SAKANAI BOY. HE CAME DOWN WITH SOME STRANGE DISEASE.
HEE HEE!
AND THEN IT HAPPENED. FOR THE FIRST TIME SINCE I LOST THEM...
...I LAUGHED AND LAUGHED AND LAUGHED.

AND I THOUGHT: THERE IS MERCY IN THE WORLD.

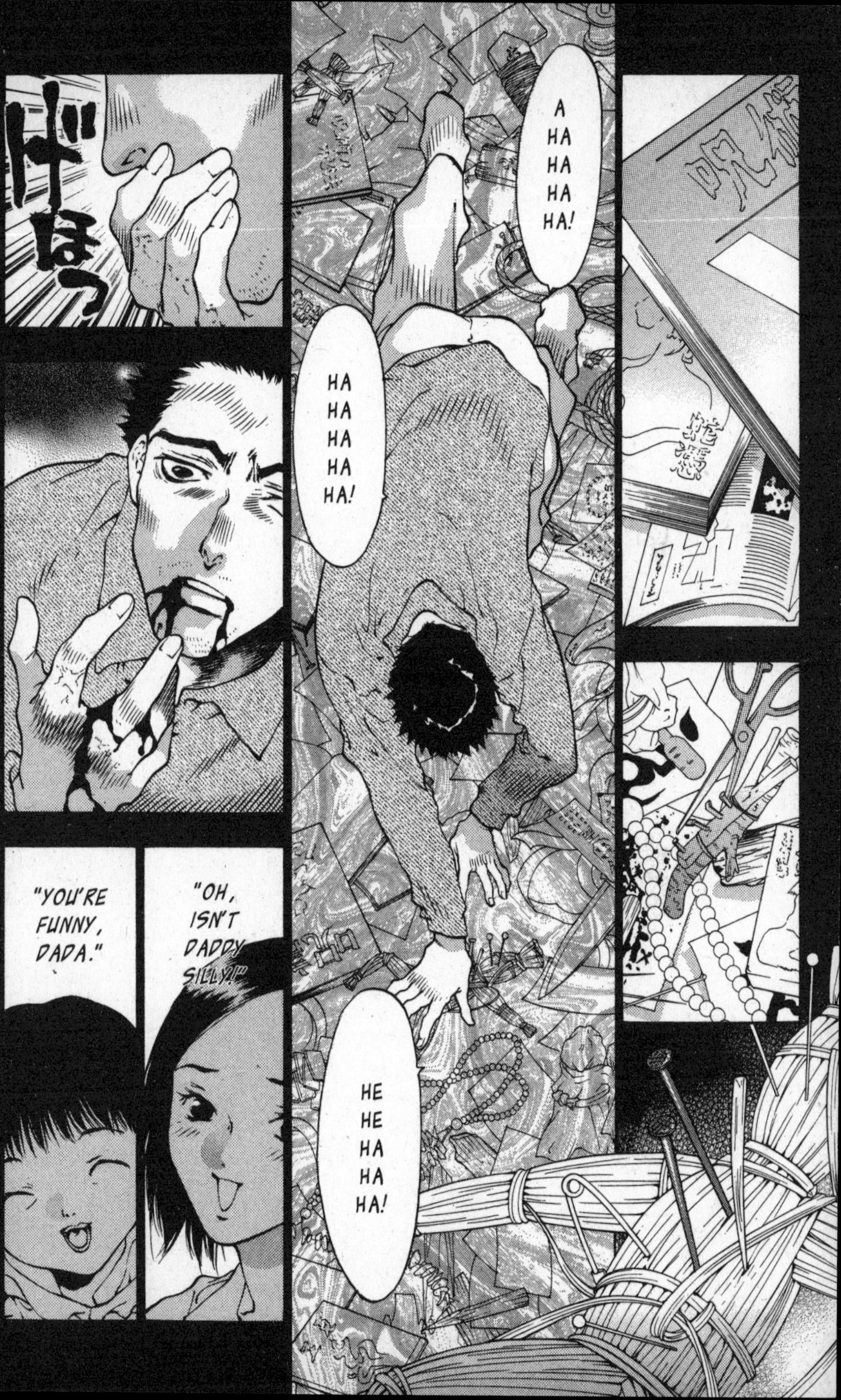

呪術
A HA HA HA HA!
HA HA HA HA HA!
HE HE HA HA HA!
げほっ
"OH, ISN'T DADDY SILLY!"
"YOU'RE FUNNY, DADA."

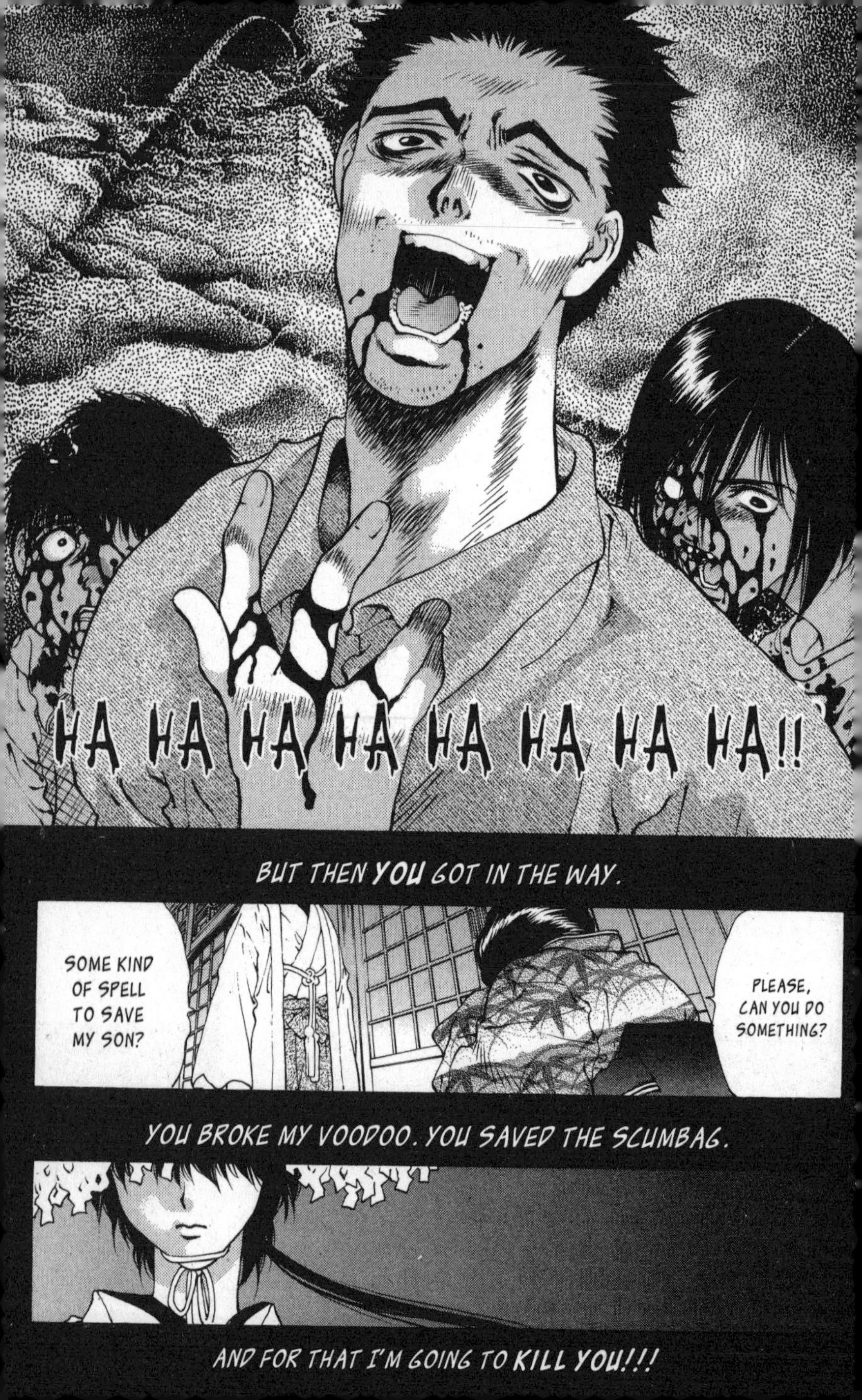
HA HA HA HA HA HA HA HA HA HA!!
BUT THEN YOU GOT IN THE WAY.
PLEASE, CAN YOU DO SOMETHING?
SOME KIND OF SPELL TO SAVE MY SON?
YOU BROKE MY VOODOO. YOU SAVED THE SCUMBAG.
AND FOR THAT I'M GOING TO KILL YOU!!!

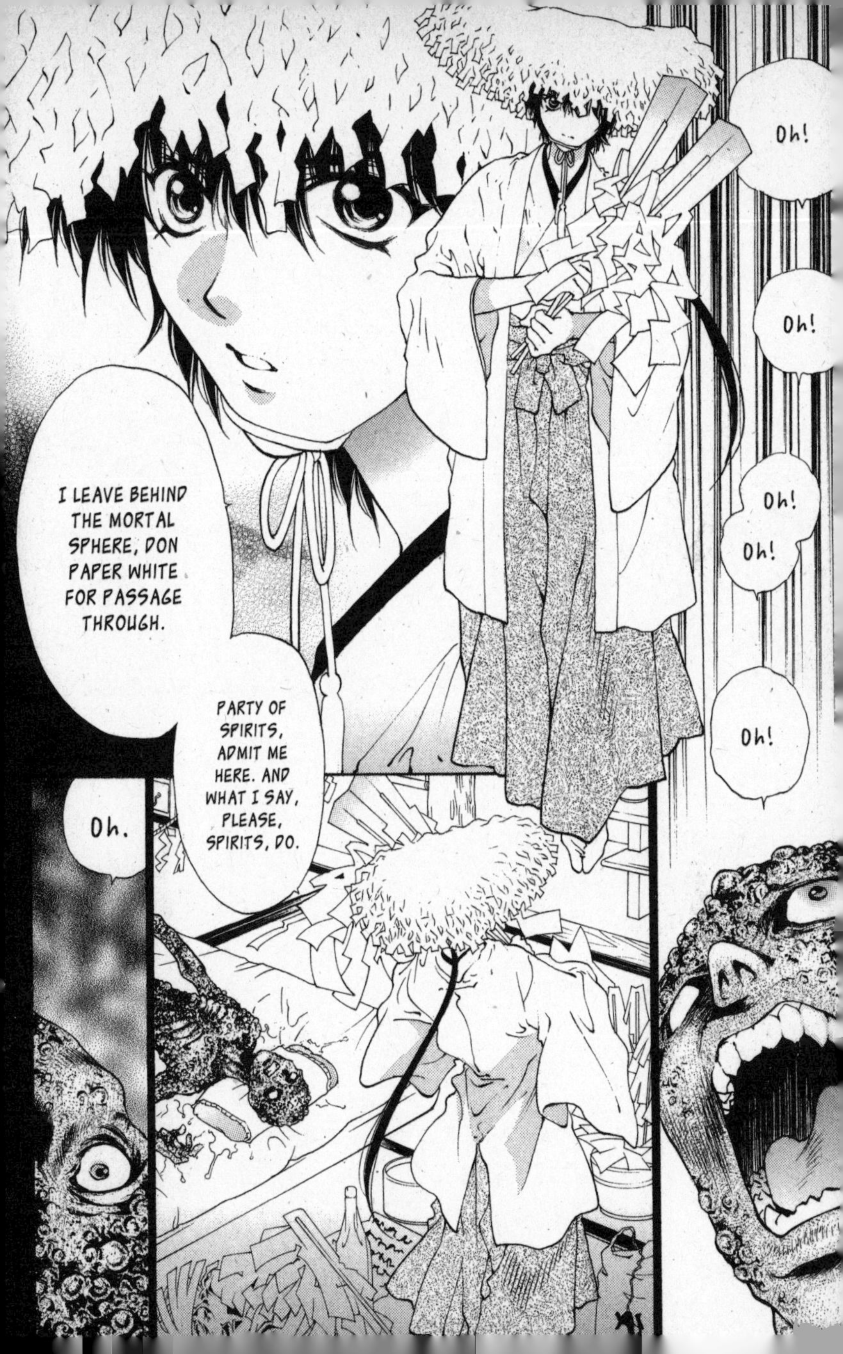
Oh!
Oh!
Oh!
Oh!
Oh!
I LEAVE BEHIND THE MORTAL SPHERE, DON PAPER WHITE FOR PASSAGE THROUGH.
PARTY OF SPIRITS, ADMIT ME HERE. AND WHAT I SAY, PLEASE, SPIRITS, DO.
Oh.

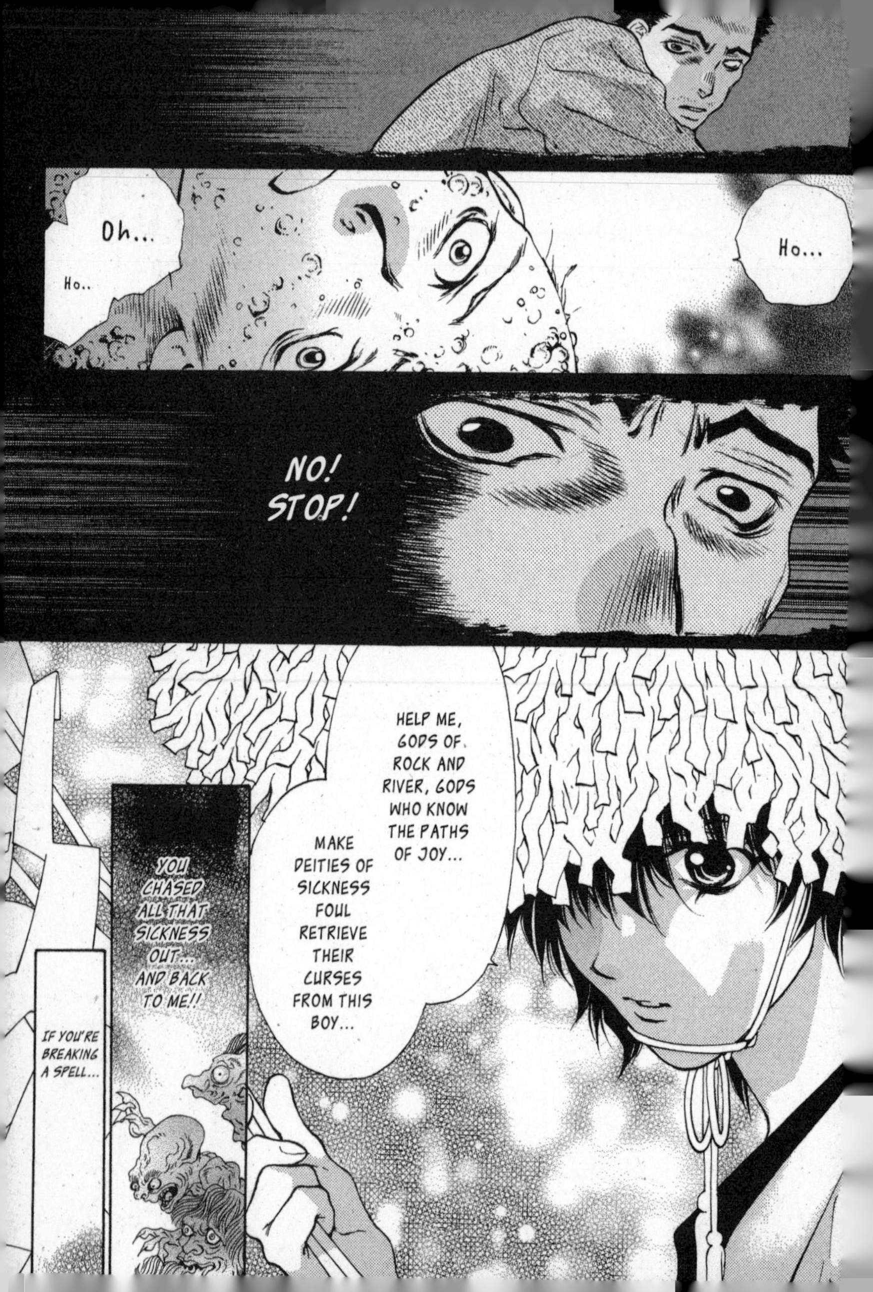
Ho...
Oh...
Ho..
NO! STOP!
HELP ME, GODS OF ROCK AND RIVER, GODS WHO KNOW THE PATHS OF JOY...
MAKE DEITIES OF SICKNESS FOUL RETRIEVE THEIR CURSES FROM THIS BOY...
YOU CHASED ALL THAT SICKNESS OUT... AND BACK TO ME!!
IF YOU'RE BREAKING A SPELL...

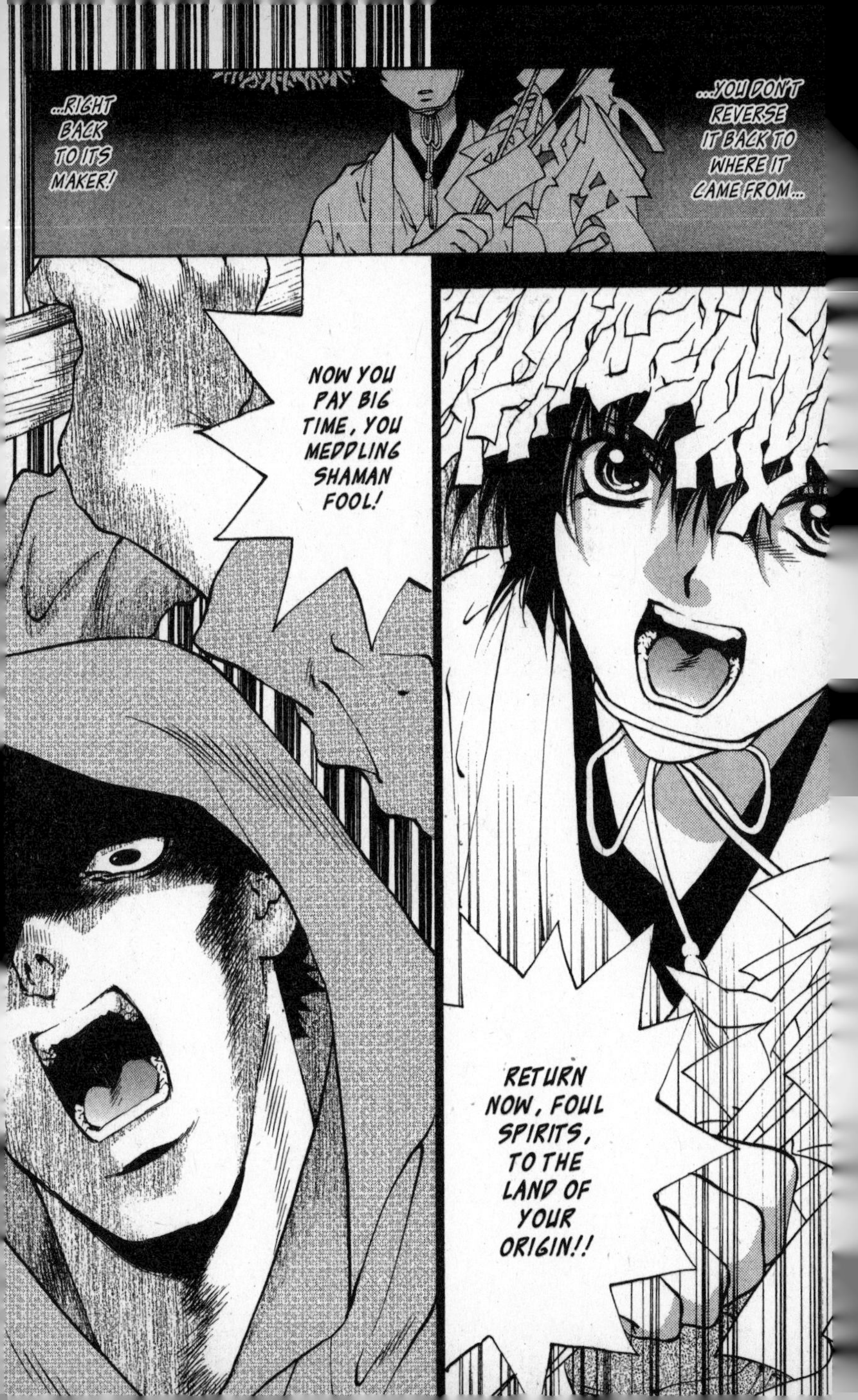
...YOU DON'T REVERSE IT BACK TO WHERE IT CAME FROM...
...RIGHT BACK TO ITS MAKER!
RETURN NOW, FOUL SPIRITS, TO THE LAND OF YOUR ORIGIN!!
NOW YOU PAY BIG TIME, YOU MEDDLING SHAMAN FOOL!

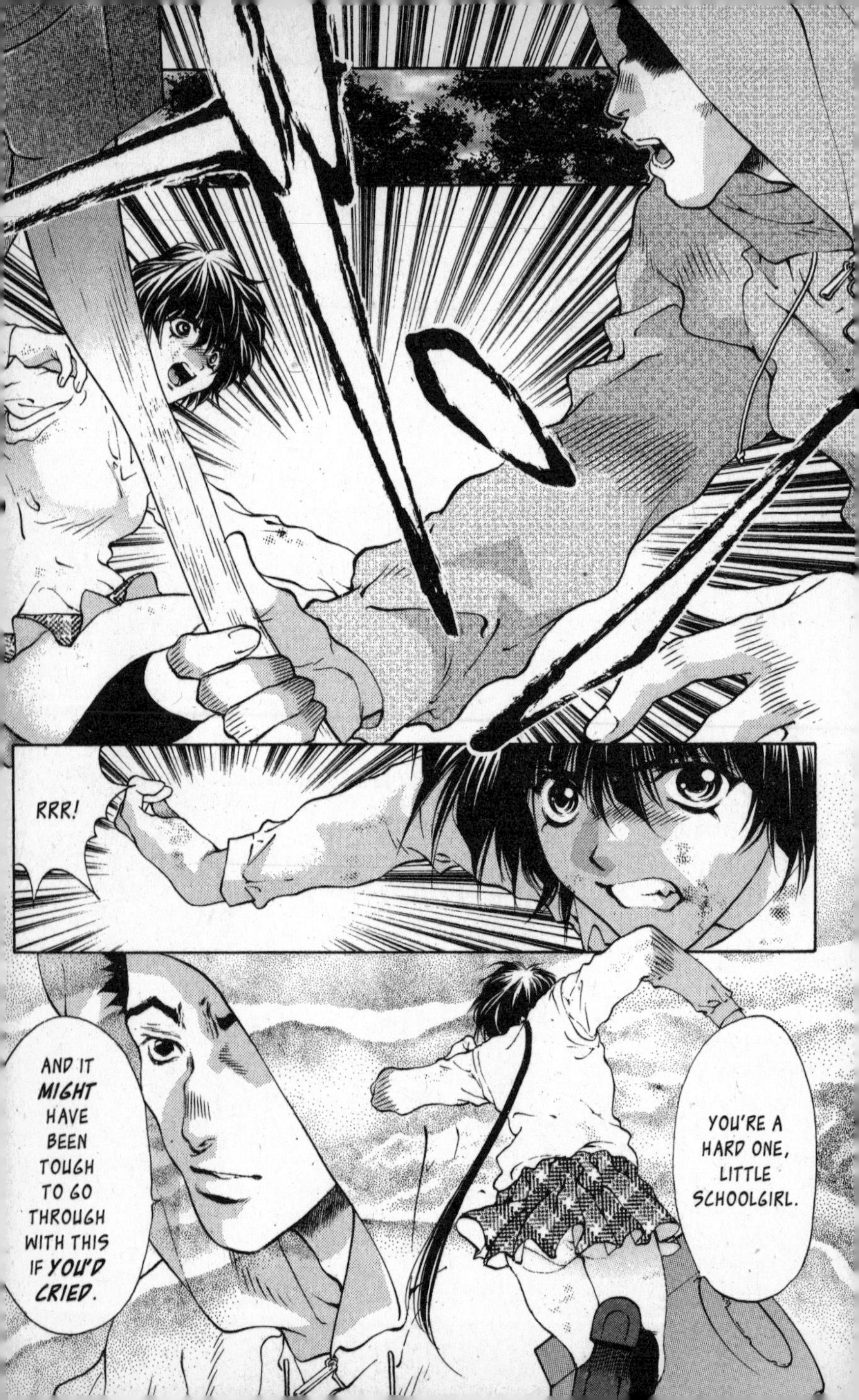
RRR!
YOU'RE A HARD ONE, LITTLE SCHOOLGIRL.
AND IT *MIGHT* HAVE BEEN TOUGH TO GO THROUGH WITH THIS IF *YOU'D CRIED*.

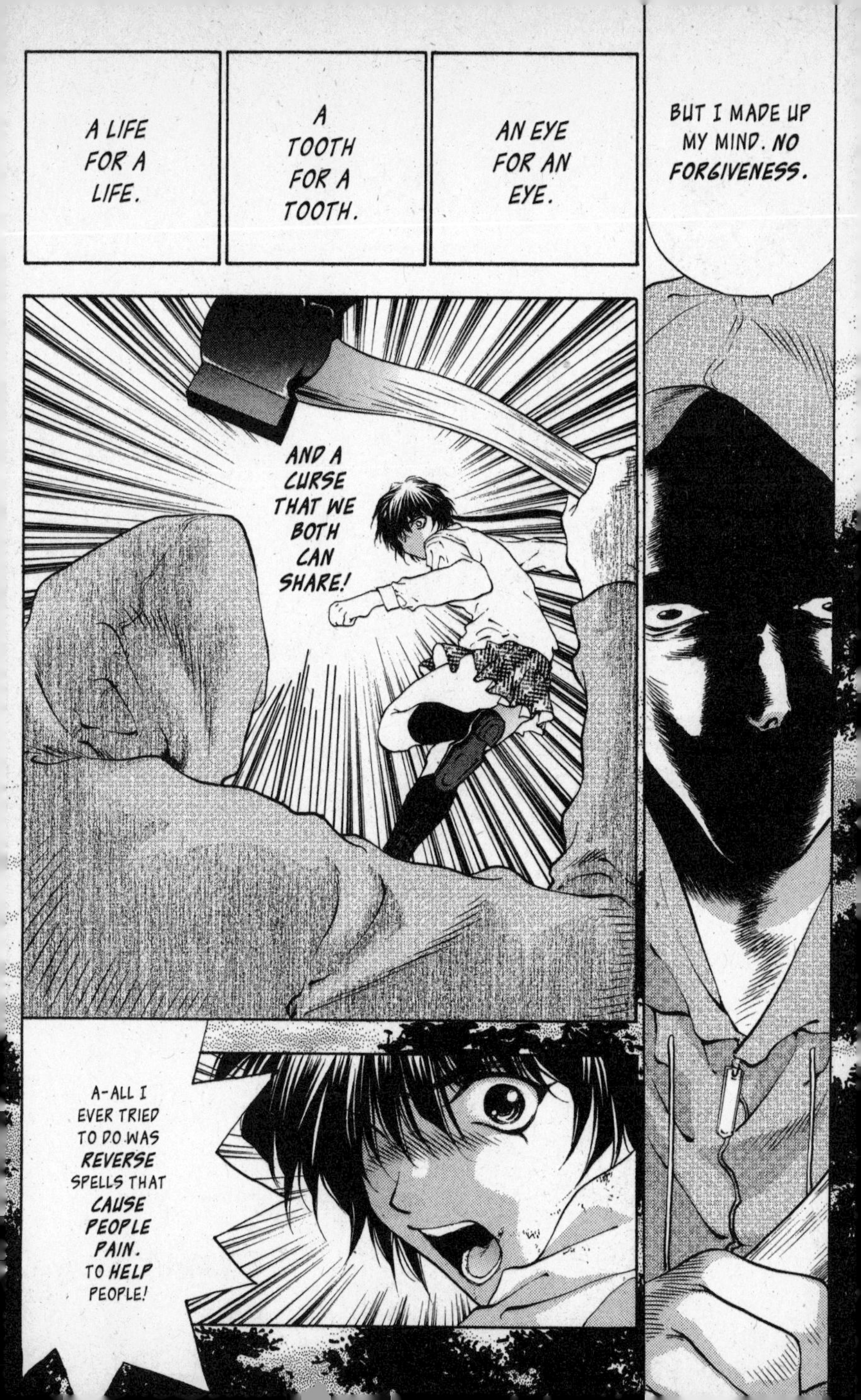

BUT I MADE UP MY MIND. NO FORGIVENESS.
AN EYE FOR AN EYE.
A TOOTH FOR A TOOTH.
A LIFE FOR A LIFE.
AND A CURSE THAT WE BOTH CAN SHARE!
A-ALL I EVER TRIED TO DO WAS REVERSE SPELLS THAT CAUSE PEOPLE PAIN. TO HELP PEOPLE!

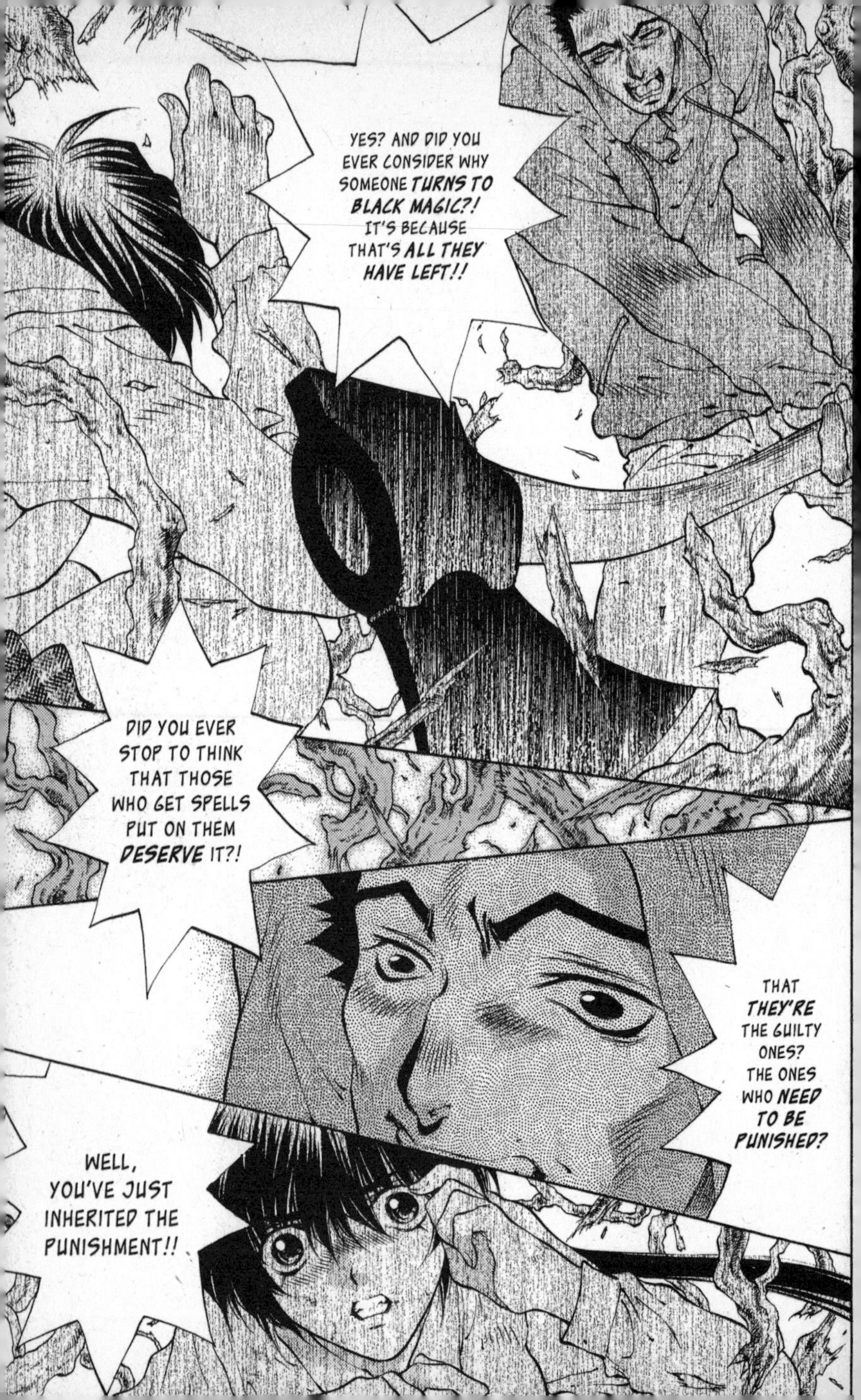
YES? AND DID YOU EVER CONSIDER WHY SOMEONE TURNS TO BLACK MAGIC?! IT'S BECAUSE THAT'S ALL THEY HAVE LEFT!!
DID YOU EVER STOP TO THINK THAT THOSE WHO GET SPELLS PUT ON THEM DESERVE IT?!
THAT THEY'RE THE GUILTY ONES? THE ONES WHO NEED TO BE PUNISHED?
WELL, YOU'VE JUST INHERITED THE PUNISHMENT!!

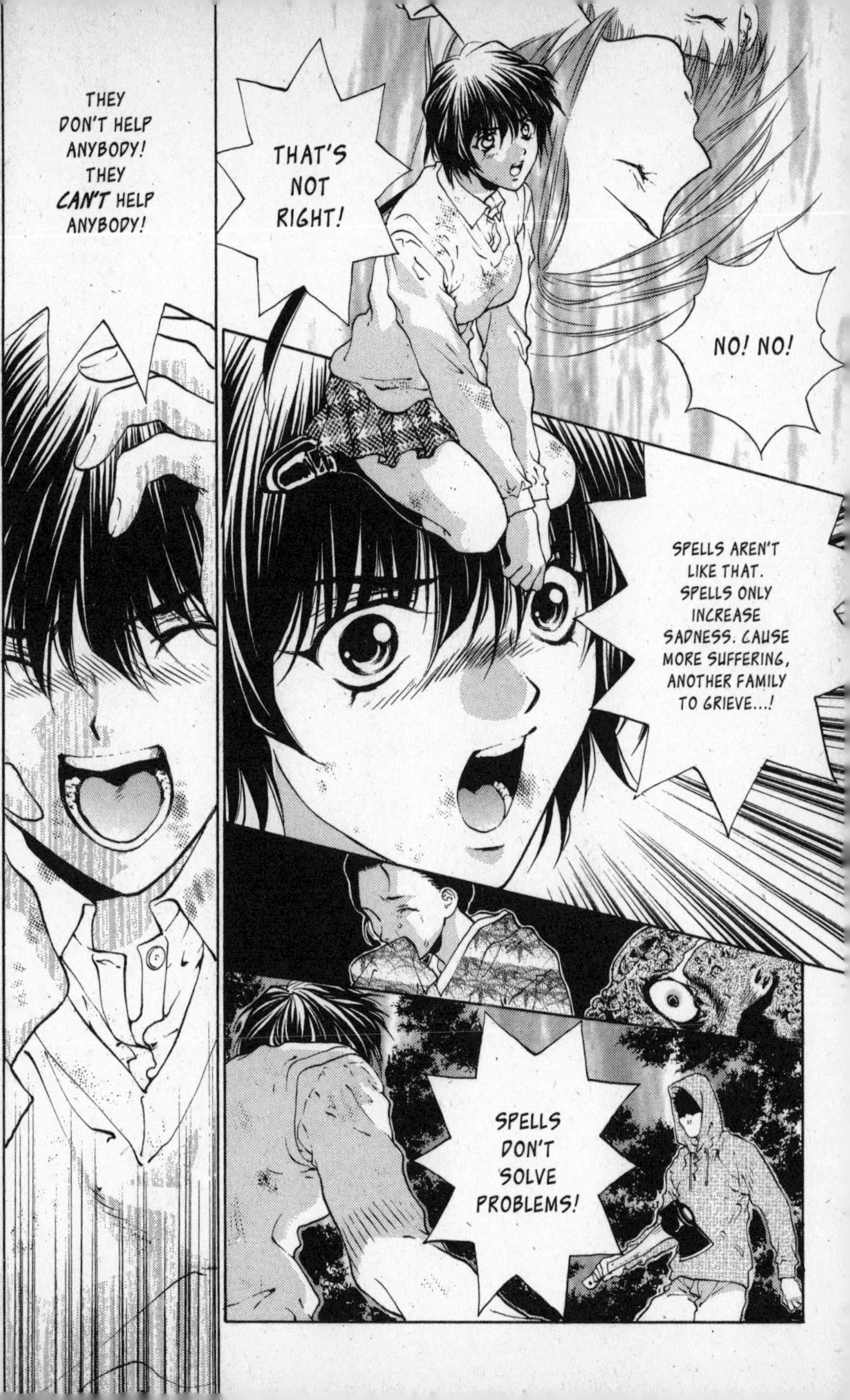

NO! NO!
THAT'S NOT RIGHT!
SPELLS AREN'T LIKE THAT. SPELLS ONLY INCREASE SADNESS. CAUSE MORE SUFFERING, ANOTHER FAMILY TO GRIEVE...!
SPELLS DON'T SOLVE PROBLEMS!
THEY DON'T HELP ANYBODY! THEY *CAN'T* HELP ANYBODY!

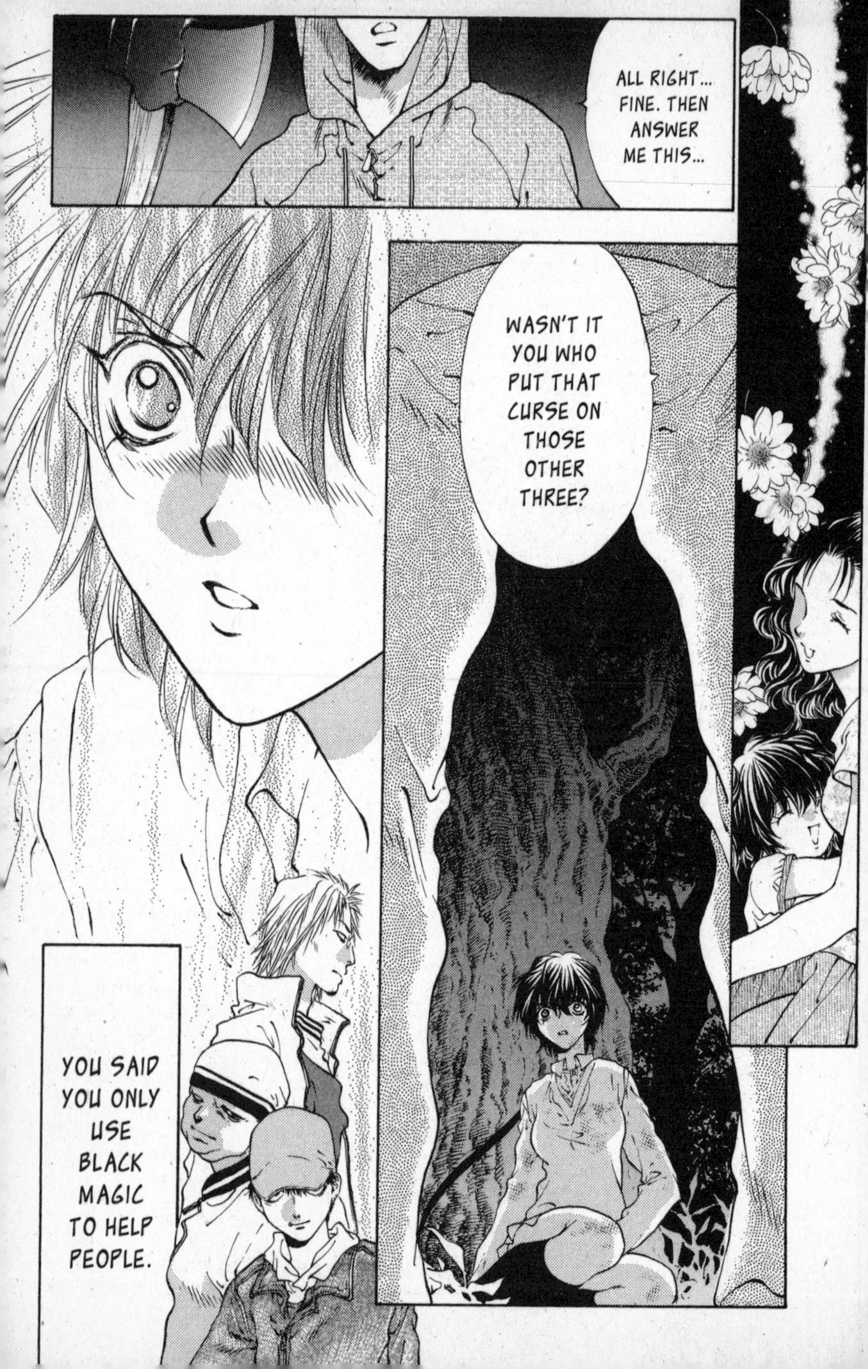
ALL RIGHT... FINE. THEN ANSWER ME THIS...
WASN'T IT YOU WHO PUT THAT CURSE ON THOSE OTHER THREE?
YOU SAID YOU ONLY USE BLACK MAGIC TO HELP PEOPLE.

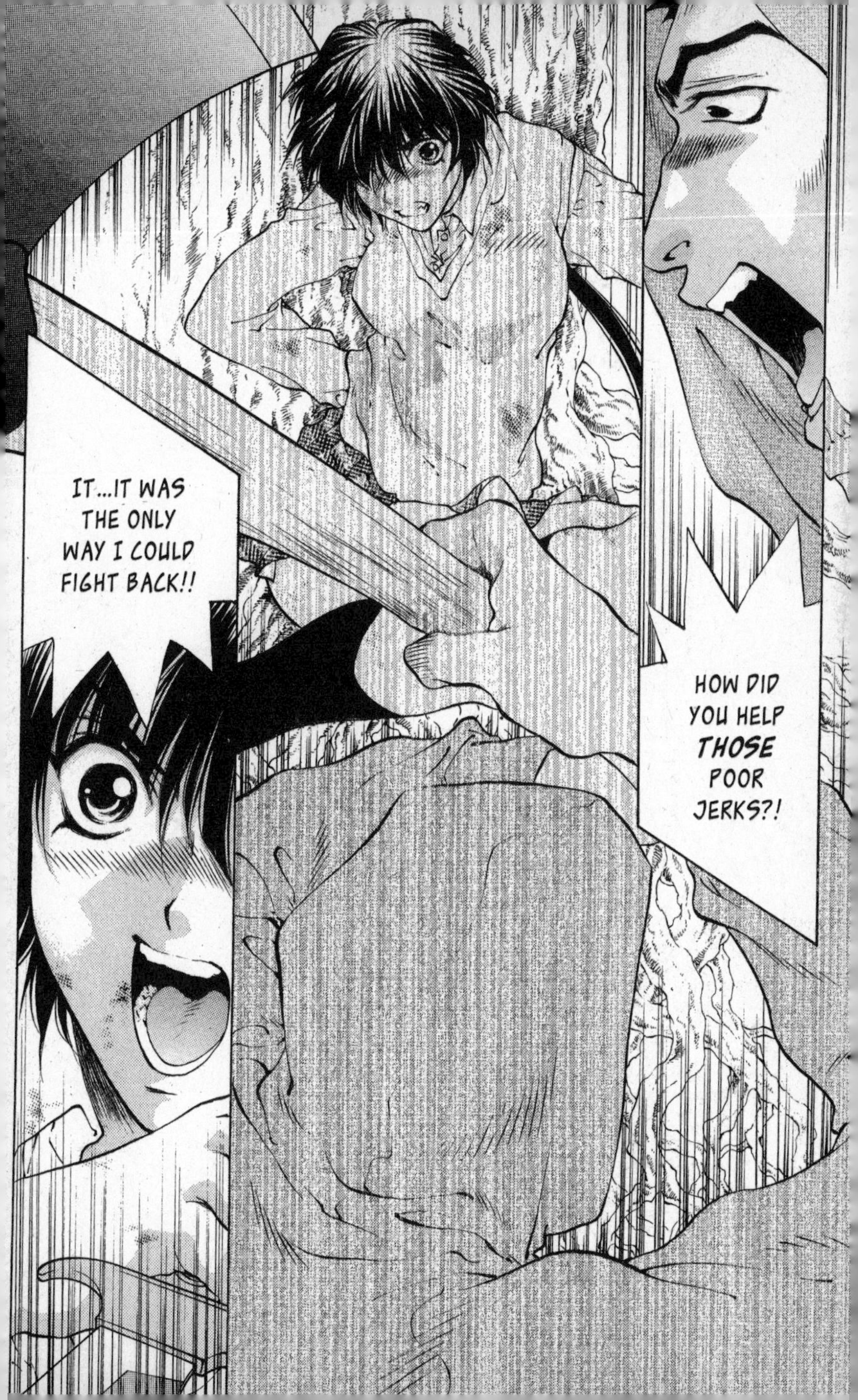
HOW DID YOU HELP **THOSE** POOR JERKS?!
IT...IT WAS THE ONLY WAY I COULD FIGHT BACK!!

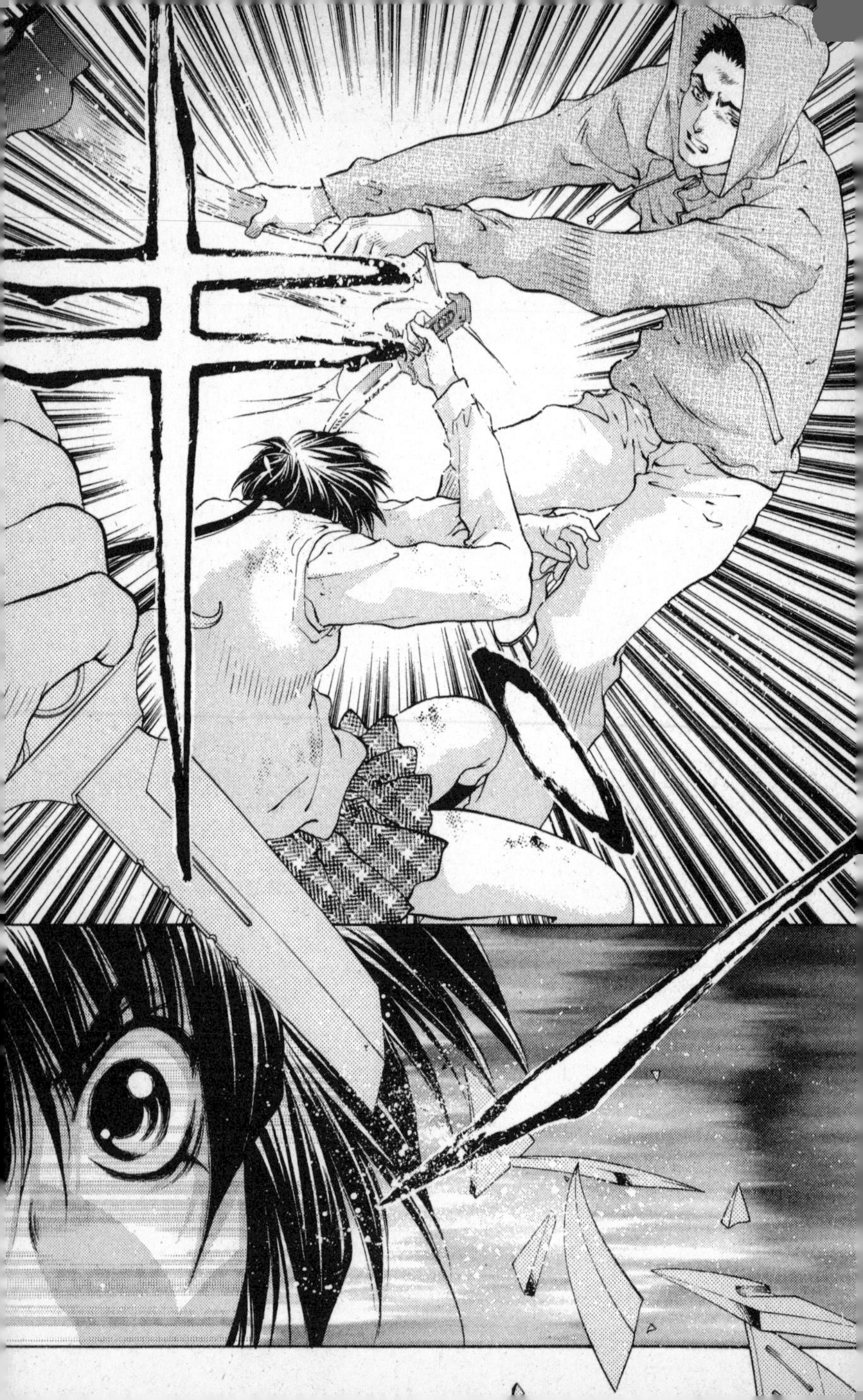

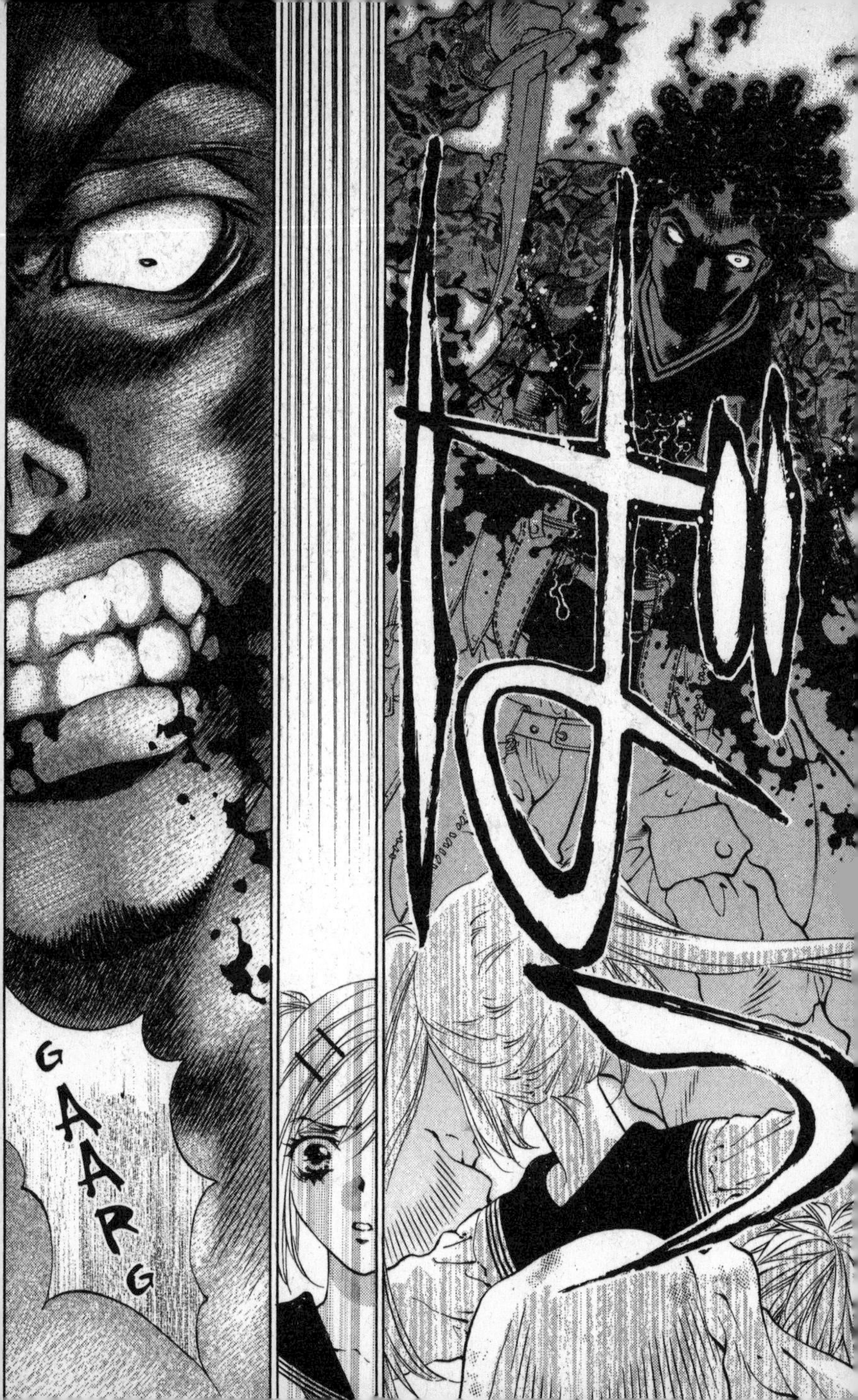
GAARG

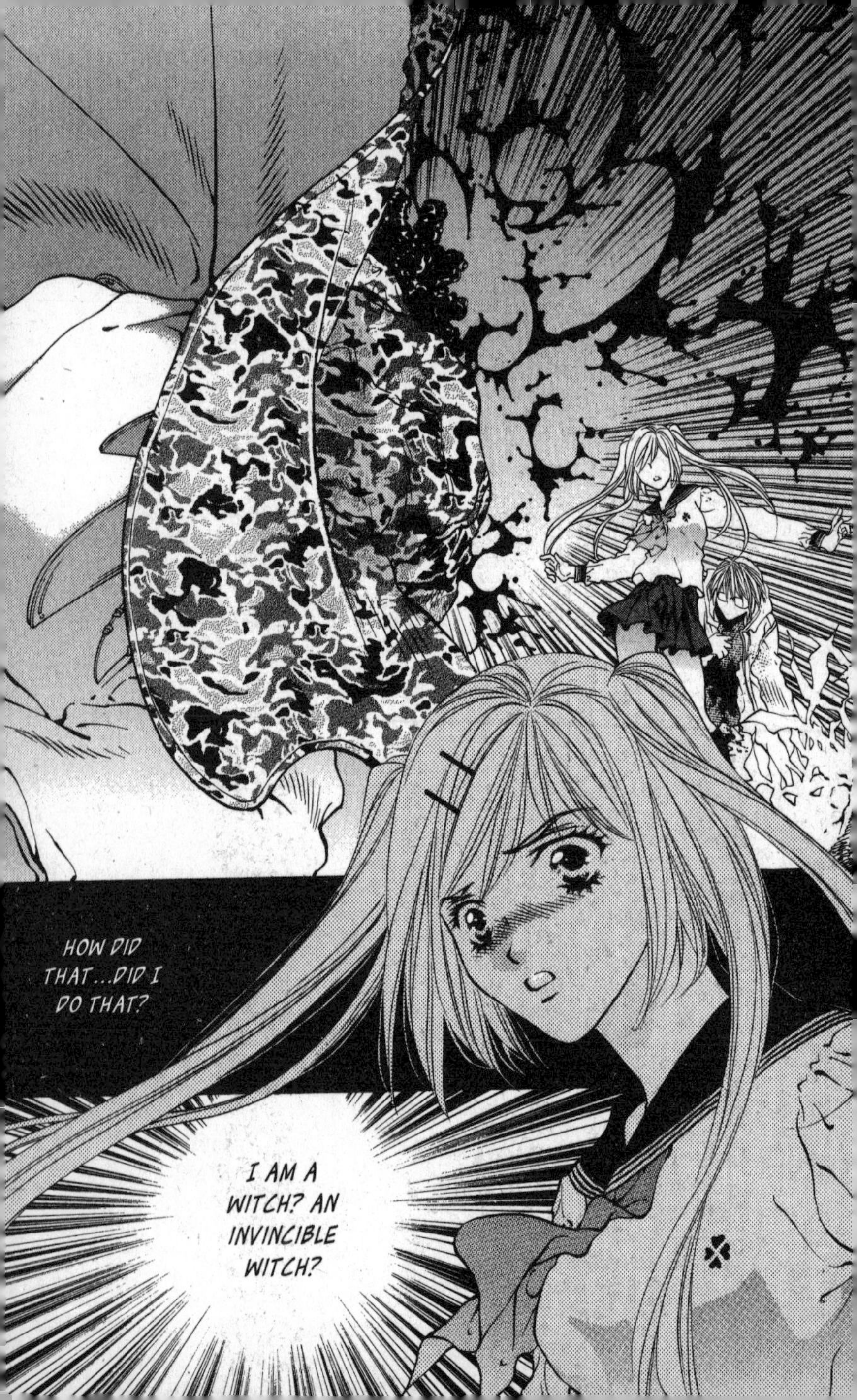
HOW DID THAT...DID I DO THAT?
I AM A WITCH? AN INVINCIBLE WITCH?

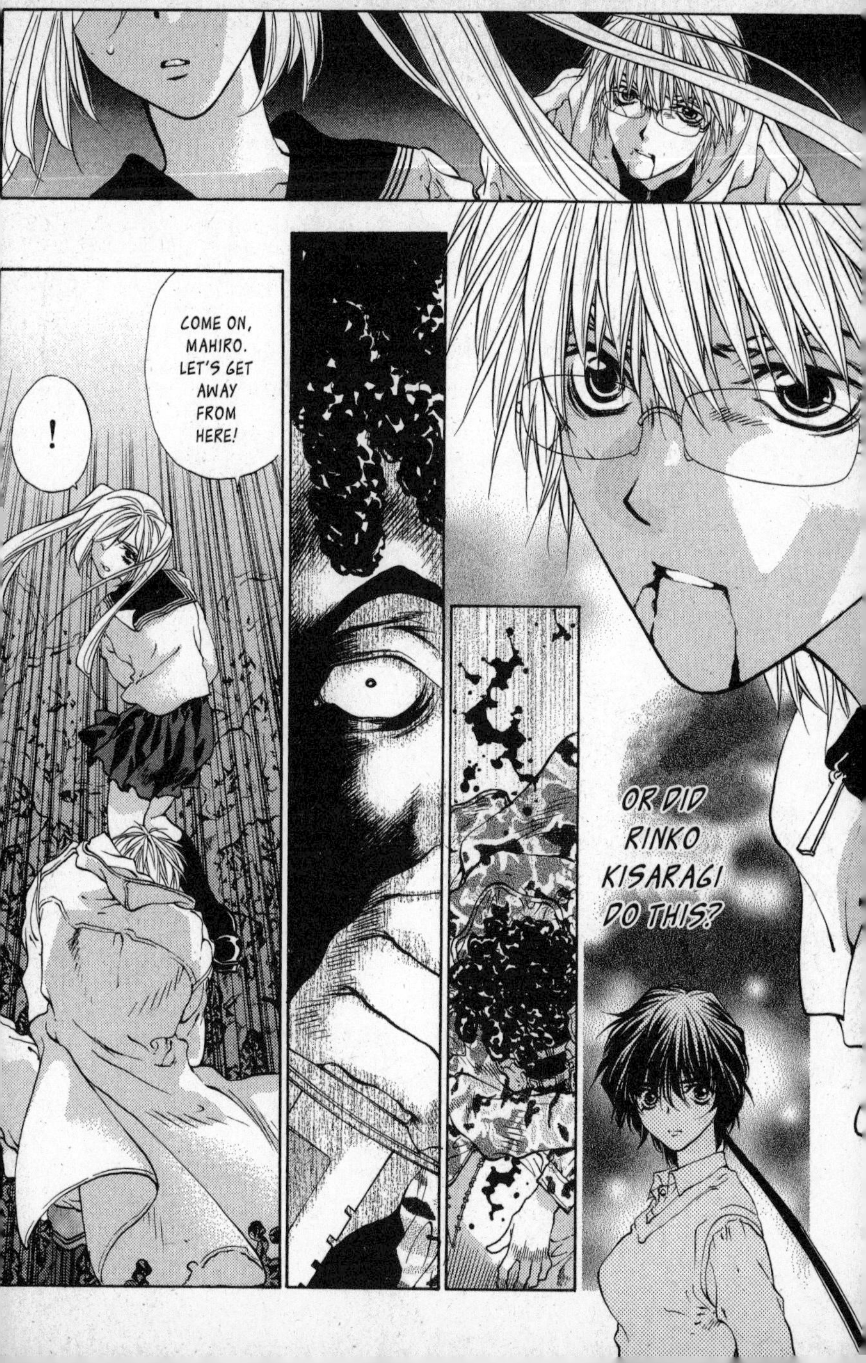
OR DID RINKO KISARAGI DO THIS?
COME ON, MAHIRO. LET'S GET AWAY FROM HERE!
!

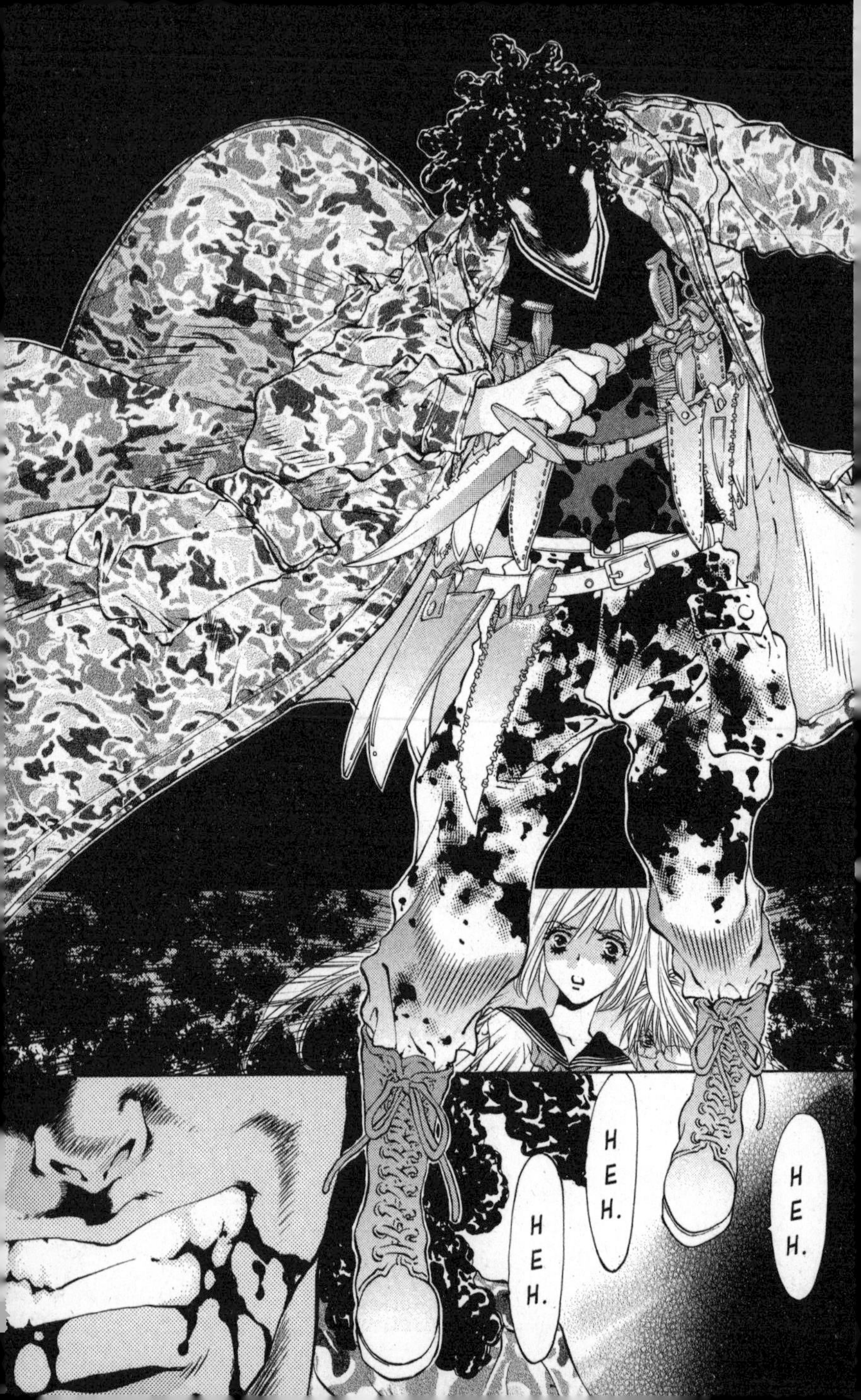
HEH.
HEH.
HEH.

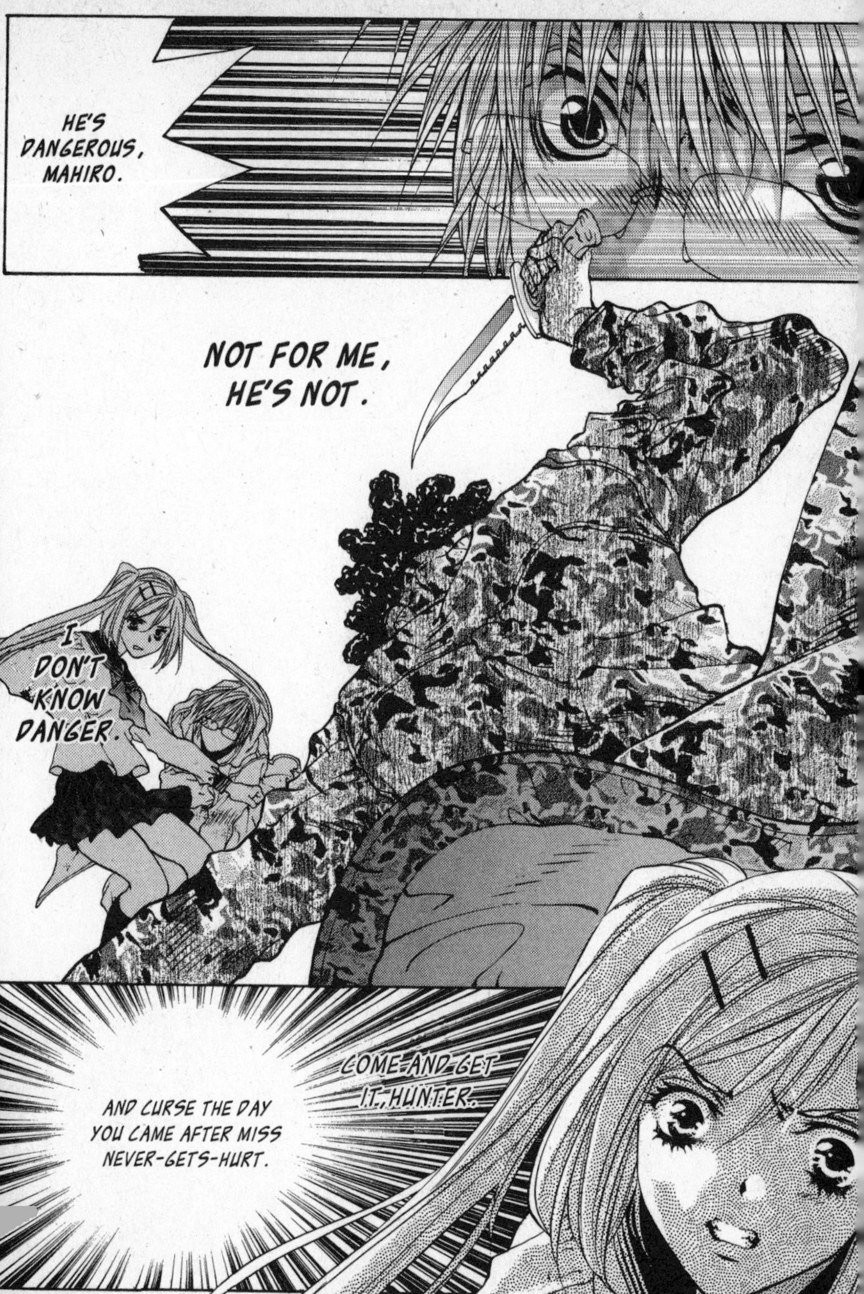
HE'S DANGEROUS, MAHIRO.
NOT FOR ME, HE'S NOT.
I DON'T KNOW DANGER.
COME AND GET IT, HUNTER.
AND CURSE THE DAY YOU CAME AFTER MISS NEVER-GETS-HURT.

第13話／完

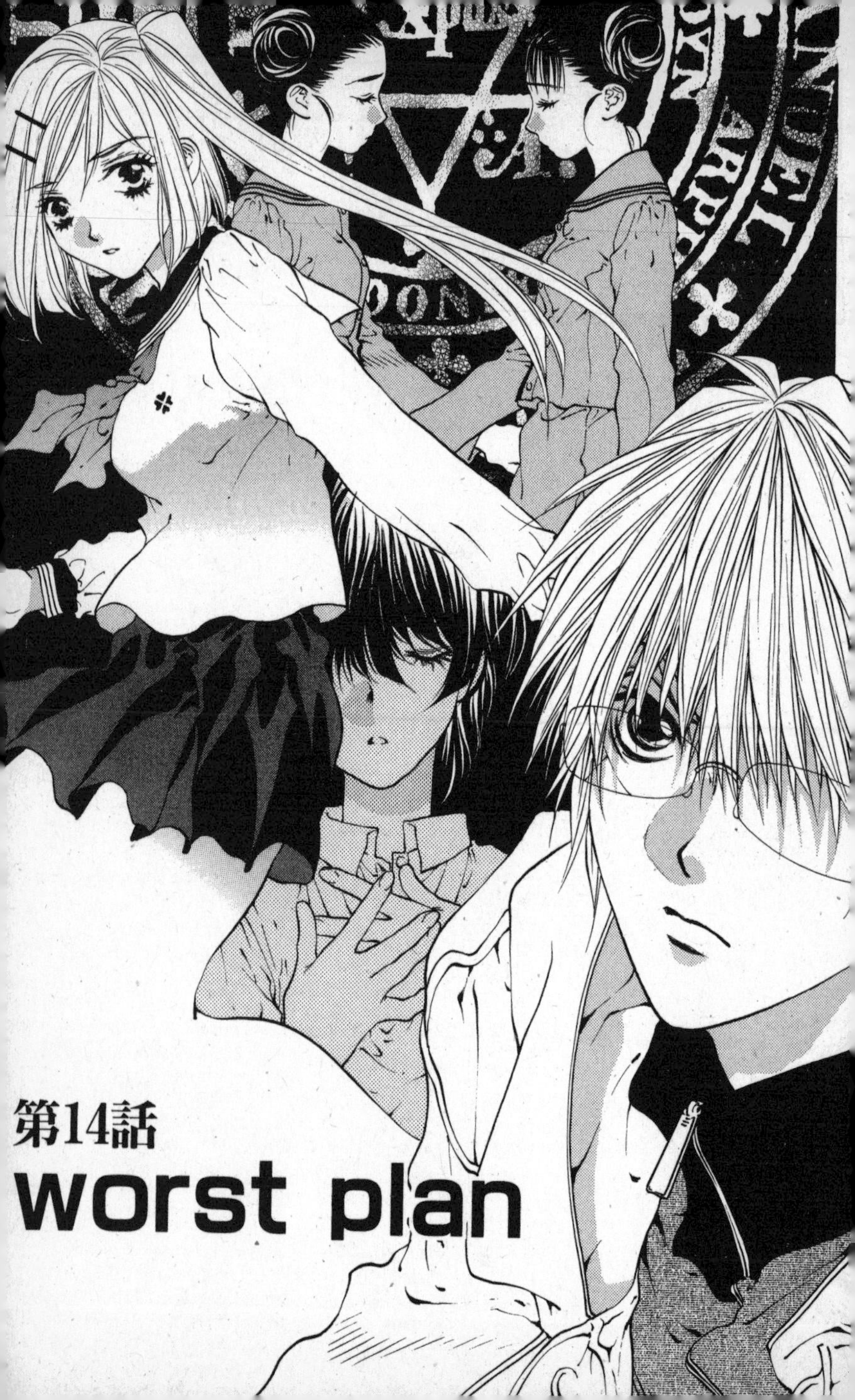

第14話
worst plan

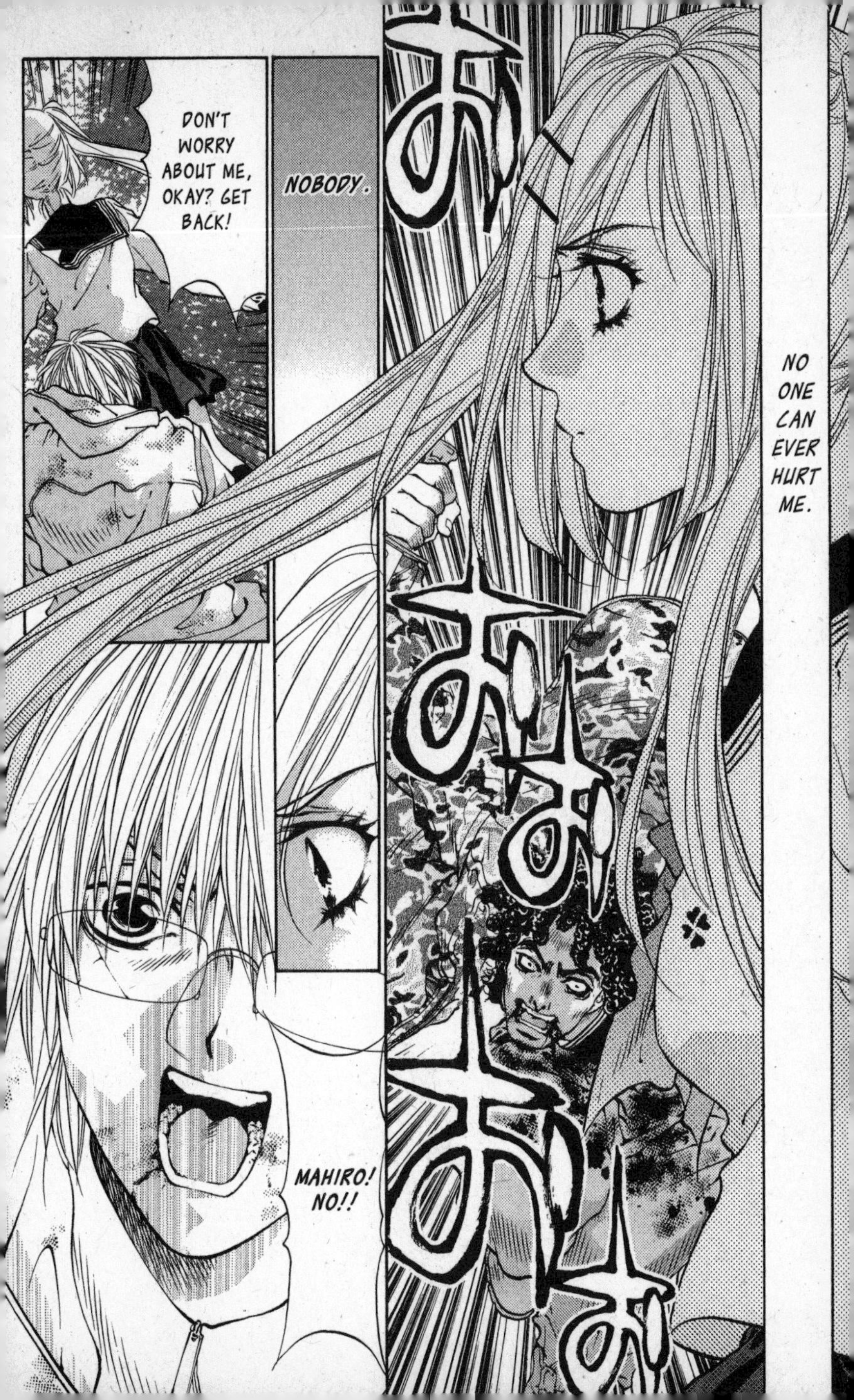
NO ONE CAN EVER HURT ME.
NOBODY.
DON'T WORRY ABOUT ME, OKAY? GET BACK!
MAHIRO! NO!!

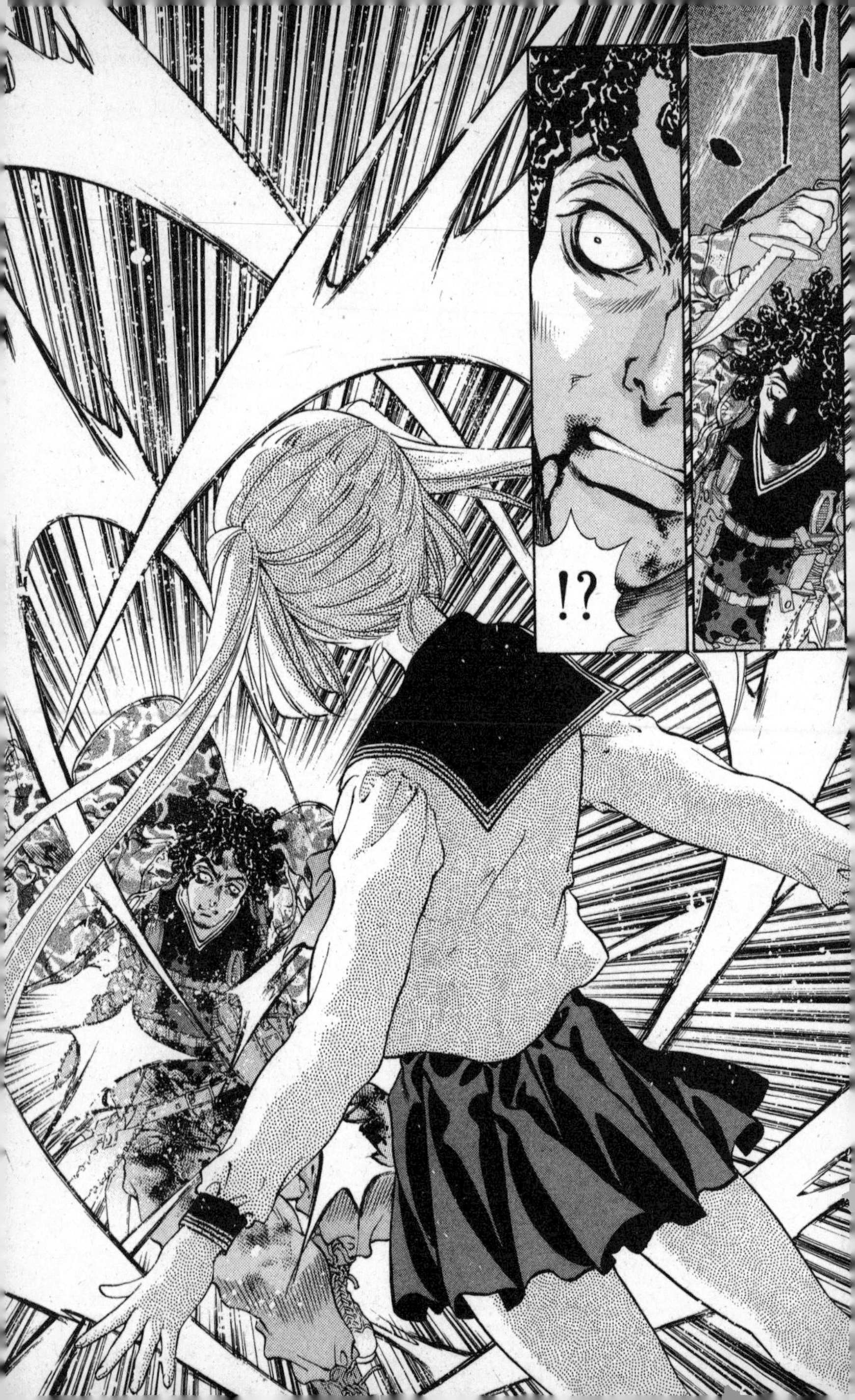
!?

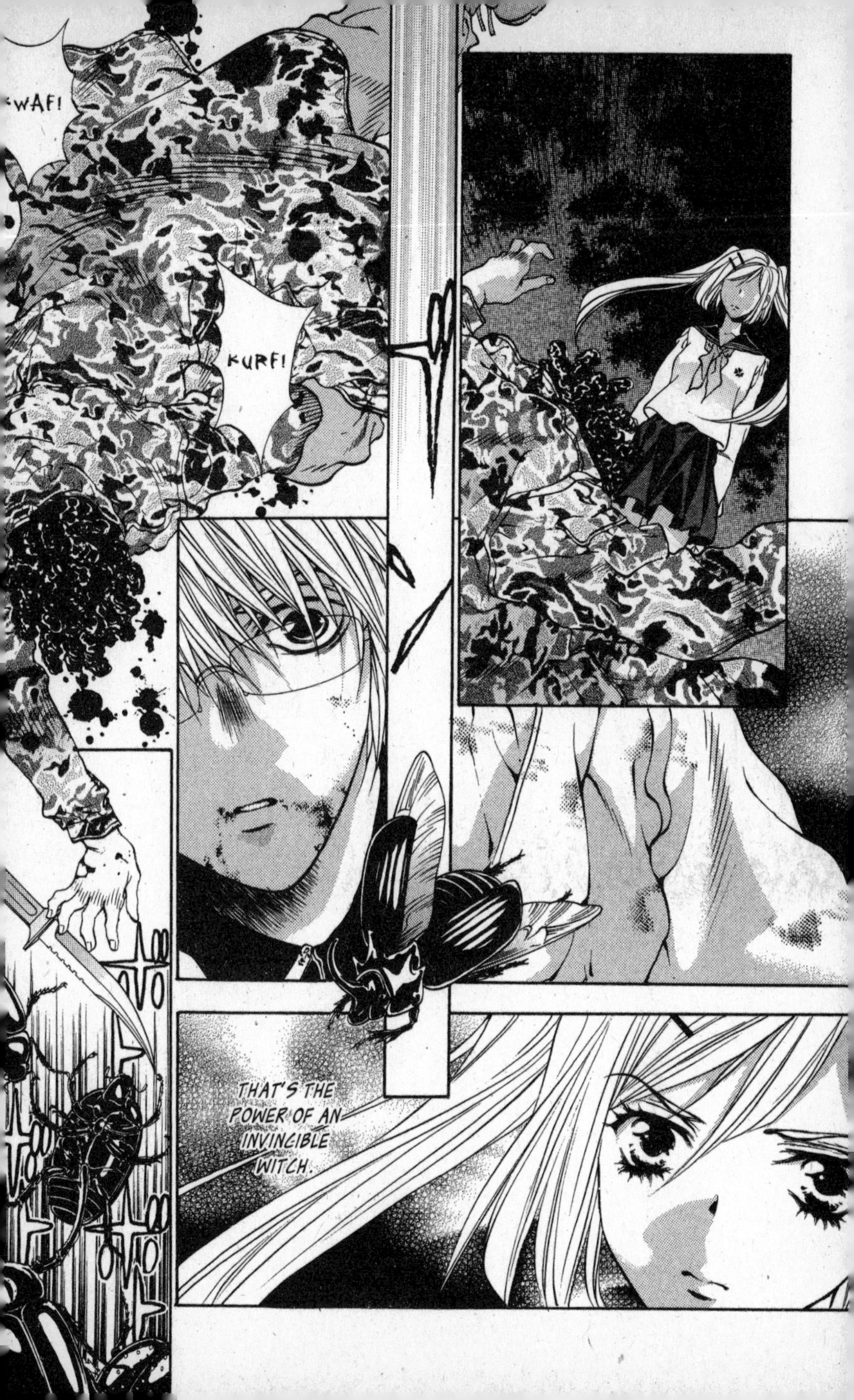
SWAF!
KURF!
THAT'S THE POWER OF AN INVINCIBLE WITCH.

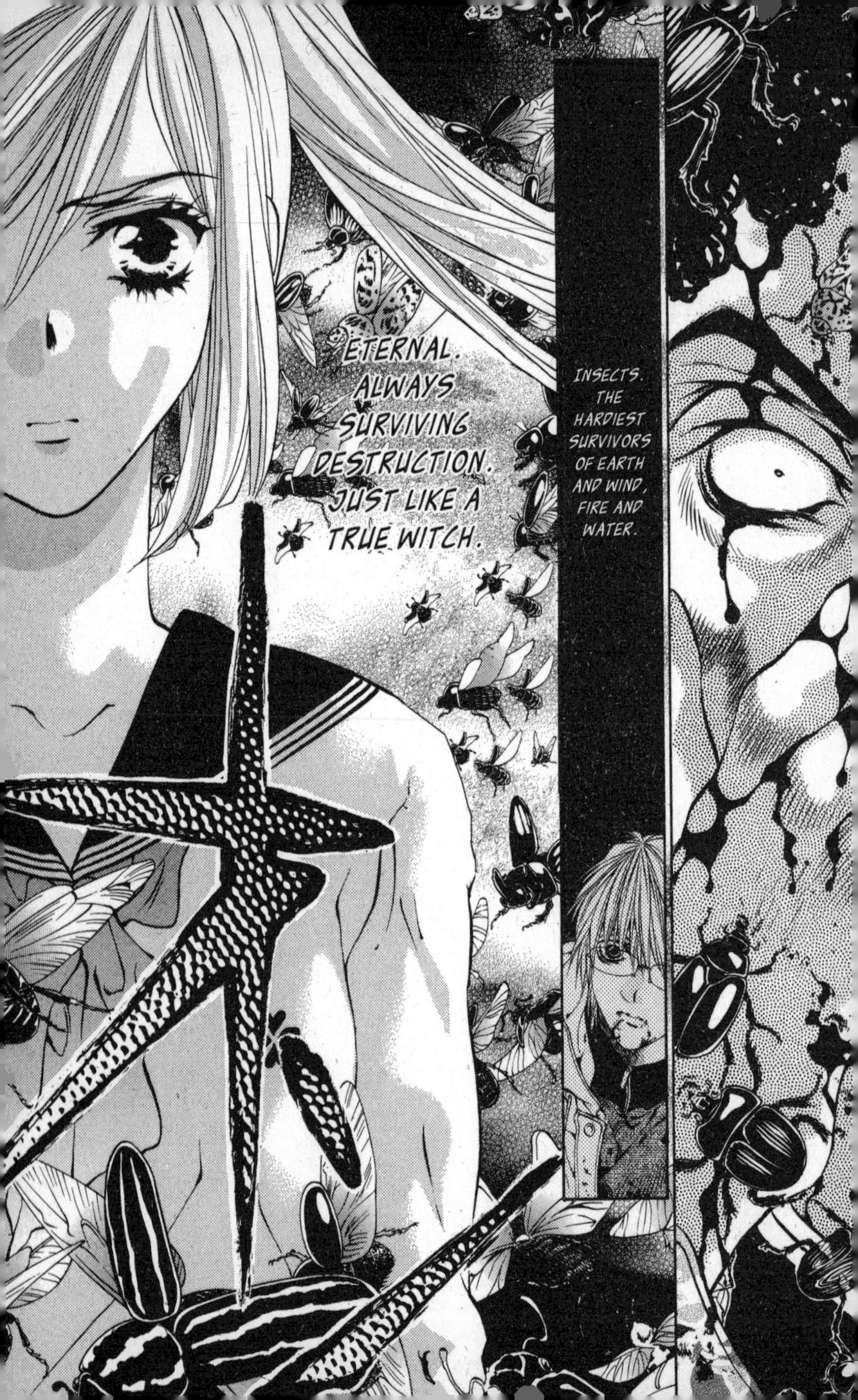
INSECTS. THE HARDIEST SURVIVORS OF EARTH AND WIND, FIRE AND WATER.
ETERNAL. ALWAYS SURVIVING DESTRUCTION. JUST LIKE A TRUE WITCH.

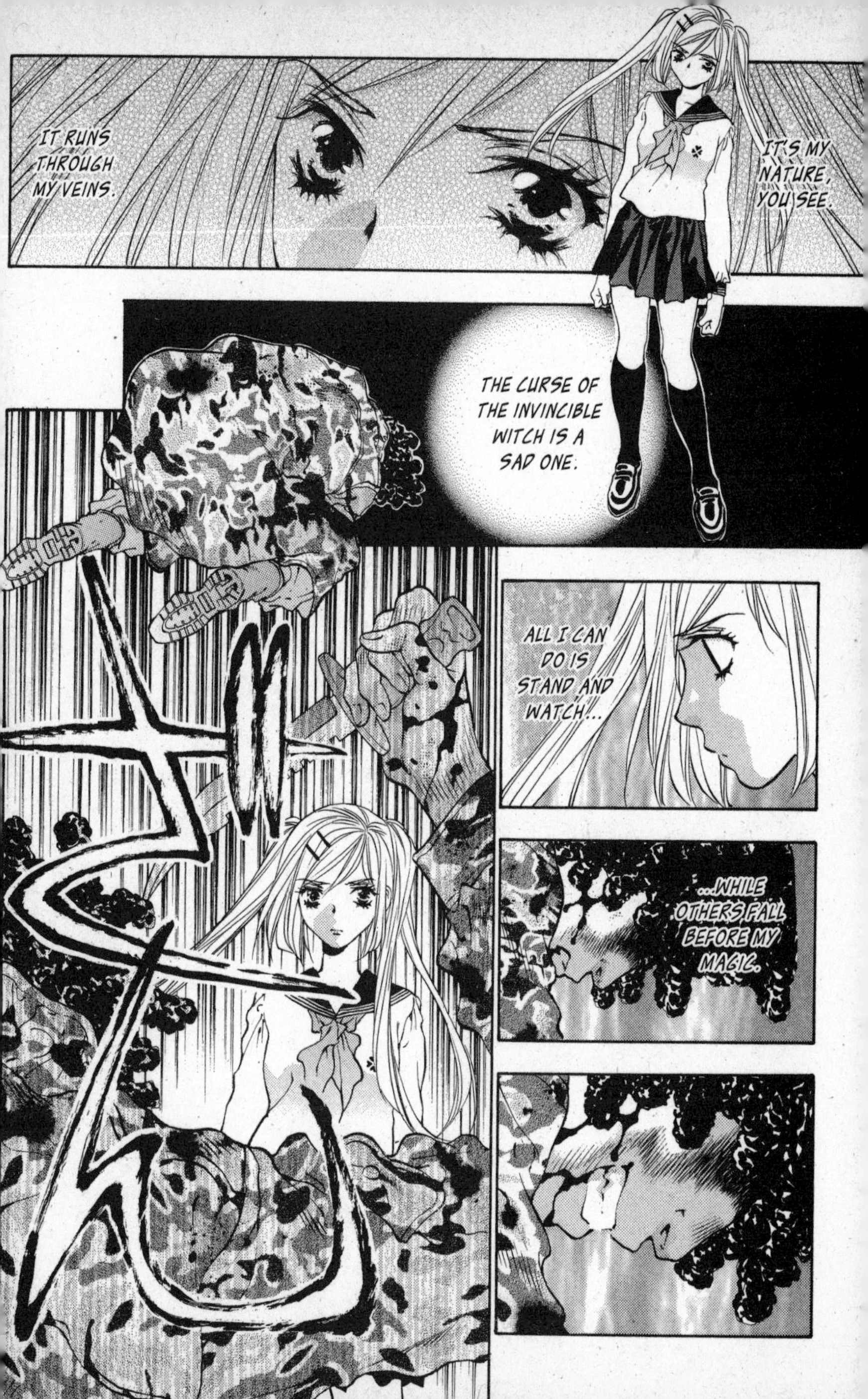
IT'S MY NATURE, YOU SEE.
IT RUNS THROUGH MY VEINS.
THE CURSE OF THE INVINCIBLE WITCH IS A SAD ONE.
ALL I CAN DO IS STAND AND WATCH...
...WHILE OTHERS FALL BEFORE MY MAGIC.

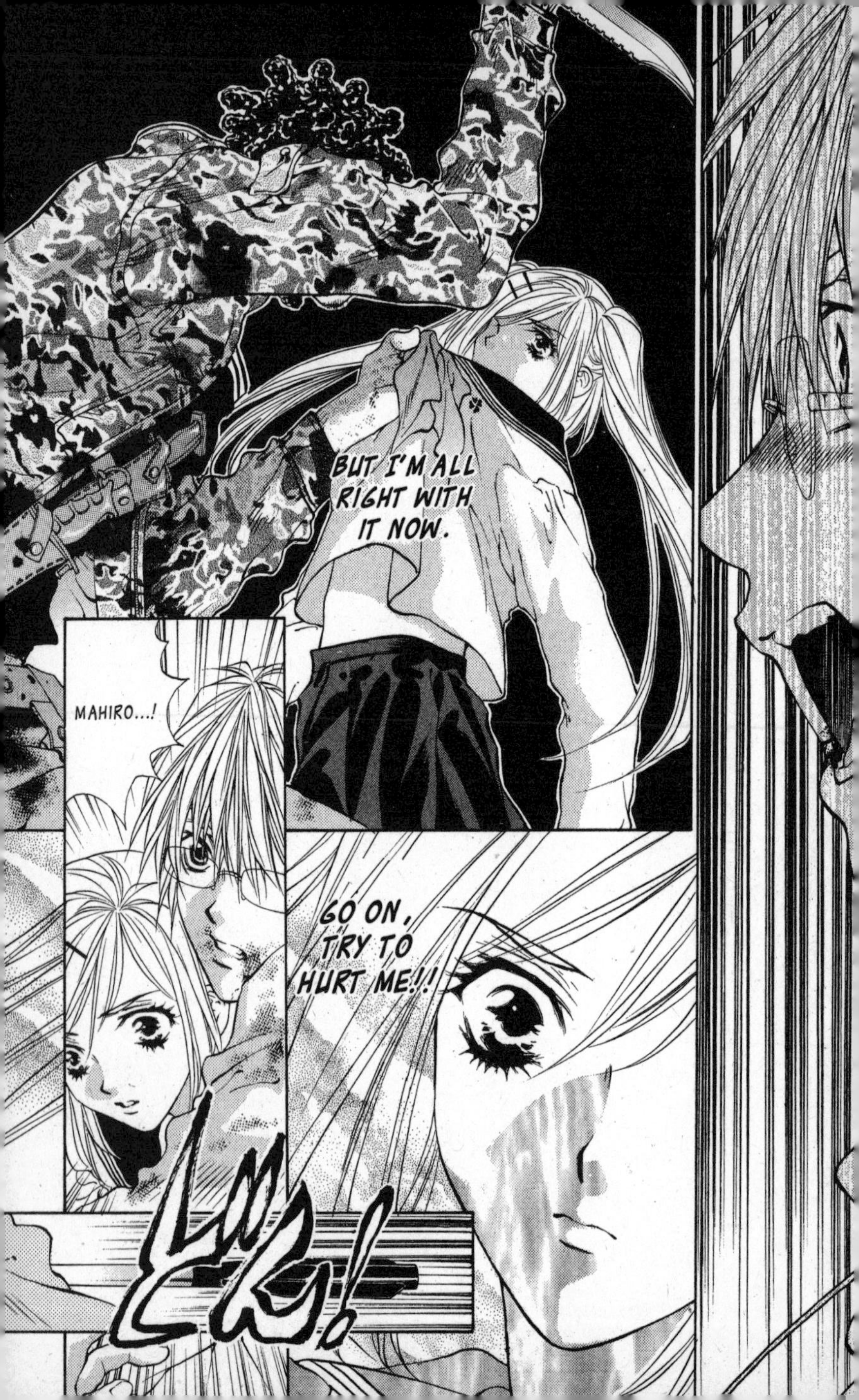
BUT I'M ALL RIGHT WITH IT NOW.
GO ON, TRY TO HURT ME!!
MAHIRO...!

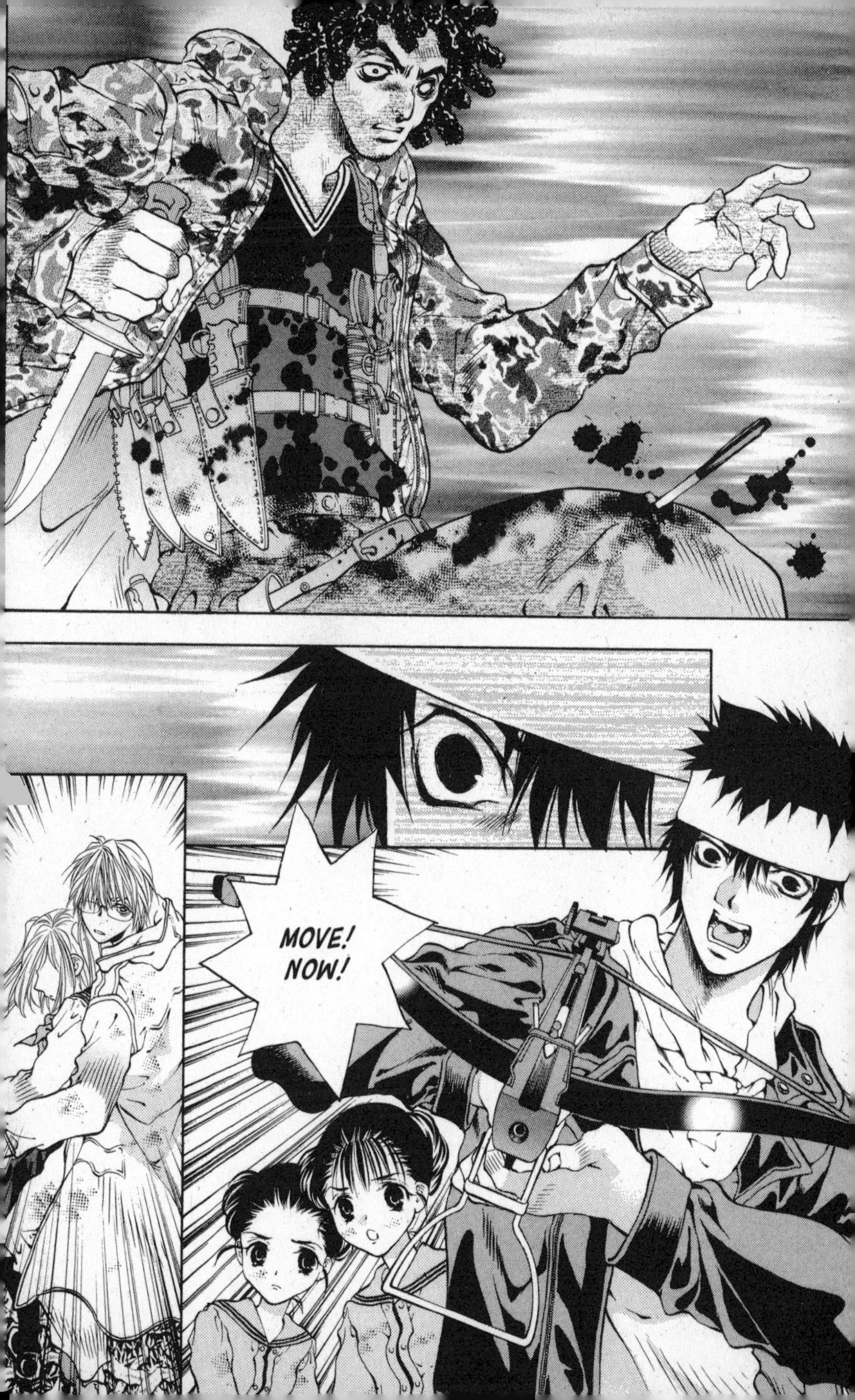
MOVE!
NOW!

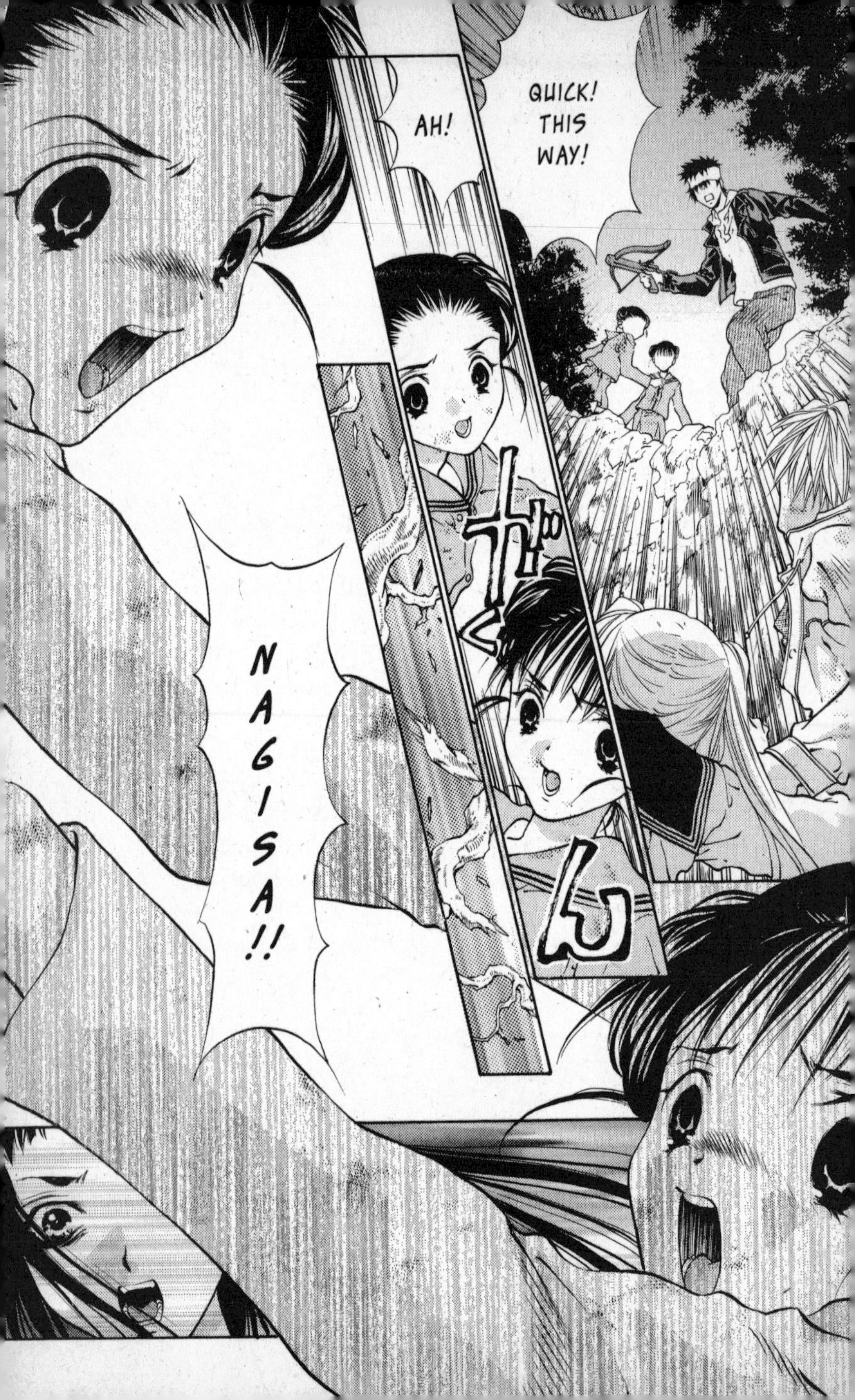
QUICK! THIS WAY!
AH!
NAGISA!!

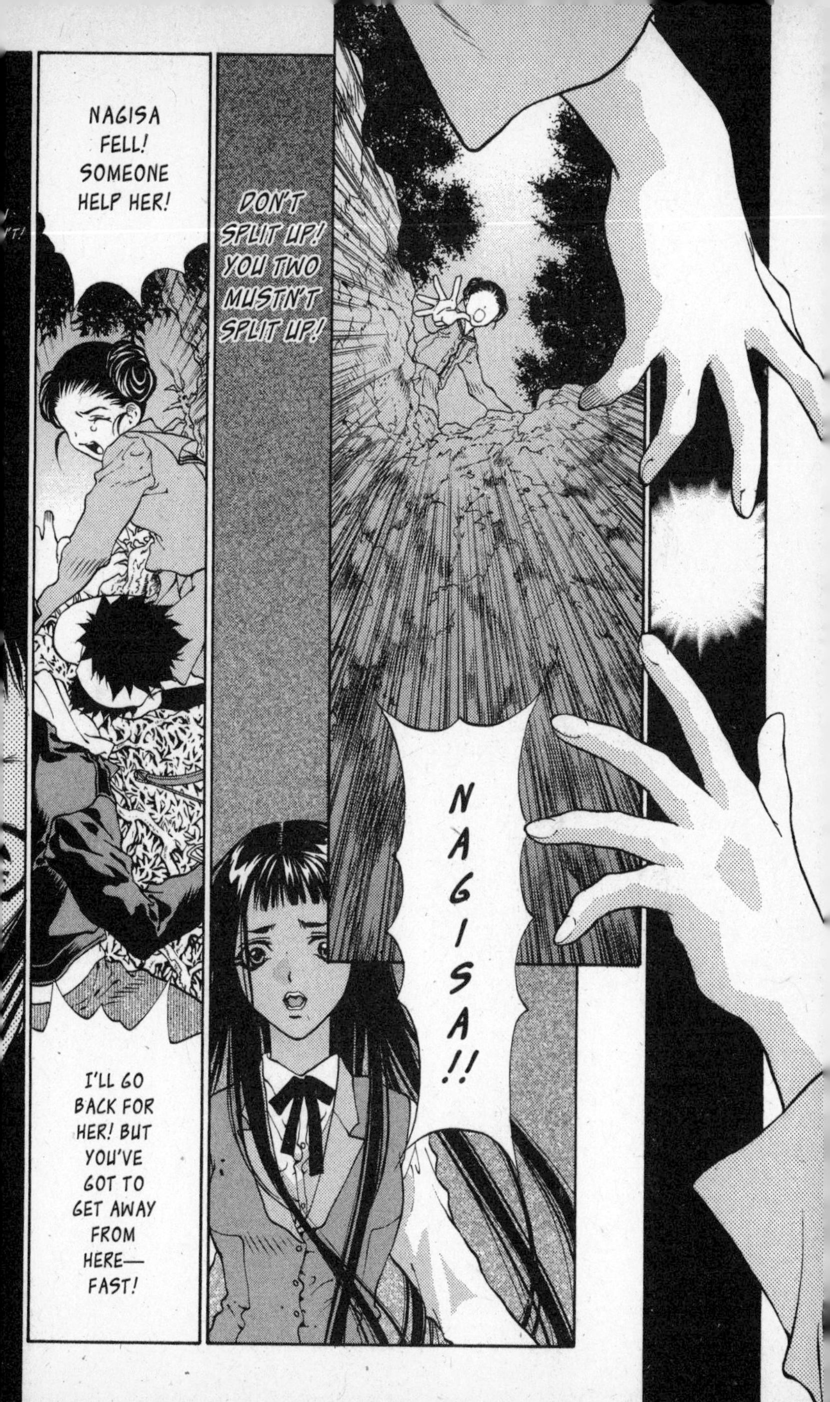
NAGISA!!
DON'T SPLIT UP! YOU TWO MUSTN'T SPLIT UP!
NAGISA FELL! SOMEONE HELP HER!
I'LL GO BACK FOR HER! BUT YOU'VE GOT TO GET AWAY FROM HERE—FAST!

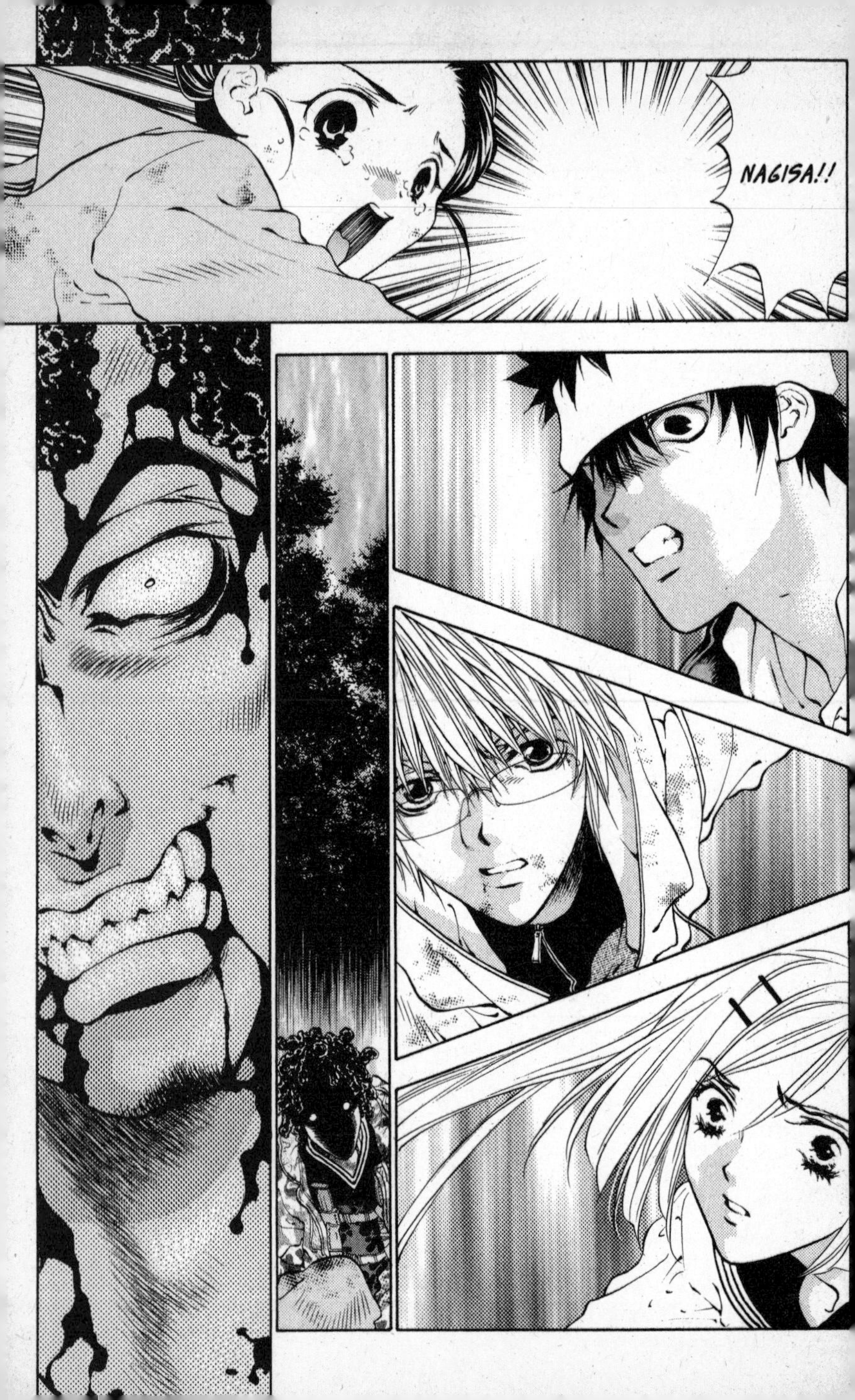
NAGISA!!

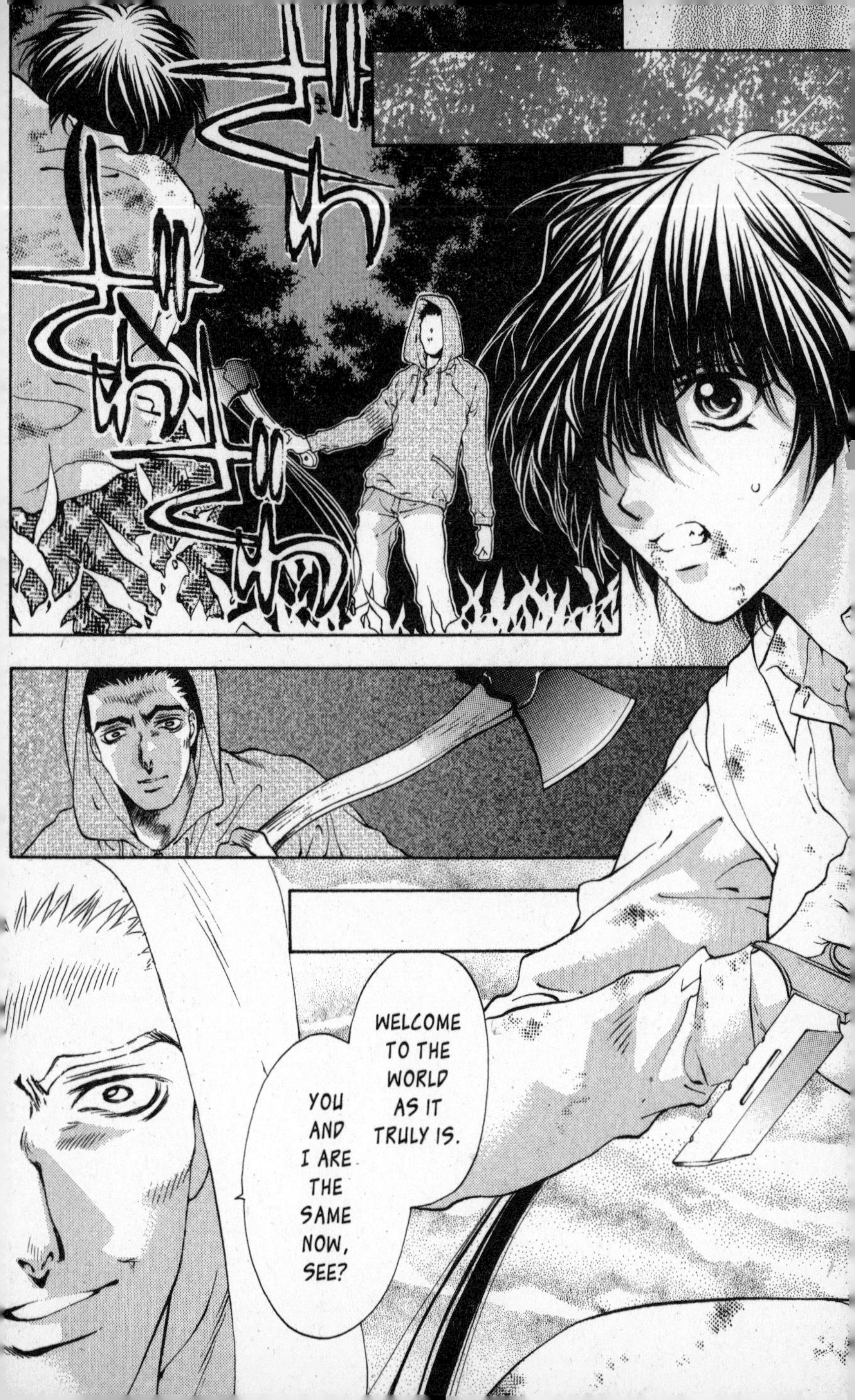
WELCOME TO THE WORLD AS IT TRULY IS.
YOU AND I ARE THE SAME NOW, SEE?

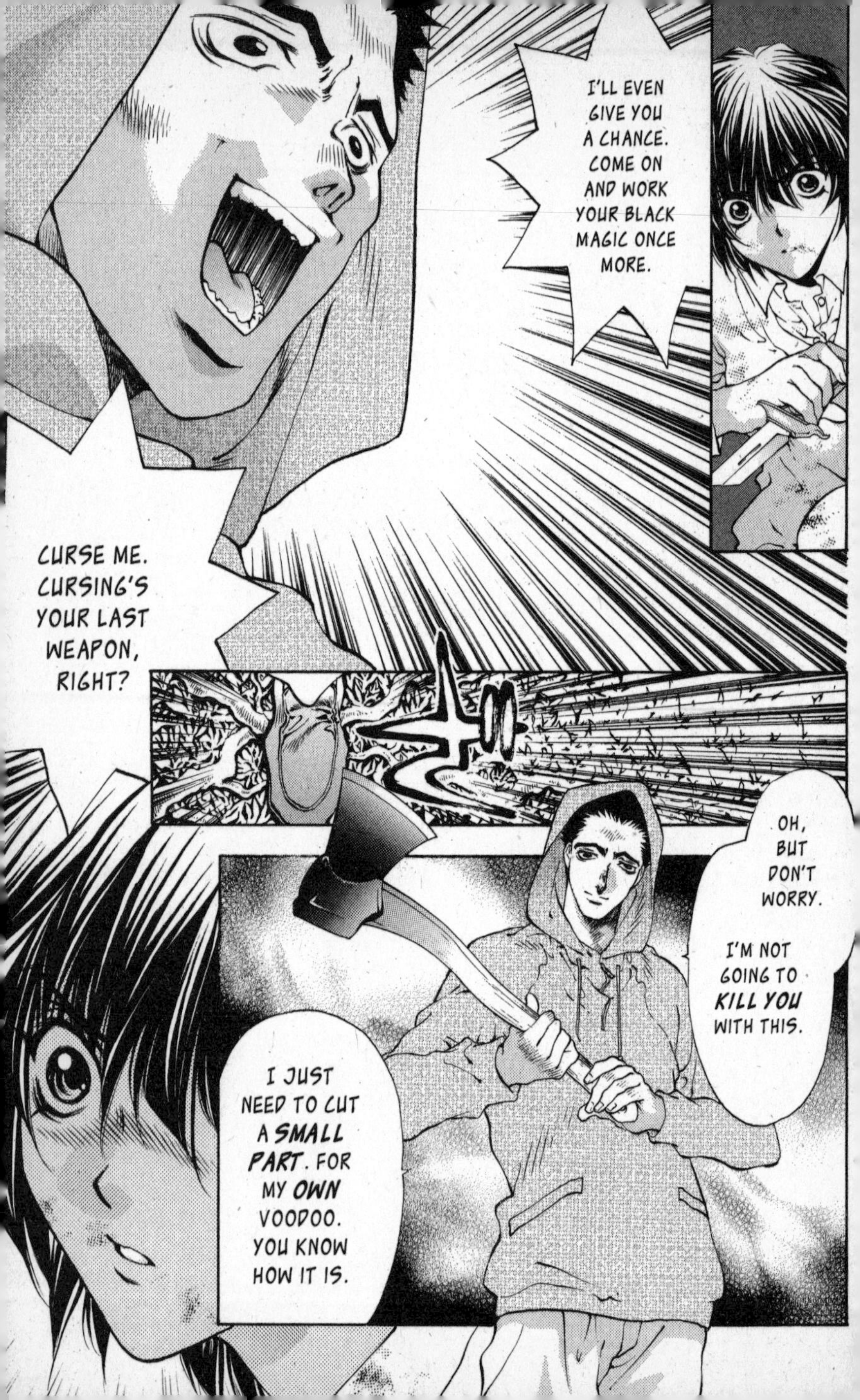
I'LL EVEN GIVE YOU A CHANCE. COME ON AND WORK YOUR BLACK MAGIC ONCE MORE.
CURSE ME. CURSING'S YOUR LAST WEAPON, RIGHT?
OH, BUT DON'T WORRY.
I'M NOT GOING TO **KILL YOU** WITH THIS.
I JUST NEED TO CUT A **SMALL PART**. FOR MY **OWN** VOODOO. YOU KNOW HOW IT IS.

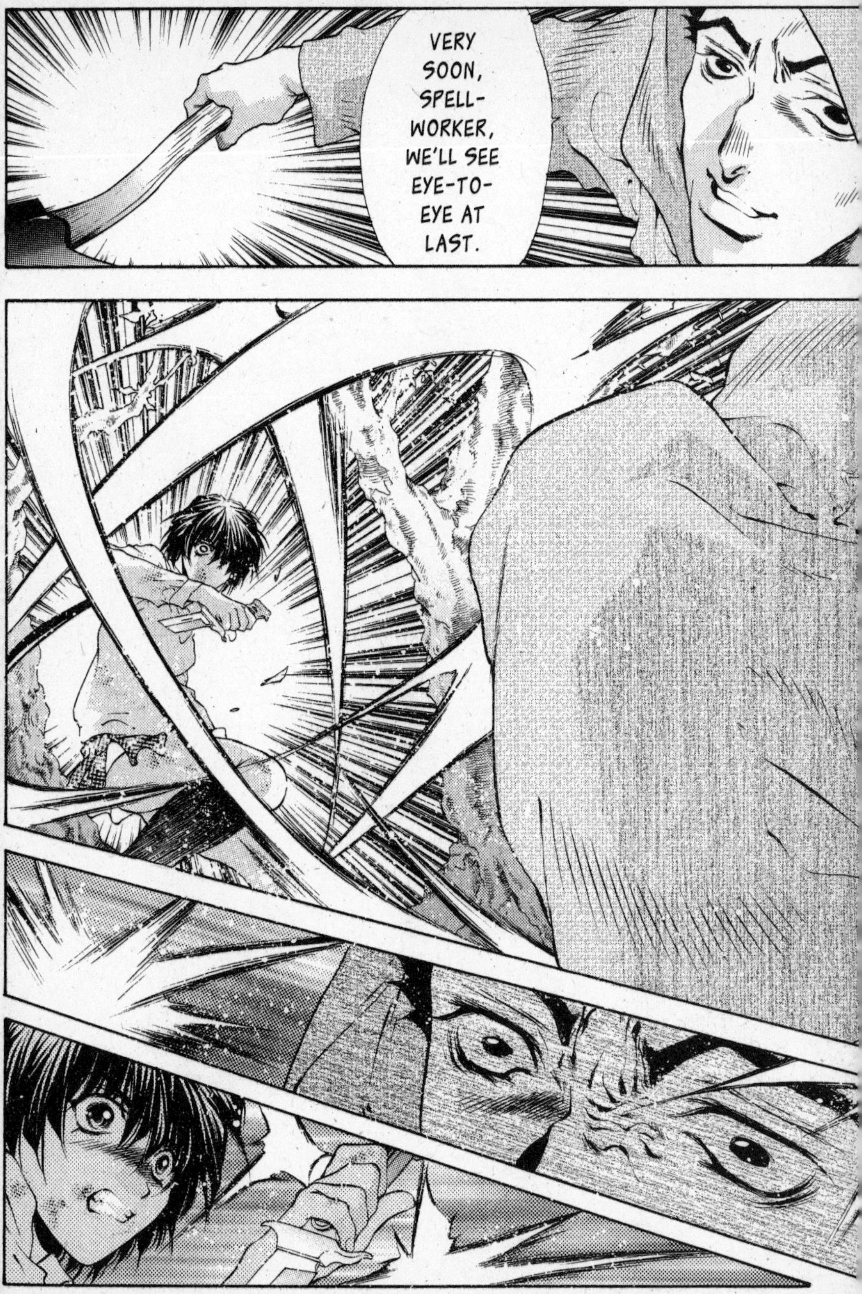
VERY SOON, SPELL-WORKER, WE'LL SEE EYE-TO-EYE AT LAST.

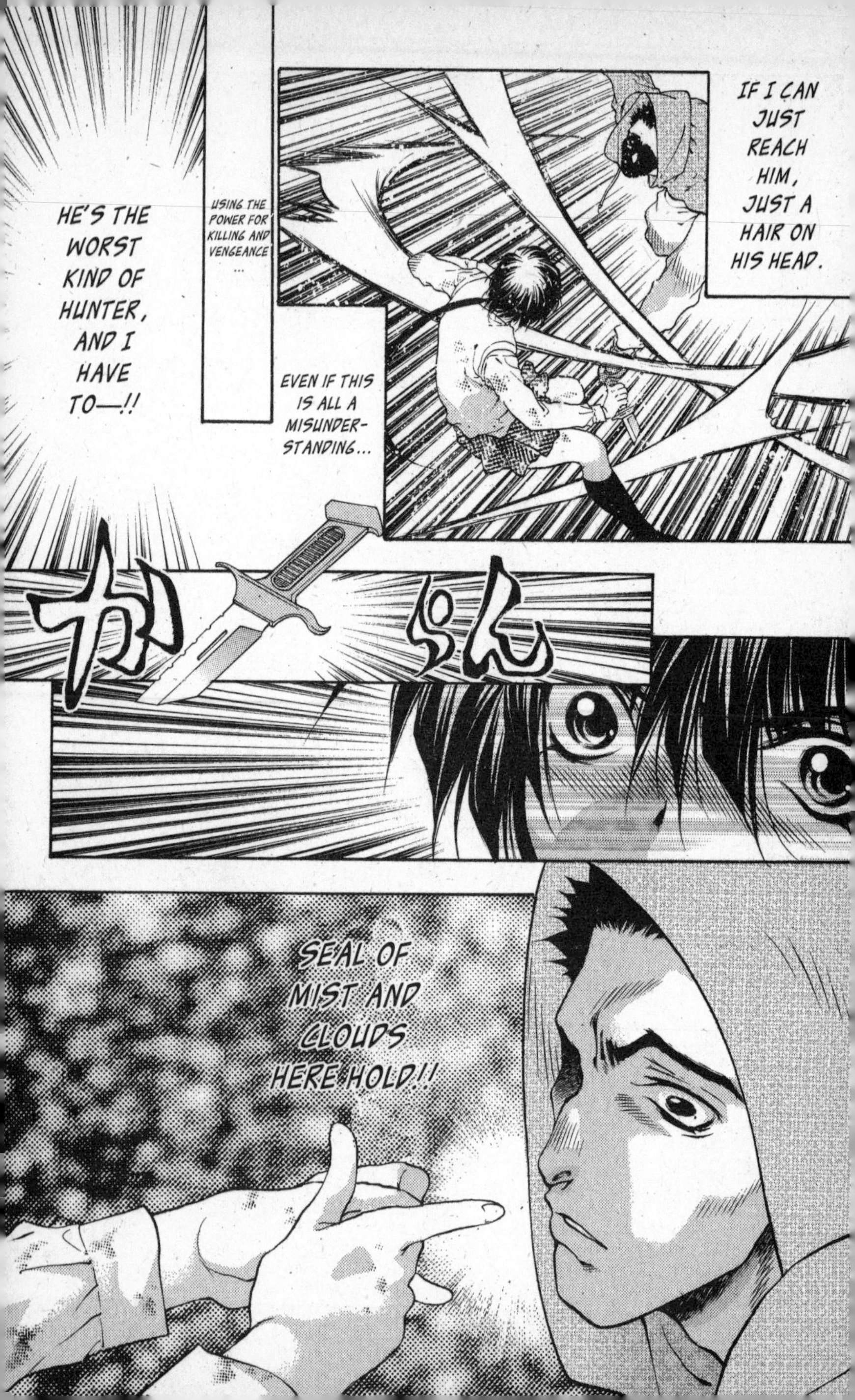
IF I CAN JUST REACH HIM, JUST A HAIR ON HIS HEAD.
EVEN IF THIS IS ALL A MISUNDERSTANDING...
USING THE POWER FOR KILLING AND VENGEANCE...
HE'S THE WORST KIND OF HUNTER, AND I HAVE TO—!!
からん
SEAL OF MIST AND CLOUDS HERE HOLD!!

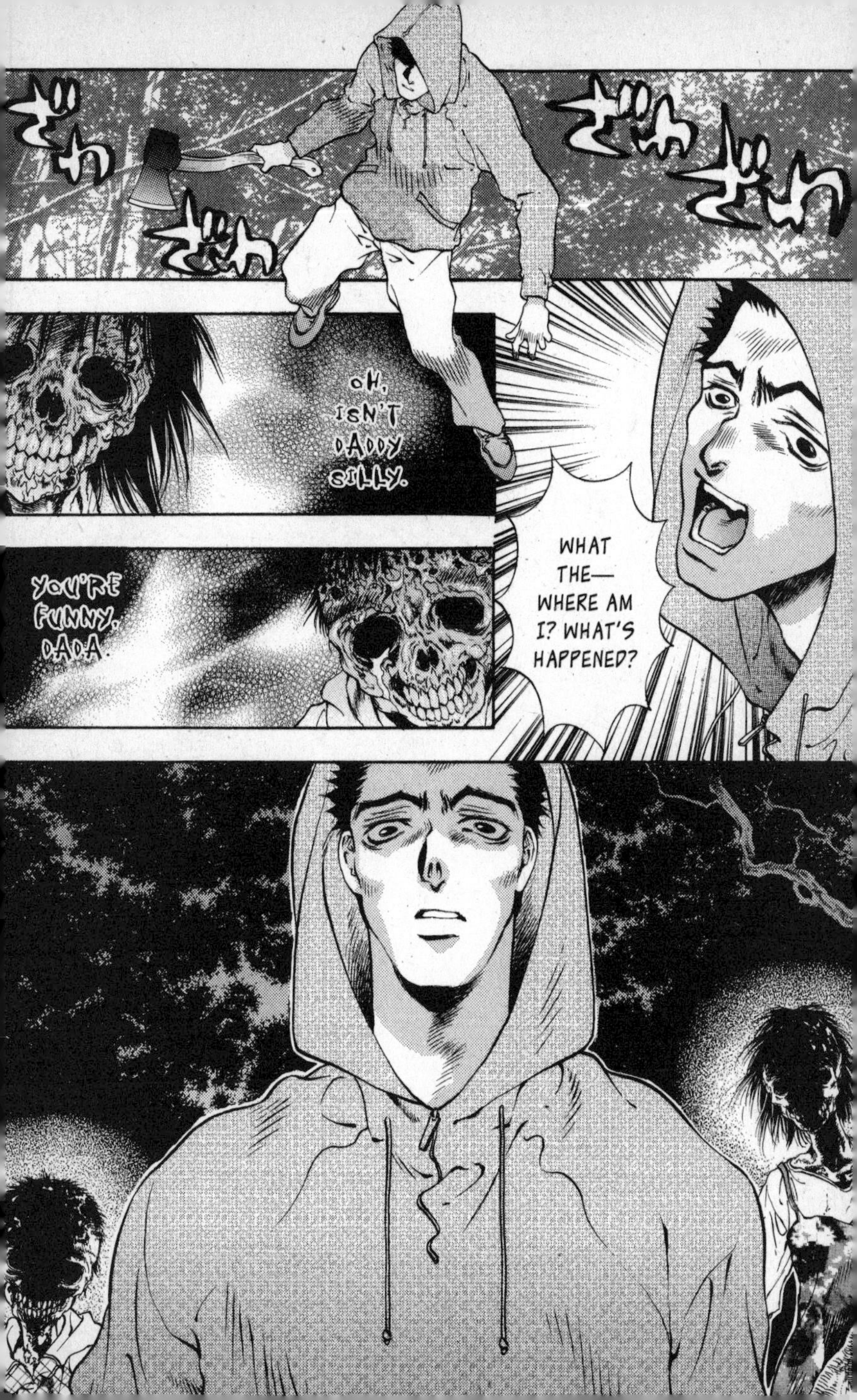
ざわ ざわ
ざわ
ざわ
WHAT THE— WHERE AM I? WHAT'S HAPPENED?
OH, ISN'T DADDY SILLY.
YOU'RE FUNNY, DADA.

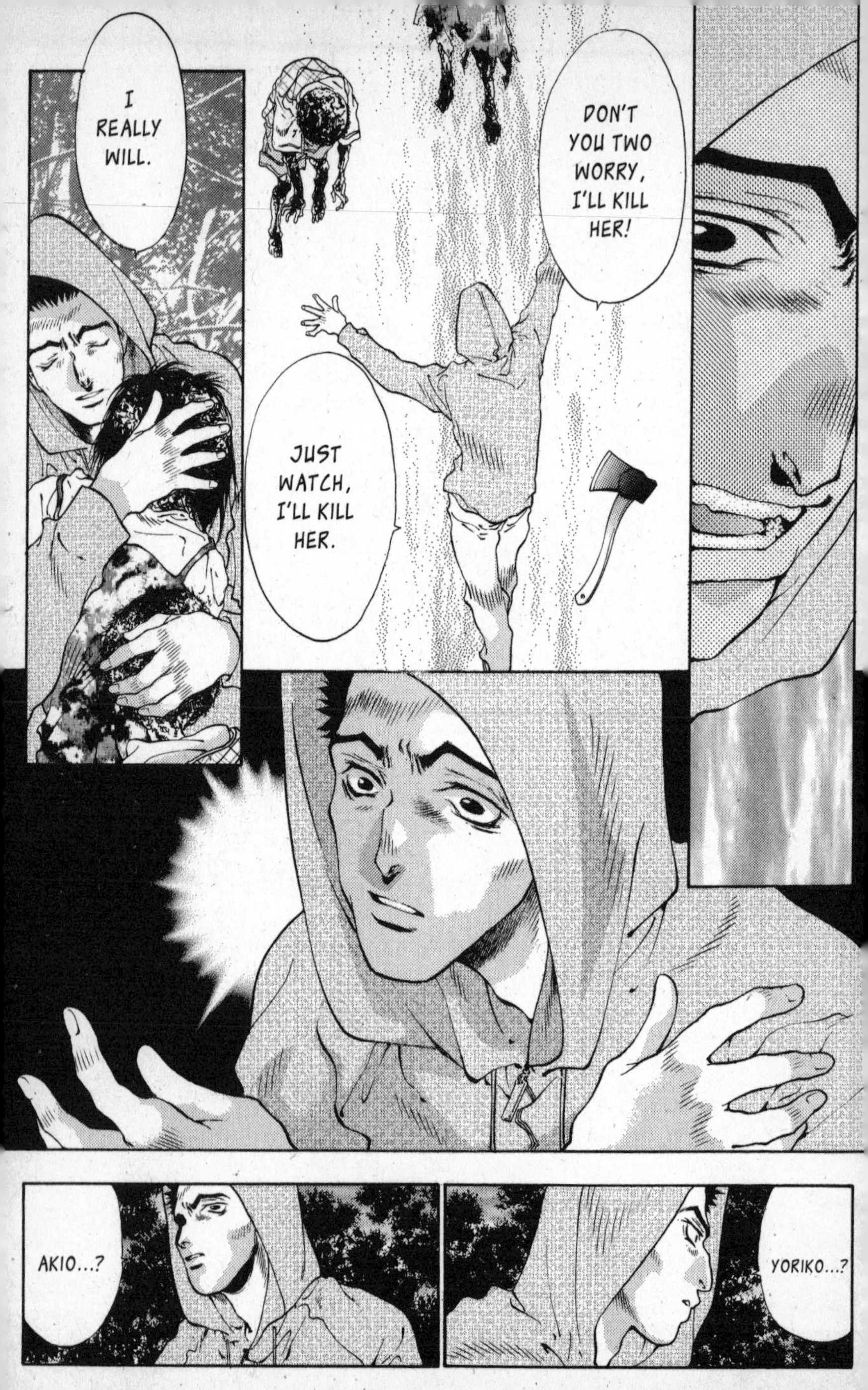
DON'T YOU TWO WORRY, I'LL KILL HER!
JUST WATCH, I'LL KILL HER.
I REALLY WILL.
YORIKO...?
AKIO...?

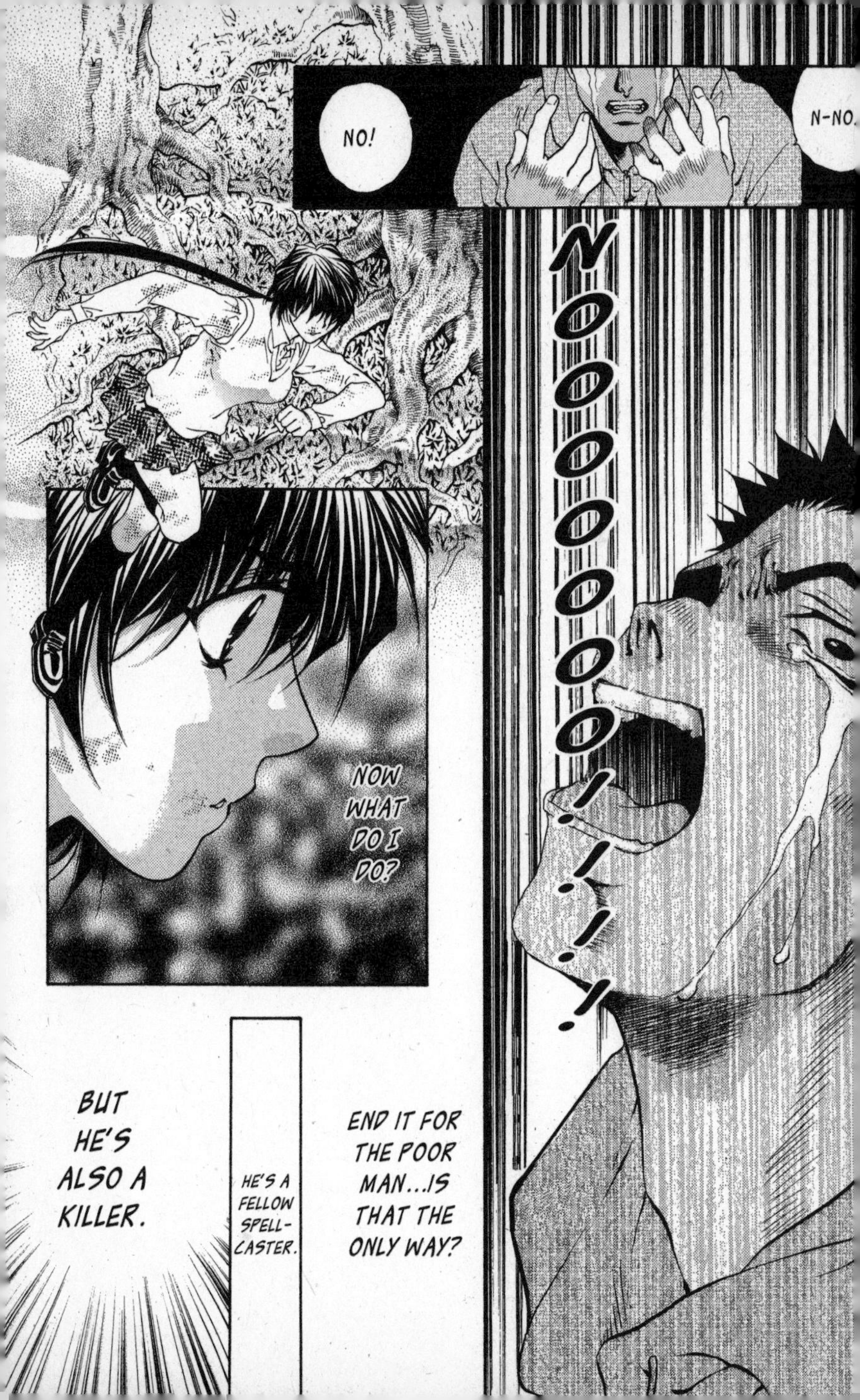
N-NO.
NO!
NOOOOOOOOOO!!!!!
NOW WHAT DO I DO?
END IT FOR THE POOR MAN...IS THAT THE ONLY WAY?
HE'S A FELLOW SPELL-CASTER.
BUT HE'S ALSO A KILLER.

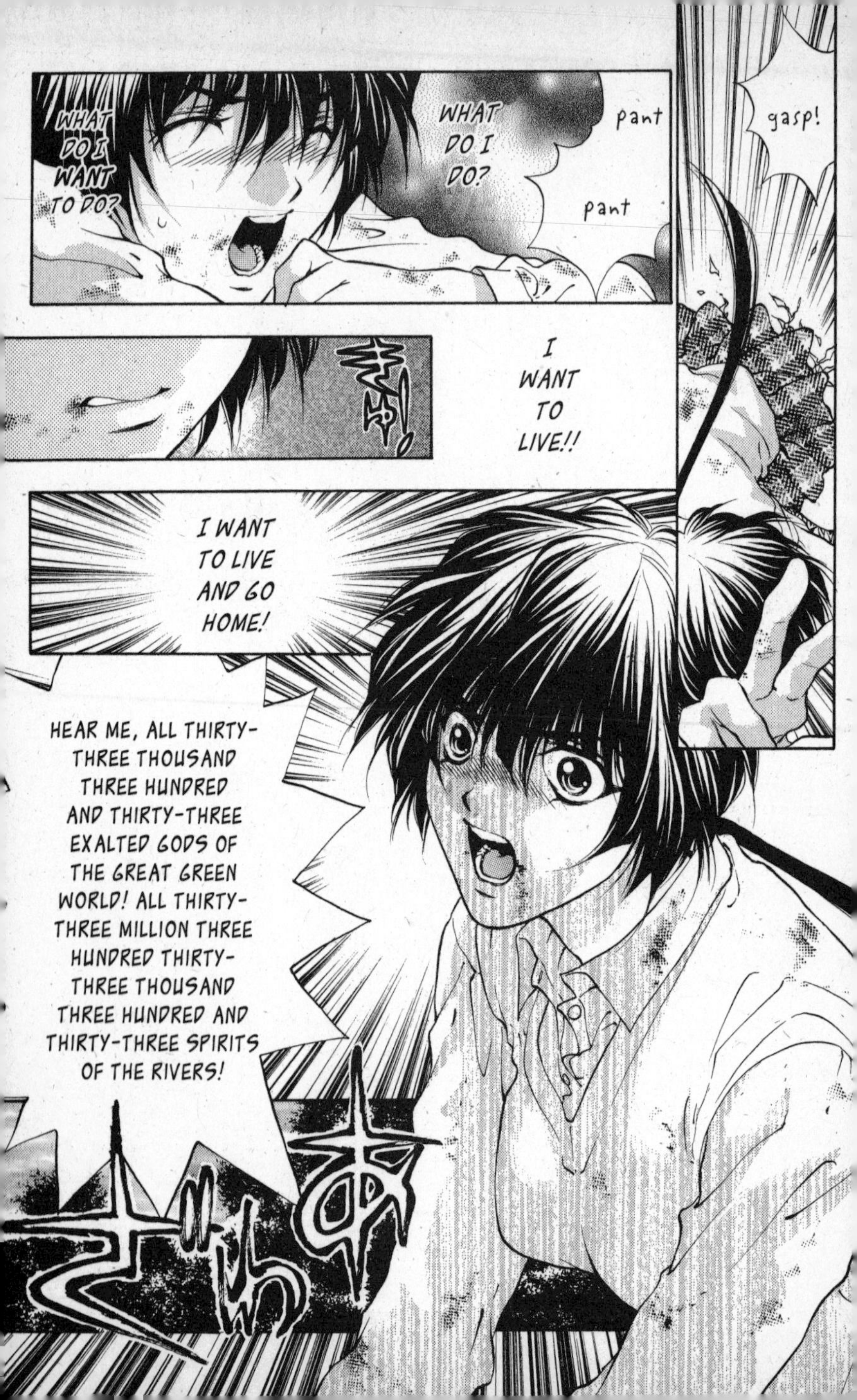
gasp!
pant
pant
WHAT DO I DO?
WHAT DO I WANT TO DO?
I WANT TO LIVE!!
I WANT TO LIVE AND GO HOME!
HEAR ME, ALL THIRTY-THREE THOUSAND THREE HUNDRED AND THIRTY-THREE EXALTED GODS OF THE GREAT GREEN WORLD! ALL THIRTY-THREE MILLION THREE HUNDRED THIRTY-THREE THOUSAND THREE HUNDRED AND THIRTY-THREE SPIRITS OF THE RIVERS!

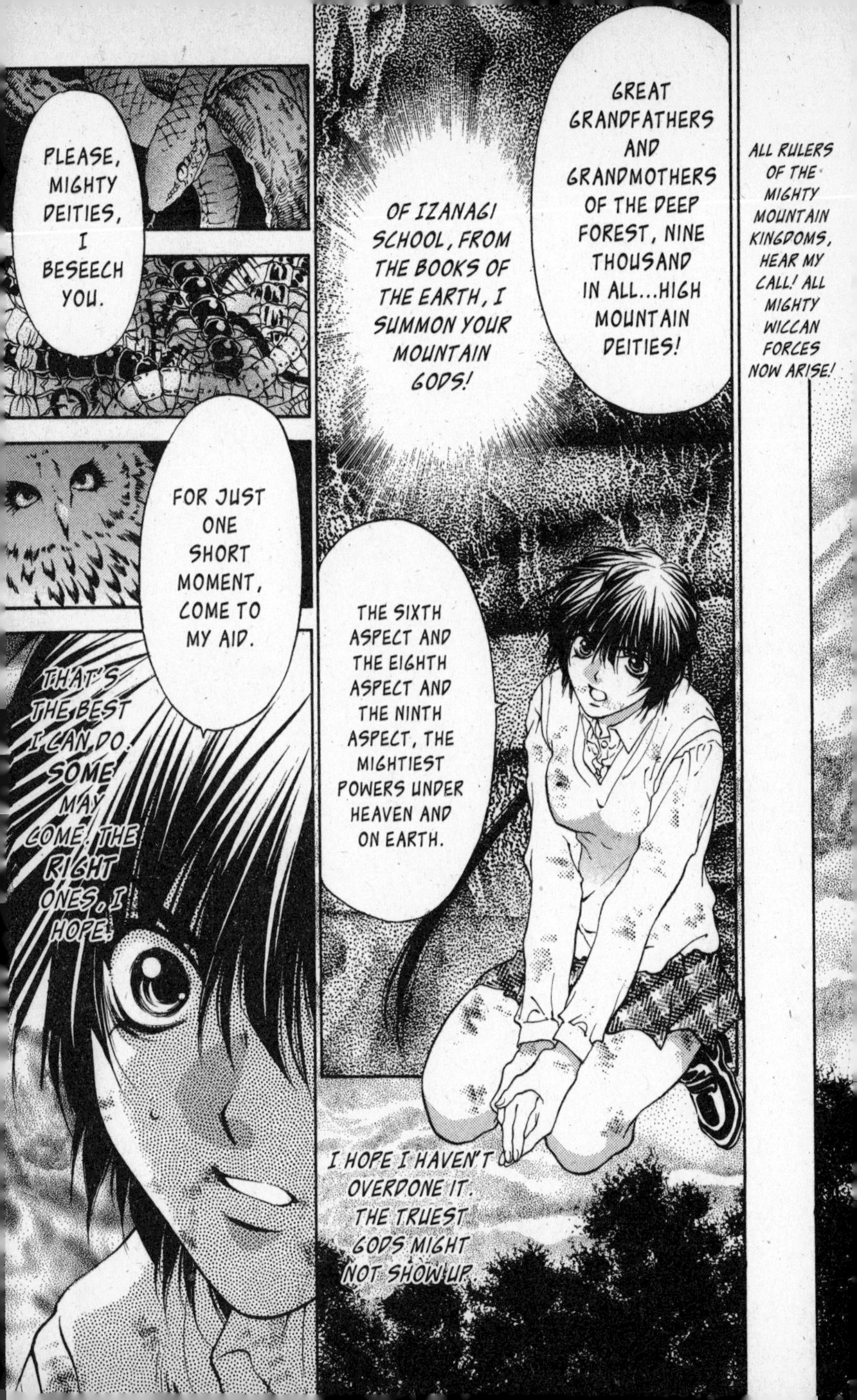
ALL RULERS OF THE MIGHTY MOUNTAIN KINGDOMS, HEAR MY CALL! ALL MIGHTY WICCAN FORCES NOW ARISE!
GREAT GRANDFATHERS AND GRANDMOTHERS OF THE DEEP FOREST, NINE THOUSAND IN ALL...HIGH MOUNTAIN DEITIES!
OF IZANAGI SCHOOL, FROM THE BOOKS OF THE EARTH, I SUMMON YOUR MOUNTAIN GODS!
THE SIXTH ASPECT AND THE EIGHTH ASPECT AND THE NINTH ASPECT, THE MIGHTIEST POWERS UNDER HEAVEN AND ON EARTH.
I HOPE I HAVEN'T OVERDONE IT. THE TRUEST GODS MIGHT NOT SHOW UP.
PLEASE, MIGHTY DEITIES, I BESEECH YOU.
FOR JUST ONE SHORT MOMENT, COME TO MY AID.
THAT'S THE BEST I CAN DO. SOME MAY COME. THE RIGHT ONES, I HOPE.

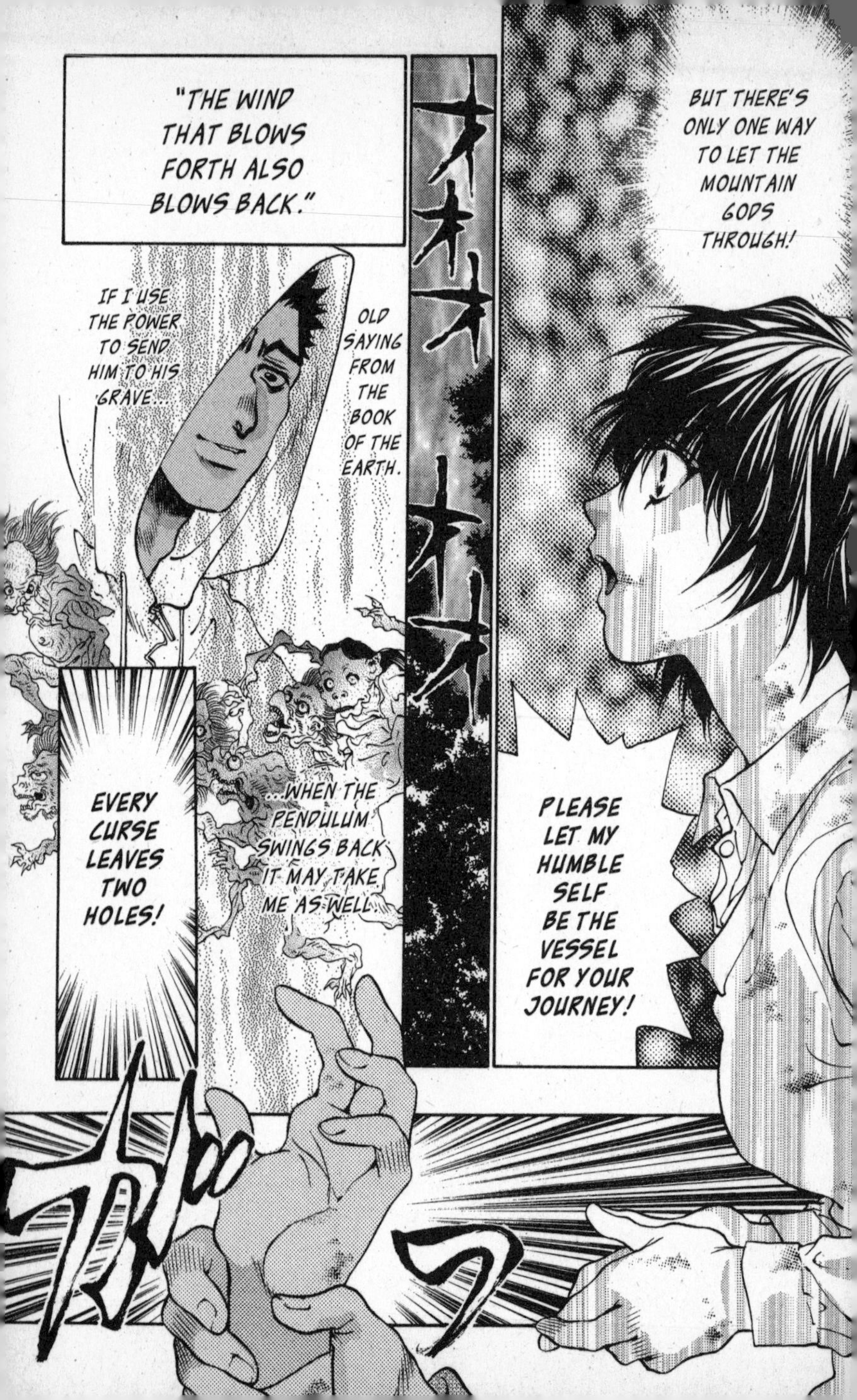
BUT THERE'S ONLY ONE WAY TO LET THE MOUNTAIN GODS THROUGH!
PLEASE LET MY HUMBLE SELF BE THE VESSEL FOR YOUR JOURNEY!
オオオオオ
"THE WIND THAT BLOWS FORTH ALSO BLOWS BACK."
OLD SAYING FROM THE BOOK OF THE EARTH.
IF I USE THE POWER TO SEND HIM TO HIS GRAVE...
...WHEN THE PENDULUM SWINGS BACK IT MAY TAKE ME AS WELL.
EVERY CURSE LEAVES TWO HOLES!

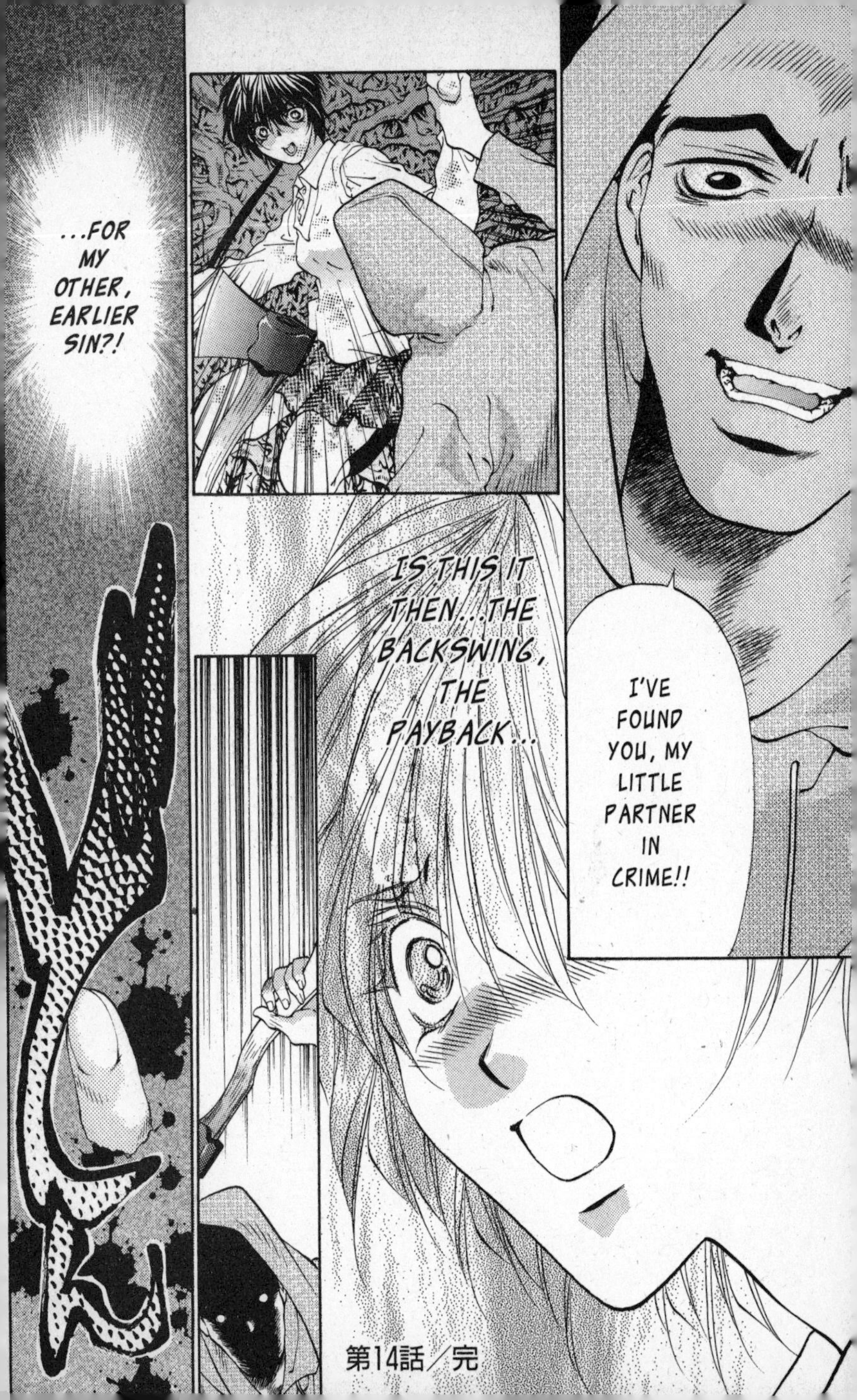
I'VE FOUND YOU, MY LITTLE PARTNER IN CRIME!!
IS THIS IT THEN...THE BACKSWING, THE PAYBACK...
...FOR MY OTHER, EARLIER SIN?!
第14話／完

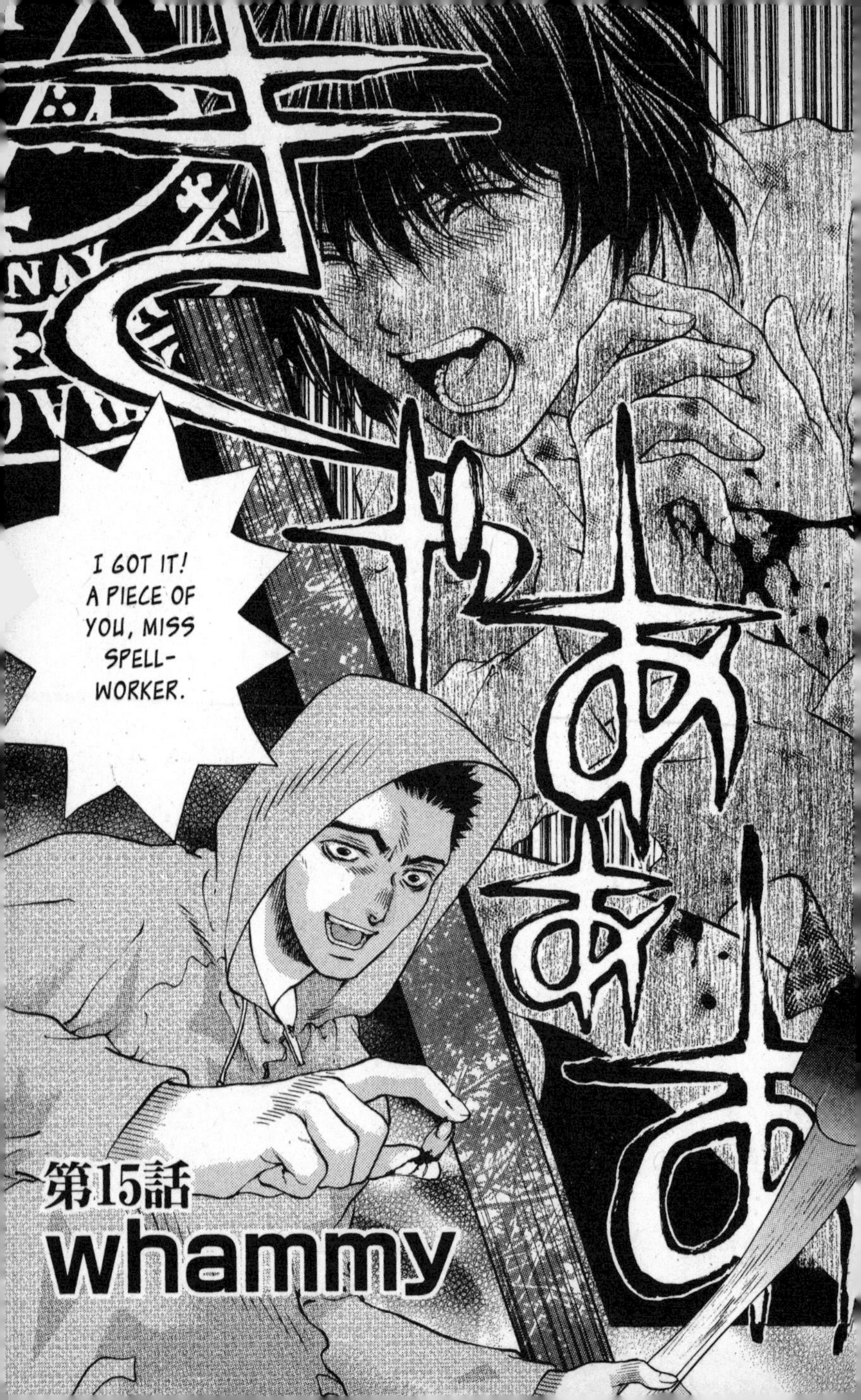
I GOT IT! A PIECE OF YOU, MISS SPELL-WORKER.
第15話
whammy

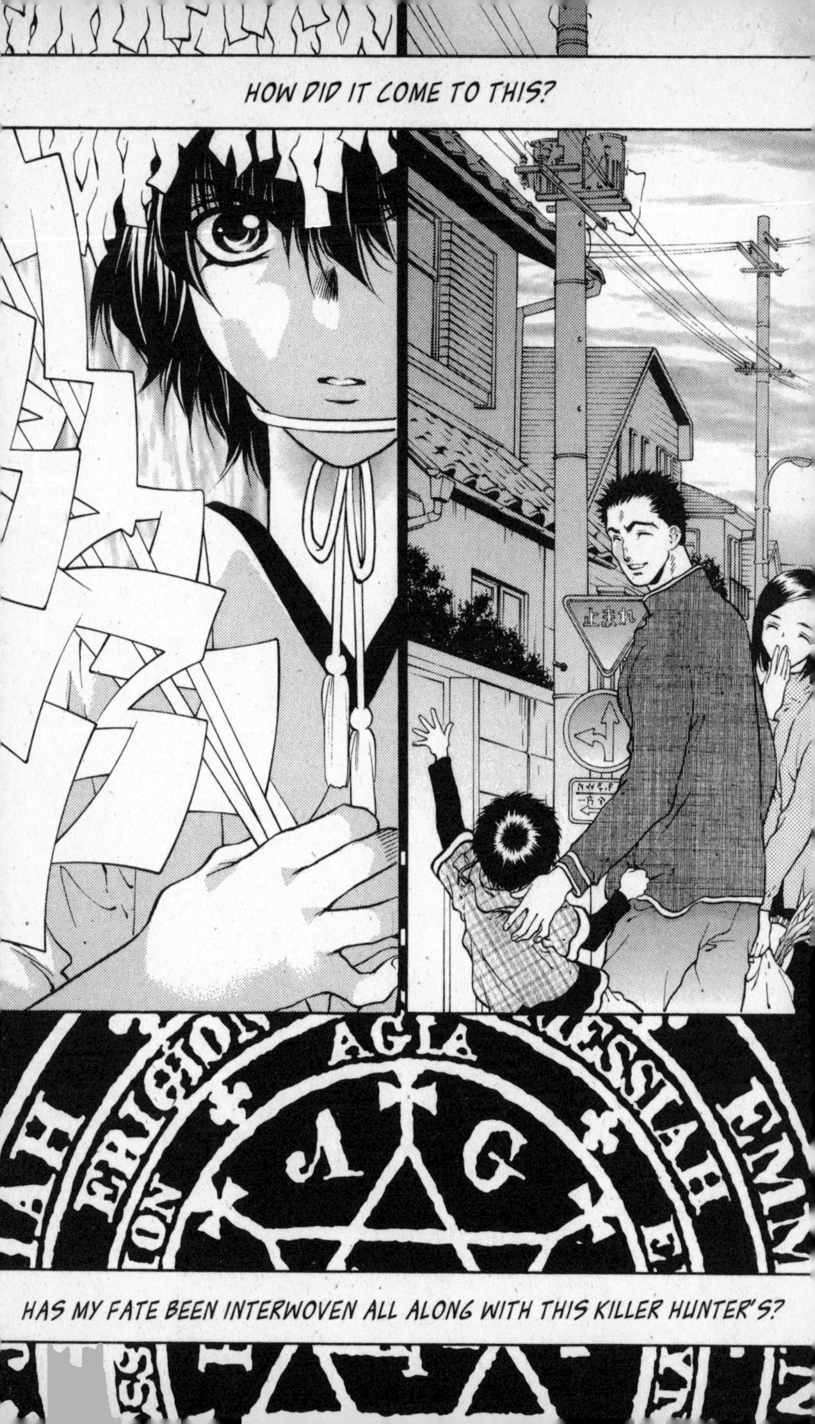
HOW DID IT COME TO THIS?
止まれ
AGLA
HAS MY FATE BEEN INTERWOVEN ALL ALONG WITH THIS KILLER HUNTER'S?

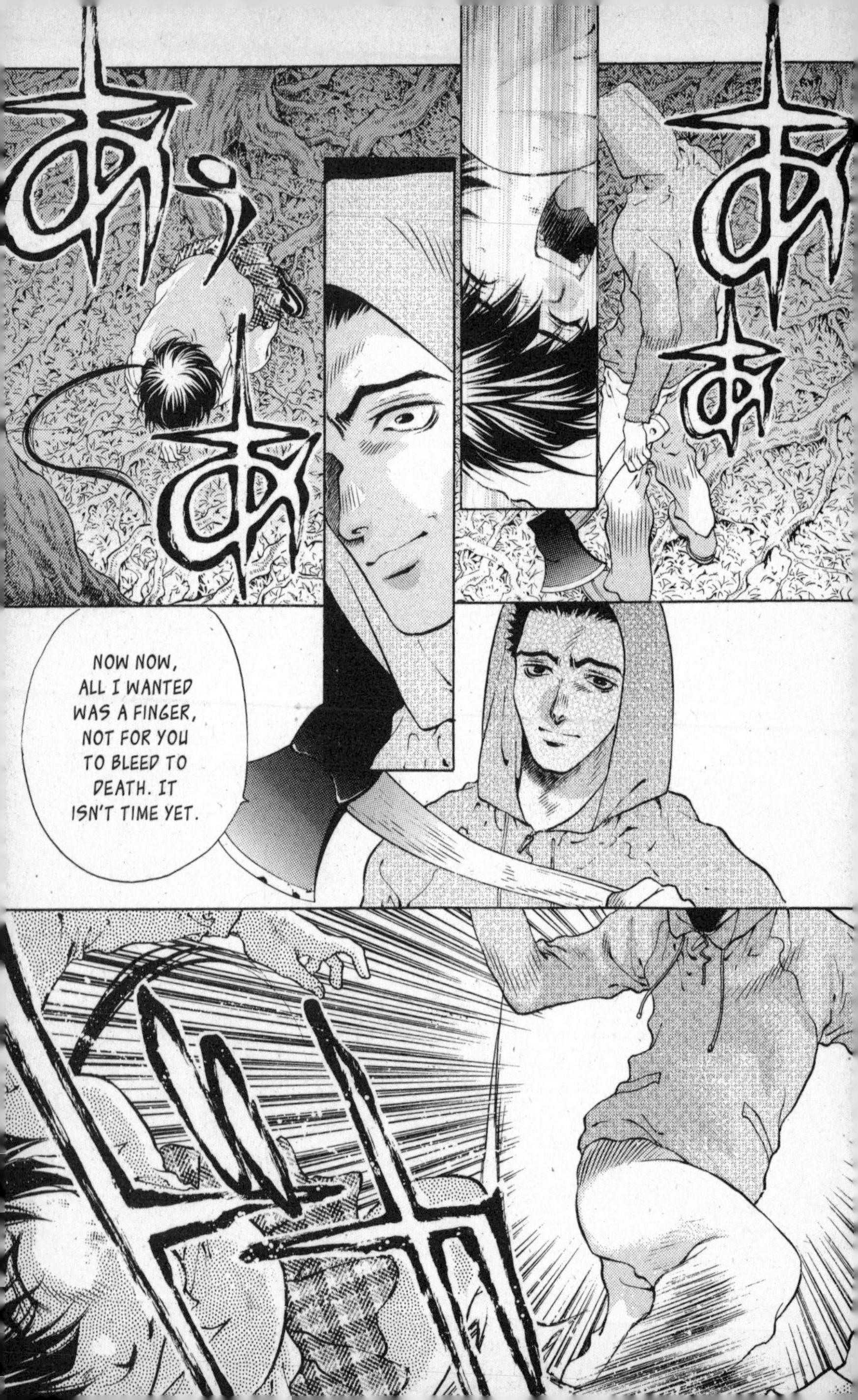
NOW NOW, ALL I WANTED WAS A FINGER, NOT FOR YOU TO BLEED TO DEATH. IT ISN'T TIME YET.

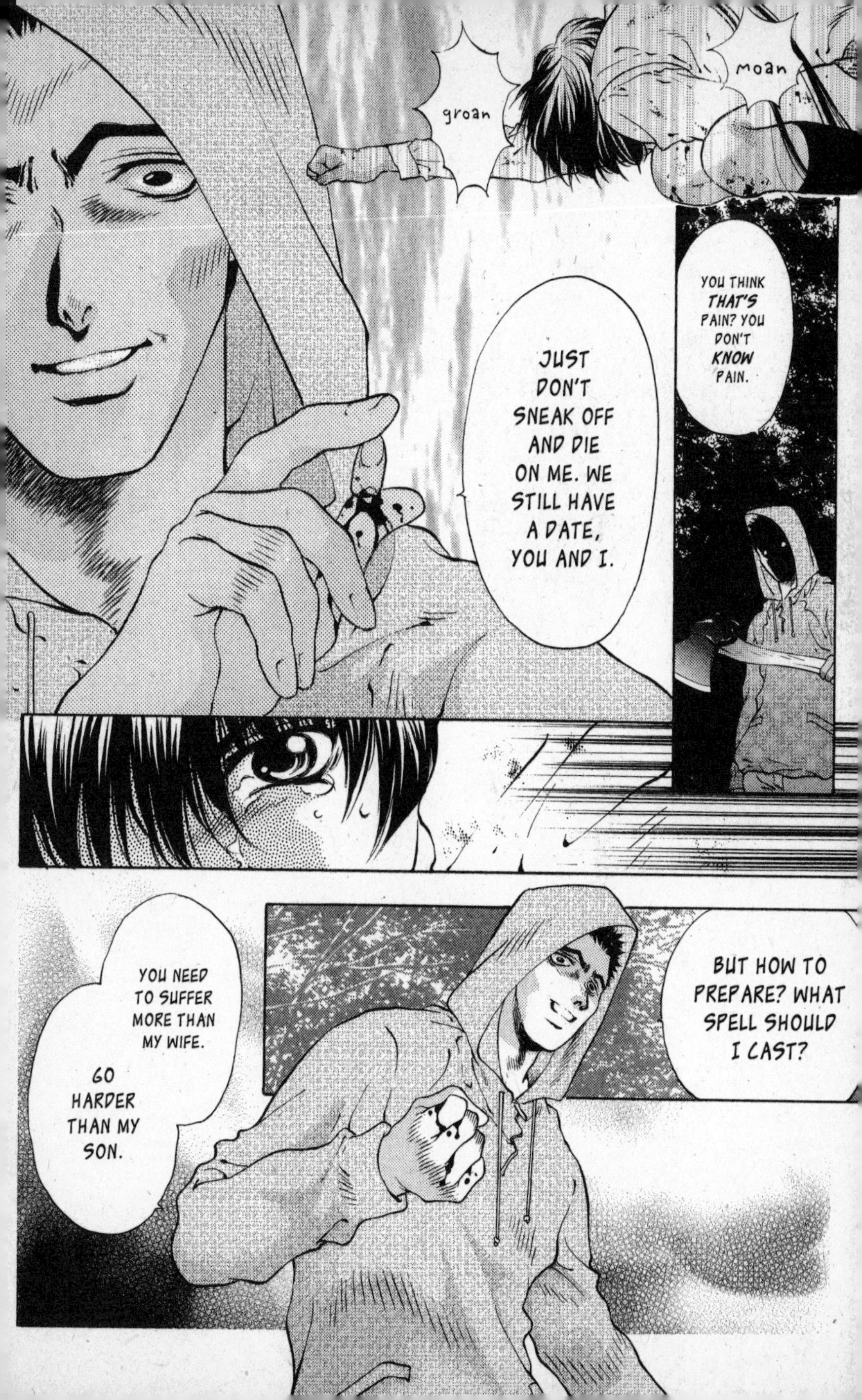
moan
groan
YOU THINK THAT'S PAIN? YOU DON'T KNOW PAIN.
JUST DON'T SNEAK OFF AND DIE ON ME. WE STILL HAVE A DATE, YOU AND I.
BUT HOW TO PREPARE? WHAT SPELL SHOULD I CAST?
YOU NEED TO SUFFER MORE THAN MY WIFE.
GO HARDER THAN MY SON.

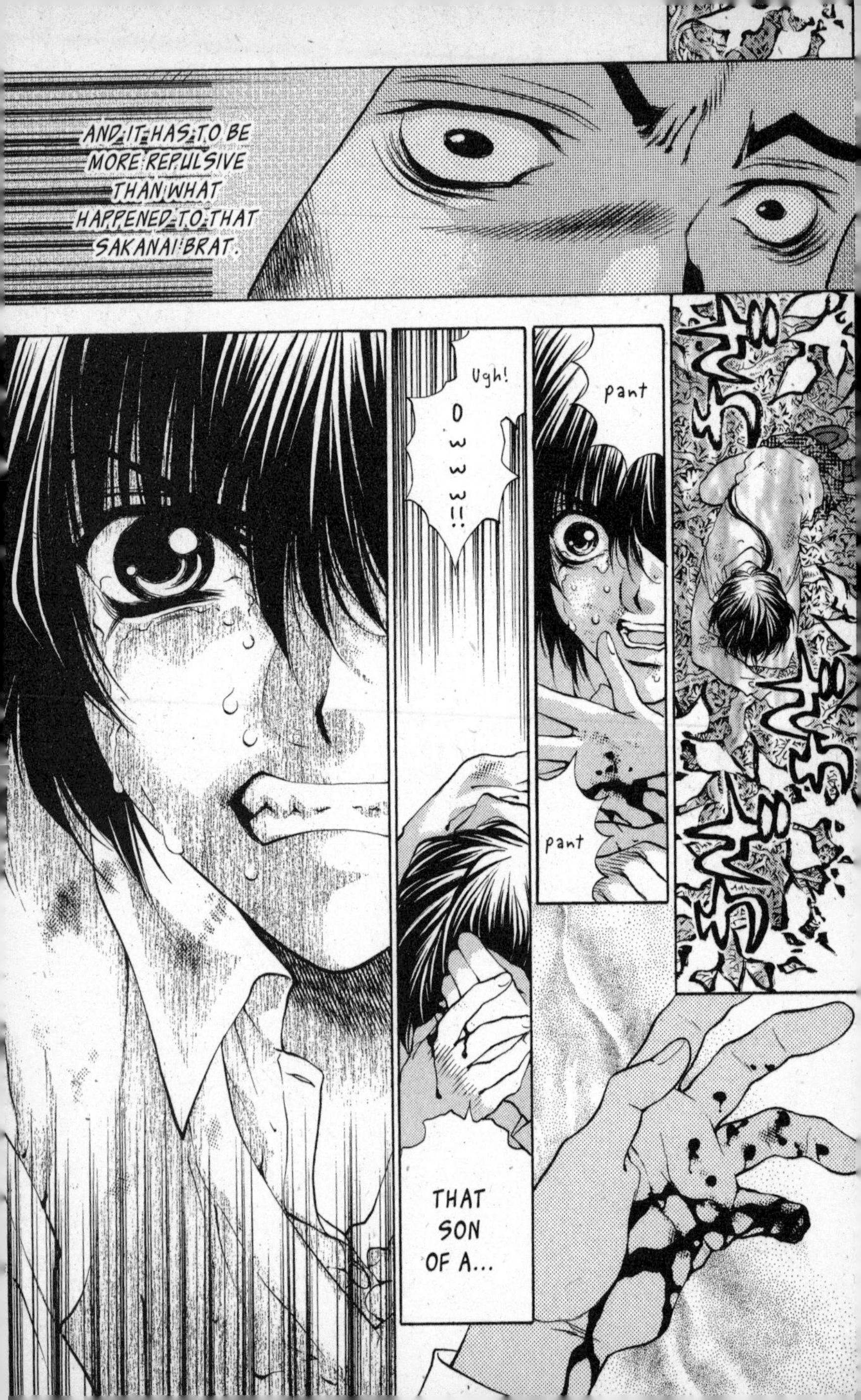
AND IT HAS TO BE MORE REPULSIVE THAN WHAT HAPPENED TO THAT SAKANAI BRAT.
pant
pant
Ugh!
Owww!!
THAT SON OF A...

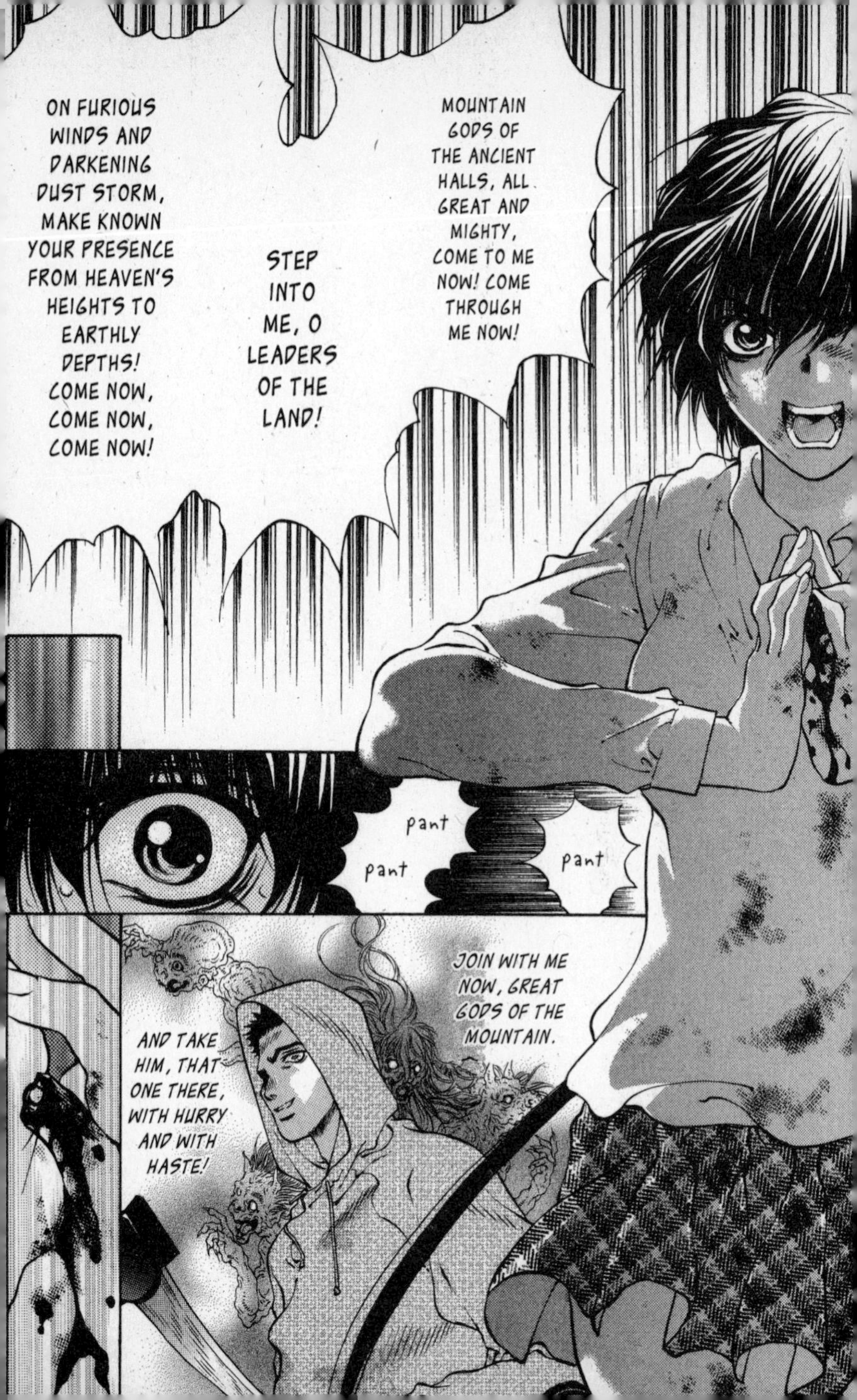
MOUNTAIN GODS OF THE ANCIENT HALLS, ALL GREAT AND MIGHTY, COME TO ME NOW! COME THROUGH ME NOW!
STEP INTO ME, O LEADERS OF THE LAND!
ON FURIOUS WINDS AND DARKENING DUST STORM, MAKE KNOWN YOUR PRESENCE FROM HEAVEN'S HEIGHTS TO EARTHLY DEPTHS! COME NOW, COME NOW, COME NOW!
pant
pant
pant
JOIN WITH ME NOW, GREAT GODS OF THE MOUNTAIN.
AND TAKE HIM, THAT ONE THERE, WITH HURRY AND WITH HASTE!

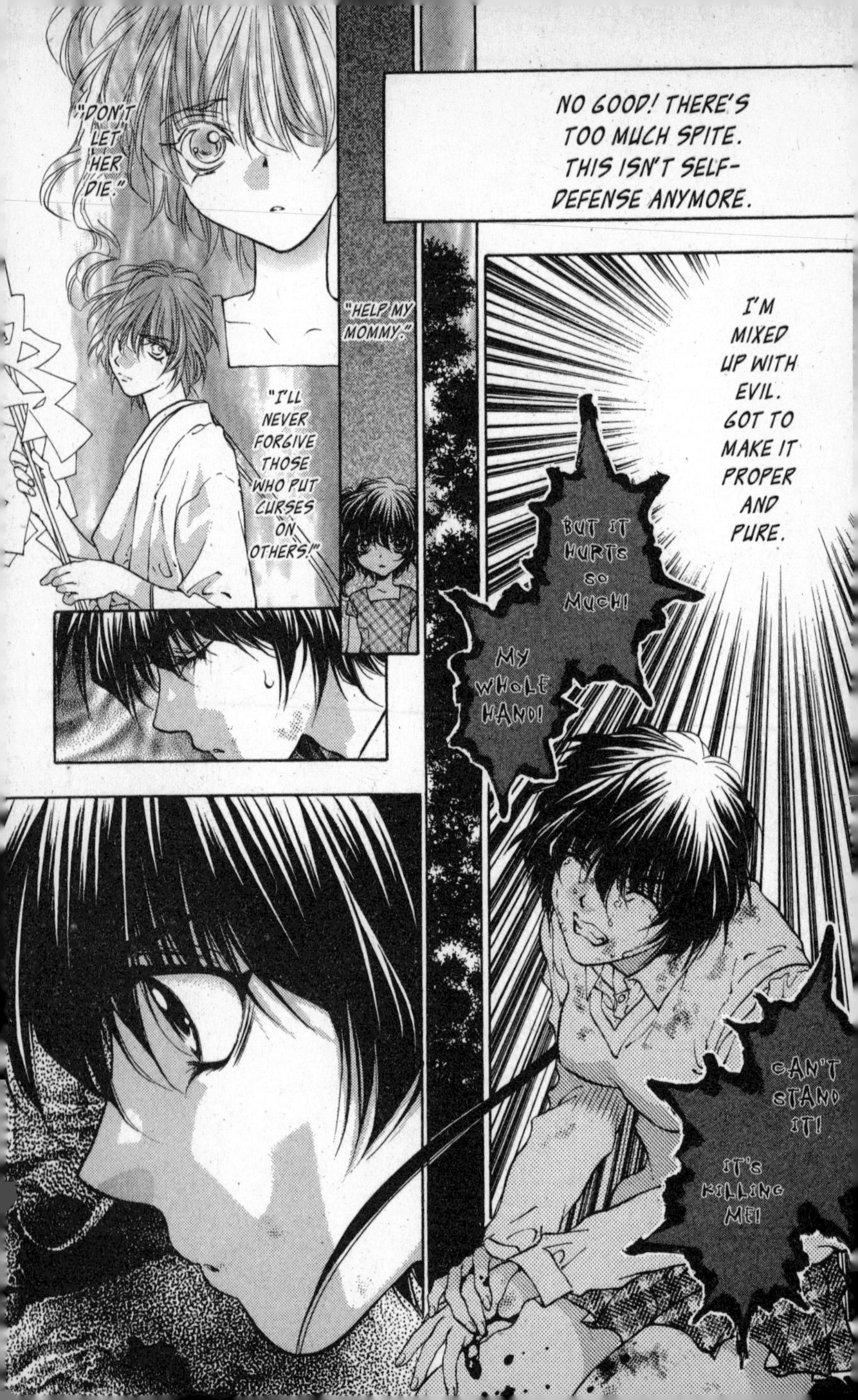
NO GOOD! THERE'S TOO MUCH SPITE. THIS ISN'T SELF-DEFENSE ANYMORE.
I'M MIXED UP WITH EVIL. GOT TO MAKE IT PROPER AND PURE.
BUT IT HURTS SO MUCH!
MY WHOLE HAND!
CAN'T STAND IT!
IT'S KILLING ME!
"HELP MY MOMMY."
"DON'T LET HER DIE."
"I'LL NEVER FORGIVE THOSE WHO PUT CURSES ON OTHERS!"

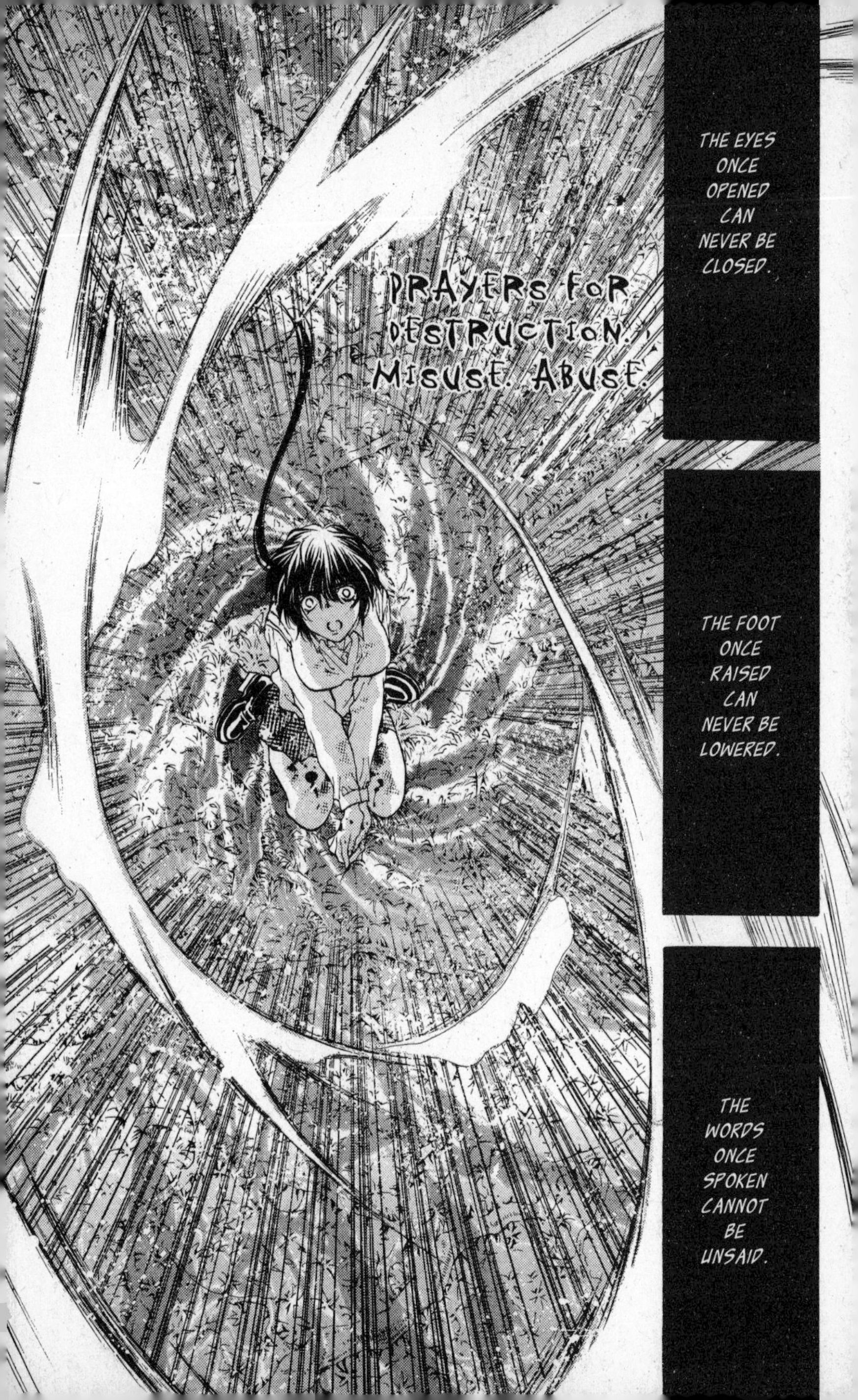
THE EYES ONCE OPENED CAN NEVER BE CLOSED.
PRAYERS FOR DESTRUCTION. MISUSE. ABUSE.
THE FOOT ONCE RAISED CAN NEVER BE LOWERED.
THE WORDS ONCE SPOKEN CANNOT BE UNSAID.

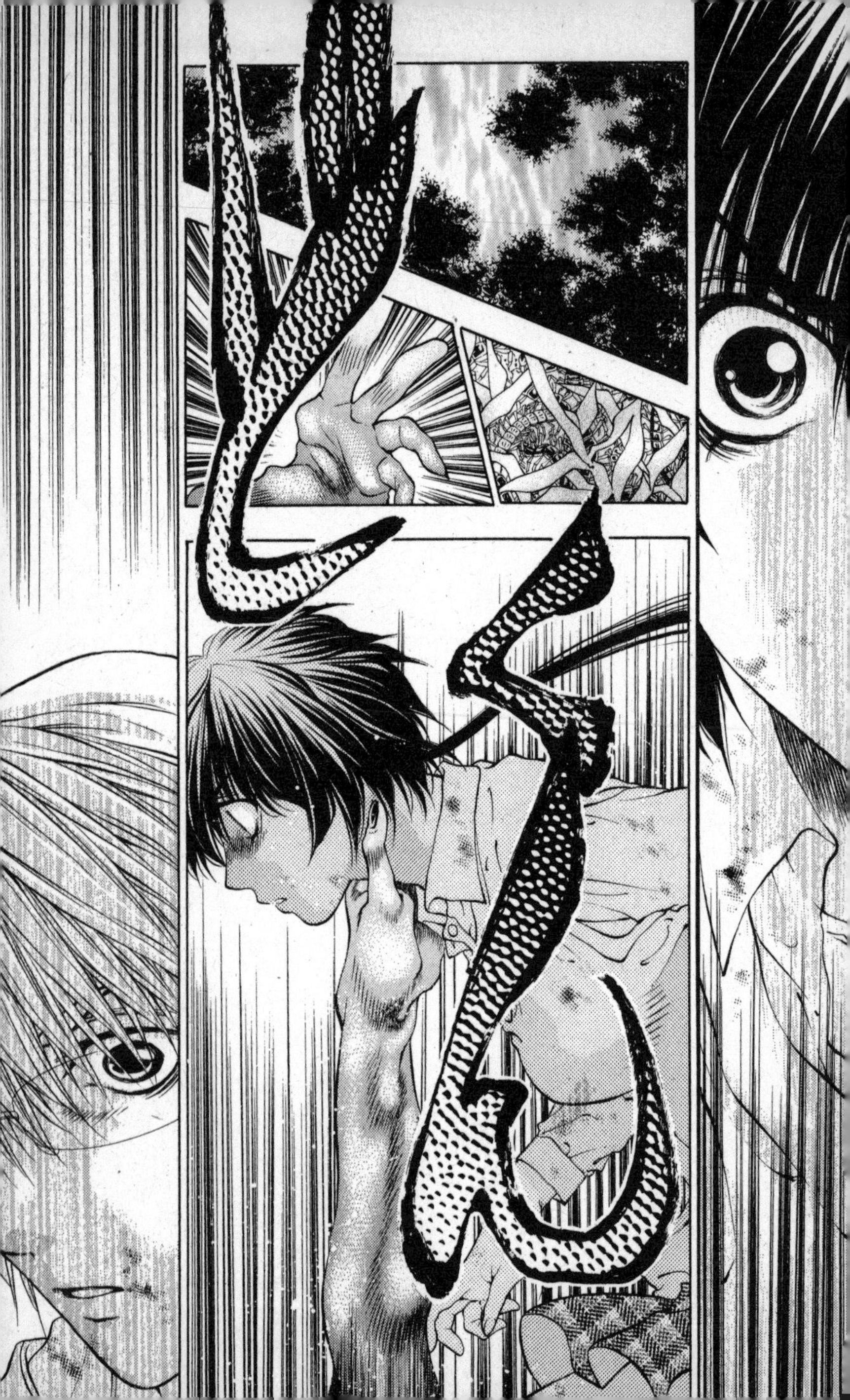

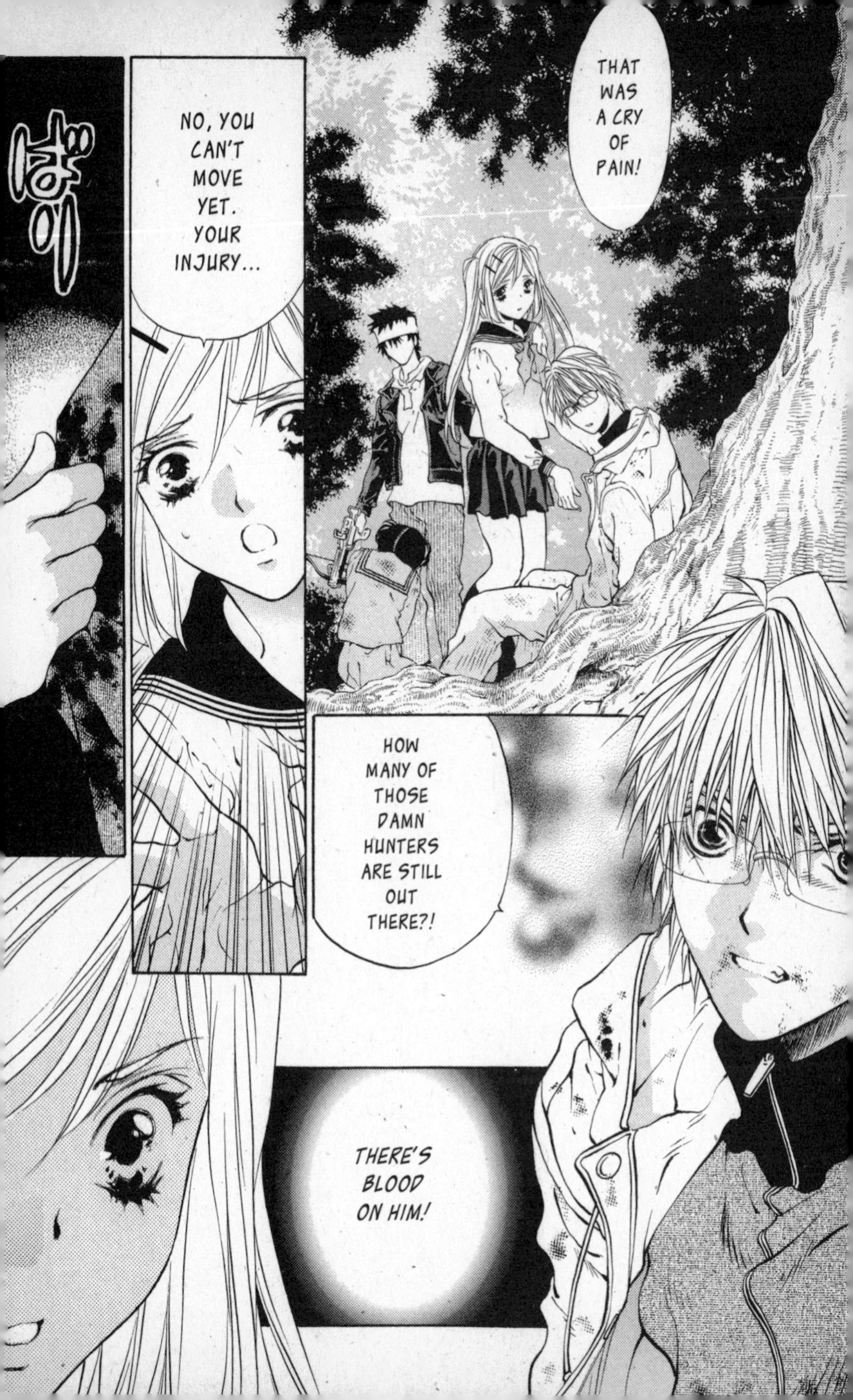
THAT WAS A CRY OF PAIN!
NO, YOU CAN'T MOVE YET. YOUR INJURY...
HOW MANY OF THOSE DAMN HUNTERS ARE STILL OUT THERE?!
THERE'S BLOOD ON HIM!

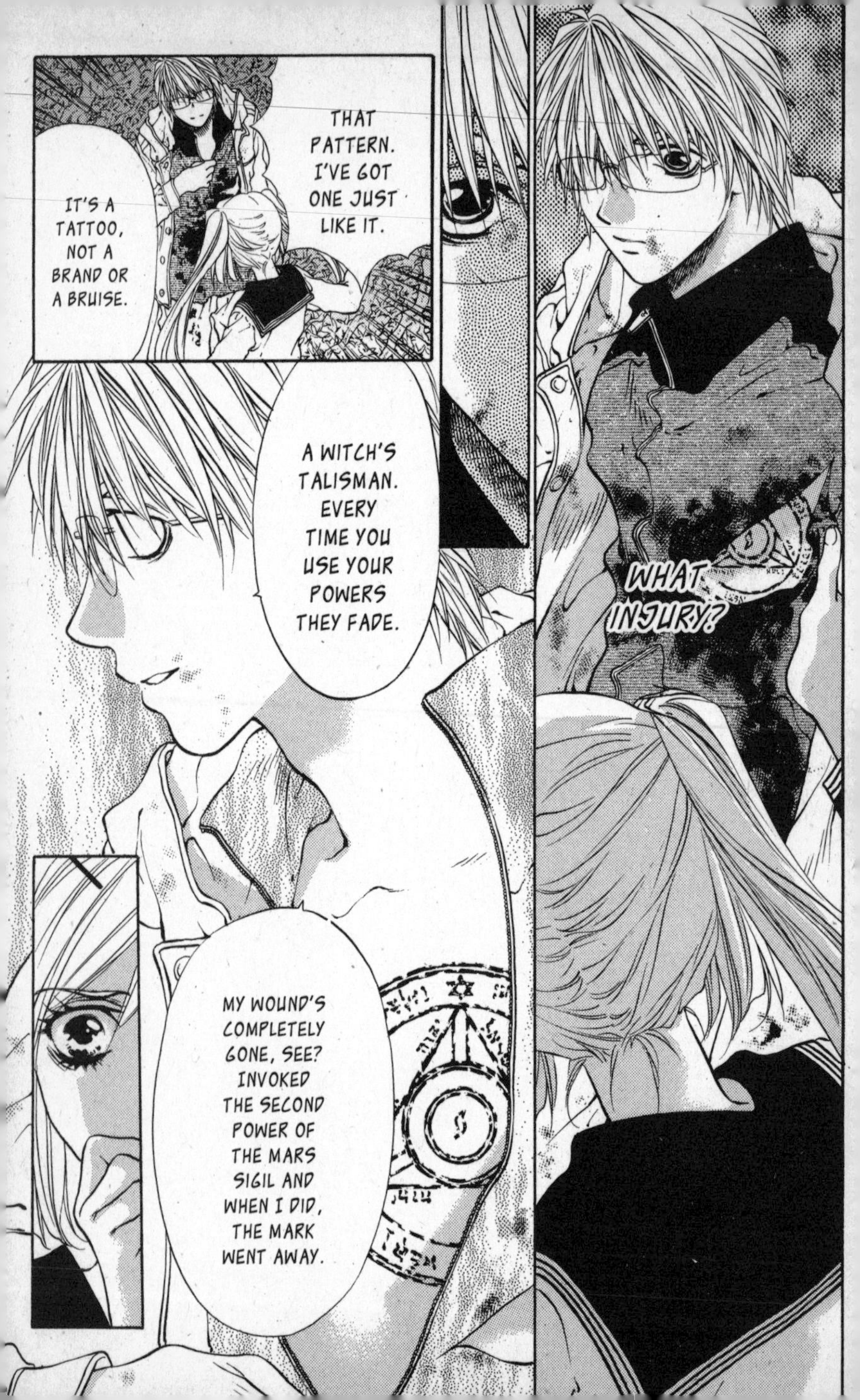
WHAT INJURY?
THAT PATTERN. I'VE GOT ONE JUST LIKE IT.
IT'S A TATTOO, NOT A BRAND OR A BRUISE.
A WITCH'S TALISMAN. EVERY TIME YOU USE YOUR POWERS THEY FADE.
MY WOUND'S COMPLETELY GONE, SEE? INVOKED THE SECOND POWER OF THE MARS SIGIL AND WHEN I DID, THE MARK WENT AWAY.

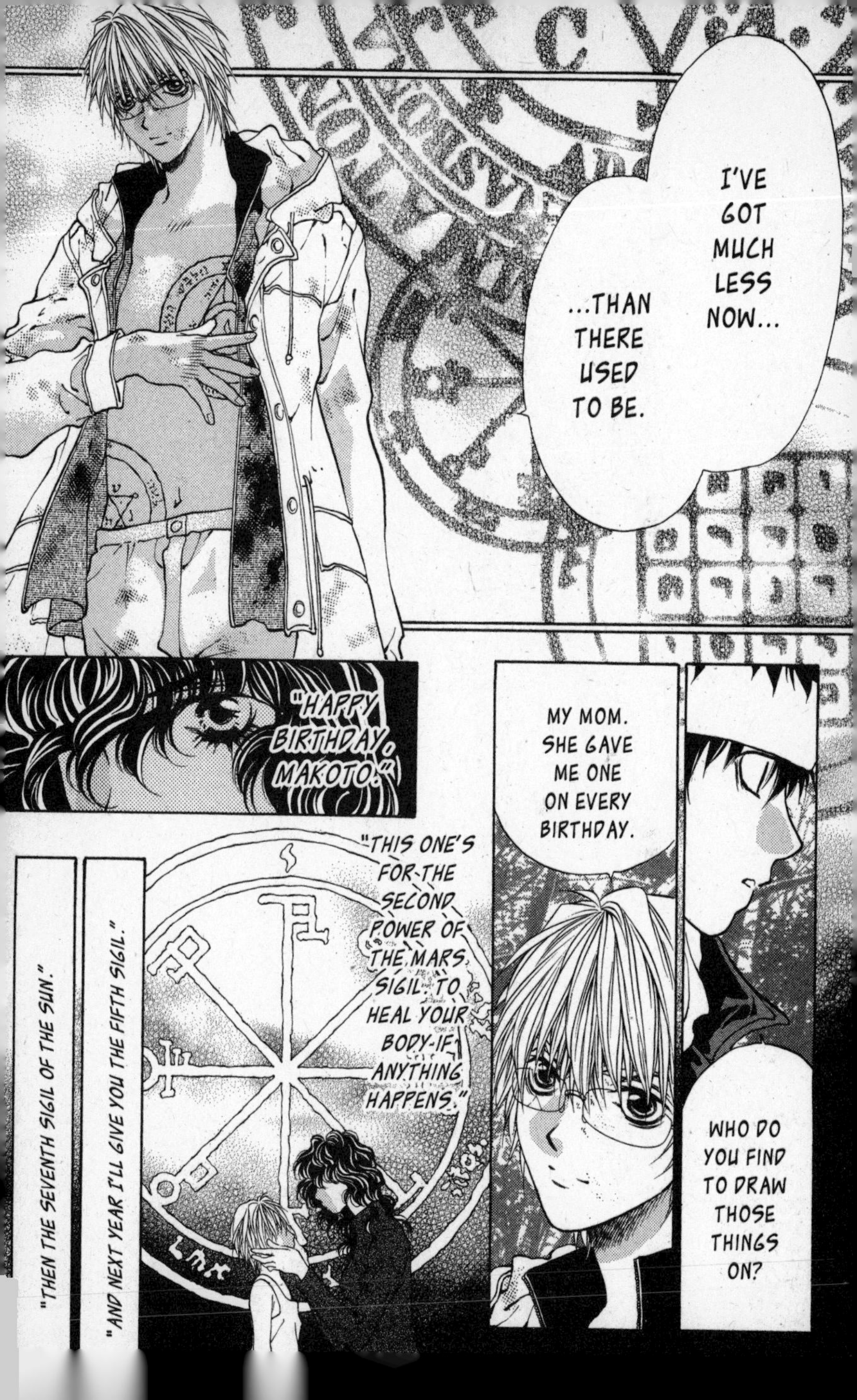
I'VE GOT MUCH LESS NOW...
...THAN THERE USED TO BE.
WHO DO YOU FIND TO DRAW THOSE THINGS ON?
MY MOM. SHE GAVE ME ONE ON EVERY BIRTHDAY.
"HAPPY BIRTHDAY, MAKOTO."
"THIS ONE'S FOR THE SECOND POWER OF THE MARS SIGIL. TO HEAL YOUR BODY IF ANYTHING HAPPENS."
"AND NEXT YEAR I'LL GIVE YOU THE FIFTH SIGIL."
"THEN THE SEVENTH SIGIL OF THE SUN."

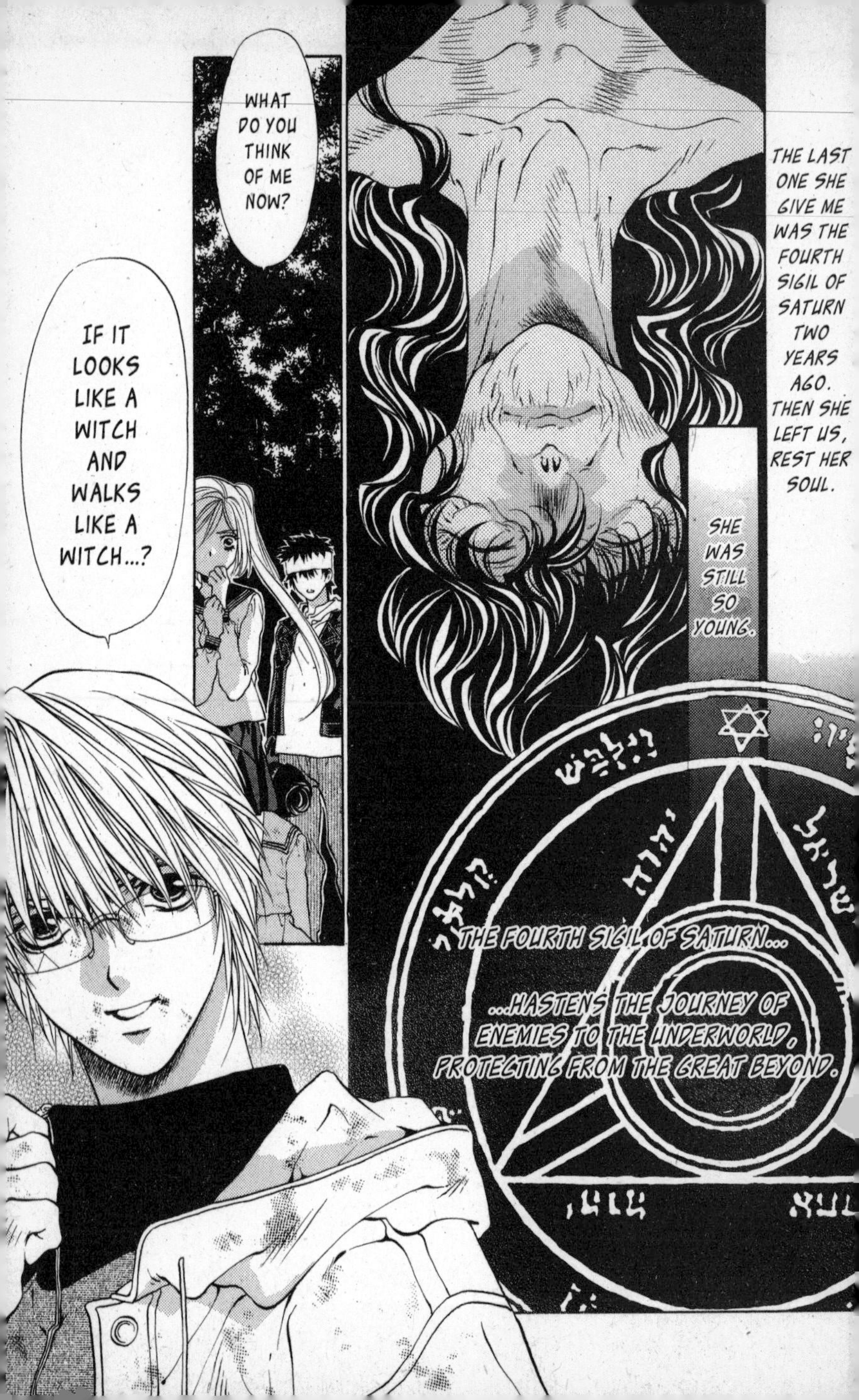
THE LAST ONE SHE GIVE ME WAS THE FOURTH SIGIL OF SATURN TWO YEARS AGO. THEN SHE LEFT US, REST HER SOUL.
SHE WAS STILL SO YOUNG.
THE FOURTH SIGIL OF SATURN...
...HASTENS THE JOURNEY OF ENEMIES TO THE UNDERWORLD, PROTECTING FROM THE GREAT BEYOND.
WHAT DO YOU THINK OF ME NOW?
IF IT LOOKS LIKE A WITCH AND WALKS LIKE A WITCH...?

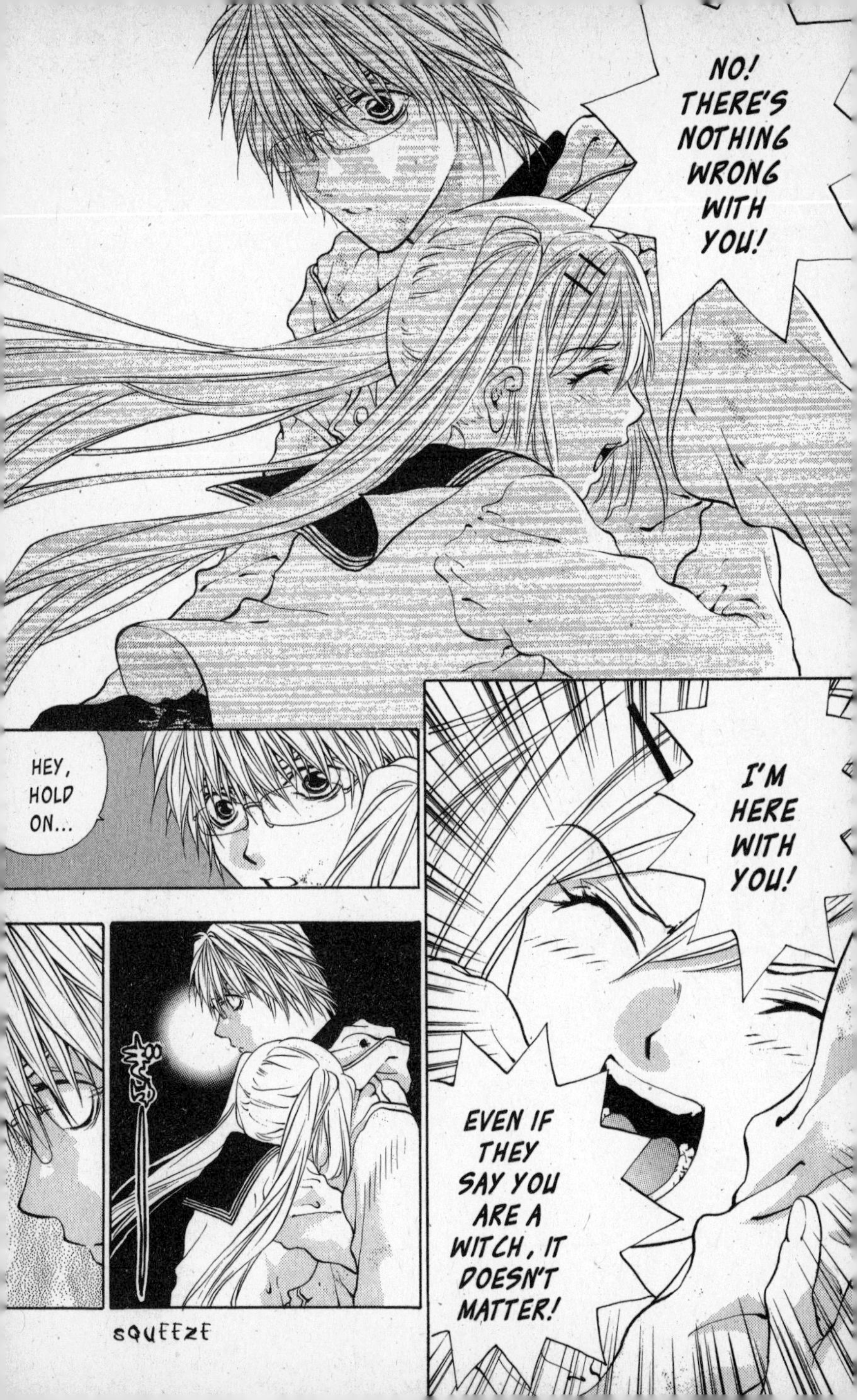
NO! THERE'S NOTHING WRONG WITH YOU!
I'M HERE WITH YOU!
EVEN IF THEY SAY YOU ARE A WITCH, IT DOESN'T MATTER!
HEY, HOLD ON...
SQUEEZE

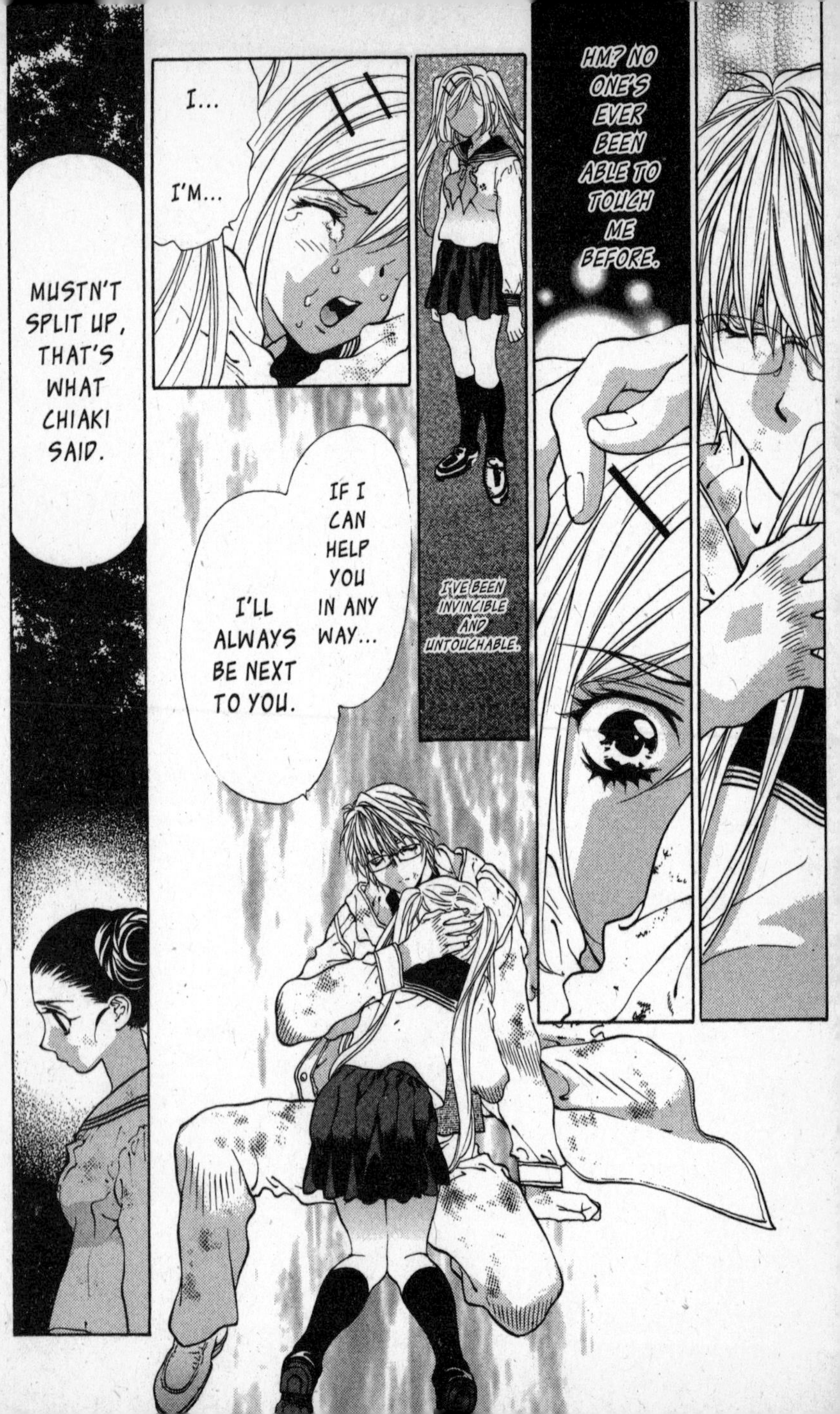
HM? NO ONE'S EVER BEEN ABLE TO TOUCH ME BEFORE.
I'VE BEEN INVINCIBLE AND UNTOUCHABLE.
I...
I'M...
IF I CAN HELP YOU IN ANY WAY... I'LL ALWAYS BE NEXT TO YOU.
MUSTN'T SPLIT UP, THAT'S WHAT CHIAKI SAID.

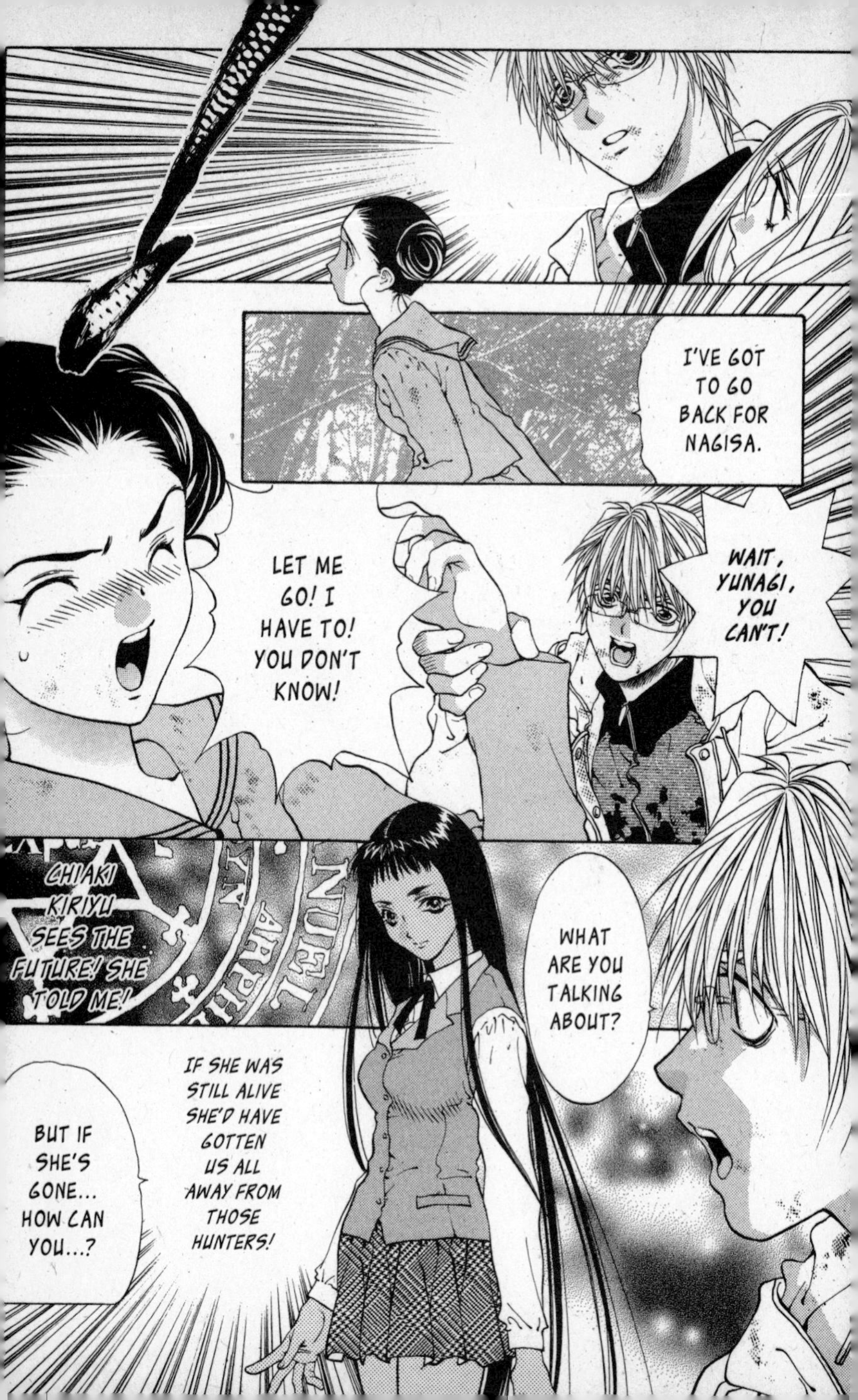
I'VE GOT TO GO BACK FOR NAGISA.
WAIT, YUNAGI, YOU CAN'T!
LET ME GO! I HAVE TO! YOU DON'T KNOW!
WHAT ARE YOU TALKING ABOUT?
CHIAKI KIRIYU SEES THE FUTURE! SHE TOLD ME!
IF SHE WAS STILL ALIVE SHE'D HAVE GOTTEN US ALL AWAY FROM THOSE HUNTERS!
BUT IF SHE'S GONE... HOW CAN YOU...?

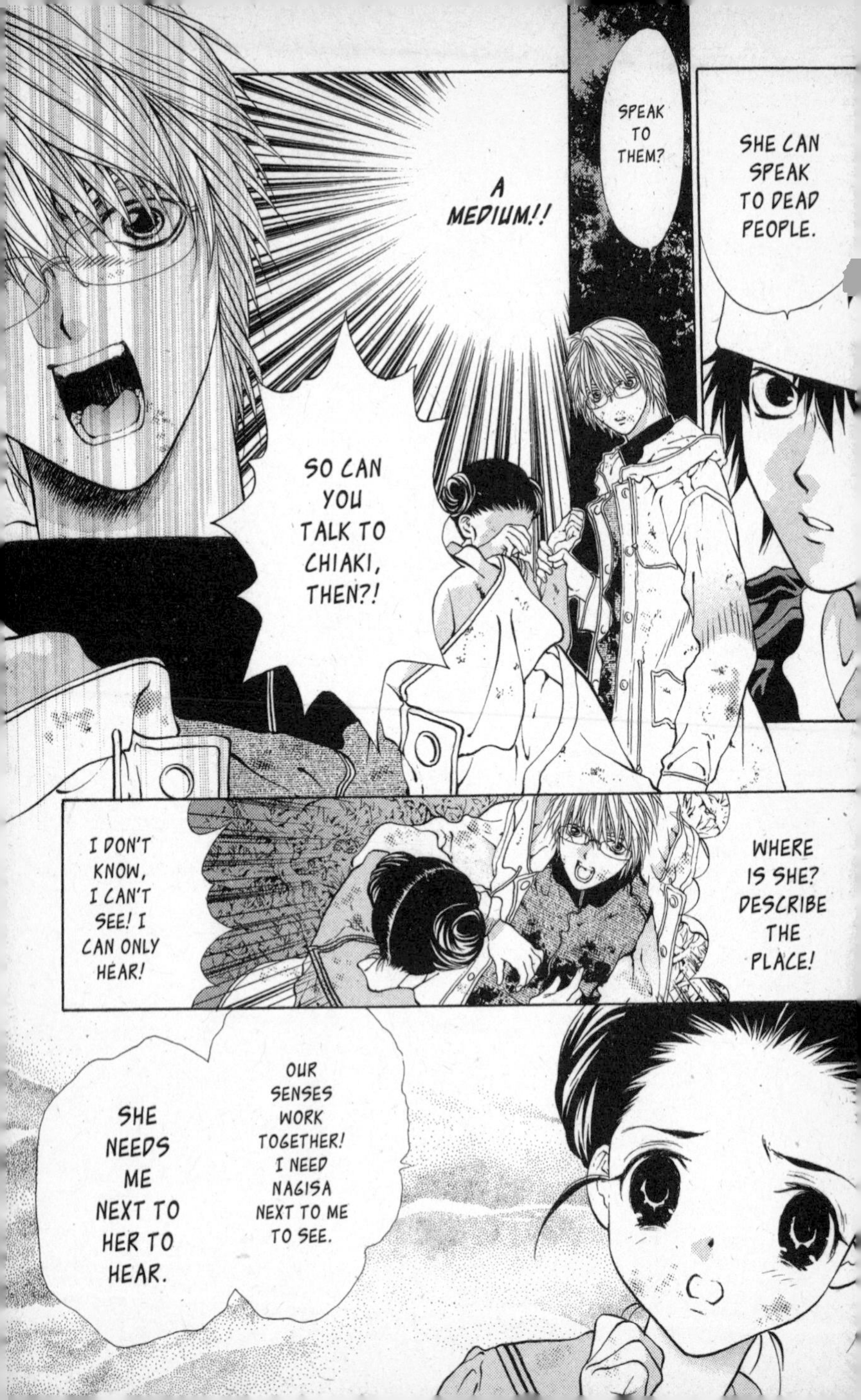
SHE CAN SPEAK TO DEAD PEOPLE.
SPEAK TO THEM?
A MEDIUM!!
SO CAN YOU TALK TO CHIAKI, THEN?!
WHERE IS SHE? DESCRIBE THE PLACE!
I DON'T KNOW, I CAN'T SEE! I CAN ONLY HEAR!
OUR SENSES WORK TOGETHER! I NEED NAGISA NEXT TO ME TO SEE.
SHE NEEDS ME NEXT TO HER TO HEAR.

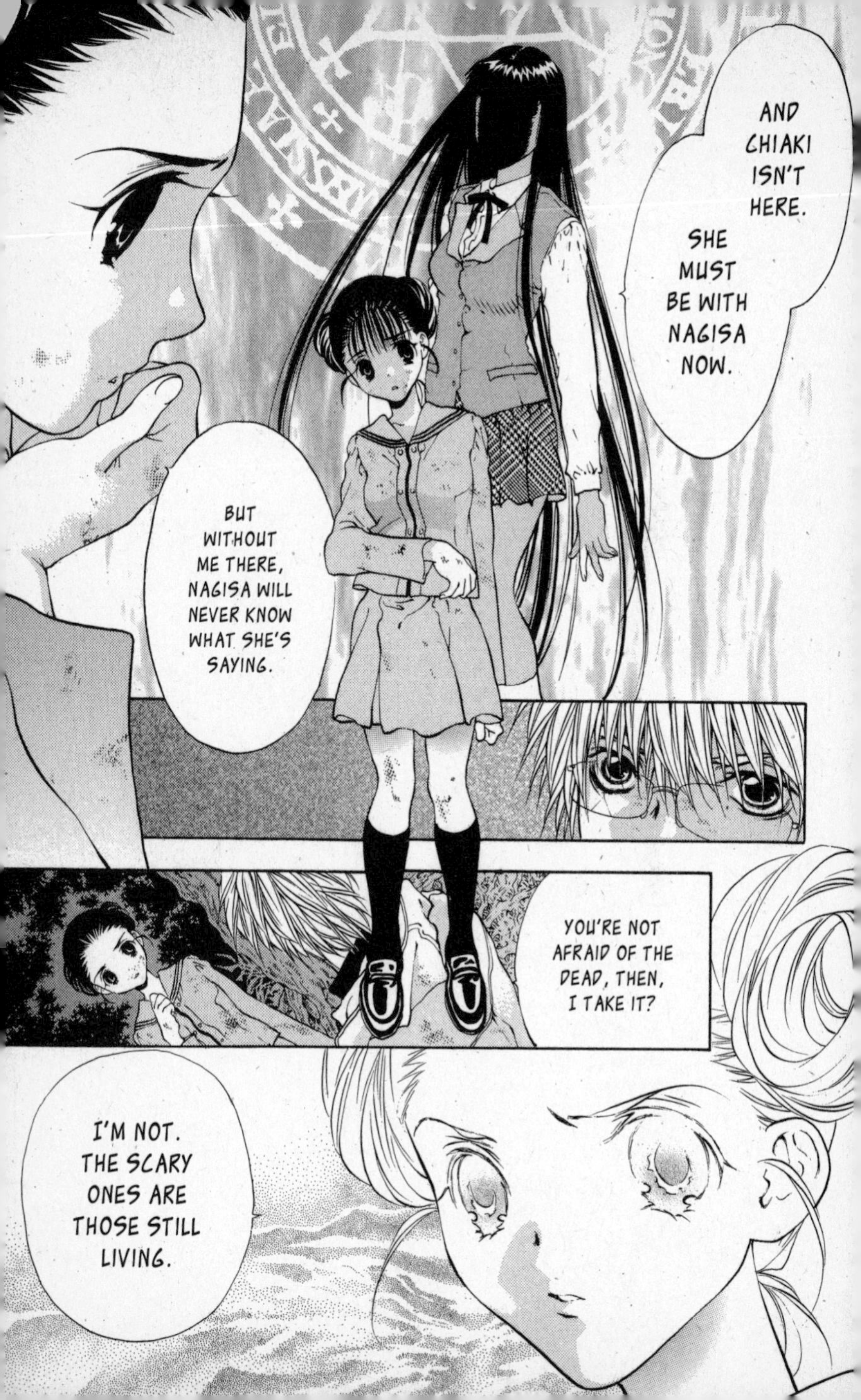
AND CHIAKI ISN'T HERE.
SHE MUST BE WITH NAGISA NOW.
BUT WITHOUT ME THERE, NAGISA WILL NEVER KNOW WHAT SHE'S SAYING.
YOU'RE NOT AFRAID OF THE DEAD, THEN, I TAKE IT?
I'M NOT. THE SCARY ONES ARE THOSE STILL LIVING.

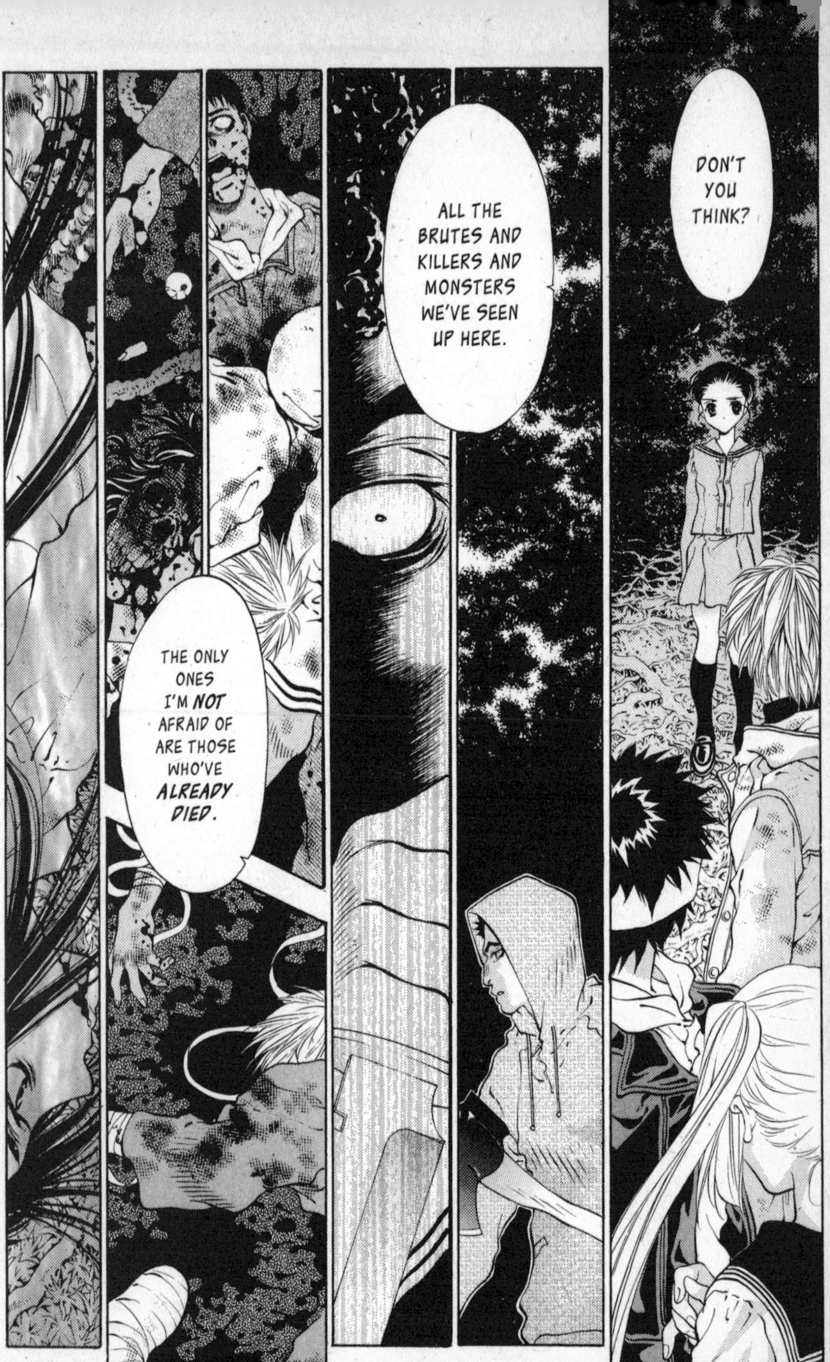

DON'T YOU THINK?
ALL THE BRUTES AND KILLERS AND MONSTERS WE'VE SEEN UP HERE.
THE ONLY ONES I'M **NOT** AFRAID OF ARE THOSE WHO'VE **ALREADY DIED**.

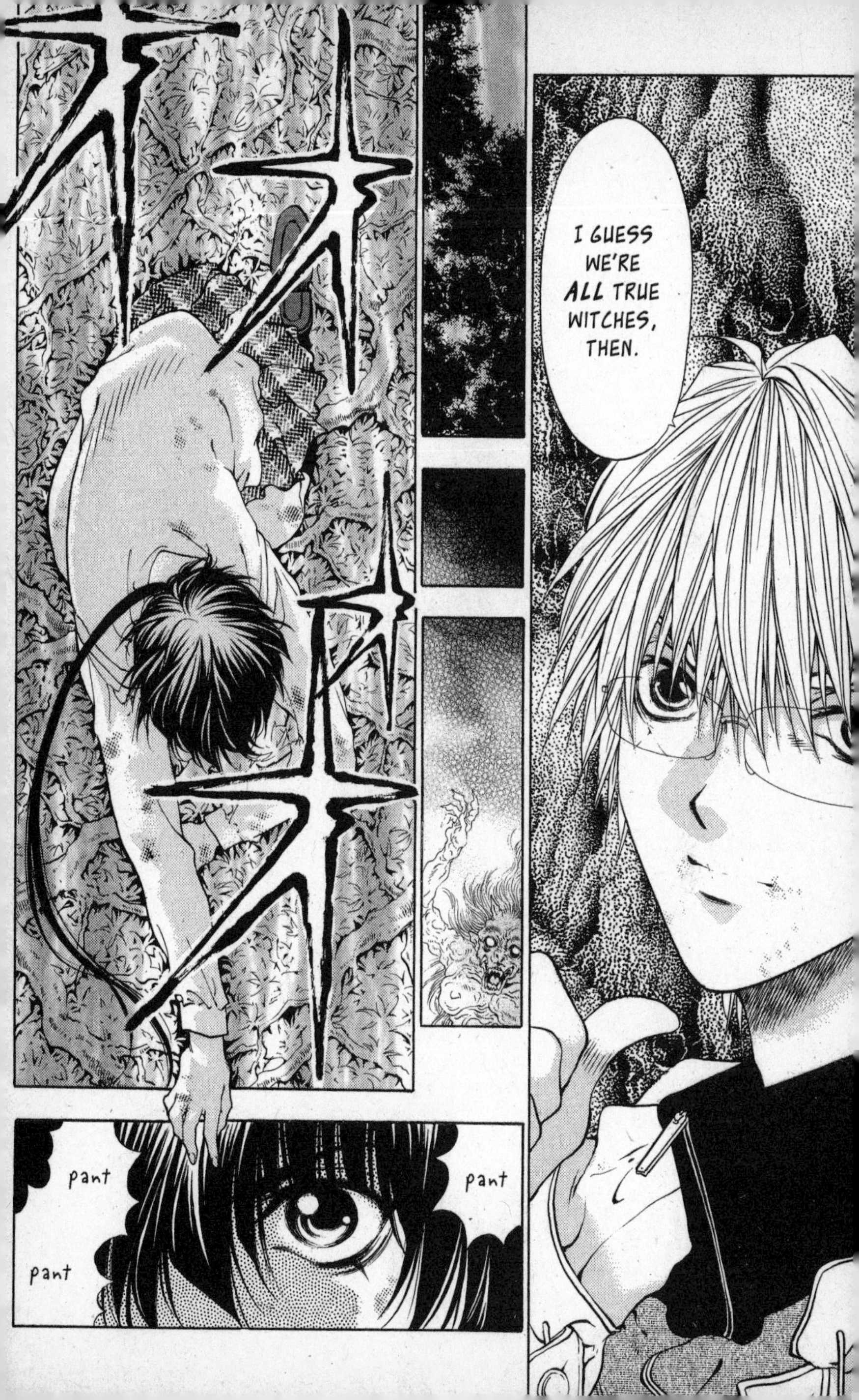
I GUESS WE'RE ALL TRUE WITCHES, THEN.
pant
pant
pant

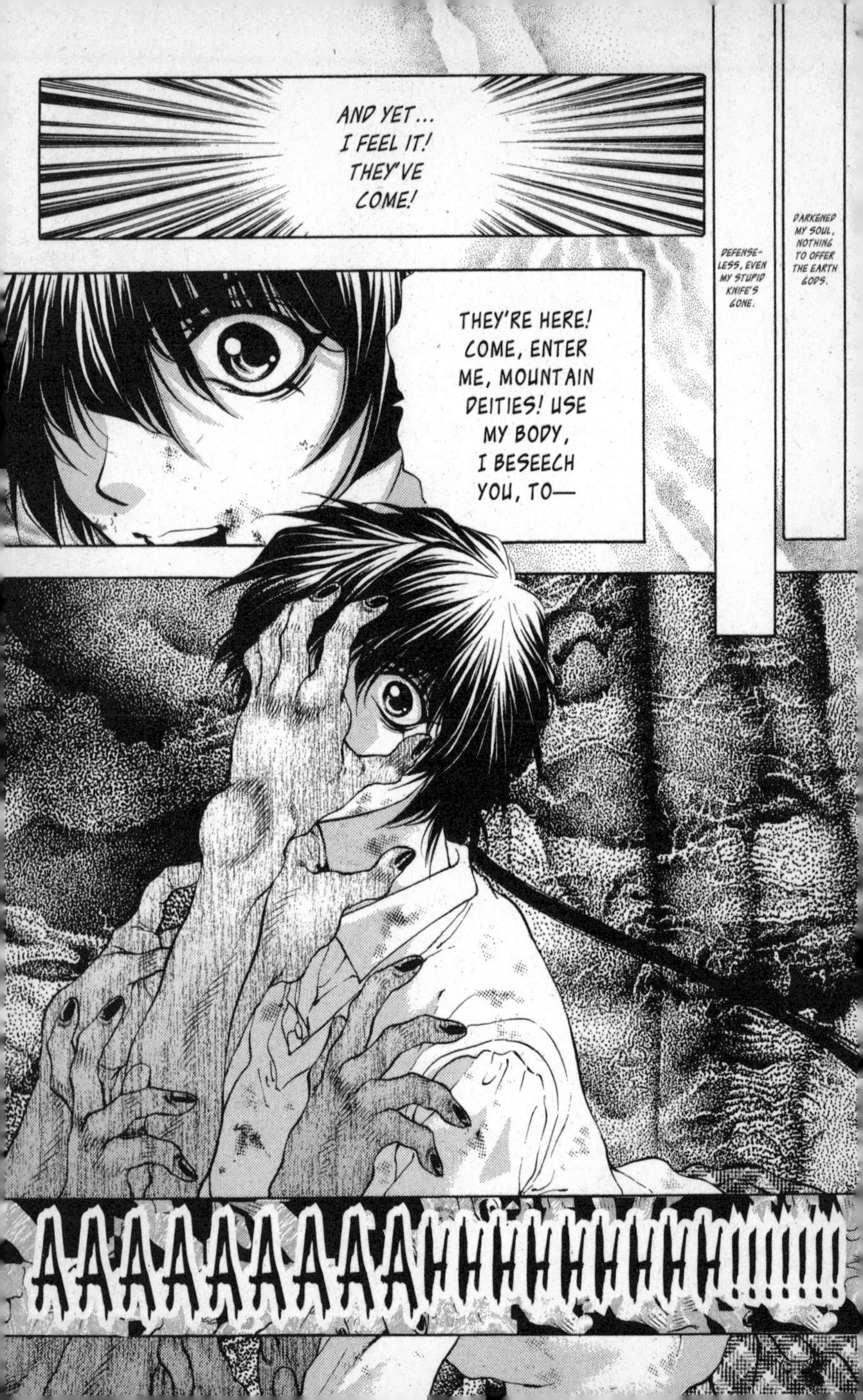
DARKENED MY SOUL, NOTHING TO OFFER THE EARTH GODS.
DEFENSELESS, EVEN MY STUPID KNIFE'S GONE.
AND YET... I FEEL IT! THEY'VE COME!
THEY'RE HERE! COME, ENTER ME, MOUNTAIN DEITIES! USE MY BODY, I BESEECH YOU, TO—
AAAAAAAAAHHHHHHHHHH!!!!!!!

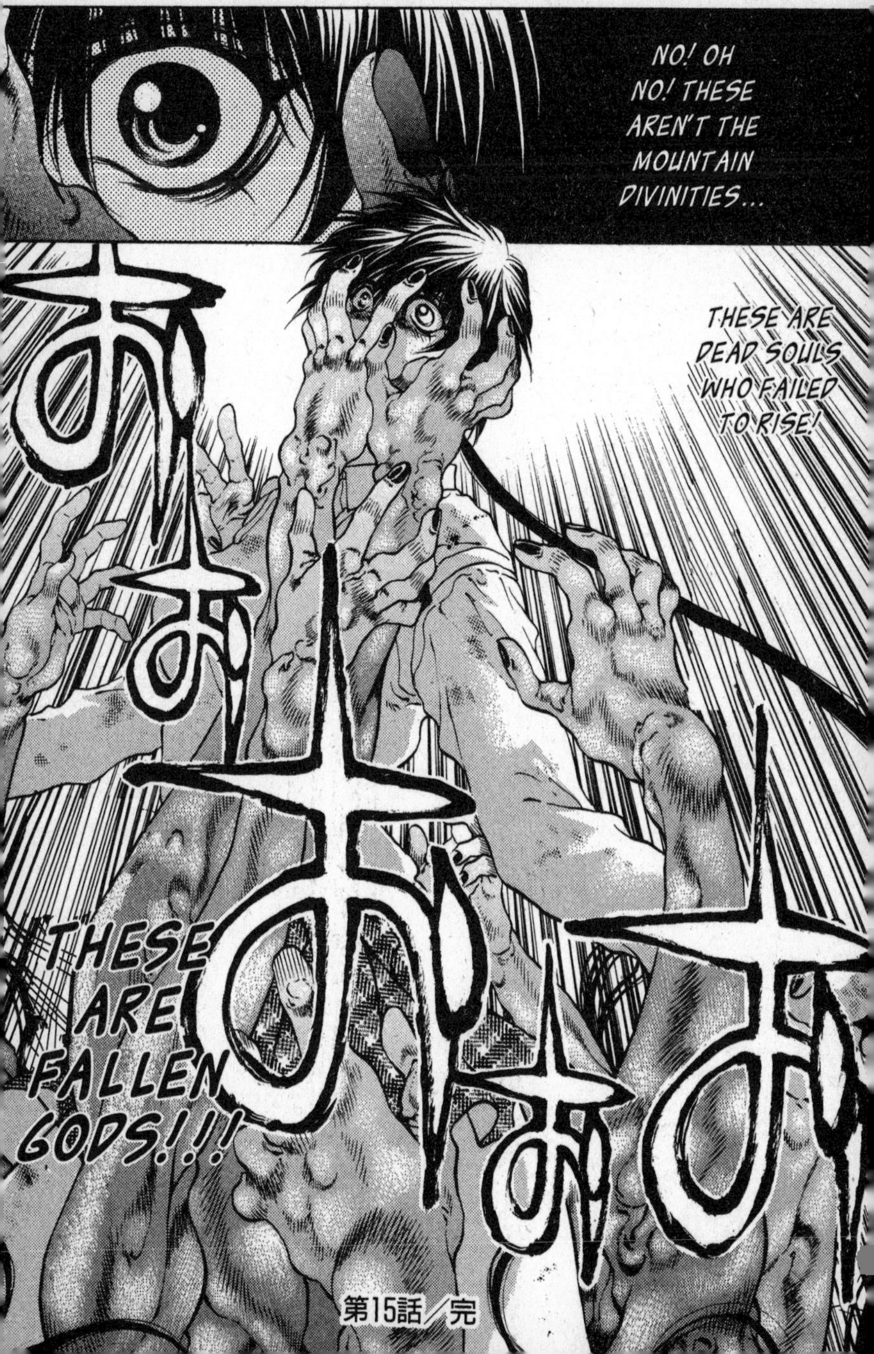
NO! OH NO! THESE AREN'T THE MOUNTAIN DIVINITIES...
THESE ARE DEAD SOULS WHO FAILED TO RISE!
おおおおお
THESE ARE FALLEN GODS!!!
第15話／完

INNOCENT W

VOLUME 2 - END

TO BE CONTINUED IN VOLUME 3